Frederick Douglass' Civil War

Frederick Douglass
Courtesy Library of Congress

FREDERICK DOUGLASS' CIVIL WAR

Keeping Faith in Jubilee

DAVID W. BLIGHT

LOUISIANA STATE UNIVERSITY PRESS
BATON ROUGE

Designer: Sylvia Malik Loftin
Typeface: Trump Mediaeval
Typesetter: The Composing Room of Michigan, Inc.

The author gratefully acknowledges the assistance of the National
Endowment for the Humanities in the completion of this book.

Chapter 5 was published in somewhat different form in *Civil War History*,
XXXI, No. 4 (December, 1985), 309–28. It is reprinted here with the
permission of the editor and the Kent State University Press. Chapter 10
appeared in *Journal of American History* (March, 1989). It appears here, in
revised form, with the permission of the editor.

Library of Congress Cataloging-in-Publication Data
Blight, David W.
    Frederick Douglass' Civil War : keeping faith in jubilee / David
W. Blight.
        p.   cm.
    Bibliography: p.
    Includes index.
    ISBN 0-8071-1463-4 (cloth); ISBN 0-8071-1724-2 (paper)
    1. Douglass, Frederick, 1817?–1895—Views on the Civil war.
2. United States—History—Civil War, 1861–1865—Afro-Americans.
3. United States—History—Civil War, 1861–1865—Influence.
4. Reconstruction.   5. Slavery—United States—Anti-slavery
movements.   I. Title.
E449.D75B55   1989
973.7'114'0924—dc19   88-29200
                                                              CIP

Louisiana Paperback Edition, 1991

00 99 98   5 4

To my mother, Martha Ann Blight,
and to the memory of my father, George Franklin Blight

We want our paper to live to record the death and burial of slavery, and to sing the glad song of jubilee to the sable millions whose cause it has thus far endeavored faithfully and fearlessly to plead. That great event, unless all signs fail, is near at hand, even at the door.

> O! speed the year of Jubilee
> The wide world o'er!

—Frederick Douglass, *Douglass Monthly,* October, 1861

CONTENTS

PREFACE

THIS WORK COMBINES MY THREE major interests in American history: the black experience, the Civil War, and intellectual history. All three subjects are crucial to understanding the shape of the American past. Events that cause a collision of ideas and passions can be fruitful vineyards for intellectual historians. Certainly, this should be the case with the American Civil War. The most important black leader and thinker of the nineteenth century was Frederick Douglass, the fugitive slave who emerged from oppression and obscurity on Maryland's Eastern Shore to become a renowned orator, editor, and autobiographer. As a black leader, Douglass became a symbol of his age, and eventually his life attracted many biographers. Until recently, however, his ideas and his psychological standing have received much less attention. This work is an intellectual biography and the first attempt to analyze the impact of the Civil War in Douglass' life and thought. I have tried to present Douglass in the midst of crisis: as interpreter, observer, advocate, and participant. I will explain his intellectual response to the Civil War, but I will also argue that Douglass saw the conflict in a spiritual framework. He interpreted the slavery issue, secession, emancipation, and the war itself as a millennial nationalist. Through a combination of secular and religious ideas, Douglass made a major contribution to the apocalypticism with which his generation made sense out of the Civil War. In varying degrees, I have tried to be biographical, speculative, and critical. Although I admit to an enduring fascination with Douglass, I hold no desire to be his apologist.

Douglass is missing from all major works on the intellectual history of the Civil War era. George Fredrickson's *The Inner Civil War: Northern Intellectuals and the Crisis of the Union*, though very useful to any student of this period, does not include Douglass. Douglass is also absent from Daniel Aaron's fine study, *The Unwritten War: American Writers and the Civil War*, and Edmund Wilson's ambitious work, *Patriotic Gore: Studies in the Literature of the American Civil War*. Although blacks are invisible altogether in Wilson's book, Douglass' speeches and editorials fit perfectly into the author's definition of the literature inspired by the Civil War.[1] One of the goals of this study is to give Douglass his place in the literary and intellectual traditions that the Civil War fostered.

The standard Douglass biographies by Benjamin Quarles, Philip S. Foner, and Nathan I. Huggins have stressed the significance of the Civil War in the black leader's life. But none has engaged in a systematic analysis of Douglass' ideas or his psychological development in relation to the war. Dickson J. Preston's *Young Frederick Douglass: The Maryland Years* is a splendid example of historical detective work, as well as a source of many insights into the youthful Douglass, his attachments to his native Maryland, and some of the conflicts between his public and private spheres. Douglass' psychological conflicts—his divided racial and social identities—have been examined by Allison Davis, in *Leadership, Love, and Aggression*, and most carefully by Peter F. Walker, in *Moral Choices: Memory, Desire, and Imagination in Nineteenth-Century American Abolition*. I have tried to heed the call for a more searching psychological analysis of Douglass made in recent review essays by Henry Louis Gates,Jr., and George Fredrickson. A major aim of my study is to demonstrate how Douglass found a much firmer social identity—a sense of nationhood—in the experience of the Civil War. I have also explored two other aspects of Douglass' psychological makeup: how he coped with the despair most blacks felt during the 1850s; and how, through war propaganda and the recruitment of black soldiers, he released a deeply felt rage against slaveholders. Waldo E. Martin's recent work, *The Mind of Frederick Douglass*, is the only systematic treatment of Douglass as a thinker. Organized topically, Martin's fine book illuminates the major currents in Douglass' thought: his inveterate optimism, his egalitarian humanism, his unbending resistance to slavery and racism, and his belief in the doctrines of progress and American providential destiny. From Martin, we learn a great deal about Douglass' character and his world view, but not as much about how his ideas ebbed and flowed in response to events. Finally, I hope that this

---

1. George M. Fredrickson, *The Inner Civil War: Northern Intellectuals and the Crisis of the Union* (New York, 1965); Edmund Wilson, *Patriotic Gore: Studies in the Literature of the American Civil War* (1962; rpr. Boston, 1984), xiii; Daniel Aaron, *The Unwritten War: American Writers and the Civil War* (New York, 1973). Only two books by James McPherson provide a systematic look at the black intellectual response to the war. See James M. McPherson, *The Struggle for Equality: Abolitionists and the Negro in the Civil War and Reconstruction* (Princeton, 1964), and James M. McPherson (ed.), *The Negro's Civil War: How American Negroes Felt and Acted During the War for the Union* (New York, 1965).

study can shed some light on the centrality of the Civil War in American history, in the black experience, and certainly in the life of Frederick Douglass.[2]

During the research and writing of this book, I have amassed many debts that I now gratefully acknowledge. I benefited from the generous aid of the research librarians at the Boston Athenaeum, the Boston Public Library, the Widener Library, Harvard University, the Frederick Douglass Papers at Yale University, the Library of Congress, the Moorland-Spingarn Research Center at Howard University, the Pennsylvania Historical Society, the State Historical Society of Wisconsin, the Rochester Historical Society, and the Bowling Green State University Library. With diligence and patience the librarians at North Central College processed my endless requests for interlibrary loans. Ed Meachen went out of his way to provide me with a research environment. I am deeply grateful to the National Endowment for the Humanities for granting me a summer stipend in 1986. North Central College further provided generous assistance through the Burlington-Northern Faculty Achievement Award in 1987.

Through the various stages of this project, many persons have encouraged and criticized my work. William Van Deburg critically read the work and has helped to shape my understanding of Douglass and black intellectual history. Jason Silverman's criticism of several chapters was very helpful, and his sincere efforts to put the resources of the Douglass Papers at Yale University at my disposal almost worked. The late Dickson Preston also read the early chapters and rendered valuable advice. Most important, he took me on a priceless tour of the Douglass sites on Maryland's Eastern Shore. Our trek through the muddy cornfield to the location of Douglass' birthplace on Tuckahoe Creek is unforgettable. The late Tom Shick encouraged the study and shared with me his wealth of knowledge and research materials on Afro-American colonization. I am grateful that I knew Tom in the fullness of his spirit. While encouraging me to pursue Douglass,

2. Benjamin Quarles, *Frederick Douglass* (1948; rpr. New York, 1968); Philip S. Foner, *Frederick Douglass* (New York, 1964); Nathan I. Huggins, *Slave and Citizen: The Life of Frederick Douglass* (Boston, 1980); Henry Louis Gates, Jr., "Frederick Douglass and the Language of the Self," *Yale Review,* LXX (Summer, 1981), 592–611; George M. Fredrickson, "Self-Made Hero," *New York Review of Books,* XXXII (June 27, 1985), 3–4; Dickson J. Preston, *Young Frederick Douglass: The Maryland Years* (Baltimore, 1980); Allison Davis, *Leadership, Love, and Aggression* (New York, 1983); Peter F. Walker, *Moral Choices: Memory, Desire, and Imagination in Nineteenth-Century American Abolition* (Baton Rouge, 1978); Waldo E. Martin, *The Mind of Frederick Douglass* (Chapel Hill, 1984).

rather than a safer and more obscure topic, Paul Boyer served as a reader of the manuscript and as an exemplary craftsman in the field of intellectual history.

For their advice and reassurance to a young historian finding his way into a well-worked field, I am beholden to Douglass scholars Waldo Martin and Peter Walker. Waldo's encouragement and criticism of the manuscript have been extremely valuable. I also owe a special debt to John Hubbell, the editor of *Civil War History*, who helped me convert chapter 5 into an article.

At North Central College, Michele Johnson, Timothy Morris, Howard Mueller, William Naumann, Barbara Sciacchitano, Thaddeus Seymour, Jack Shindler, and James Taylor supported my efforts to complete the writing with patience and friendship. To Barbara, Howard, and Tim, I owe much special gratitude. Francine and Edward Navakas shared every stage of this work; their friendship and rich literary knowledge have been indispensable. Without Ed's interpretation of Lowell's "For the Union Dead," I might never have found an ending for the final chapter. Meredith Russell was a mainstay of moral support through the perils of publishing and many other duties. I was fortunate to have Marlene Carlson type the final draft with her customary skill and professionalism.

At Harvard University Nathan Irvin Huggins and David Herbert Donald have been gracious with their time and support. As a Douglass scholar himself, Nathan's advice has been extremely valuable; his work has long been a model for me in the field of Afro-American history. At Louisiana State University Press, my editor, Margaret Dalrymple, has been a delight to work with; Margaret's keen observations and commitment to my work have been a sustaining force for many months. For sharing their insights, courtesies, and time I am also indebted to Richard Blackett, Catherine Clinton, Carolivia Herron, David Howard-Pitney, Michael Kammen, Janet Lang, Dan B. Miller, Douglas T. Miller, Daniel T. Rodgers, Donald Rogers, Layn St. Louis, David Thelen, William Trollinger, Clarence E. Walker, and students too numerous to name at two institutions, who listened to more perhaps than they ever wanted to know about Frederick Douglass and the meaning of the Civil War.

I owe my greatest debt to Richard Sewell, who urged me to think for myself, while providing an impeccable model of scholarship to follow. His unfailing support and friendship have been indispensable. His painstaking criticism of both my ideas and my prose has sharpened my perceptions, saved me from numerous errors, and improved the work immeasurably. Dick has taught me much about clear thinking and clear writing. I take full responsibility, of course, for all remaining errors and imperfections.

My gratitude to my mother, Martha A. Blight, goes deeper than acknowledgments can convey. My brother, James G. Blight, has influenced me in unique and lasting ways. To him I owe motivations known only to persons from the east side of Flint, Michigan, who seek a life of the mind and imagine themselves scholars. Finally, I owe a very special thanks to Karin Beckett for her caring, her criticism, her patience, and her devotion.

LIST OF ABBREVIATIONS

DM   *Douglass Monthly,* published in Rochester,
                   1859–63.
FD Papers (LC)   Frederick Douglass Papers. Library of Congress.
FDP   *Frederick Douglass's Paper,* published in
                   Rochester, 1851–59.

FREDERICK DOUGLASS' CIVIL WAR

1 / Keeping Faith in Jubilee: Sources of Hope in the Pre–Civil War Thought of Frederick Douglass

A man's troubles are always half disposed of, when he finds endurance his only remedy.
—Frederick Douglass, *My Bondage and My Freedom*, 1855

Would that this might be the year of the jubilee to those now toiling millions! Would that this were the day of release. But no wavering shadow of this coming event falls upon our vision. We walk by faith, not by sight.
—Frederick Douglass, *Douglass Monthly*, January, 1859

THE CIVIL WAR WAS THE CRUCIBLE in which slavery was destroyed and the American Union tested and preserved. These two great questions—slavery and the survival of the Union—continue to mark the war's centrality in American history. For black Americans, the war took on the deepest possible meaning: it was both an end and a new beginning of a long struggle to achieve freedom and dignity out of oppression. The war came as the fulfillment of prophecy, but only after a period of despair. For antebellum black leaders, the 1850s was a decade of increased activity and organization, but also a time of great disappointment. After lifetimes of struggle against slavery and racial caste, and in the wake of setbacks like the Fugitive Slave Act, the Kansas-Nebraska Act, and the Dred Scott decision, northern black leaders suffered a crisis of faith in America. During the 1850s, some opted for schemes of emigration to Africa or the West Indies. Most who remained in the United States strove to build institutions of black self-improvement, joined forces with organized abolitionism, suffered discouragement, and relied on a variety of ideological, spiritual, and psychological resources to sustain their hope. By the late 1850s Afro-American intellectuals had reached a crossroads. Ironically, on the eve of revolutionary changes in American race relations, most black leaders saw a future for their people as dismal as the past had ever been.

At the center of this crisis stood Frederick Douglass, the most influential black leader of the mid-nineteenth century. By the late 1850s, Douglass was already a symbolic personality, a fugitive slave who had risen from bondage and established himself as one of the foremost orator-editors of the abolition movement. During his twenty-one years as a slave, he had suffered all the privations and brutalities of slavery. But he was no ordinary fugitive when he escaped from his native Maryland in 1837. His boyhood had provided privileges few other slaves enjoyed: a lengthy stay with a benevolent master in Baltimore who had nurtured him to literacy; exposure to religious ideas that gave him confidence in the future; and enough sources of self-esteem to give him a sense of personal destiny. With luck, pluck, and remarkable inner gifts, Douglass stole his own freedom. His public career as an abolitionist began in 1841 when he became a lecturer with William Lloyd Garrison's Massachusetts Antislavery Society. From then until the Civil War, Douglass challenged slavery and racism as few others could. By the 1850s he was revered in most antislavery circles in the British Isles, and both loved and resented among American abolitionists. As he spoke with grace and eloquence from countless platforms on two continents, and wrote with increasing skill and force, Douglass presented the greatest living challenge to the American paradox of slavery and freedom.

This was the Douglass of fame and symbol, the living monument who commanded respect but could not change history. Indeed, Douglass contributed enormously to his own symbol by publishing two autobiographies by 1855.[1] But beneath the surface of the symbolic black leader (fugitive slave risen to international reformer) dwelled an increasingly frustrated man. Acutely aware of his specialness but equally cognizant of the powerlessness of black leaders in the 1850s, Douglass struggled to understand the limits imposed upon him by a racist society at the same time he sought the limits of his own mind and will. According to Douglass, the black intellectual of the mid-nineteenth century was "isolated in the land of his birth—debarred by his color from congenial associations with whites . . . equally cast out by the ignorances of the blacks." Fifty years later, W. E. B. Du Bois wrote his famous description of the "double-consciousness" of the black man who struggled with being "an American, a Negro; two souls, two thoughts, two unreconciled strivings; two warring ideals

1. Frederick Douglass, *My Bondage and My Freedom* (1855; rpr. New York, 1969); Frederick Douglass, *Narrative of the Life of Frederick Douglass, An American Slave, Written By Himself* (1845; rpr. New York, 1963). For an analysis of the manner in which Douglass used the autobiographical method to preside over his biographers and create his own historical image, see Walker, *Moral Choices*, 212–14, 223–28. Walker has demonstrated quite persuasively that there are many pitfalls for historians who accept Douglass' own portrayal of his "consistent personality" over time.

in one dark body." The antebellum generation of black leaders lived with an especially painful sense of this isolation, split-consciousness, and frustration. Their challenges included not only the fashioning of strategies for elevation and emancipation, not only the development of their own sense of identity, but the very preservation of faith in the cause of black freedom. To assume the role of "black leader" in the mid-nineteenth century was squarely to confront American racism. In many ways, Frederick Douglass represents a small but important group of black intellectuals who were divided men in a dividing country.[2]

From the time he moved to Rochester, New York, and launched his independent career as an abolitionist editor in 1847, there is no more pervasive theme in Douglass' thought than the simple sustenance of *hope* in a better future for blacks in America. His thousands of editorials and speeches reflect a preoccupation with the tensions between hope and despair among a people struggling for liberation and survival. To a degree Douglass possessed a naturally sanguine disposition, and although he rejected orthodoxy, he exhibited an abiding religious faith. As a public man, Douglass was as determined and self-confident as any black leader of his time; he was not easily diverted from his dream of black freedom and a just America. But like all black leaders, Douglass lacked elective sanction and an organized constituency. Douglass experienced deep personal discouragement in the 1850s as he struggled to lead his people through a time symbolized by the words of Chief Justice Roger B. Taney in the Dred Scott decision: black people were "beings of an inferior order . . . so far inferior, that they had no rights which the white man was bound to respect."[3] Blacks would not be alone in their resistance to such ideas, but their cause seemed only bleaker in the final years of America's road to disunion. In order to understand the significance of the Civil War in Douglass' life and thought, we must first examine the roots of his preoccupation with hope and despair in the 1850s.

To Douglass, providing hope seemed to be a sacred duty, given the deepening frustration blacks felt in the 1850s. He would utilize any meager "sign" of progress in the antislavery cause as a means of bolstering confidence and perseverance. Because they had always sur-

2. *FDP*, March 4, 1853; W. E. B. Du Bois, *The Souls of Black Folk* (1903; rpr. New York, 1969), 45. The sense of powerlessness exhibited by black leaders in the 1850s is a major theme in Jane H. Pease and William H. Pease, *They Who Would Be Free: Blacks' Search for Freedom, 1830–1861* (New York, 1974), 298.

3. Quoted in Don E. Fehrenbacher, *The Dred Scott Case: Its Significance in American Law and Politics* (New York, 1978), 347.

vived the "terribleness of the past," Douglass believed, blacks were especially well equipped to face the "inflexible realities" of the present. "We should not as an oppressed people grow despondent," he wrote in 1855. "Fear and despondency prevent us from working . . . with that hopeful spirit which causes us to keep our head above the waters. . . . If we can at the present crisis, catch but one soft, low whisper of peace to our troubled souls, let us cling to it. Let us rejoice in Hope." This vague call for persistence rested, in part, on the romantic notion that black people possessed a kind of natural hopefulness forged by necessity under bondage. History had bred into blacks a "tenacity of life" and "powers of endurance" unique to their race. Douglass tried to buoy the spirits of his readers with the claim that by nature "the poor bondman lifts a smiling face above the surface of a sea of agonies, *hoping on, hoping ever.*" Douglass never fully resolved his simultaneous beliefs in special racial gifts and the Enlightenment notion of a common human nature, in black uniqueness as well as human unity. This should come as no surprise; it was a dualism espoused by virtually all black thinkers in the nineteenth century.[4]

During a time when most blacks perceived their lot in American society as worsening, Douglass' constant appeals for hope took on a strained and abstract quality. His vagueness was due, in part, to the natural tension between hope and gloom among reformers who sought to challenge or overthrow the institutions of their society. In 1859, Douglass contended that where he could not provide "visible evidences of progress," he did not wish to deceive with "illusions of hope." His usual solution for this tension was to deliver ringing testaments of faith in the moral righteousness of the cause of black freedom, to seek the deeper levels of spirit and consciousness where permanent manifestations of hope are born. Douglass was one of the nineteenth century's greatest orators, and his writings exhibit a similar style. He performed tirelessly as the preacher of a black civil

4. "The Doom of the Black Power," *FDP*, July 27, 1855; "The Claims of the Negro Ethnologically Considered," address delivered at Western Reserve College, July 12, 1854, in Philip S. Foner (ed.), *The Life and Writings of Frederick Douglass* (5 vols.; New York, 1950), II, 308. These expressions of the natural characteristics of blacks have an interesting similarity to some of George Fredrickson's analysis of "romantic racialism" in the white mind of the nineteenth century. See George M. Fredrickson, *The Black Image in the White Mind: The Debate on Afro-American Character and Destiny, 1817–1914* (New York, 1971), 97–129. On Douglass' paradoxical beliefs in racial uniqueness and human unity, see Martin, *Mind*, 198–202. Martin also stresses Douglass' expression of "exemplary perseverance" on the part of blacks, both as Africans and as Americans.

religion. His weekly and monthly editorials (often as many as five in each issue of his paper) were analyses of current affairs, but more often than not they resonated like sermons of deliverance. No matter how bleak the prospects nor how discouraging the course of events, Douglass assumed the responsibility of reviving hope and promising an ultimate triumph.[5]

Douglass' expressions of hope took many forms. He frequently appealed to the "abstract righteousness" of the antislavery cause, cautioning his readers to remember that they were living through the "seed time" of a great reform. The "harvest" would come in natural course. "Rely upon it," he urged, "we have not written, spoken, or printed in vain—no good word can die, no righteous effort can be unavailing in the end." Douglass tried to give these vague exhortations a footing in an optimistic conception of human nature. "An abstract belief in slavery," he claimed, "can only thrive in the dark, and cannot abide the light." Douglass envisioned human nature as ultimately good. He believed that the deepest roots of human nature lay in its "best elements," which were "beyond the power of slavery to annihilate." Although sorely tested, Douglass never ceased believing that he lived in a moral universe. Because slavery was an evil so monstrous, the antislavery movement (a cause so just) simply had to triumph.[6]

Douglass carried his moral determinism a step further by frequently comparing the struggle between slavery and freedom to similar conflicts in nature itself. The causes from which the abolition movement sprung were nothing new: "like the great forces of the physical world, fire, steam, and lightning, . . . [they had] slumbered in the bosom of nature since the world began." They were like "precious gems in the hillsides, whereon the shepherdboy sings, unconsciously his evening song . . . awaiting the thoughtful discoverer, and

5. "Progress of Slavery," *DM*, August, 1859. On Douglass' ability as a preacher, see Quarles, *Douglass*, 14; William L. Andrews, "Frederick Douglass, Preacher," *American Literature*, LIV (December, 1982), 592–96; and Lenwood G. Davis, "Frederick Douglass as a Preacher, and One of His Last Most Significant Letters," *Journal of Negro History*, LXVI (Summer, 1981), Documents Section, 140–43, which includes two letters by Douglass indicating the extent of his interest and involvement as a preacher with the African Methodist Episcopal Zion Church.

6. "1859—The New Year," *DM*, February, 1959; "A Fulcrum for the Antislavery Lever," *DM*, June, 1860; "The Antislavery Movement," lecture delivered to the Rochester Ladies' Antislavery Society, January, 1855, in Foner (ed.), *Life and Writings*, II, 357. Another excellent example of Douglass' conception of the "inherent righteousness" of the antislavery cause, and the fact that he did not wish his ideas to be taken as "mere rhetorical flourish," is in "The Doom of the Black Power."

the skillful workman to bring them forth in forms of beauty, power, and glory."[7] Thus, believing that the cause of black freedom was somehow a part of nature's course, Douglass spoke resounding but anxious words of hope in the 1850s. He combined the romantic faith in human goodness with the rational claims of the natural rights tradition to forge a view of human nature that usually sustained him against the odds.

Typical of most American thinkers of his time, Douglass' appeals to "nature" and "inherent righteousness" were part of his larger belief in the doctrine of progress and in a providential theory of history. Douglass never systematically tried to write a philosophy of history, but his writings and speeches are replete with the idea of divine direction of human affairs. To Douglass, progress was essentially moral and, ultimately, irrepressible. In one of his pleas for steadfastness in 1856, Douglass proclaimed to his readers that first principles could sustain them. "Endure unto the end," he argued, "there is about Truth an inherent vitality, a recuperative energy. . . . Progression is the law of our being."[8] Against the anachronism of American slavery, the doctrine of progress made an excellent theoretical weapon. According to Douglass, slavery was so abhorrent to enlightened human nature that it simply could not bear discussion over time. "It is against nature," he declared in 1853, "against progress, against improvement, and against the government of God." In Douglass' view, the bondsmen had allies in every advancement in technology, education, and transportation. Like nature, this romantic view of history demanded an ultimate order to events and, above all, divine direction. Douglass' struggle to sustain faith in abolition and in America relied heavily on his conception of Providence, on God's design against which slavery and oppression simply could not prevail. Acknowledging that the cause of blacks had reached a "seemingly desperate case" in 1853, and claiming that he was "not a hopeful man," Douglass answered the inquiry: "Will our enemies prevail in the execution of their designs? In my God and in my soul I believe they *will not*."[9]

7. "The Antislavery Movement," 336. On Douglass' optimism and view of human nature, see Martin, *Mind*, 20–22, 132–33, 172–73, 185.

8. "The Suffrage Question," *FDP*, April 25, 1856. For additional analysis of Douglass' view of progress and history, see Huggins, *Slave and Citizen*, 74–75; and Vincent Harding, *There Is a River: The Black Struggle for Freedom in America* (New York, 1981), 148–49.

9. "The Present Condition and Future Prospects of the Negro People," speech delivered at the annual meeting of the American and Foreign Antislavery Society, New York

Although contemptuous of the clergy and scornful of orthodoxy through most of his life, Douglass held religious convictions that buoyed his spirit and molded his temperament. His religion was honed in the experience of slavery, reawakened in his years as a fugitive slave, and reinforced by Garrisonian abolitionism. As a fugitive slave in New Bedford, Massachusetts, in 1839, Douglass made a formal commitment to Christianity by becoming a licensed preacher in the African Methodist Episcopal Zion Church.[10] He also gave ample testimony to the significance of religion in his early life. In *My Bondage and My Freedom,* he stated that his "religious nature was awakened" at the age of thirteen. "I cannot say that I had a very distinct notion of what was required of me," wrote Douglass, "but one thing I knew very well—I was wretched, and had no means of making myself otherwise." He turned to prayer and to a personal faith, as he put it, "in Jesus Christ, as the Redeemer, Friend, and Savior of those who diligently seek Him." Here was Christian doctrine expressed in its simplest terms.[11]

While in Baltimore the adolescent Douglass also turned to an intensely religious old black man named Uncle Lawson. The impressionable slave boy became "deeply attached" to the drayman, describing him in the autobiographies as his "spiritual father." Douglass spent countless hours in Lawson's shack reading the Bible aloud. The old man seems to have inspired young Frederick with a sense of hope

---

City, May, 1853, in Foner (ed.), *Life and Writings,* II, 253, 250. For an analysis of the attachment of black intellectuals to the providential theory of history, see Leonard I. Sweet, *Black Images of America, 1784–1870* (New York, 1976), 69–124.

10. See Andrews, "Frederick Douglass, Preacher," 592–96. Douglass made this claim in a letter written in 1894, solicited by one of the AMEZ church's early historians, James W. Hood. In his article, Andrews reprints the letter in full. Douglass declared that his connection with the church began in 1838 and that "as early as 1839 I obtained a license from the Quarterly Conference as a local preacher, and often occupied the pulpit by request of the preacher in charge" (*ibid.,* 596). Testimony to Douglass' formal associations with the AMEZ church throughout his life is also found in David Henry Bradley, Jr., *A History of the A.M.E. Zion Church, 1796–1872,* (2 vols.; Nashville, 1956), I, 111–12. On Douglass the preacher, also see Robert G. O'Meally, "Frederick Douglass's 1845 Narrative: The Text Was Meant to be Preached," in Dexter Fisher and Robert B. Stepto (eds.), *Afro-American Literature* (New York, 1979), 192–211. Douglass' writing style has often been described as oratorical or suited for the platform. But O'Meally's argument, as reflected in his title, also helps to explain the motivations behind Douglass' writings, in editorials as well as the autobiographies. On Douglass' early religion, see William L. Van Deburg, "Rejected of Men: The Changing Religious Views of William Lloyd Garrison and Frederick Douglass" (Ph.D. dissertation, Michigan State University, 1973), 62–80; and Preston, *Young Frederick Douglass,* 92–104.

11. Douglass, *Bondage and Freedom,* 166–67.

and self-confidence. Lawson informed Douglass that God had great plans for him, that a special destiny lay ahead. It is difficult to measure Lawson's influence on Douglass' developing mind, since the autobiographies are the only source for this episode. But Douglass did develop a sense of special destiny. Indeed, he wrote the three autobiographies, in part, as a means of authenticating this conception of self. Uncle Lawson was at least one influential source of the idea of a benevolent and millennial God, a God who had the welfare of the downtrodden at heart, and who would one day intervene on their behalf. Uncle Lawson's instructions, wrote Douglass, "were not without their influence upon my character and destiny. He threw my thoughts into a channel from which they have never entirely diverged." Moreover, Douglass felt "assured, and cheered on . . . believing that my life was under the guidance of a wisdom higher than my own."[12]

Douglass' God was the God of black Christianity: benevolent and loving, but also a deliverer with a special concern for the oppressed. In general religious outlook, Douglass was a nineteenth-century millennialist. He was not an "evangelical" Christian in any strict sense, but his views of God and history squarely placed him in the millennial tradition. By the 1850s, his thought exhibited virtually all the religious and secular tenets of millennialism: eschatological symbolism, God's second coming and retributive justice, and the American sense of mission as a "redeemer nation." Whether derived from biblical prophecy or expressed in a more ambiguous and secular way, these beliefs were widespread in mid-nineteenth-century America. Douglass garnered long-range hope for the cause of black freedom from faith in an apocalyptic God who could enter history and force nations, like individuals, to chart a new course. This faith did much to shape Douglass' interpretation of the sectional crises of the 1850s and especially of the Civil War that followed.[13]

12. *Ibid.*, 168–69. On the influence of Uncle Lawson, also see Preston, *Young Frederick Douglass*, 97–98; and Andrews, "Frederick Douglass, Preacher," 592–93.

13. The literature on millennialism is extensive. Most helpful to me have been James H. Moorhead, *American Apocalypse: Yankee Protestants and the Civil War, 1860–1869* (New Haven, 1978), 1–128; James H. Moorhead, "Between Progress and Apocalypse: A Reassessment of Millennialism in American Religious Thought, 1800–1880," *Journal of American History*, LXXI (December, 1984), 524–42; Ernest Lee Tuveson, *Redeemer Nation: The Idea of America's Millennial Role* (Chicago, 1968), 1–90, 187–214; Ira Brown, "Watchers for the Second Coming: The Millennial Tradition in America," *Mississippi Valley Historical Review*, XXXIX (December, 1952), 441–58; David E. Smith, "Millennarian Scholarship in America," *American Quarterly*, XVII (Fall, 1965), 535–49; and J. F. Maclear, "The Republic and the Millennium," in Elwyn A. Smith (ed.), *The Religion of the Republic* (Philadelphia, 1971), 183–216.

Douglass arrived at this spiritual understanding of history—a mixture of millennialism, progress, and apocalypticism—by less formal means than traditional theologians, but by the 1850s it had shaped his thinking and provided perhaps the deepest layer of his prewar hope. Douglass' millennialism was optimistic and activist at the same time. Waiting for the "jubilee" of black emancipation and the fulfillment of America's national destiny required patience, but also "earnest struggle"; it demanded faith, but also great "suffering." His famous statement about agitation in 1857 has stood the tests of time and numerous protest ideologies: "If there is no struggle there is no progress. . . . Power concedes nothing without a demand. It never did and it never will." But for Douglass, millennial symbolism was not merely a rhetorical device. It was a real source of faith, not simply a benign spiritual exercise. He hoped that his listeners would live to see "a celebration of the American jubilee," Douglass declared at a speech on West Indian emancipation in 1857. "That jubilee will come," he promised. "You and I may not live to see it; but . . . God reigns, and slavery must yet fall; unless the devil is more potent than the Almighty; unless sin is stronger than righteousness, slavery must perish, and that not very long hence." The progress of history, the purpose of America, and the destiny of his own people were all essentially moral. "There was something God-like" in the British decree of emancipation in the West Indies, Douglass claimed. He knew that the political and historical circumstances of British emancipation were more complex than spiritual imagery could convey, but he could not resist calling the event a "wondrous transformation" and a "bolt from the moral sky." He called on black Americans to see West Indian emancipation as "a city upon a hill" to light the way toward their own new history.[14] The deepest source of Douglass' hopes lay where all great dreams are preserved: in the spiritual and moral imagination.

Douglass' millennialism was never without his persistent scorn for religious hypocrisy. To Douglass, pious slaveholders were the most dangerous kind. He despised the use of Christianity to defend slavery and relished every opportunity to condemn the practice. In an almost perverse way, Douglass seemed to gather strength from attacking religious hypocrisy, which he saw as a spiritual disease striking "at the freedom of the national mind." He viewed "slaveholding religionists" in two ways: they were the Slave Power's most dangerous weapon, and the most vulnerable target for abolitionists' attacks.

14. Speech, "West Indian Emancipation," delivered at Canandaigua, New York, August 4, 1857, in FD Papers (LC), reel 14, pp. 22, 6, 9.

When condemned in 1859 for his "tirade of abuse" against the northern clergy, Douglass defended his religious skepticism: "Forever would we prefer the fellowship of the skeptic who recognizes us as men," he wrote, "to the devout saint who can only regard us . . . as excluded from the dignity of humanity. Forever commend us to a sound man in preference to a rotten religionist." To Douglass, racial equality before God was self-evident. From religion he demanded honesty and a gospel of liberation. He was especially attracted to the brand of Unitarianism preached by the Boston iconoclast Theodore Parker. Douglass was a moral determinist who put part of his faith in a millennial God, but he expected nothing of history without human will and fiery activism.[15]

Douglass' beliefs in God's retributive justice and in history as progress were widely shared by black thinkers. Letters and articles in the *Christian Recorder*, a black newspaper published in Philadelphia by the African Methodist Episcopal Church, reflect the same preoccupations in the decade before the Civil War. Columns abound on such topics as the "Nature of Christian Hope" and the "Providences of God." The Reverend J. P. Campbell, the *Christian Recorder*'s first editor, assumed a similar role to that of Douglass—a promoter of black optimism and self-confidence. As a minister must, Campbell

15. "Slaveholding Religion," *DM*, October, 1860. For Douglass' hatred of pious slaveholders, see his *Bondage and Freedom*, 196–97, 258. Douglass was attacked by the *Congregational Herald* for his hostile views toward northern clergy after a western speaking tour. See *DM*, April, 1859. On Douglass' admiration for Parker, see "Death of Theodore Parker," *DM*, July, 1860. "Ten thousand times over would we prefer the religion of Theodore Parker," Douglass wrote, "with its downright honesty . . . its honor to man as man, without respect to color . . . than that miserable trash passing as Evangelical religion." On the changes in Douglass' religious outlook, see Martin, *Mind*, 173–82. Martin charts a course for Douglass from "divine determinism" to religious "liberalism" and "humanism." According to Martin, this process had already begun in the mid-1850s as Douglass became involved in political abolitionism and emphasized human will over religious faith. Although Martin's analysis of the "demystification" of Douglass' religion is very interesting, he underestimates the significance of millennialism in the black thinker's mind. From my reading of the sources, Douglass did not abandon a "sacred world view" and develop a "supremely rational view" as readily as Martin indicates. Human will and divine power were equal forces in much of nineteenth-century millennial thought. Much recent scholarship has stressed this ambiguity and dualism in millennialism. See especially Moorhead, "Between Progress and Apocalypse," 524–33. Moorhead demonstrates persuasively how for many northern Protestants millennial symbolism "could shift, almost effortlessly, from a religious to a political context." For another call for greater awareness of the ambiguity in millennialism, see James West Davidson, *The Logic of Millennial Thought: Eighteenth-Century New England* (New Haven, 1977), 28–36. On the growth of Douglass' religious liberalism, also see William L. Van Deburg, "Frederick Douglass: Maryland Slave to Religious Liberal," *Maryland Historical Magazine*, LXIX (Spring, 1974), 27–43.

would occasionally try to define the idea of faith to his readers. He argued that where "experience" offered blacks few reasons for confidence in their lot, only faith could provide "evidence" for hope. Moreover, Campbell trumpeted the "law of progress" as boldly as any other black leader. "We are progressive beings," he wrote, "God has made us to be eternally progressing."[16] There is nothing surprising in these expressions of faith and optimism; one expects such views from religious leaders. But no amount of theorizing about the nature of Christian faith could completely submerge the parallel assertions of anxiety and, at times, an underlying pessimism in black opinion. Without a spiritual anchor to rely upon, without a God of justice to overrule a society that promised only injustice, without the simple but powerful theory that history is a process where things somehow get better, and without a fierce commitment to agitation, black leaders could not realistically have continued to exhort their people to remain hopeful of a life of opportunity and dignity in the face of oppression.

Some very conservative opinions about black prospects also appeared in the *Christian Recorder* in the 1850s. Some contributors urged waiting for a better world in the hereafter, others simply counseled patience and moderation through petitioning state legislatures, while a few even took the self-improvement formula to the extreme of denouncing agitation altogether. By witnessing black elevation, wrote one correspondent, whites "would be compelled upon their own principle to grant us our rights." Few black leaders ever gave up on this central premise of the self-improvement doctrine, but the lessons of the 1850s refuted the notion that virtue would ultimately be its own reward. Reverend J. P. Campbell's angry responses to these conservative assertions demonstrated his commitment to black self-reliance. As for rights, he argued, "we have to wait for nothing, the right is a natural one."[17]

16. See *Christian Recorder* (Philadelphia), August 17, 1854, September 16, 1854, October 2, 1854, February 1, 1855, August 18, 1855, January 19, 1861. For the Campbell quotations, see *ibid.*, October 2, 1854, September 16, 1854.

17. *Ibid.*, May 1, 1855, September 16, 1854, April 4, 1855. On the nature of black religion under slavery and freedom, see Albert J. Raboteau, *Slave Religion: The Invisible Institution in the Antebellum South* (New York, 1978); and Monroe Fordham, *Major Themes in Northern Black Religious Thought, 1800–1860* (Hicksville, N.Y., 1975). For analysis of the attachment of black leaders to the self-improvement formula, see Frederick Cooper, "Elevating the Race: The Social Thought of Black Leaders, 1827–1850," *American Quarterly*, XXIV (December, 1972), 604–25; and David W. Blight, "In Search of Learning, Liberty, and Self-Definition: James McCune Smith and the Ordeal of the Antebellum Black Intellectual," *Afro-Americans in New York Life and History*, IX (July, 1985), 7–25.

This mixture of faith and agitation characterized the black struggle. Although the bedrock of black Christian faith remained the conception of a protective and delivering God, the tension between belief and reality caused anxiety for many blacks. For a man like Douglass, who was not a clergyman and preferred religious skepticism to formal theology, the belief in progress and Divine Providence served well to buttress a sagging confidence in the future of blacks in America. But as an agitator and a reformer, Douglass could never be fully satisfied with a reliance on faith alone. As the prospects of blacks darkened in the 1850s, he yearned more and more to see the signs of progress in passing events. Any faith so sorely tested demands at some point what Douglass would later call the "facts of experience." Occasionally Douglass found great encouragement from the "experience" of his speaking tours. His ceaseless travel and contact with audiences gave him reassurance for his efforts. In late winter, 1859, Douglass engaged in a month-long, western speaking tour that took him to Illinois, Wisconsin, and Michigan. He delivered nearly fifty speeches and came back "gratified" and with "cause to rejoice." His positive reception at so many stops, he wrote, was "soul-cheering to observe."[18]

An examination of Douglass' pre-Civil War thought reveals an intellectual and emotional balancing between hope and gloom. By 1861, in a remarkable lecture entitled "Life Pictures," Douglass wrote: "all subjective ideas become more distinct, palpable, and strong, by the habit of rendering them objective, and all wishes and aspirations, all hopes or fears grow stronger as we give them honest expression in words, forms, or colours. This weapon can be potent in the hands of the bigot and fanatic, or in the hands of the liberal and enlightened." In expressions reminiscent of the optimism of Walt Whitman, Douglass appeared confident in the humanism of the American people. Frustratingly vague at times, even mystical in many of his oratorical flourishes, Douglass contended that "amidst all the gloom, there is life, and therefore, hope. Humanity is a great worker, and sometimes works wonders. Armed with its God-like forces, it is master of all situations, and is a full match for all adversities." Man's limitless potential to conquer evil and to overcome the tragic undertones of history was a favorite theme for the former fugitive slave who was acutely aware that he had defeated great odds

18. "The Proclamation and a Negro Army," speech delivered at Cooper Institute, New York, February, 1863, in Foner (ed.), *Life and Writings*, III, 328; "My Recent Western Tour," *DM*, April, 1859.

in his own life. His romantic and Transcendentalist faith in human potential came at least in part from his own experience, but he had also honed his convictions about human perfectability under the tutelage of the Garrisonian abolitionists in the 1840s. But for the black reformer, no matter how outwardly sanguine about his belief that "life is agitation and agitation progress," when philosophy met experience, the strain and frustration were immense.[19]

Some of Douglass' optimism emerged from a sense of obligation, though much of it was also a product of his passionate humanism. From the mid-1850s to the outbreak of the Civil War, however, Douglass found it difficult to remain consistently hopeful. His discouragement found expression in many ways. The black leader's frustration began and ended with his personal awareness of the depth of American racism. In many of his editorials and speeches Douglass seems a lonely voice crying out into the wilderness of racial hatred. In 1853 he characterized the position of northern free blacks as "anamolous, unequal, and extraordinary." From these careful but telling words, Douglass moved quickly to bitter descriptions of the effects of prejudice, as he lectured his audience of white abolitionists. "Aliens we are in our native land," he proclaimed. Political and religious principles "are construed and applied against us. We are literally scourged beyond the beneficent range of both authorities, human and divine. . . . American humanity hates us, scorns us, disowns and denies in a thousand ways, our very personality." To Douglass, fugitive slaves like himself had only fled from the "hungry bloodhound" of the South to the "devouring wolf" of the North. All efforts to fashion hope and plan strategies for elevation or abolition had to confront this greatest of all obstacles—racial prejudice.[20]

A half-century later W. E. B. Du Bois described the entire history of Afro-Americans as a "longing to attain self-conscious manhood." This dehumanization of blacks under generations of slavery and caste was a theme that permeated Douglass' thought on the eve of the Civil War. "We are coolly put on trial for our manhood," he lamented in a speech first delivered in 1858. The "vital question" at stake in the great sectional crisis, he argued, was not "whether slavery shall be extended or limited, whether the South shall bear rule or not— but . . . whether the four million now held in bondage are men and

19. "Life Pictures," also alternately entitled "Lecture on Pictures," delivered November 14, 1861, Syracuse, New York, and during winter, 1861, at the Parker Fraternity Course, Boston, in FD Papers (LC), reel 14, pp. 4, 13, 21.

20. "The Present Condition and Future Prospects of the Negro People," 243–44. On Douglass' confrontation with racial ideology, see Martin, *Mind*, 109–35.

entitled to the rights and liberties of men." Whether in the political or social arena, in personal or institutional relations, antebellum blacks understood that the questions of slavery and race were a measure of black humanity and of the extent to which American society would recognize it. In the term *manhood*, the combined anguish and hope of generations met and found meaning. Hence, the participation of black soldiers during the Civil War would take on great significance as a quest for the irrevocable recognition of manhood and citizenship. Black leaders were quick to see that at the center of the national controversy over slavery rested not only the meaning of race in an expanding American republic, but the very future of black people in that society. For a black abolitionist long struggling to convert an unwilling society to abolition, there were many signs of hope in the political storm over slavery in the 1850s. But in neither North nor South could black leaders escape the daunting reality of racism.[21]

Ignorance and fear, the age-old essence of racial prejudice, were constant themes in Douglass' prewar rhetoric. "No people are more talked about and no people seem more imperfectly understood," he complained. "Those who see us every day seem not to know us." The root of the problem was the same in both sections. Southerners were "moving heaven and earth to get more Negroes into the United States," but only as slaves; and in the North, Douglass charged, blacks were "denounced as exotics." Both sections, he insisted, were "animated by the same devilish pride and cupidity." When the war broke out in 1861, Douglass' rhetoric became more directly concerned with identifying racism as the "real enemy" of the Union and especially of the antislavery cause. But for all abolitionists, especially a black leader committed to both abolition and racial uplift, the act of understanding and identifying the true character of the "enemy" had been many years in practice. This acute awareness of the power and depth of American racism makes the fortitude and sustenance of hope among black leaders in the troubled fifties all the more remarkable.[22]

Black abolitionists often found the prejudice they encountered

---

21. Du Bois, *Souls*, 45; "The Races," speech delivered at various locations during 1858–61, in FD Papers (LC), reel 14, pp. 2, 9.

22. "The Races," 1; *DM*, August, 1859. Douglass was here responding to an article in the Philadelphia *North American* that argued that free blacks were unfit for citizenship in America. Douglass contended that blacks were not hated as much for their blackness as they were for their aspiration to "free" status, thus posing a moral, psychological, and economic threat to the white majority. Douglass further captured the age-old motives in claims of Negro inferiority when he wrote in this same article: "The meanest and stupidest tyrant that ever breathed can find in the character of the oppressed an apology for his oppression."

within the antislavery movement to be most grating of all. Some were clearly more sensitive than others, and some, notably black Garrisonians such as William Cooper Nell and Charles Lenox Remond, maintained closer ties with white abolitionists. But all were aware that in the United States the linkages between black and white abolitionists, though in some ways essential and rewarding, were fragile and often temporary. In Great Britain the interracial relationships of abolitionists were quite a different matter, and Douglass was perhaps the most conspicuous example of how important the British connection could be to American reformers. But in the anguished fifties, Douglass and many of his black colleagues lashed out frequently at the racism they experienced among their American antislavery friends. In 1856, Douglass found encouragement in the resurgence of political antislavery sentiment in the country. He was "pleased that the whites are finding that they cannot degrade their black brother without sharing his degradation," but, he added, "we grieve to find that under the shelter of this mode of attack the fell spirit of Negro hate can hide itself."[23]

Racial prejudice pervaded and sometimes overwhelmed the consciousness of virtually all antebellum black intellectuals. Samuel Ringgold Ward, a fugitive slave who emigrated to Canada, then to England and finally to Jamaica, spoke eloquently for every free black when he described prejudice as "the ever-present, ever-crushing Negro-hate, which hedges up his path, discourages his efforts, damps his ardour, blast his hopes, and embitters his spirits." The psychological impact of racism was so profound that Ward wondered that "the mass of us are not either depressed into idiocy or excited into demons." As one of the most embittered of the black elite, Ward despaired of understanding the actual cause of prejudice—to him, "American" and "Negro-hater" were nearly "synonymous terms." Despair over the power of white prejudice also gripped the spirits of James McCune Smith, the highly educated black physician-reformer in New York City. Smith felt "not only deeply injured, but grossly misunderstood" by most whites. "Our white countrymen do not know us," he wrote in 1860; "they are strangers to our characters, ignorant of our capacity, oblivious to our history." Whether educated and successful or illiterate and poor, there seemed to be no way for

23. "The Unholy Alliance of Negro Hate and Antislavery," *FDP*, April 5, 1856. On the associations of black abolitionists with Britain, see R. J. M. Blackett, *Building an Antislavery Wall: Black Americans in the Atlantic Abolitionist Movement, 1830–1860* (Baton Rouge, 1983).

northern blacks to find recognition of their humanity, much less their equality. The degradation of blacks had become a social custom in America. "What American artist has not caricatured us?" complained Smith. "What wit has not laughed at us in our wretchedness? What songster has not made merry over our depressed spirits: What press has not ridiculed and condemned us?" When Douglass, Ward, Smith, or other black intellectuals contemplated the future, their instinctive hopes for an immediate end to slavery, for human dignity and equality, were darkened by the clouds of American racism.[24]

These constant reflections by black leaders on the nature and depth of white racism demonstrate their profound awareness that at the core of the slavery controversy lay the issue of *race*. Far more had to be overcome than the political hegemony of the Slave Power, for the obstacle was far greater than slavery itself. Perhaps more than anything else, these reflections illuminate the sense of powerlessness felt so deeply by black leaders, who desperately wanted to control their own futures and the destiny of their people. Douglass summed up the deepest yearnings of free blacks in the phrase "practical recognition of our Equality." "This is what we are contending for," he argued. "It is what we have never received." Without this source of inspiration and psychic survival, Douglass feared "the almost insoluble problem of our future destiny."[25]

In spite of this daunting realization of the power of white racism, Douglass never ceased exhorting his people to self-reliant activism. Indeed, the lack of organization and apparent indifference among many northern blacks angered him and became yet another variable in his effort to sustain hope. Douglass knew its causes—illiteracy, poverty, discrimination, the denial of human rights, and the absence

24. Samuel Ringgold Ward, *Autobiography of a Fugitive Negro* (1855; rpr. New York, 1968), 28–29, 39; James McCune Smith, "The Suffrage Question," a broadside written by Smith for the New York City and County Suffrage Committee of Colored Citizens, September, 1860, in McPherson (ed.), *The Negro's Civil War,* 272. For analysis of the nature and depth of white racial attitudes in antebellum America, see Winthrop D. Jordon, *White Over Black: American Attitudes Toward the Negro, 1550–1812* (Chapel Hill, 1968), 315–573; Leon F. Litwack, *North of Slavery: The Negro in the Free States, 1790–1860* (Chicago, 1961), 30–186; and Fredrickson, *Black Image in the White Mind,* 1–129. For an analysis that corroborates my portrayal of the sensitivities to white racism among black leaders, see George A. Levesque, "Boston's Black Brahmin: Dr. John S. Rock," *Civil War History,* XXVI (December, 1980), 326–46.

25. "Self-Elevation—Rev. S. R. Ward," *FDP,* April 13, 1855. Douglass was reacting to a letter (part of a series) from Ward entitled "The Modern Negro—No. II," London, March, 1855, published in the same issue. Ward vigorously and bitterly attacked what he perceived as the racism of most Quakers and Garrisonians, whose treatment of black abolitionists Ward likened to the "animus of the overseer."

of politicization—but like many other black leaders, he had no patience with what he considered unjustifiable indifference. Inspired by the emergence of the Republican party and by "Bleeding Kansas," he chastised the "do-nothing tactics" of his fellow black leaders during the election campaign of 1856, challenging them to discard their "masterly inactivity" and join the canvass. In what seemed to him a new and hopeful political climate, Douglass spared nothing in condemning those who "float quietly with the current, allowing others to win and bestow the freedom which we lazily propose to enjoy." Black inactivity would only "prove the charges of our enemies true," he maintained. In 1857, the black orator said that he expected and could withstand any insult from white racists, but "the stolid contentment, the listless indifference, the moral death which reigns over many of our people . . . beats down my little flame of enthusiasm and leaves me to labor half robbed of my natural force." He found black apathy "humiliating," and every time he spoke or wrote about it, he tried to convert the issue into a manifesto for struggle and self-help. Douglass had maintained hope by linking black liberation to Providential destiny, but he knew that nothing was possible without "sacrifice" and "earnest struggle." Through his frequent harangues against black indifference, Douglass vented frustration and kept his own flame burning. Whether in editorials or from the platform, these appeals were altar calls by a black leader exhorting his flock to action and perseverance.[26]

In the late 1850s, Douglass struggled to sustain his spiritual hopefulness. He seemed to preserve an inner resolve where few outward signs of hope were apparent, but his rhetoric betrays fear and a grasping, almost desperate, claim to the righteousness of the antislavery cause even if its failure seemed imminent. In the wake of the Dred Scott decision, Douglass found himself wrestling with the manifold discouragements of his people. "They fling their broad and gloomy shadows across the pathway of every thoughtful colored man in this country," he painfully admitted. In an eloquent lament, Douglass expressed the horrible uncertainties of the moment:

I see them clearly and feel them sadly. With an earnest, aching heart, I have long looked for the realization of the hope of my people. Standing as it were, barefoot and treading upon the sharp and flinty rocks of the present, and looking out upon the boundless sea of the future, I have sought in my humble way, to penetrate the intervening mists and clouds, and perchance, to descry

26. "The Do-Nothing Policy," *FDP*, September 12, 1856, in Foner (ed.), *Life and Writings*, II, 403–405; "West Indian Emancipation," 19–22.

in the dim and shadowy distance the white flag of freedom, the precise speck of time at which the cruel bondage of my people should end, and the long entombed millions rise from the foul grave of slavery and death. But of that time, I can know nothing, and you can know nothing. All is uncertain at this point.[27]

These remarks are a measure of both Douglass' frustration and his sense of duty.

Douglass' speeches and editorials are interspersed with the dual, and at times contradictory, expressions of a passionate writer revealing his personal analysis of events while at the same time performing as the spokesman for black hopes. That he had this personal outlet—the regular columns in his newspaper and frequent speeches—may partly explain why he could remain more optimistic than most black leaders. In the course of one speech or essay, Douglass could bitterly attack the U.S. government, harangue the Garrisonians, and lash out at American racism, yet manage to convert these visions of gloom into appeals for resistance. His constant activity, extensive correspondence, and his many antislavery contacts in the United States and Great Britain afforded Douglass a flow of information and ideas. Most important, through his writings and speaking he could purge his own despair, thereby releasing some of the inevitable tensions and confused rhetoric of a black abolitionist seeking radical and immediate goals that seemed virtually unattainable.

Douglass relied heavily on his newspaper as an intellectual and a psychological outlet that provided him a vehicle by which he could freely express his views and reinvigorate his spirits. He claimed that there were times when he almost gave up on the paper. "But . . . it was the best school possible for me," he recalled. "It obliged me to think and read, it taught me to express my thoughts clearly." The paper made him self-reliant and gave him a sense of liberation through language. "I had an audience to speak to every week." Douglass wrote, "and must say something worth their hearing or cease to speak altogether." He relished what he called this "sting of necessity." The paper, he claimed, gave his life "motive power"; as long as it lived, Douglass seemed to believe, the cause of black freedom lived as well.[28]

In the 1850s Douglass' paper was frequently in danger of financial ruin; its survival was a cause of constant emotional strain for an

27. "The Dred Scott Decision," speech delivered at the anniversary of the American Abolition Society, New York City, May 14, 1857, in FD Papers (LC), reel 14, p. 28.
28. Douglass, *Life and Times*, 264.

editor just learning his trade. Indeed, the paper probably would have folded were it not for two people: the abolitionist-philanthropist Gerrit Smith, and the Englishwoman Julia Griffiths. Smith's substantial contributions kept Douglass' paper afloat during the first several years of its existence. For psychological and emotional support, however, Douglass turned to Griffiths, a woman he met in 1845 at Newcastle-upon-Tyne during his initial tour of Great Britain. Griffiths moved to America in 1848 and settled in with the Douglass family in Rochester; for seven years she served Douglass as business manager, fund-raiser, editorial assistant, and even nursemaid. During this period of Douglass' quest for professional independence and his transformation into a political abolitionist, Griffiths was perhaps the most important personal influence in his life. She was certainly his most cherished friend.[29]

Douglass' relationship with Griffiths became a cause of great controversy by 1851. Beneath his ideological split with the Garrisonians festered the claim—made by Garrison himself—that the black editor carried on an affair with this unmarried white woman living in his own home. By 1852 Griffiths became a major focus of the Garrisonians' vilification of Douglass. There is no evidence of a sexual relationship between the editor and his assistant, although Griffiths did appear to be at least one cause of considerable discord in Douglass' home. In August, 1851, Griffiths wrote to Smith describing Douglass as "extremely depressed" about the financial status of the newspaper and "a considerable increase of those home trials about which I spoke to you." Griffiths did not elaborate on the "home trials" in any surviving letter.[30]

Although Douglass' wife, Anna, denied any friction caused by Griffiths, the contrast between the two women must have been troubling to the entire family. Anna was illiterate and largely uninvolved in Douglass' professional life. She managed a tidy house, prepared her husband's clothes for his frequent travel, raised four children (often on meager funds), and kept the home fires burning during Douglass' long absences. The Douglasses' daughter Rosetta described her mother as a "housekeeper" who "drew around herself a certain re-

29. Most Douglass biographers have dealt with his relationship with Julia Griffiths. See Martin, Mind, 40–44, 137–38; and Quarles, Douglass, 102–107.

30. Julia Griffiths to Gerrit Smith, August 26, 1851, in Gerrit Smith Papers, Syracuse University. For Garrison's reaction to Griffiths, see William Lloyd Garrison to Samuel J. May, Jr., March 21, 1856, in Louis Ruchames (ed.), The Letters of William Lloyd Garrison (4 vols.; Cambridge, 1975), IV, 391; Liberator (Boston), November 18, 1853, December 2, 1853, December 16, 1853; and FDP, December 9, 1853.

serve." Anna was uncomfortable in the "drawing room" and possessed almost no "knowledge of books," remembered her daughter. In Douglass' career, Anna remains largely a silent presence, a woman mired in domesticity, her husband's "helpmate" who managed his private affairs but could never be his intellectual companion. "Father was mother's honored guest," Rosetta recalled. "He was from home so often that his homecomings were events that she thought worthy of extra notice."[31] Undoubtedly, Douglass and Anna shared an abiding love during their forty-four years of marriage, but this picture of Douglass' domestic situation makes the presence of the refined and intelligent Englishwoman all the more interesting. Although she may have caused more discord than we shall ever know, Griffiths was indispensable to Douglass. For seven years she was his anchor on a troubled journey, both public and private.

Although sources are slim, Douglass' relationship with Griffiths is not completely shrouded in mystery. Douglass certainly did not hide anything himself; he was open about his affection for Griffiths as well as his mutual attraction with white women generally.[32] But whatever the extent of their personal relationship, Griffiths was Douglass' most important source of professional aid and personal support. Intermittently, she mothered him, criticized his writings, raised money that kept him solvent, and gave him a sorely needed source of intellectual and emotional stimulation. The image of Frederick Douglass as a strong, even arrogant, personality who molded his own destiny has been hard for biographers to resist, but it must be tempered with the knowledge that during the crucial period of his emergence as an independent thinker (1848–1855) he leaned on Julia Griffiths, his highly skilled, fiercely loyal cohort. Without her, Douglass may not have maintained faith in his paper and, therefore, in himself.

During the early 1850s Griffiths carried on a frequent correspondence with Gerrit Smith, discussing abolitionist issues and requesting money (with considerable success). In these letters, the clearest picture we have of the private Douglass emerges. Griffiths made constant reference to Douglass' "sickness," especially respiratory and throat ailments. In 1850 she described Douglass as incapacitated with "a grave attack of what we believe to be inflammatory rheu-

31. Rosetta Douglass Sprague, "My Mother As I Knew Her," speech delivered to the WCTU, Washington, D.C., May 10, 1900, published in pamphlet, 1934, in FD Papers (LC). For Anna's denials, see her letter to Garrison, *Liberator*, December 2, 1853.

32. On Douglass and white women, see Martin, *Mind*, 43. For the significance of his relationship with his second wife, Helen Pitts (who was white), see Walker, *Moral Choices*, 259–61.

matism"; he had suffered "three severe falls" and was "incapable of using his limbs to any extent." In December, 1851, Douglass was "entirely laid up" with an "ulcerated" throat.[33] These are but two of the many descriptions of his ill health in the early 1850s. Griffiths often attributed Douglass' illness to stress: "Although the seat of the disease is the throat," she wrote in July, 1851, "I am inclined to think that serious anxiety for his paper has much to do with it." In December, 1852, Griffiths wrote of Douglass' desperate need for "some portion of quiet" in order to write, and she complained of her own "chief difficulty" in convincing "those individuals who have no idea of *mental labor*" that quiet and solitude were essential for his work. This was no doubt a reference to Douglass' family, perhaps especially to Anna. This letter was written shortly after Griffiths had moved out of the Douglass home into her own residence.[34]

Griffiths was not only Douglass' assistant who drafted some of his editorials (from dictation) while he was sick, she was also his protector. In an 1851 letter to Smith that she labeled *"Private,"* Griffiths communicated her "frightful apprehension" that the "immense anxiety (pecuniary and family) is begging to affect our friend Frederick's mind." She feared that Douglass was losing "his balance of mind" and told Smith in confidence that the editor had talked of "going crazy." Griffiths stressed that she did not leave Douglass' side for long during his tribulations; she read aloud and sang some of his favorite "hymns and psalms." She begged Smith to write a "bright commendatory letter" to the depressed Douglass. In the meantime, like a good Victorian woman, Griffiths promised to "do all in my power to tranquilize him . . . and . . . not feather my fears to anyone."[35]

Griffiths' letters must be read with caution. Many of her missives to Smith were, at least in part, requests for money, and her image of a sick and depressed Douglass may have been somewhat embellished in order to loosen Smith's purse strings. But sincerity pervades all the letters, and Griffiths was much more than merely a fawning Victorian lady. She was proud of her role as Douglass' assistant. From her descriptions, we get at least a partial picture of a man prone to fits of anxiety over the ambitious course he had charted. At times, Douglass must have felt isolated in Rochester, a lonely voice speaking with a

33. Griffiths to Smith, ? 1850, December 13, 1851, both in Gerrit Smith Papers. Other examples of letters about Douglass' illnesses include Griffiths to Smith, Saturday Morning, 1850, July 10, 1851, and Smith to Griffiths, July 25, 1851, all in *ibid.*
34. Griffiths to Smith, July 23, 1851, December 18, 1852, both in *ibid.*
35. Griffiths to Smith, November 24, 1851, in *ibid.* On Griffiths' role as fund-raiser, see Griffiths to Smith, February 22, 28, 1851, July 10, 1851, all in *ibid.*

newspaper that could only survive through abolitionists' philanthropy. He seemed convinced of his life's calling as an editor-orator, but at times he could only have wondered how he might really have an effect, how he could ever persuade men to change some of their deepest convictions.

It was characteristic of Douglass in the 1850s to grasp hope from the midst of despair. In part, this was a rhetorical device, a product of the *duty* of hope, but the conversion of gloom into promise also reflects the fortitude and stoicism essential to Douglass' work. In his scheme of history, an evil so great as slavery might thrive and gain longstanding advantage, but slavery, like all forms of tyranny, warred endlessly with natural law and the ultimate justice of Divine Providence. Eventually, the evil would become so great, such an all-consuming threat to human liberty, that it would explode and meet destruction by its own folly. In Douglass' view, liberty "may to human appearances be dead, the enemy may rejoice at its grave, and sing its funeral requiem, but in the midst of the triumphal shout, it leaps from its well-guarded sepulchre, asserts the divinity of its origins, flashes its indignant eye upon the affrighted enemy, and bids him prepare for the last battle, and the grave."[36] Appeals to the abstract righteousness of the antislavery cause and to the indestructibility of liberty came from genuine resources of faith in Douglass' mind, and they exploded with literary power on the pages of his newspaper and from countless platforms. But one cannot help wondering about the effect of these appeals on his black reading or listening audience. The troubled and unjust world of antebellum northern blacks offered few reasons for optimism. Their task was survival; success went to those most resilient and able to improvise. Douglass was an improvisational writer and orator, fashioning hope out of the hard lives of his people wherever he could find it.

Douglass often had little to rely upon apart from his own imagination and his oratorical skill to lift the spirits of his people. Straining to foster hope by any means possible, he frequently argued that the larger the victory for slavery, the more vulnerable the institution became to ultimate destruction. His speech on the Dred Scott decision is an excellent case in point. Acknowledging that many blacks now considered the dream of emancipation completely lost, he insisted on "a brighter view." "David . . . looked small and insignificant when going to meet Goliath, but looked larger when he had slain his foe," argued Douglass. "Thus hath it ever been," he continued,

36. "The Doom of the Black Power."

"oppression organized as ours is, will appear invincible up to the hour of its fall."[37]

The David and Goliath metaphor illustrates an important mixture in Douglass' rhetoric. On the one hand, the choice of a biblical reference in which the small and righteous rise up to slay a huge and evil foe betrays the fear and anxiety of the black leader who felt a profound sense of powerlessness. It was almost as if Douglass was pleading with his fellow blacks not to lose hope, to *believe* they would triumph no matter how dark the hour. On the other hand, his imagery also demonstrated once again the faith, however tattered, that slaveholders and their northern apologists were digging their own graves. When events like the Dred Scott decision led to crisis and gloom, Douglass fell back on his spiritual reserves and relied upon prophecy. In the advances of the Slave Power, he believed "the finger of the Almighty may be seen bringing good out of evil . . . hastening the triumph of righteousness." He urged his listeners to hold fast to their belief in natural rights and reason, and to meet the Taney decision "with a cheerful spirit." "This very attempt to blot out forever the hopes of an enslaved people," Douglass claimed, "may be one necessary link in the chain of events preparatory to the downfall, and complete overthrow of the whole slave system."[38]

There can be no doubt that Douglass held these beliefs dearly. The notion of God's retributive justice was a powerful force in his mind and, therefore, in his social analysis. But he was a black abolitionist editor and social critic as well as a spiritual leader, and balancing these two roles was difficult. As a humanist, drawing heavily on his faith in the natural rights tradition, he could cheerfully declare:

As the intellect enlarges, and the scope of reason is extended, and the sympathies are purified, the abhorrence of slavery must increase. In these truths, our faith in the ultimate triumph of freedom finds firm anchorage ground. These truths give us more than mere prophetic assurance that the world will continue to move. They enable us to ask with hopeful confidence,

> 'What voice shall bid the progress stay,
> Of truth's victorious car?
> What arm arrest the growing day,
> Or quench the solar star.'[39]

But for every one of these romantic and hopeful statements, there were just as many pessimistic, bitter exclamations about the plight of American blacks. Thus, in the Dred Scott speech, Douglass at one

37. "The Dred Scott Decision," 28–29.
38. *Ibid.,* 33, 32.
39. "A Fulcrum for the Antislavery Lever."

point expressed resounding confidence in American character, the federal government, and the Constitution, but in the next breath he attacked the "moral blindness of the American people."[40] Bridging this gap between faith and reality was the principal intellectual, spiritual, and psychological challenge of the middle period of Douglass' life.

As with most devoted reformers, Douglass' rhetoric was a release for his most heartfelt spiritual and intellectual convictions, but, quite naturally, it also became an outlet for his deepest and most painful frustrations. Hence, we find an ambiguous, roller-coaster quality in Douglass' thought and spirits in the late 1850s. He was absolutely certain of his own basic beliefs and of the righteousness of the cause of abolition, and he espoused wholeheartedly the doctrine of black self-improvement, but there were so few specific and tangible ways that a black editor-orator could truly affect what in 1860 Douglass called the "terrible paradox of passing history." Ultimately, Douglass could only suggest that the explanation for the paradox of slavery and freedom lay in the "narrow and wicked selfhood" of the American people. This was partially a reflection on human nature, but, most important, yet another broadside at American racism.[41]

By the eve of the Civil War, there were many political developments in which Douglass found reasons for continued hope—most notably, the emergence of the Republican party. But like so many others among his black colleagues, his patience had run thin. At the beginning of 1859, Douglass confessed to a low and "saddened" spirit: "How long! How long! O Lord God of Sabbath!" he moaned, "shall the crushed and bleeding bondsman wait? . . . O! who can answer—who can tell the end we long to know?" Douglass was especially discouraged that, in his view, much of the vitality had dissipated from the abolition movement, and he frequently appealed for a return to "pure" antislavery doctrines and tactics, to the moral fervor of the early abolitionists. By August, 1860, in an editorial entitled "The Prospect in the Future," Douglass concluded that the antislavery cause was "shrouded in doubt and gloom." "The labors of a quarter of a century," he wrote, had "reached a point of weary hopelessness." From Douglass' perspective, the most dispiriting fact was the failure of moral suasion to produce practical results. The majority of Ameri-

40. "The Dred Scott Decision," 35–36.
41. "The Prospect in the Future," *DM*, August, 1860, in Foner (ed.), *Life and Writings*, II, 495. The roots and endurance of Douglass' hope and faith are themes developed in Harding, *There Is a River*, 239–40, 242–45, 248–49.

cans, even those emotionally moved, seemed only to regard the most profound efforts of abolitionists as a "grand operatic performance." "Reason and morality," lamented Douglass, "have emptied their casket of richest jewels into the lap of this cause in vain."[42]

These occasional bouts with cynicism, as well as the vacillation between hope and surrender, represent the painful confusion of a black intellectual seeking to overthrow racial oppression in a society where at times every conceivable interest seemed conspired to prevent it. For Douglass and other black leaders, ideological and psychic survival depended on an acute awareness of the obstacles amassed against them, and of the limitations of their own resources. It depended on the strength, as Douglass put it, to "work and wait." Still riding the crest of the wave of hope and emotion created by John Brown's raid, and shortly after returning from his second triumphal journey to England in July, 1860, Douglass wrote privately: "The times are just now a little brighter; but I will walk by faith, not by sight, for all grounds of hope founded on external appearance have thus far signally failed and broken down under me."[43] Religious and secular *faith* would remain his reserve of strength and justification. For Douglass, the eve of the Civil War was a time of anguish and excitement, a time for accelerated efforts to bring prophecy and human agency together at one of history's rare moments of opportunity.

42. *DM*, February, 1859; "The Prospect in the Future," 494.
43. Douglass to William Still, Rochester, July 2, 1860, in Foner (ed.), *Life and Writings*, II, 488.

2/THE POLITICS OF HOPE AND PRINCIPLE IN THE 1850S

The time has passed for an honest man to attempt any defense of a right to change his opinion as to political methods of opposing Slavery. Antislavery consistency itself, in our view, requires of the Antislavery voter that disposition of his vote and his influence, which, in all the circumstances and likelihoods of the case tend most to the triumph of Free Principles in the Councils and Government of the nation. . . . Right Antislavery action is that which deals the . . . deadliest blow upon Slavery that can be given at that particular time. Such action is always consistent, however different may be the forms through which it expresses itself.
—Frederick Douglass, *Frederick Douglass's Paper* August 15, 1856

FREDERICK DOUGLASS' EXHORTATION to "work and wait" implied not only a stoic faith unique to black leaders in America but a political consciousness as well. In the 1850s Douglass experienced a political awakening. After breaking with the Garrisonians in the late 1840s and establishing an independent newspaper in Rochester, he increasingly embraced political abolitionism. Indeed, he assumed the roles of black social critic and national political commentator. Douglass' increasing concern with national affairs and his development as a political actor are crucial to an understanding of his eventual interpretation of secession and the Civil War.

Douglass' course was typical of the many abolitionists who came to see political action as essential to any antislavery progress. Although he began his career under the tutelage of the Garrisonians, developing deep personal ties and ideological commitments to Wendell Phillips and to Garrison himself, he eventually found their rigid doctrines of moral suasion, nonvoting, and disunionism lacking in the political climate of the 1850s. With most abolitionists, Douglass came to see slavery as an evil of the broadest dimension, a system rooted in racism and woven deep into the social fabric. But it was also the cause of great sectional conflict, a potential threat to national existence, and therefore an immensely political problem. As a black abolitionist committed to a "root and branch" abolition of slavery as well as to the elevation and equality of his people, Douglass took heart in the rising sectional crises over the expansion of slavery. The growing challenge to the existence of slavery in the western territories offered abolitionists new opportunities to question its morality everywhere in America.

Through the course of the 1850s Douglass' work defined his life and rendered him more and more a public and, therefore, a political man. He struggled to publish his newspaper as a weekly, traveled and spoke widely throughout the northern states, and attended every major black convention (except those concerned with emigration). He became a principal architect of black self-help plans, such as manual-labor schools, preached the doctrine of self-reliance, and made his newspaper a major forum for debate over the entire scheme of black self-improvement. He attended political party conventions and became an active campaigner, first for the Liberty and Free-Soil parties and eventually for the Republicans. He harbored fugitive slaves and spirited at least one hundred to freedom in Canada from his home in Rochester. In 1855, the same year that his assistant Julia Griffiths returned to England, Douglass published his second autobiography, *My Bondage and My Freedom*. Douglass wrote about his life, at least in part, as a public man, wishing to use his own example to the fullest possible good for his people. Inherently, his autobiographies were political acts.

By liberating himself from Garrisonian doctrine, rejecting virtually all forms of colonization, and embracing American nationalism and mission, Douglass came to believe that only through national conflict and direct federal action would black freedom and equality become possible. But like most black leaders, he could speak and write about events but rarely control them. As a people without political leverage but at the heart of sectional controversy, blacks occupied a peculiar position; they were part of the "cause" of a great social problem without having much sway over the "effects" that would determine their fate. In his third autobiography, Douglass described his feelings during the immediate prewar period: "I confess to a feeling allied to satisfaction at the prospect of a conflict between the North and South. Standing outside the pale of American humanity, denied citizenship, unable to call the land of my birth my country, and adjudged by the Supreme Court of the United States to have no rights which white men were bound to respect, . . . I was ready for any political upheaval which should bring about a change in the existing condition of things."[1] Beneath these yearnings was the belief that any open dispute over slavery would help to expose the moral conflict that lay at its root. Beneath them also was a black abolitionist wishing for political conflict that could forge revolutionary change.

Douglass' espousal of political abolitionism was gradual, and only

1. Douglass, *Life and Times*, 329.

slowly and reluctantly did he arrive at a positive view of political parties. From 1841 to 1847, the Garrisonian school of abolition molded his thinking; his emergence as a brilliant orator took place within the contours of moral suasion. But as Douglass grew in stature and self-confidence, and especially after the establishment of his own newspaper in 1847, his thinking shifted as well. Organized political abolitionism was nearly a decade old on June 14, 1848, when Douglass attended his first official political gathering, a meeting of the National Liberty party in Buffalo. This small group, led by Gerrit Smith, the New York philanthropist-reformer, consisted of old Liberty party members attempting to give their "one-idea" party a broader base. Douglass, as a new resident of western New York (he had relocated in Rochester and had begun publishing the *North Star* in the fall of 1847), found himself increasingly attracted to the Liberty party's doctrine. In the early 1840s he had spoken favorably of the emergence of a political organization that demanded the abolition of slavery as a moral wrong and advocated the rights of free blacks; now he lived and worked in a new environment, under the influence of a more versatile yet no less ardent brand of abolitionists who were creating just such an organization.[2]

Like all other Americans keenly interested in the slavery question, Douglass had been attracted to the territorial problem through the annexation of Texas and the Mexican War. As the struggling editor of his own newspaper, he seized the issue of slavery expansionism. "I like radical measures," he announced in a speech at Syracuse in 1847, "whether adopted by Abolitionists or slaveholders. I do not know but I like them better when adopted by the latter." The coincidence of the Mexican War and Douglass' quest for personal and ideological independence from the Garrisonians served to hasten his espousal of political antislavery. The more openly he discussed slavery's expansion, the more intensely he focused on southern power and northern subservience. In January, 1848, Douglass condemned the Mexican War as a "slaveholding crusade" that had loosed ambition, tyranny, and aggression throughout the land, all in the name of the spread of slavery. According to Douglass, the country was ruled by "demogogues," and the people were trapped "within the bewildering meshes

---

2. Leon F. Litwack, "The Emancipation of the Negro Abolitionist," in Martin Duberman (ed.), *The Antislavery Vanguard: New Essays on the Abolitionists* (Princeton, 1965), 146–49; *North Star*, June 23, 1848; Quarles, *Douglass*, 143; Foner (ed.), *Life and Writings*, II, 68–69; Richard H. Sewell, *Ballots for Freedom: Antislavery Politics in the United States, 1837–1860* (New York, 1976), 101.

of their political nets." He called upon all Americans to flood Congress with petitions to end the war.[3]

Throughout the spring and summer of 1848, Douglass satirized the coming presidential election and condemned the two existing parties (Whigs and Democrats) as the "property of the slaveholder." Still spouting Garrisonian notions about a "slaveholding Constitution" and the necessity of disunion, Douglass saved special chastisement for the political behavior of northerners. Northern Whigs and Democrats were "infatuated and deluded" to imagine that they could truly affect the outcome of the election. "Slavery," Douglass argued, "the old President-making power, is still on the throne." Although his rhetoric at this stage of his career was fraught with fear, oversimplification, and near cynicism, the political reality of the slavery controversy had captured Douglass. After lamenting the moral bankruptcy of all existing political parties, Douglass nevertheless asserted his belief that "there are yet a few in each political party who would be pleased to have the coming contest waged on the principle of the Wilmot Proviso."[4] He could still attack parties with Garrisonian moral vengeance, but in so doing, his underlying hope that a new antislavery party might somehow arise in the North emerged.

Around the principle of the Wilmot Proviso—resistance to slavery's expansion—a new party was taking root. At Buffalo in August, 1848, the Free-Soil party was born amid huge crowds and great excitement. Douglass and several other black leaders attended. Although he tried to sustain a detached role at the convention, Douglass was called upon to speak. A throat ailment prevented anything but a short statement, but Douglass was clearly impressed and encouraged. In the weeks preceding the Free-Soil convention, he had urged voting abolitionists to support the Liberty party's nominee, John P. Hale, but in September, as Hale stepped aside, Douglass gave the endorsement of the *North Star* to the Free-Soil ticket of Martin Van Buren and Charles Francis Adams. Although it most closely represented abolitionist principles, the Liberty party, Douglass concluded, "was advan-

3. "American Slavery," speech delivered at Market Hall, Syracuse, New York, September 24, 1847, in Foner (ed.), *Life and Writings*, I, 269; *North Star*, January 21, 1848.
4. *North Star*, March 17, 1848, July 7, 1848, March 17, 1848. In a debate over appropriations for the Mexican War, on August 8, 1846, David Wilmot, a Democrat from Pennsylvania, proposed an amendment requiring that slavery be prohibited in any new territory acquired from Mexico. The amendment became known as the "Wilmot Proviso." It passed the House on two occasions but was defeated both times in the Senate. Nevertheless, it became an ideological guidepost in the slavery expansion controversy.

taged by the Free Soil Party by the superiority of its circumstances."[5] This was the initial shift from principle to expediency in Douglass' career as a political abolitionist. Indicative of many similar shifts to follow, it marks the start of a process whereby Douglass agonized between a moral world-view and the realities of political power, between detachment and action, between militancy and accommodation, and between the warring ideals of his inner self.

Douglass' conversion to political abolition did not occur overnight, but he had discovered a new and irresistible ideology. His drift away from the Garrisonians accelerated the more he came under the influence of the Sage of Peterboro, Gerrit Smith. Few American reformers demonstrated such zeal and dedication to the cause of blacks as did Smith. Although his support was faltering at first, by 1840 he became a founder of the Liberty party; moreover, his seemingly limitless purse financed not only abolition societies, parties, and publications, but efforts at black elevation and education as well. By the mid-1850s, no black American was more indebted to Smith's generosity and support than Frederick Douglass. Not only did Smith underwrite Douglass' newspaper in its early years, but he helped guide the black editor's ideological transformation. If William Lloyd Garrison was a fatherly figure in Douglass' life, then Gerrit Smith was his mentor.[6]

To the Garrisonians, Douglass quickly became an apostate, not only through his flirtations with political parties but also because of his adoption of an antislavery interpretation of the Constitution. By March, 1849, Douglass informed Smith that his paper's editorial

5. *Ibid.*, September 10, 1848; Quarles, *Douglass*, 144–45. For the Free-Soil convention, see Sewell, *Ballots for Freedom*, 156–63. For the reactions of black leaders generally to antislavery political parties, see Benjamin Quarles, *The Black Abolitionists* (New York, 1969), 168–96.

6. On Gerrit Smith, see Ralph Volney Harlow, *Gerrit Smith: Philanthropist and Reformer* (New York, 1939), an old but useful biography. For analysis of the nature and significance of the Gerrit Smith group of abolitionists, see Lawrence J. Friedman, "The Gerrit Smith Circle: Abolitionism in the Burned-Over District," *Civil War History*, XXVI (March, 1980), 18–38. A more thorough elaboration on the Smith circle of abolitionists and their philosophy of cultural voluntarism is in Lawrence J. Friedman, *Gregarious Saints: Self and Community in American Abolitionism, 1830–1870* (New York, 1982), 92–126.

Numerous letters from Douglass and Julia Griffiths to Smith in the Gerrit Smith Papers (Syracuse University Library) document Smith's financial support of Douglass. Many of Douglass' letters to his mentor begin with expressions of gratitude for yet another contribution to his paper or his personal support. In 1860 Douglass published the figure of $1,200 as the total of Smith's contributions for the paper. In all likelihood that figure was probably low. The subject of Smith's financial support was a sensitive issue for Douglass, and one over which he suffered a great deal of guilt and anxiety. He summed up the meaning of Smith's generosity in response to questions raised in an

stance was somewhere between the Garrisonians and the Liberty party. He did not clarify what he meant by this distinction but assured Smith that the *North Star* was "not a party paper" even though he was "not disposed to denounce as knaves those who believe that voting is a duty."[7]

"Nonvoting" was the easiest of the Garrisonian doctrines for Douglass to discard. The meaning of slavery in relation to federal law proved more problematic. Only through a slow and troubled process did Douglass embrace Smith's view that the Constitution empowered—even required—Congress to abolish slavery in the southern states by direct legislation. Pioneered by the New York abolitionist Alvan Stewart, this argument gained wider adherence from the writings of William Goodell and Lysander Spooner in the mid-1840s.[8] By the time Douglass moved to Rochester in 1847, this version of the antislavery interpretation of the Constitution had become a central premise among Gerrit Smith's circle of abolitionists in the Burned-Over District. They pointed to constitutional guarantees of habeas corpus and a "republican form of government" for every state, the libertarian features of the Preamble, the enabling clause, and especially to the Fifth Amendment's declaration that no person could "be deprived of life, liberty, or property, without due process of law" as proof that the federal government was constitutionally obligated to abolish slavery everywhere.

This view differed markedly from that championed by the Ohioan Salmon P. Chase. Beginning also in the early 1840s, Chase argued that the "intentions" of the Founding Fathers were for a speedy aboli-

---

article in another black journal, the *Anglo-African:* "Exaggerated stories of immense sums of money given us by Mr. Smith, set in motion by those who have desired to find an ignoble motive for our agreement with his opinions, have no doubt injured the paper in many quarters; but on the other hand, the fact that Gerrit Smith honored us with his friendship and his confidence, has greatly sustained and strengthened us for many years past" (*DM,* August, 1860). On Garrison's influence, see Douglass to Charles Sumner, September 2, 1852, in Foner (ed.), *Life and Writings,* II, 210–11. Douglass describes his relationship to Garrison as "like that of a child to a parent."

7. Douglass to Smith, March 30, 1849, in Gerrit Smith Papers.

8. Luther R. Marsh (ed.), *Writings and Speeches of Alvan Stewart on Slavery* (New York, 1860); William Goodell, *Views of American Constitutional Law in Its Bearing Upon American Slavery* (n.p., 1844); Lysander Spooner, *The Unconstitutionality of Slavery* (2nd ed.; 1845; rpr. New York, 1965). On the arguments of Stewart, Goodell, and Spooner, see Jacobus ten Broek, *The Antislavery Origins of the Fourteenth Amendment* (Berkeley, 1951), chap. 3; William W. Wiecek, *The Guarantee Clause of the U.S. Constitution* (Ithaca, 1972), 155–65; Eileen Kraditor, *Means and Ends in American Abolitionism: Garrison and His Critics on Strategy and Tactics, 1834–1850* (New York, 1967), 186–95; and Sewell, *Ballots for Freedom,* 94–95.

tion of slavery. He believed that slavery was a creature of state law and therefore merely "local" in America. The federal government had the power, said Chase, to abolish slavery in all places where it had exclusive jurisdiction (the District of Columbia and the territories). Hence, the duty of abolitionists was to restrict and circumscribe slavery, and through pressure over time, eventually force the South to emancipate its slaves by state action. By the mid-1850s Chase's view became the constitutional basis of the Republican party's doctrine of nonextensionism. Whether either of these viewpoints captured the true sentiments of the Founding Fathers is dubious, but they gave the abolition movement a new political persuasion whereby constitutional principle could be elevated above constitutional practice.[9]

Douglass' gradual conversion to the idea that the Constitution could be a radical antislavery instrument serves as an interesting barometer of his espousal of political abolitionism. By early 1849, he had stepped beyond the hardened Garrisonian conception of the Constitution as a proslavery covenant with evil. In a letter to Salmon Chase, Douglass declared himself "satisfied that if strictly construed according to its reading" the Constitution was "not a pro-slavery instrument," although the "original intent" of the founders and the meaning given it by the Supreme Court had made it so. Actual provisions of the document, coupled with moral and natural law, made the Constitution a source of antislavery principles, but history, Douglass seemed to be saying, had made it proslavery in practice.[10]

By April, 1850, in the midst of the crisis over the Compromise of that year, Douglass was still perplexed on the Constitution question: "Liberty and Slavery—opposite as Heaven and Hell—are both in the Constitution," he wrote. But this was precisely its "radical defect"; it offered no resolution for the "war of elements which is now rocking the land." To those who saw in the Constitution the instruments of freedom and justice, Douglass gave his "sympathies" but not his "judgment." He concluded that, for the present, the Constitution was "at war with itself." The mind of the young black editor was sometimes in a similar state.[11]

9. On Smith's view of the Constitution, see Sewell, Ballots for Freedom, 94–95; and Friedman, "The Gerrit Smith Circle," 29–30. On Douglass' espousal of Smith's view, see Martin, Mind, 36–38. On Chase's view, see Eric Foner, Free Soil, Free Labor, Free Men: The Ideology of the Republican Party Before the Civil War (New York, 1970), 73–77, 83–87. On Chase, also see Chase to Douglass, January 23, 1849, and Douglass to Chase, February 2, 1849, in Foner (ed.), Life and Writings, I, 352–53.

10. Douglass to Salmon P. Chase, North Star, February 8, 1849.

11. North Star, April 5, 1850.

January, 1851, found Douglass not yet convinced that the Constitution empowered Congress to abolish slavery in the states, but he was much more impressed with Smith's reasoning. Admitting to Smith that their "personal acquaintance" had greatly affected his thinking, Douglass declared himself "so much impressed . . . that I have about decided to let slaveholders and their Northern abettors have the laboring oar in putting a proslavery interpretation on the Constitution." Douglass had almost swallowed the theory whole, but he still had some reservations: "I am sick and tired of arguing on the slaveholders' side of this question," he complained, "although they are doubtless right so far as the intentions of the framers of the Constitution are concerned." Smith's arbitrary determination that because slavery was such a moral outrage it could never achieve "legal" status troubled Douglass, who still wondered about the confusion between moral perceptions and "American legal authority." Despite these reservations, Douglass assured his mentor that he had "ceased to affirm the proslavery character of the Constitution."[12]

Douglass' increasing political consciousness led him inexorably to a radical antislavery view of the Constitution, and by July, 1851, his conversion was complete. Although he still preferred to have the debate focused on the document itself rather than on the "intentions" of the Founding Fathers, Douglass declared that he too believed that the framers saw slavery as "an expiring institution" and sought "to make the Constitution a permanent liberty document." His reasoning came from an admixture of selective historical perception and moral outlook. Douglass always garnered hope from America's founding creeds, and in his view the Constitution—its republicanism and protection of individual rights—provided a legal foundation for the earlier promise in the Declaration of Independence. Without this promise and foundation, Douglass' vision of a future for blacks in America would have crumbled. If the Constitution enshrined slavery and made American citizens "mere bodyguards of human fleshmongers," Douglass argued, "then we freely admit that reason, humanity, religion and morality alike demand that we do spurn and fling from us with all possible haste and holy horror that accursed Constitution, and that we labor, directly and earnestly, for revolution, at whatever cost and at whatever peril." His maturing commitment to political action forced a choice: either the Constitu-

12. Douglass to Smith, January 31, 1851, in Gerrit Smith Papers.

tion was a "warrant for the abolition of slavery in every state in the union," or else the only alternative was violent revolution. Many black leaders had already suggested that the latter path might be the only recourse for their people (most notably, David Walker and Henry Highland Garnet), and Douglass had learned much from their arguments. This contrast of extreme alternatives demonstrated the bankruptcy of Garrisonian principles for Douglass, but it also suggests that, whereas desperation is often the seedbed of revolution, it can be the source of a hard-earned political realism as well.[13]

By 1852, Douglass' struggle with the Constitution question had ceased. At Pittsburgh on August 11, in an impromptu speech before the Free-Soil convention, Douglass was at his oratorical best. Attacking the Fugitive Slave Act, he argued that if, as some contended, the law was "constitutional," then "it would be equally the legitimate sphere of government to repeal it." Taking this newly radical position, the Free-Soil party itself had declared the Fugitive Slave Act unconstitutional, but at the 1852 convention, most Free-Soilers (they had now changed their name to Free Democrats) opposed additional radical proposals from Gerrit Smith that would have endorsed equal political rights for blacks and women and declared slavery a form of "piracy" that was illegal everywhere. Douglass declared himself squarely in Smith's minority camp: "I am proud to be one of the disciples of Gerrit Smith," he announced, "and this is his doctrine. . . . Human government is for the protection of rights; and when human government destroys human rights, it ceases to be a government and becomes a foul and blasting conspiracy; and is entitled to no respect whatever." Douglass declared that his purpose at the convention was to represent the principles of the Liberty party, which he did with vehemence and distinction. He lectured the dele-

13. "Is the United States Constitution For or Against Slavery?" *FDP*, July 21, 1851, in Foner (ed.), *Life and Writings*, V, 196, 192–93; Douglass, *Life and Times*, 262. David Walker, a Boston free black, published his *Appeal* in 1829. It was a radical antislavery pamphlet that called, in part, for violent slave resistance. At the 1843 National Negro Convention in Buffalo, Garnet delivered an address in which he called for militant slave resistance. "Brethren arise, arise!" said Garnet, "strike for your lives and liberties. Now is the day and hour. Let every slave throughout the land do this, and the days of slavery are numbered." For Garnet's "Address," see Sterling Stuckey (ed.), *The Ideological Origins of Black Nationalism* (Boston, 1972), 172–73. Douglass led the opposition to the convention's adoption of Garnet's message, defeating it by one vote. Douglass and Garnet carried on a feud of varying intensity through most of their lives. Later, he would come to share Garnet's view of slave insurrections as just and even desirable, but in 1843 Douglass' opposition to the advocacy of slave insurrection reflected his devotion to the Garrisonians.

gates on the "impossibility of legalizing slavery," urged a crusade to destroy slavery everywhere and not just in the territories, and challenged his audience to be concerned with "right" and not with numbers of votes. Douglass was preaching his newly learned brand of abolitionism at a political convention, and he seemed to revel in the effort.[14]

This conversion, like others, presented a new dilemma. For the next decade, Douglass repeatedly confronted the maxim that politics and perfectionism do not mix. In 1851–52 he remained ostensibly a member of the all-but-defunct Liberty party and aided Gerrit Smith's persistent efforts to keep the fledgling organization alive in New York. But as the 1852 elections approached, Douglass characteristically entertained notions of coalition with the Free-Soil movement. In February, 1852, he wrote to Smith: "I do confide in your judgment as to all matters touching the cause of human freedom. I cannot promise that I could follow if you should go for disbanding the Liberty Party, but I will promise to stand by that party if you say *stand!*"[15] This was a promise Douglass would never be able to keep. His pattern of shifting party allegiances and endorsements was already well founded, and he steadily came to believe that no opportunity for political advantage against slavery should be ignored. As Douglass' grasp of political reality and of the rigid limitations of his own position grew, he yearned for any means to link the cause of black liberation more closely with the national government.

From mid-summer until early fall of 1852, Douglass worked for a merger of the Liberty and Free-Soil parties. His hopes rose after his speech and warm welcome at the Free-Soil convention in August, and he wanted the remnants of the Liberty party to strive to imbue the Free-Soilers with more radical principles. In September, Douglass wrote a ringing endorsement of the Free-Soil ticket of John P. Hale and George W. Julian, contingent upon the replies of the candidates to two questions sent them by the Liberty party. The second of these queries—"whether you believe that slavery . . . is a naked piracy around which there can be no legal covering"—shows the stamp of

14. Sewell, *Ballots for Freedom*, 245–47; "The Fugitive Slave Law," speech delivered at the National Free-Soil Convention, Pittsburgh, August 11, 1852, in Foner (ed.), *Life and Writings*, II, 206–209.

15. Douglass to Smith, February 19, 1852, in Gerrit Smith Papers. In this letter, Douglass asked Smith's views on the Liberty party's possible absorption into a new and larger antislavery party. Also see Quarles, *Douglass*, 147–48.

Gerrit Smith and ruined the chances for political unity in the anti-slavery ranks in 1852.[16]

Douglass adhered to this principle of the illegality of slavery and the government's power to abolish it everywhere, but the bulk of his editorial endorsing the Free-Soilers reveals a mind torn between moral principle and political action. Douglass urged Liberty men to remember that a vote could seldom represent all of one's moral convictions: "The fallacy here," he admonished his radical colleagues, "is in the assumption that what is morally right is, at all times, equally politically possible." Sounding like a veteran politician, Douglass cautioned patience and flexibility; all reforms, he argued, must experience slow growth "until they gain a sufficient number of adherents to make themselves felt at the ballot box." He offered a "rule" for political action: "the voter ought to see to it that his vote shall secure the highest good possible, at the same time that it does no harm." Waxing sanguine and preaching expediency, Douglass insisted that the Liberty and Free-Soil parties occupied "common ground." The difference between them, he argued, was "exceedingly slight . . . verbal, rather than real."[17]

These were not the sentiments of a moralist taking the highest ground. To a significant extent, however, the Free-Soil party of 1852 was a radical antislavery organization, and Douglass, quite naturally attracted to its standard, was expressing his best aspirations for political action against slavery. Although he could encourage forebearance from radicals for the "half-loaf" of the Free-Soil party, he himself was impatient for results. Once converted to political abolitionism, Douglass demanded more of it than it could ever give, more than simply organized adherence to principle, even if such steadfastness might serve to spread the faith. This stance would cause him recurring hope throughout the 1850s, but also great indecision and disappointment.

In the wake of all this activity and rhetoric, Douglass again demonstrated his political fickleness by shifting his support back to the Liberty party. Hale and Julian ignored the "questions" presented them by the Liberty devotees, and by October Douglass withdrew his support from the Free-Soil ticket. Although the performances of both parties in the fall elections were dismal, Douglass found solace in the election of Gerrit Smith to the United States Congress. Running as an independent candidate, Smith had surprisingly captured the Twenty-

16. Douglass to Smith, July 15, 1852, in Gerrit Smith Papers; *FDP*, August 20, 1852.
17. *FDP*, September 10, 1852.

Second District of New York. "The cup of my joy is full," wrote the active campaigner to his mentor. Douglass' pattern of shifting political allegiances would continue throughout the 1850s; moreover, his devotion to the unpredictable ideas of Gerrit Smith would occasionally waver. But by the time of the Kansas-Nebraska Act and the birth of the Republican party in 1854, Douglass had wrestled for at least six years with balancing principles and expedience, forebearance and opportunism.[18]

Douglass' initial reaction to the Kansas-Nebraska Act was a mixture of outrage and refurbished hope. In his view, the repeal of the Missouri Compromise resulted from the "villainy of the slave power" and the "pusillanimity of the North." "The Republic swings clear from all her ancient moorings," he rejoiced, "and moves off upon a tempestuous and perilous sea. Woe! woe! woe to slavery! Her mightiest shield is broken . . . and for one, we now say . . . , let the battle come." He was encouraged by the increasing severity of the various drafts of the Kansas-Nebraska bill. "If we must have the repeal of the Missouri restriction," Douglass wrote privately, "let nothing be done to soften the measure." With good reason, he anticipated a political awakening in the North and a rise in antislavery sentiment, and he welcomed the splintering of political parties along sectional lines with the excitement of a frustrated reformer discovering new justification for his cause. "Let the old parties go to destruction," Douglass urged, "and henceforth let there be only a free party, and a slave party." The issue thus clarified, slavery could be more readily attacked along abolitionist lines from within the structure of American politics. The conflict was never so clear-cut as Douglass wished, but in the emergence of the Republican party and in the political storm over slavery in Kansas, he saw fresh hopes. Where the arguments of abolitionists had failed, perhaps Providence, the forces of history, and skillful opportunism could yet convulse American society to confront itself.[19]

Despite frequent discouragement, Douglass always believed that attitudes could be reshaped, if not by moral conversion then by the

---

18. *FDP*, October 15, 1852; Douglass to Smith, November 6, 1852, in Gerrit Smith Papers. For Douglass' joy over Smith's election, also see Douglass to Samuel J. May, November 10, 1852, in Foner (ed.), *Life and Writings*, V, 262. On Douglass' political flip-flopping, see Martin, *Mind*, 33–35.

19. *FDP*, May 26, 1854; Douglass to Smith, May 19, 1854, in Gerrit Smith Papers. For the reactions of political abolitionists generally to the Kansas-Nebraska Act, see Sewell, *Ballots for Freedom*, 254–66; E. Foner, *Free Soil*, 93–95; and William E. Gienapp, *The Origins of the Republican Party, 1852–1856* (New York, 1987), 72–87.

sheer weight of the evil of slavery and its threat to the liberties of all Americans. While the concept of an "irrepressible conflict" frightened white northerners and southerners, to Douglass it was an idea to be seized and exploited. He sought not to assuage fears of the impending crisis but to hasten its coming. In November, 1855, Douglass proclaimed: "The hour which shall witness *the final struggle* is on the wing. Already we hear the booming of the bell which shall yet toll the death knell of human slavery." He exploited every opportunity to expose the "irreconcilable hostility" between North and South over the slavery question. Natural law and a just God made conflict a certainty and a good thing. "As a nation," Douglass exhorted, "if we are wise, we will prepare for the last conflict, . . . in which the enemy of Freedom must capitulate." He hoped that a new antislavery ideology would emerge to unburden the slavery debate of further compromises. "Truth and Error, Liberty and Slavery, in a hand-to-hand conflict," wrote the visionary editor, "this is what we want; this is what we will have."[20]

Territorial expansion and the audacity of slaveholders themselves had opened the door for new hope, new ideology, and a new politics in America. Amid the sectional tensions of the 1850s, Douglass' task was to help drive the cause of black liberation more and more to the center of national affairs. Slavery was no longer a topic confined to churches, parlors, reform journals, and street corners; it was the cause of open political strife that would forever change America's party structure. The abolitionist ideal of a two-party system sharply divided by the moral question of slavery seemed somewhat realistic during the Kansas crisis. "The disintegration of the once powerful political parties," wrote Douglass, "is a cheering and significant sign of the times. The throne of the despot is trembling to its deep foundations. There is a good time coming." Vague as these expressions are, they represent Douglass' belief that the more slavery expansionism divided American politics, the more openly the nation would be forced to confront the humanity of blacks.[21]

Wishing for conflict and waiting for events, Douglass found encouragement in the nation's alarm. In 1860, he reacted to the breakup of the Democratic party with a combination of fear, glee, and righteous vindication. Admitting that the Union now appeared doomed and the future full of uncertainty, he nevertheless confessed to feeling

20. *FDP*, November 16, 1855. Also see Douglass' editorial, "Irrepressible Conflict," *DM*, October, 1859.
21. *FDP*, November 16, 1855.

"mightily excited about the matter." Douglass mocked the Democrats for splitting because "the head of the sable Africans was thrust between them as an apple of discord." Could it be possible, Douglass satirized, that the Democrats (if not the nation) would finally be "prevented from making a President by the ever-lasting Negro! Has it come to this . . . can nothing bind these intrusive sons of Ham? Are they so irrepressible that they come unbidden to Democratic communion tables, and thrust their dividing heels into the dish of Democratic love feasts?[22]

Douglass had long argued that blacks were the *conscience* of America. If slavery as a political issue could be more and more mingled with the cause of black freedom, then blacks might yet be the beneficiaries of disunion. "Slavery is the great test question of our age and nation," wrote Douglass in 1859. "It, above all others, enables us to draw the line between the precious and the vile, whether in individuals, creeds, sects, or parties." In Douglass' mind, the issue of slavery divided good from evil in America like "the distinctness of summer-lightening upon a black cloud." Ultimately, slavery would become a moral question for *all* Americans, liberating some and corrupting others. The survival of America's shared sense of mission between northerners and southerners depended upon how the questions of slavery and race were resolved. Douglass shared deeply with whites this sense of American mission, but in his view, before America's messianic destiny could be fulfilled, the nation had to be awakened to its folly.[23]

As Douglass' political consciousness grew, his grasp of political rhetoric increased as well. In the concept of the Slave Power, he found a means to convert the enemy of black people into the enemy of all Americans. The idea of a "Slave Power conspiracy" was at least as old as the 1820s, but in the 1850s (especially in the wake of the Kansas-Nebraska excitement) it became the staple of political antislavery rhetoric. Douglass adopted this rhetoric and exploited it to the fullest. In a speech at the annual meeting of the American and Foreign Antislavery Society in May, 1853, he laid out his understanding of the Slave Power: it was "a purely slavery party," he believed, and its branches reached "far and wide in the church and in the state." In Douglass' view, this rapidly growing conspiracy was driven by five "cardinal objects": first, the complete suppression of all antislavery

22. *DM*, June, 1860.
23. *DM*, July, 1859.

discussion; second, removal of all free blacks from the United States; third, perpetual guarantees for slavery in the West; fourth, the "nationalization" of slavery and its recognition by every state in the Union; and fifth, the extension of slavery to Mexico and South America. In this early assessment of the Slave Power, Douglass captured most of the essential features of the theory that would eventually bring unity to antislavery politics. These "designs," it was said, had taken on their own relentless, enveloping character, corrupting institutions and men alike. The Slave Power, Douglass argued, demanded that its adherents "unite in a war upon free speech, upon conscience, and to drive the Almighty from the councils of the nation." Slavery was no longer merely a moral wrong committed against black slaves in the South. It "shot its leprous distillment through the life-blood of the nation" and threatened the liberties of all Americans, white as well as black.[24]

Douglass was quick to see the appeal of the Slave Power idea. The corruptive influence of slavery had long been a central feature of his writing and oratory; now he could expose the multitude of evils slavery fostered and the degeneracy of slaveholders themselves to a widening white audience. A chance arose to make significant political and ideological gains through old arguments whose veracity he had never doubted. It had not been the primary concern of a black spokesman to expose slavery's threat to the liberties of white men, but Douglass was learning never to miss an opportunity to link the cause of black freedom to the preservation of white freedom. The Slave Power's "first purpose," he therefore surmised, was the stifling of free speech. "One end of the slave's chain must be fastened to a padlock in the lips of northern freemen," Douglass wrote, "else the slave will himself become free."[25]

To Douglass, understanding the Slave Power meant coming to grips with the "enemy." "We ought to know who our enemies are," said Douglass in 1853, "where they are, and what are their objects and measures." Analysis of the Slave Power idea, though, brought awareness of the complexity and vastness of that enemy, which, ac-

24. "The Present Condition and Future Prospects of the Negro People," 245–48. For analysis of the Slave Power concept and its use in political antislavery, see E. Foner, *Free Soil*, 73, 87–102; Sewell, *Ballots for Freedom*, 86–89, 102–106, 152–53, 199–201, 257–60; and Gienapp, *Origins*, 71–72, 76–77, 357–65. For the origins of the use of the term *Slave Power*, see E. Foner, *Free Soil*, 90, 96; David Brion Davis, *The Slave Power Conspiracy and the Paranoid Style* (Baton Rouge, 1969), 14–18.

25. "The Kansas-Nebraska Bill," speech in Metropolitan Hall, Chicago, October 30, 1854, in Foner (ed.), *Life and Writings*, II, 323.

cording to Douglass, inherently sought dominion over the western territories, hegemony in all branches of the federal government, and control over the mind and spirit of the citizenry. "Slavery aims at absolute sway," he argued, "and to banish liberty from the republic. It would drive out the schoolmaster and install the slave-driver, burn the schoolhouse and install the whipping post, prohibit the Holy Bible and establish the bloody slave code, dishonor free labor with its hope of reward, and establish slave labor with its dread of the lash." The monster's survival depended upon its own aggressiveness and the weakness of its victims, so its corruptive power became its charm and its own best ally. As most abolitionists saw it, the Slave Power's invisible curse destroyed the moral sensibilities not only of southerners but of northerners as well. Hence, in antislavery rhetoric, the Slave Power became a national sickness that threatened everything sacred in America.[26]

In Douglass' analysis of the Slave Power, he expressed all the forebodings shared by other abolitionists. He stressed the threat to America's national character, to its principal myths and doctrines; he feared for America's national mission, its inherited destiny as a beacon of democracy and liberty for the world (a destiny Douglass dearly wished to share); and he repeatedly characterized the struggle against the Slave Power as a test of America's collective moral rectitude, an idea he would amplify even further in his interpretation of the Civil War. But unlike many political abolitionists, Douglass saw the Slave Power idea as more than a conservative and defensive doctrine used to protect majority rule and free labor. In his search for the "real enemy" and the fullest advantage of a powerful idea, Douglass carried his analysis of the Slave Power much further. By showing its influence on the northern mind, he coupled anti-Slave Power propaganda with attacks on racism itself.[27]

To Douglass, the slavery question was more than a contest for power or the preservation of liberty. Confrontation with the Slave Power, the black editor hoped, would bring an even larger confrontation with the question of *race*. Again, seeking to join the cause of black freedom to America's political reorganization, Douglass wished to provide this new "lever of antislavery feeling" with a "fulcrum of moral principle on which to act." The propaganda advantages of the Slave Power idea were profound, but Douglass seemed

26. "Present Condition and Future Prospects," 247; *FDP*, February 24, 1854. Also see Douglass' editorial, "Slaveholding Religion."
27. On Slave Power as a defense weapon, see E. Foner, *Free Soil*, 86.

aware that real black liberation awaited cataclysmic events and even deeper conversions.[28]

Slavery expansionism had forced a sectional and political crisis, but Douglass wanted the controversy to cause Americans to look inward and not simply to the West or to Washington. Recognition of black humanity and the necessity of abolition were his ultimate goals. The question of whether black people had rights exceeding those of a horse, Douglass claimed, formed "the grand hinge of American politics." This oversimplified the slavery controversy, of course, but Douglass would not allow the Slave Power theory to deflect attention from his conception of the real enemy. He was always on guard against the practice of "opposing slavery and hating its victims," a problem that the Slave Power frenzy only exacerbated in some quarters of the North.[29]

Moreover, as a radical abolitionist and relative novice in the craft of politics, Douglass condemned all forms of "compromise" with the South. As David B. Davis has shown, abolitionists came to view the Slave Power as the "great American enemy," a force of evil with which there could be no compromise.[30] Indeed, one of Douglass' greatest hopes for the Slave Power argument was that it would end the effort for consensus on the slavery question. He pleaded with his readers to see the "true issue" in the Kansas-Nebraska controversy. To insist on preservation of the Missouri Compromise, he argued, would only be "honor among thieves," since further compromises with slavery would ignore the immorality of slavery and disregard the fate of blacks. Seeking consensus with the Slave Power, Douglass wrote, was "thawing a deadly viper, instead of killing it." Douglass knew that the sense of betrayal in the North over the repeal of the Missouri Compromise was a potent force for the antislavery cause, but discussion of the Slave Power could be put to a greater purpose, he hoped, than to wrangle about geography and political advantage. "The real issue to

28. *DM*, June, 1860.

29. *DM*, October, 1860; *FDP*, April 5, 1856.

30. Davis, *Slave Power Conspiracy*, 63–86. Davis makes the essential point that the identification of a "perfect enemy" helps to shape the social purpose and identity of a people. Also valuable is Larry Gara, "Slavery and the Slave Power: A Crucial Distinction," *Civil War History*, XV (March, 1969), 5–18. Gara's separation of the Slave Power concept from genuine abolitionism (concern for free blacks as well as for slaves) is instructive. Douglass' rhetoric, however, demonstrates that among radical abolitionists the Slave Power idea could be exploited as a political and ideological force without resorting to the racist underpinnings so pertinent in Gara's thesis. Douglass made the Slave Power rhetoric his own (another means to expose American racism), while utilizing it in the same fashion as his white colleagues. Mid-nineteenth-century black leaders lived with many dualities, and this was perhaps a welcomed one.

be made with the slave power," Douglass charged, "is this: Slavery, like rape, robbery, piracy or murder, has no right to exist in any part of the world—that neither north or south of 36 deg. 30 min. shall it have a moment's repose, if we can help it." To break the American tradition of compromise would take a mighty effort and a powerful threat to liberal values. In the Slave Power, Douglass believed the "perfect enemy" had been found, but the battle against the fear and practice of compromise was one he would fight through the war years and beyond.[31]

Some of the inherent qualities of the Slave Power allayed Douglass' fears of further compromises. Just as America's destiny was to enlighten the world and build an empire of liberty, so it seemed that the slaveholders' destiny was to destroy themselves. Douglass took heart in what abolitionists perceived as the natural aggressiveness of the slave system. Like most "monsters" of literary origin, slavery found sustenance only through mobility and expansion. Coining a new label for the same idea, Douglass referred to slavery in an 1855 editorial as the "Black Power." Slavery's path of destruction was wide, he observed, but "while crushing its millions, it is also crushing itself." Slavery, Douglass contended, would go the way of all absolute despotisms, overreaching its limits in the quest to destroy freedom. In a flourish of hope, he envisioned a new era precipitated by the tyranny of the Slave Power:

It [Slave Power] never wore an aspect so repulsive as it does today. It has made such a frightful noise of late that the attention of the world is directed toward it. The passage of the Fugitive Slave Act, and the Nebraska Bill; the recent marauding movements of the oligarchy in Kansas, all the ebullitions of its pent-up wrath, are fatal stabs in the monster's side. The antislavery sentiment of the North has been strengthened and increased by these developments; indeed, the Abolitionists have now a most potent ally in the Slave Power. Slaveholders are unconsciously performing good service in the cause of liberty.

Douglass' estimate of northern public opinion pointed to a significant change. Instead of regarding abolitionists as merely fanatics "crying wolf," the masses now perceived the evil in their midst and themselves cried "kill the wolf."[32]

In the character of the slaveholder himself, Douglass found a personal manifestation of the perfect enemy. At an early stage in his career, his diatribes against slaveholders took on the style of war

31. *FDP*, February 24, 1854; Davis, *Slave Power Conspiracy*, 84.
32. *FDP*, July 27, 1855.

propaganda. In his eyes the perfect enemy was a *hated enemy*, the embodiment of the evil that had to be eradicated. Consideration of violence as a tactic and especially the advent of the Civil War would eventually intensify this aspect of Douglass' rhetoric, but before 1861 he had ample practice at exposing what he perceived as the degeneracy of the master class. "The slaveholder is not satisfied to associate with men in the Church or in the State," he warned the Rochester Ladies' Antislavery Society in 1855, "unless he can thereby stain them with the blood of his slaves." The black orator's challenge was to convert this rekindled fear into a general conviction. "To be a slaveholder is to be a propagandist from necessity," Douglass contended. From experience he knew that the abolitionist's work was the same.[33]

Although he overestimated the slaveholders' sense of guilt, the psyche of the master class was one of Douglass' favorite subjects. Slavery's aggressiveness derived in part, he argued, from the psychological fears and needs of debased slaveholders. At least partially aware that they deserved punishment, they shuddered at the prospect. "They who study mankind with a whip in their hands will always go wrong," Douglass charged. "They only *see without*, the qualities they feel within themselves. . . . Pride, self-love, cruelty, brutality and revenge." Slaveholders were at least half-conscious that they had created a monster, and only by making it the "pet monster of the American people" could they preserve it. Slavery could only survive, he maintained, "by keeping down the undergrowth morality which nature supplies." The sensibilities of each newborn babe had to be hardened against the power of natural law, and the morality of a nation had to be shaped to sustain a wholly immoral institution. "The slave power must go on its career of exactions," Douglass asserted, "till the timidity which concedes shall give place to courage which shall resist." With each victory of the Slave Power came renewed opportunities to fling abolitionists' principles far and wide, but proslavery triumphs in national affairs seemed so resounding that the black abolitionist could only wonder where next to turn his voice, lest it be drowned out.[34]

Douglass' analysis of the Slave Power and, for that matter, all public

33. "The Antislavery Movement," 358.
34. "The Presidential Campaign of 1860," speech at a celebration of West Indian Emancipation, August 1, 1860, in Foner (ed.), *Life and Writings*, II, 503, 505; *DM*, September, 1860; "Antislavery Movement," 358–59.

issues demonstrates the complexity of his many roles. As a radical abolitionist and black editor, he was the symbolic spokesman of his people, and his life had to serve as an on-going illustration of their aspirations. He represented slaves, freedmen, and the black elite all at once. Simultaneously, he attacked the Slave Power in the South and racism in the North as equally ominous threats to the future of blacks, and he performed what could be called the "duty of hope" in a society where institutions and leaders seemed impervious to the notion of racial justice. He spoke for a largely uneducated and disfranchised people with little if any political leverage. With this dilemma, to whom did Douglass speak? Did anyone really listen?

As an editor and especially as an orator, Douglass directed much of his rhetoric at his white audience. If white attitudes were not influenced, if antislavery and antisouthern sentiment could not be fomented among white northerners, if the law and the United States government remained a fortress for slavery and white supremacy, then perhaps the destiny of blacks did not lie in America. But as we shall see later, Douglass despised the notion of colonization. To him, it abandoned hopes, destroyed dreams, and violated his sense of personal and national identity. He frequently lamented the peculiar plight of Afro-Americans as outcasts in their native land. Blacks were "becoming a nation in the midst of a nation which disowns them," he charged in 1853. But it was precisely through this sense of alienation and outrage that Douglass strove to affect the minds of whites. It is impossible to measure his actual impact on white attitudes, but his genius was clearly in his oratory and few ever matched his platform skills. Moreover, in the idea of the Slave Power, Douglass discovered perhaps the best possible means to bridge the chasm between blacks and the minds and institutions of the American people. Referring to the races and not to sections, Douglass claimed that "for weal or for woe this nation is united." "We are one nation," he maintained, ". . . if not one in immediate condition, at least one in prospects." *Prospects* were all a black leader could look to in the 1850s, and the Slave Power's aggressions might yet lend reality to hope.[35]

By entering the debate over the Slave Power, Douglass found himself playing two divergent roles: the black representative and voice of the slaves, and the political abolitionist concerned about national destiny and the welfare of the Union. His purpose was always to

35. "Present Condition and Future Prospects," 246.

capture the new awareness about slavery and to convert it into an increased concern for black freedom. The two roles both conflicted with and served each other. If he could link white fears of a slaveholding conspiracy to black suffering, a common cause might yet be struck where only racism had reigned before.

Ever-conscious of his specialness, Douglass exploited his own symbolism whenever possible. His speeches in the 1850s increasingly combined his own remarkable "story" with harangues against the Slave Power. As slaves were daily brutalized, so too all Americans risked the steady dehumanization that slavery wrought. "As a colored man there are peculiar reasons for my speaking," Douglass told an assemblage of abolitionists in 1853. "The man struck is the man to cry out," he continued, ". . . I am placed among the victims of American oppression. I view this subject from their standpoint and scan the moral and political horizon of the country with their hopes, their fears, and their intense solicitude." In October, 1854, Douglass' speaking tour found him in Chicago addressing a large gathering at Metropolitan Hall on the topic of the Kansas-Nebraska bill. Reacting to the charge that he was an "intruder" in the backyard of the unpopular bill's author, Stephen A. Douglas, the black Douglass exploited the moment to assert the "special reasons" for his right to speak. Beyond his "constitutional" as well as "natural right" to speak on any subject, Douglass described his peculiar role:

The people in whose cause I come here tonight are not among those whose right to regulate their own domestic concerns is so feelingly and eloquently contended for in certain quarters. They have no Stephen Arnold Douglas . . . to contend . . . for their Popular Sovereignty. They have no national purse—no offices, no reputation, with which to corrupt Congress, or to tempt men, mighty in eloquence and influence into their service. Oh, no! They have nothing to commend them but their unadorned humanity. They are human—that's all—only human. . . . I knew this suffering people; I am acquainted with their sorrows; I am one with them in experience; I have felt the lash of the slave driver, and stand up here with all the bitter recollections of its horrors vividly upon me.

An important aspect of the antebellum black leader's duality is thus revealed. Douglass wished to be accepted "simply as an American citizen having a stake in the weal or woe of the nation," as he asserted in the Chicago speech, but he was also the unique black voice, a former slave, America's awful paradox in the flesh, and he knew he must cultivate both images at once. He must be at one with his people and at the same time strive to make their cause at one with that of the nation. A chosen people and a suffering people might yet find common ground through a compelling myth and a shared sense of peril.[36]

How, though, were the two causes of black freedom and national destiny to become inseparable? By what vehicle or through what institution could such a union be struck? After 1854, the object of Douglass' hopes in this regard increasingly became the Republican party. In the potential of the antislavery coalition mustered by the Republicans Douglass found a recurring antidote for the many setbacks of the 1850s.

More than any other single issue before the war, Douglass derived his sense of political pragmatism from coming to grips with the Republican party. His reactions ranged from vehement opposition to cautious support, from hope to frustration and confusion. Two contradictory themes seem to run through all of Douglass' rhetoric regarding the Republican party. He demanded adherence to abolitionist principles (both for himself and for organizations). The "freesoil" position, therefore, offered him little satisfaction, and he took every opportunity to expose its deficiencies. But simultaneously he found it impossible to resist the appeal of a broad coalition that could discredit slavery, even if it fell short of calling for complete abolition and equal rights for blacks. Douglass was learning to be a realist and an opportunist, while also trying to preserve the moral integrity of his abolitionism.

From 1854 until the Civil War, Douglass found much to attack in the Republican party. At times he condemned "free soilism" and the Slave Power with the same vehemence. "Free soilism is lame, halt, and blind," wrote Douglass in 1855, "while it battles against the spread of slavery, and admits its right to exist anywhere." His editorials occasionally burned with bitterness over the nonextension argument. "Instead of walking straight up to the giant wrong and demanding its utter overthrow," he complained, "we are talking of limiting it, circumscribing it, surrounding it with free states, and leaving it to die of inward decay. A theory more fanciful and false, for getting rid of slavery, it would be difficult to conceive of." Nonextensionism seemed an inadequate response to cries for freedom and

36. *Ibid.*; "The Kansas-Nebraska Bill," 316–19.

justice. "Were we to relinquish our present position on the slavery question and join the Republican Party," contended Douglass, "we should feel that we were retrograding, instead of advancing."[37]

As the presidential election year began in 1856, Douglass tried to maintain his radical, uncompromising opposition to the Republicans. He argued forcefully that the survival of the abolition movement depended on "the soundness of its principles." The Republican party, he asserted, possessed "not a single warm and living position . . . except freedom for Kansas" and represented only a "sinuous political philosophy, which is the grand corrupter of all reforms." As the title of his editorial stated, Douglass sought to do his "duty as an antislavery voter." That "duty" demanded a steadfast adherence to principles and meant continued stress on the "sin" of slavery and the impossibility of property in man. It meant, at least at this point, the preservation of his "antislavery integrity." True to principle, Douglass performed as the dutiful abolitionist, standing on what he called the "true ground upon which to meet slavery." But this was only one sense of duty in his mind. He was equally committed to the duty of hope and equally aware of the political ground upon which slavery had to be met.[38]

The nonextension argument not only evoked the "true" abolitionist side of Douglass but exposed his pragmatism. From its beginning, Douglass perceived the potential of the Republican party to control federal power and impugn slavery. He saw no alternative but to exploit any advantage he could find against slavery. "I am willing to accept a judgment against slavery, whether supported by white or black reasons," he declared in 1857, "though I would much rather have it supported by both. He that is not against us is on our part."[39] Douglass had difficulty at times deciding whether the Republicans were for or against the cause of black freedom, but he could not resist hitching his hopes to the new party's future.

Douglass' denunciations of the Kansas-Nebraska Act led almost inevitably to tacit support of the emerging Republican party. The Kansas controversy had become "the great question of the age," he announced in the fall in 1854, and his enthusiasm for the way slavery had surged into national affairs prompted him to devise his own strangely naïve scheme for making Kansas a free state. In September, 1854, Douglass proposed an ambitious emigration plan by which one

37. *FDP*, August 24, 1855; *FDP*, December 7, 1855.
38. *FDP*, April 25, 1856; *FDP*, August 24, 1855.
39. "The Dred Scott Decision," in FD Papers (LC).

thousand free black families from northern cities would be resettled in Kansas. His "army of One Thousand families" was to be organized and financed by northern philanthropy, making the most of the free-soil fervor of the moment. "The true antidote . . . for *black slaves*," argued Douglass, "is an enlightened body of black freemen." This was Douglass at his most impractical. At times he needed to throw his dreams out to his readers, to envision the world as he wished it to be, and the excitement over Kansas and the Republicans seemed to offer a brief interlude when dreams were possible. But it is astonishing that Douglass could exhibit real confidence in this emigration plan and contend that white northerners would accept and support such a bold scheme. He seems for once to have forgotten the basic racism that underlaid the free-soil impulse. Douglass' plan conveniently ignored the fact that the "free labor" ideology around which the Republican party formed meant free *white* labor to most northerners.[40]

Douglass soon abandoned what he admitted was an "imperfectly presented" scheme. It is possible that he launched this plan because he knew it had no chance to succeed and therefore was a safe rhetorical adventure, but he also saw his emigration scheme as an opportunity for blacks to become actors in the sectional crisis, to enter the fray with everyone else. Douglass explained his emigration plan as a quest by blacks for recognition and citizenship rights. He also recommended it as a way to meet the "slaveholder on his own ground," to forcefully engage in the conflict between slavery and freedom by taking the greatest advantage of the Kansas-Nebraska excitement. So anxious was he to push the cause of black freedom into the national limelight that he could suspend his own sense of reality (northern racism—the "enemy" within) and propose that "white working men flock into the territory of Kansas by the thousands. There is room and work for all. Will the people of the North aid such a movement as is here contemplated? We believe they will, and will do so joyfully."[41] To stop merely the spread of slavery in the territories did not meet Douglass' criteria for "true" abolitionist ideology, but from the vantage point of 1854, it certainly provided new hope and new ways to attack slavery.

From such a combination of confusion, idealism, and frustration,

40. "The Kansas-Nebraska Bill," 320; *FDP*, September 15, 1854.
41. *FDP*, September 15, 1854. For Douglass' initial optimism about the emergence of the Republicans, also see the editorial, "The End of All Compromises with Slavery—Now and Forever," *FDP*, May 26, 1854. On "free labor" ideology, see E. Foner, *Free Soil*, 9–39; and Gienapp, *Origins*, 355–57.

Douglass interpreted the meaning of the Republican party. In July, 1855, he beheld the "doom" of the Slave Power "written in unmistakable characters by the great Republican Movement which is sweeping like a whirlwind over the Free States." Because it did "not go far enough in the right direction," Douglass declared that he could not "join" the party. He rejoiced, nevertheless, in the new party's possibilities. "It evinces the fact of a growing determination on the part of the North," he wrote, "to redeem *itself* from bondage."[42] Once smitten by the potential of the Republican party, Douglass never abandoned hope that such limited means might produce more radical ends.

The presidential elections of 1856 and 1860 vividly illustrate Douglass' equivocal responses to the Republican party. By 1855, the Liberty party still struggled for survival under a new name—the Radical Abolitionist party. Gerrit Smith was still its chief sponsor and Douglass remained a loyal member. Throughout 1855 and most of 1856, Douglass zealously preached the doctrines of the Radical Abolitionists, especially the constitutional duty of the federal government to abolish slavery everywhere. As late as June, 1856, he strongly backed the ticket of Smith and Samuel McFarland of Virginia, while denouncing the limited aims of the Republicans. Suddenly, however, with the campaign in midstream, he flip-flopped, shocking his closest associates by enthusiastically endorsing John C. Frémont for President.[43]

Douglass refused to acknowledge the charge of inconsistency in his sudden switch of allegiances. "The difference between our paper this week and last week," he contended, "is a difference of Policy, not of Principle." In an eloquent appeal for expediency and coalition politics, he argued that results (at least the hope of them) were just as important as principles. The most vital concern for abolitionists, Douglass maintained, was "to strike hardest, where the slaveholders felt most keenly." The deadliest blow to the Slave Power, he surmised, would be the election of a Republican president. In spite of the Republicans' lack of genuine abolitionist convictions, Douglass urged his radical friends to "take them, . . . not merely for what they are but for what we have good reason to believe they will become." The Republicans were the "most numerous" antislavery organization and

42. *FDP*, July 25, 1855.

43. Douglass to Smith, August 14, 1855, in Gerrit Smith Papers; *Proceedings of the Radical Abolition Convention, June 26–28, 1855* (New York, 1855); Quarles, *Douglass,* 156–61; *FDP*, June 10, 1856.

therefore the "most likely to achieve a valuable victory." The Republicans could be effective, Douglass concluded, whereas the Radical Abolitionists were too "isolated" and operated like "dwellers in the mountain peaks of the moral world." The doctrines of the unconstitutionality of slavery and the federal government's right to legislate abolition everywhere required much time and agitation before they could carry the day; nonextensionism and fear of the Slave Power, however, had captured the northern imagination. Hence, Douglass argued, support for the Republican party was the "path of duty" in order to accomplish "a possible good thing" while larger aims could wait.[44] Compared to his voluminous writings about the necessity of preserving "principles" within antislavery politics, this indeed seemed like a striking change, but the Republican endorsement in 1856 only conformed to the pattern Douglass established in 1848 and 1852 when he supported the Free-Soil party. In the Liberty party and its doctrinal successors, Douglass always had a party for his principles, but in the Republican party, as with the Free-Soilers before, he found a party for his hopes.

The duty of hope and the duty of principle were once again in conflict, and Douglass agonized over the impossible task of reconciling them. He had learned two different kinds of thinking, one moral and one political, and with divided and confused loyalties, he had to do both at once. He could "afford to be calm" under censure and rebuke, Douglass wrote to Gerrit Smith. "I support Frémont as the best thing I can do *now,* but without losing sight of the great doctrines and measures, inseparable from your great name and character."[45] Douglass had grown immensely in his path of intellectual self-discovery, and he wanted his ideological father to understand, if he could not approve.

Between the elections of 1856 and 1860, Douglass drifted into periods of great discouragement when the Republican party once again became the object of his scorn. Emigration and the potential uses of violence dominated the anguished minds of most black leaders during these years, and Douglass' responses to these issues will be assessed in later chapters. The gloom of the late fifties, though, inevitably affected his ability to sustain hope in a party that simply did not move in the manner he had wished. Supplanted by the territorial problem, the entire antislavery movement (as Douglass de-

44. *FDP,* August 15, 1856. On the question of Douglass' consistency with principles and politics, see Martin, *Mind,* 36.
45. Douglass to Smith, August 31, 1856, in Gerrit Smith Papers.

fined it) had lost momentum. According to him, the crisis in Kansas demonstrated that there was really very little difference between Democrats and Republicans. "Neither party aims to be entirely just and humane to the black man," complained an angry Douglass. "The first would admit the black man into Kansas as a *slave*," he contended, "and the other would seem to wish to exclude him as a *freeman*." Despised and unwanted, the message was clear to Douglass: a "free" Kansas meant the exclusion of blacks. The racist underpinnings of the nonextension argument had become all too apparent.[46]

In 1859 Douglass' hopes for the Republican party seemed to be bitterly disappointed. Nothing shocked him more than the designs of some southerners to reopen the African slave trade and the indifference with which northerners met the challenge. One of his greatest fears, he declared, was the "ever credulous and politically imbecile North." In Douglass' judgment, the character of the Republican party had fallen to "an inconsistent, vascillating, crooked, and compromising advocacy of a good cause."[47] In October, 1859, at this low ebb in his spirits, the actions of John Brown at Harpers Ferry cast the slavery controversy in a new light. Douglass' hopes revived as he fled to England in search of emotional and financial support, as well as refuge from federal arrest for his alleged complicity in Brown's conspiracy.

With its potential for a conclusive conflict between slavery and freedom, the election of 1860 once again forced Douglass to confront the meaning of the Republican party. Shortly after returning from his five-month sojourn in the British Isles, he wrote an affectionate public letter to his English friends. Grateful for their many private kindnesses, Douglass informed his supporters that he believed his public work had never been so necessary. He anticipated the election of a Republican president but declared that "the real work of abolitionizing the public mind will still remain." Assuming his election-year role, Douglass girded up for another walk along the thin line between endorsement and denunciation of the Republicans. "The Republican Party," he told his British friends, "is . . . only negatively antislavery.

46. *DM*, August, 1859.
47. *DM*, August, February, 1859. Douglass also expressed his sense of betrayal with the Republican party in an editorial in *DM*, May, 1859. "Its members will everywhere as individuals denounce the slave system as a foul and damning immorality," he complained, "but when they act as a party, they find it convenient to act on the suggestion of a false and demoralizing philosophy, and to give the lie collectively to what they hold as true individually."

It is opposed to the *political power* of slavery, rather than to slavery itself." But this was an election year, a time for adaptation and re-kindled hope. The Republicans, he concluded, possessed great poten-tial because they could "humble the slave power and defeat all plans for giving slavery any further guarantees of permanence." Abolition would follow in the process, and Douglass promised to work faithfully for the Republican party's triumph.[48]

Douglass seemed at times to suspend his own memory in order to reverse his judgments. In a June, 1860, editorial, he wrote a laudatory description of Abraham Lincoln, the newly nominated Republican candidate. Douglass was disappointed with the Chicago platform, but in Lincoln he saw promise, a man with "great firmness of will . . . a radical Republican . . . fully committed to the doctrine of the 'irrepressible conflict.' " Although he regretted the Republicans' lack of abolitionism and would have preferred the "brave and inspir-ing march of a storming party," in its absence he would settle for "the slow processes of a cautious siege." On July 2, however, Douglass wrote to Gerrit Smith in a confused tone: "I cannot support Lincoln," he asserted, "but whether there is life enough in the Abolitionists to name a candidate, I cannot say. I shall look to your letter for light on the pathway of duty." And then, in August, he published an editorial in which he proclaimed that the "vital element" of the Republican party was its "antislavery sentiment." "Nothing is plainer," argued Douglass, "than that the Republican Party has its source in the old Liberty Party." It would "live or die," he contended, "as the abolition sentiment of the country flourishes or fades." Douglass was once again vexed by his simultaneous commitments to moral principle and political action.[49]

Douglass' fluctuating responses to the Republican party depended upon his audience and his angle of vision at a given time. His letters to Gerrit Smith concentrate on "principles" and are full of deference to his ideological mentor and financial benefactor, whereas his public editorials are the anguished and searching efforts of a black leader to understand an amalgam of political interests and a party that seemed to both hate and champion his people. The American party system was undergoing a revolution and the nation teetered on the brink of

48. Douglass to "My British Antislavery Friends," May 26, 1860, in *DM*, June, 1860.
49. On Douglass' suspension of memory, see Harding, *There Is a River*, 239. Harding contends that Douglass occasionally engaged in "certain acts of self-inflicted amnesia" about the immediate past. *DM*, June, 1860; Douglass to Smith, July 2, 1860, in Gerrit Smith Papers; *DM*, August, 1860.

disunion; party lines and political persuasions were blurred and un-predictable. In this fluid political atmosphere, Douglass' dilemma was not unique.[50] When he scanned the Republican leadership, his vision often came to rest on Charles Sumner, the radical senator from Massachusetts. Occasionally, Sumner's imposing and heroic figure blocked Douglass' vision, preventing him from seeing the more con-servative elements in the Republican coalition, but it was Sumner's presence as a Republican in the United States Senate that inspired Douglass to assert that the "abolition element" might yet prove to be the root stem of the party. To Douglass, Sumner was the "Wilberforce of America," and he operated in the presence, if not the possession, of power. Douglass looked to Sumner's example with a combination of envy, admiration, and hope. Most important, Sumner *was* a Re-publican who "dared to grapple directly with the hell-born monster itself," moved beyond rhetoric about the Slave Power, and attacked the "brutal barbarism of slavery itself."[51]

Despite his vacillation and lack of political leverage, Douglass' re-actions to the Republican party did reflect some firm goals and intel-lectual tendencies. His endorsement of the Republicans echoed pri-marily the arguments of the radical wing of the party. He saw nonextensionism as merely the first step in a comprehensive, con-stitutional plan to eradicate slavery in the South, morally discredit-ing the institution and eventually destroying it through federal action. But Douglass also voiced the sentiments of moderate Repub-licans who sought the "denationalization" of slavery. Advocates of denationalization, an argument advanced most prominently by Salmon P. Chase, sought to turn slavery in upon itself where it would suffocate and die. Wherever federal jurisdiction existed—the District of Columbia, the territories, foreign and interstate commerce, the postal service, the Fugitive Slave law—these Republicans would ei-ther deny slavery protection or openly attack it. Douglass was greatly encouraged by the denationalization theory: "It will be a great work accomplished," he wrote after the Chicago convention in June, 1860, "when this Government is divorced from the active support of the inhuman slave system." He wanted to "pluck executive patronage"

50. Quarles, *Douglass*, 162–63. Quarles attributes Douglass' sudden conversion to the Republicans to the fluid political climate of the time, but also to his "resilient mind." This is a brief but apt characterization of an on-going intellectual process for Douglass.

51. *DM*, August, 1860; "The Presidential Campaign of 1860," 506–507. For Doug-lass' reactions to Sumner's "Barbarism of Slavery" speech, see "The Speech of Senator Sumner," *DM*, July, 1860.

away from southerners and "turn the tide of the National Administration against the man-stealers of this country." Thus Douglass
combined radical rhetoric with moderate methods to define the antislavery aims of the Republican party. Whatever the pace and means,
he saw that enough Republicans shared the same goal: the ultimate
extinction of slavery.[52]

Although frustrated with its limited aims, the very fact that the
Republican party represented a *coalition* of interests appealed to
Douglass. He frequently discussed the diversity of motives that produced the "great tide of opposition to slavery." All elements of the
free-soil ideology seemed welcome in 1860 if they contributed in
some way to electing a Republican president.[53] As an opportunist
representing a largely disfranchised and enslaved people, Douglass
yearned to affect power. Since at least 1848, he had fought endlessly
with himself and his colleagues over whether the United States government was an enemy or a potential friend to Afro-Americans. Only
by broadening the antislavery base could federal power be wrested
from the slaveholders and transformed into the agent of black freedom. Whether the product of human will, the hand of God, or the
force of events, this at least was the substance of Douglass' dream. In a
lecture at Glasgow, Scotland, in March, 1860, Douglass summed up
his political aims:

My position now is one of reform, not revolution. I would act for the abolition
of slavery through the Government—not over its ruins. If slaveholders have
ruled the American Government for the last fifty years, let the antislavery
men rule the nation for the next fifty years. If the South had made the Constitution bend to the purposes of slavery, let the North now make that instrument bend to the cause of freedom and justice. If 350,000 slaveholders
have . . . been able to make slavery the vital and animating spirit of the
American Confederacy for the last 72 years, now let the freemen of the North,

52. "The Chicago Nominations," *DM*, June, 1860, in Foner (ed.), *Life and Writings*,
II, 485. On the radical and moderate arguments of the Republican party and how they
coalesced in antislavery commitment, see Sewell, *Ballots for Freedom*, 308–15. On
Chase and the denationalization idea, see Sewell, *Ballots for Freedom*, 304, 312–13;
and E. Foner, *Free Soil*, 83–84. Whether held by radicals or moderates, the idea that
slavery was a "local" institution and that the federal government could be "divorced"
from it became a staple belief for all Republicans.
53. *DM*, August, 1860. In his editorial, "The Republican Party," Douglass acknowledged that "opposition to slavery is supported by different reasons." He then described
at length these various reasons, including the racist motives for exclusion of blacks
from western territories. He seemed to be straining to convince himself that the core
idea that would preserve the party was "the fact that the slave is a man." For Douglass'
grasp of the "free labor" ideology of the Republican party, see his editorial, "The
Chicago Nominations"; also E. Foner, *Free Soil*, 301–17; and Sewell, *Ballots for Freedom*, 292–354.

who have the power in their own hands, and who can make the American Government just what they think fit, resolve to blot out forever the foul and haggard crime.[54]

It must be noted that this speech was delivered before a Scottish audience (where Douglass was extremely popular) as part of a fund-raising tour to support his newspaper, and it must also be viewed in the context of the Harpers Ferry excitement in America and Douglass' involvement with John Brown. Although open in his celebration of Brown, Douglass was not about to praise the idea of slave insurrection before such an audience. Nevertheless, his hopes for the seizure of federal power were only rendered possible at this juncture by the presence of the Republican party. Freedom achieved through the government would mean a very different future for blacks than that gained by violent revolution.

Douglass' response to the Republican party also reflects his seemingly instinctive aversion to dogma and orthodoxy. He could preach adherence to abolitionist principles as strongly as anyone, but underneath Douglass' radicalism ran a strain of pragmatism that rendered him uncomfortable with rigid doctrine. Douglass detested the feuding and factionalism that divided abolitionists, though he often argued vehemently on one side or the other of these conflicts. His well-documented break with the Garrisonians demonstrated his quest for intellectual independence and a less dogmatic approach to abolition. Under the influence of Gerrit Smith, he found a broader, more flexible ideology that offered greater means if not better results in attacking slavery, but even in the company of the most radical of political abolitionists he could not find complete satisfaction. The repeated failures of the Liberty and the Radical Abolition parties were due, in Douglass' view, to doctrinal disputes: "They [Radical Abolition party] have again and again allowed themselves to fall out by the way," he charged in 1860, "and quarrel with each other about minor points, about side issues, political theories and theological dogmas." From his perspective, Douglass found the dogmatic mind offensive and ineffective.[55]

Douglass was especially disgusted when religious orthodoxy divided abolitionists. Lacking theological training, his mind recoiled from religious quarrels. Although deeply spiritual in his own way, he

54. "The Constitution of the United States: Is It Proslavery or Antislavery?" speech delivered at Glasgow, Scotland, March 26, 1860, in Foner (ed.), *Life and Writings*, II, 480.
55. *DM*, November, 1860. Douglass' editorial, "New Trouble Between Old Friends," stresses doctrinal conflicts between William Goodell and Gerrit Smith.

demanded that religious ideas serve the abolitionist and not impede his "usefulness." This may account in part for his political resiliency, since his distaste for dogmatism in religion carried over into politics. He owed allegiance to no church and to no body of doctrine for its own sake, and he tried to maintain the same flexibility toward political parties. In many ways, he was still practicing the adaptability he had learned as a slave on Maryland's eastern shore. Whether scheming to steal time for reading as an eleven-year-old, plotting his own escape to freedom at twenty, or struggling to survive as a black editor at age forty-three, Douglass had long known that only through his own resourcefulness and opportunism would he best serve himself and the needs of his people. Ultimately, he did not judge Republicans by their religious orthodoxy or by their abolitionist zeal. He recognized their "tendencies," sought their help, hitched a qualified portion of his hope to their wagon, and with great impatience waited for them to play their appointed role in the drama of progress.[56]

In the 1860 election, Douglass resolved to vote for Gerrit Smith but to work and hope for a Republican victory. He tried to explain this contradiction by claiming that because abolitionists were moral reformers they had a responsibility to vote their principles. By "bearing aloft the unsullied banner of pure Abolitionism," Douglass believed that the "antislavery integrity" of the movement would be preserved.[57] In these anguished times, he still found it difficult to bridge the gap between pure abolition and antislavery politics. He could not find peace on either side, so, knowing that the votes of radical abolitionists (especially black ones) could hardly turn an election, he safely cast his vote with his "soul" while eagerly awaiting the crisis a Republican victory would bring. Personally, he threw his vote away in 1860; then, as a social reformer, he prepared to help push the new politics of antislavery along the course of abolition.

Herein lies the ultimate meaning of the Republican party for Douglass—its potential to cause southern reaction and sectional conflict. In a speech on the presidential campaign in August, 1860, Douglass tried to clarify his position: "I would gladly have a party openly combined to put down slavery at the South. In the absence of such a party, I am glad to see a party in the field against which all that is slaveholding, malignant, and Negro-hating, both in the North and the South, is combined." Whatever aroused the ire of the Slave Power and forced it to react was in some way the friend of the slave. "The slaveholders

56. *Ibid.*; Preston, *Young Frederick Douglass*, 83–156.
57. *DM*, October, 1860.

know that the day of their power is over," Douglass assured his readers, "when a Republican President is elected." More than anything else, the black editor wanted to hasten a decisive national conflict over slavery. For this reason above all others, he found himself compelled to support the Republican party. At the very least, southern fears of Lincoln's potential victory served as "tolerable endorsements of the antislavery tendencies of the Republican Party."[58]

To understand the political thought of Frederick Douglass, one must not be dismayed by his inconsistency. He was thoroughly human, complex, and contradictory; occasionally he was simply confused. He was performing many roles and forever balancing the duty of principle with the duty of hope. Douglass possessed a remarkably adaptable temperament and a powerful personal will, and he would find hope wherever he could. Owing a great debt to his abolitionist mentors and benefactors, he found it very difficult to break with them, yet if advantage could be gained by staking out his own ground or embracing a new idea or party, no bond of friendship or ideology would stop him. Until the Gilded Age, his moral rage against slavery and racism never found rest in any political organization. But on the eve of the secession crisis in 1860, Douglass still worked and waited, anxiously wrestling with the dream that the federal government might yet be the agent of black liberation.

58. "The Presidential Campaign of 1860," 514–15.

3/LET THE CONFLICT COME: DOUGLASS AND THE SECESSION CRISIS

The contest must now be decided, and decided forever, which of the two, Freedom or Slavery, shall give law to this Republic. Let the conflict come.
—Frederick Douglass, *Douglass Monthly*, March, 1861

For this consummation we have watched and wished with fear and trembling. God be praised! that it has come at last.
—Frederick Douglass, *Douglass Monthly*, May, 1861

It is something to couple one's name with great occasions, and it was a great thing to me to be permitted to bear some humble part in this, the greatest that had thus far come to the American people. It was a great thing to achieve American independence when we numbered three millions, but it was a greater thing to save this country from dismemberment and ruin when it numbered thirty millions.
—Frederick Douglass, *Life and Times of Frederick Douglass*, 1881

THE ELECTION OF 1860 WAS A unique presidential contest in American history, the only time when the losers refused to accept the result. Abraham Lincoln's election provided southern secessionists with an issue over which they might take their states out of the Union, and the very meaning and existence of an American nation lay in the balance. The 1860 election had offered clear choices to the American electorate, but in its aftermath, the options facing most Americans were less clear. Were southern leaders in earnest about their "revolution," or was their rhetoric just so much bluster? If disunion did occur, would it be a peaceful process? Would the lame-duck Buchanan administration respond with coercion, concessions, or drift? What of the newly elected Lincoln—how would this Republican president respond to secession once in power? And what of the abolitionists? If the bulk of the slave states succeeded in separating from the Union, what would it mean for those who represented thirty years of antislavery agitation? These questions, and more, troubled Frederick Douglass in the wake of Lincoln's election. As the secession crisis developed, Douglass confronted it with a combination of fear, exhilaration, and confusion. In disunion and the coming of the Civil War, Douglass would rediscover the depths of his radical abolitionism, his commitment to his race, and his psychological attachment to American nationalism.

On election day, November 6, 1860, Douglass was in Rochester, working from morning until night at the polls, both guarding against fraud and button-holing voters. While placing his long-range hopes in a Republican victory, Douglass' most immediate concern was the proposal on the New York state ballot to abolish the $250 property qualification for black voters. This movement for equal suffrage had attracted the racist scorn of Democrats and only limited endorsement from Republicans, but for black leaders it was the cause of a vigorous campaign. Coordinated from New York City under the leadership of the black physician and reformer James McCune Smith, the campaign for black suffrage distributed thousands of copies of a tract, *The Suffrage Question in Relation to Colored Voters in the State of New York*. In the three months prior to the election, Douglass traveled the backroads of western New York and distributed 25,000 copies of the tract.[1]

Universal suffrage was a party issue in New York. A constitutional amendment providing equal suffrage had passed the legislature in 1857 but was never brought to a referendum. In 1860 the measure was reenacted with almost unanimous Republican support and solid Democratic opposition. In the campaign, however, most Republican newspapers and speakers quietly ignored the referendum, fearing that it might hurt Lincoln's chances of winning the state. After Lincoln carried New York by fifty thousand votes, Douglass was encouraged by the Republican victory, but the resounding defeat of the black suffrage measure left him bitter and disillusioned. What the Republican legislators had enacted, they treated with too much indifference at the polls. Although over half the Republican voters approved black suffrage, most of the rest abstained, and the amendment lost by a margin of 337,984 to 197,503. However, the fact that most New York Republican leaders had long supported black suffrage must not be overlooked; moreover, in the context of 1860, the level of the vote in favor of black political rights in New York is remarkable.[2]

But to black leaders like Douglass, the more important fact was

1. The suffrage amendment had passed the Republican-dominated New York legislature. The New York City and County Suffrage Committee of Colored Citizens coordinated the campaign. See "The Suffrage Question in Relation to Colored Voters in the State of New York," New York, 1860 (pamphlet); Quarles, *Douglass*, 166–67; McPherson, *Struggle for Equality*, 25–26.

2. On black suffrage in New York, see Phyllis F. Field, *The Politics of Race in New York: The Struggle for Black Suffrage in the Civil War Era* (Ithaca, 1982), 114–46; Phyllis F. Field, "Republicans and Black Suffrage in New York State: The Grass Roots Response," *Civil War History*, XXI (June, 1975), 136–47; Sewell, *Ballots for Freedom*, 333–34; E. Foner, *Free Soil*, 285–86.

that the insidious property requirement for blacks still stood, while white voters could march to the polls as freely as ever. Douglass felt betrayed by Republican silence on the suffrage issue: "The blow is a heavy and damaging one," he wrote. "Every intelligent colored man must feel it keenly." The defeat of the suffrage amendment served as yet another reminder of the powerlessness of black Americans. "We do not even wring from this vote the poor consolation that anybody was afraid of our influence or power," Douglass complained. "The victory over us is simply one of blind ignorance and prejudice."[3] Douglass saw a clear message in the suffrage vote. As political partici- pants, blacks were still almost completely subjugated, their voice almost inaudible in the American electorate. This discouragement notwithstanding, Douglass went on to interpret the larger meaning of Lincoln's victory, striving in his usual way to convert defeat into renewed fervor.

At the very least, Douglass believed, Lincoln's election had broken the hold of the South on the United States government, and a funda- mental challenge, however limited, had been mounted to the politi- cal power of slavery. To Douglass, the "chief benefit" of the election was the "canvass itself." Despite the "cowardly disclaimers and mis- erable concessions" by some Republicans, the mere dissemination of antislavery ideas provided an end in itself. Blacks were still denied citizenship rights, and their cause, Douglass suggested, had only en- tered national politics by a back door; in New York, they had been treated like "the black baby of Negro suffrage . . . thought too ugly to exhibit on so grand an occasion." Although the cause of black libera- tion seemed shunted away and out of sight, Douglass believed that it had nevertheless gained greater consequence with the Republican victory. Now, if only the nation could be forced into sufficient disar- ray, there might yet be real cause for rejoicing in the election of an "antislavery reputation" to the presidency.[4]

In the wake of the election of 1860, Douglass yearned for what we might call a politics of disorder. Throughout the Afro-American expe- rience, the greatest advances for black liberation and equal rights have come during periods of political and social upheaval, and in the secession winter of 1860–61, Douglass understood that political tur- moil might facilitate black advancement. He was no better equipped to predict the consequences of secession than any of his contempo- raries, but what he seemed to want was a political rupture that would

3. "Equal Suffrage Defeated," *DM*, December, 1860.
4. "The Late Election," *DM*, December, 1860; "Equal Suffrage Defeated."

force both a legal and a military confrontation between North and South. Sufficient civil strife would force the reluctant Republicans to use coercive powers to weaken and then destroy slavery in the South. Douglass' sentiments were those of an antislavery propagandist who wanted to focus the secession question squarely on slavery itself. To Douglass, civil war was frightful, but by February, 1861, he cast the dreaded prospect in typically positive and apocalyptic language: The "God in history everywhere pronouncing the doom of those nations which frame mischief by law," Douglass claimed, had caused a "concussion . . . against slavery which would now rock the land." National will had not solved the problem: "If there is not wisdom and virtue enough in the land to rid the country of slavery," he claimed, "then the next best thing is to let the South go . . . and be made to drink the wine cup of wrath and fire, which her long career of cruelty, barbarism and blood shall call down upon her guilty head." Douglass could not easily define the course of the disorder he sought, but there can be no question that he welcomed disunion with millennial expectation.[5]

Obviously, Lincoln's election altered the balance of power in America. A sectional election had produced a northern president opposed to the extension of slavery, and if Republican will was firm, the North was no longer bound by history and fear to southern proslavery interests. Douglass guardedly hoped that Lincoln's election would awaken the nation to "the consciousness of new powers, and the possibility of a higher destiny than the perpetual bondage to an ignoble fear."[6] Until the new president's response to secession materialized four months later, Douglass maintained a careful distinction between Lincoln himself and the "possibility" his election had fostered.

Douglass' immediate interpretation of the election reflected his experience as well as the charged atmosphere of December, 1860. Great changes might be possible, but only if events and ideas combined in ways that even a sanguine black editor could not expect. Not yet knowing how secession would cause Republicans to become more intractable on nonextensionism, he feared that antislavery moderation in the White House might spell the end of radical abolition

5. "The Union and How to Save It," *DM*, February, 1861, in Foner (ed.), *Life and Writings*, III, 64–65. For the idea of a "politics of disorder" and its role in American society, see Theodore J. Lowi, *The Politics of Disorder* (New York, 1971), 53–61, 170–85.

6. "The Late Election."

across the North. Although he had been wishing for such a development for years, Douglass was not yet able to envision just how the "Union" would become a moral force linked to abolition. He could not fully embrace the ideology of the Republicans; occasionally he even doubted the resolve of southern fire-eaters.

On the eve of South Carolina's secession, Douglass was not convinced that enough radical disposition existed on either side to cause an open split, especially one that would lead to war. In spite of all the secessionist rhetoric, he contended that the South had over-reacted to Lincoln's election and had misinterpreted his intentions. Because of his high office and his lack of radical convictions, Douglass argued, Lincoln could become the abolition movement's "most powerful enemy." With cynical disregard for the more hopeful expressions contained in the same editorial, Douglass claimed that "the present alarm and perturbation will cease; the southern fire-eaters will be appeased and will retrace their steps—there is no sufficient cause for the dissolution of the union." For more than a decade Douglass had watched southern power appeased and the slavery controversy compromised, and he had learned to expect sectional crises to end in reconciliation. In December, 1860, he doubted that the result of the latest crisis would be any different.[7]

Douglass' confusion over the range and intensity of the secession movement was typical of most northerners. As historian David Potter has demonstrated, Republican reactions to the threat of secession early in the crisis ranged primarily from indecision to incredulity. The logic of secession, both legal and moral, had long been debated in America; moreover, southerners had long rehearsed its rationale by 1860. But no one knew what secession would mean in practice. Although there was ample evidence of Republican resolve on the territorial question, Douglass feared other concessions by the North if secession swept the Deep South. In his view, the Union might be saved for all the wrong reasons. Although slaveholders might not realize it, Douglass predicted (with ironic accuracy, at least for the short-run) that slavery would be "as safe, and safer, in the Union under such a President [Lincoln] than it can be under any President of a Southern Confederacy." Through secession, Douglass imagined, the South might invite some form of coercion that could threaten slavery in the existing states, whereas, temporarily at least, by the South's staying in the Union slavery might remain untouched. Douglass did

7. *Ibid.*

not have a crystal ball and the long-range implications of Lincoln's election were not apparent in much of the black editor's rhetoric, but there is no doubt that without secession and war, slavery would have lived a great deal longer in the United States. As for Douglass' disbelief that secession would really occur in December, 1860, his views were quite consistent with those of most Republicans. Underestimation of secessionist fervor and overestimation of southern unionism were viewpoints shared widely in the North. What Douglass dreaded most was that the ritual of compromise would once again preserve sectional harmony at the expense of black freedom.[8]

Douglass found little encouragement in the behavior of the northern public. The bulk of white northerners had always viewed abolitionists with suspicion and contempt, and with the threat of disunion in the air and abolitionists railing against compromise, hostility to antislavery agitators rose to new levels of violence. On December 3, 1860, at Tremont Temple in Boston, Douglass was scheduled to deliver a speech on the first anniversary of the execution of John Brown, but a mob led by hired thugs broke up the meeting. In the ensuing fight, Douglass was thrown down a staircase, but not before he "fought like a trained pugilist." The roots of this renewed hostility were, in large part, economic. By December, 1860, northern workingmen, along with merchants, shipowners, and cotton manufacturers, were deeply worried about the impact of possible disunion, while bankers and industrialists squirmed as the prices of stock declined markedly. The specter of financial ruin caused the spirit of political conciliation to revive, and the conservative and Democratic press teemed with procompromise sentiment and incendiary attacks on abolitionists. While southern conventions debated secession, mob violence against antislavery speakers occurred in several northern cities in the first two months of 1861. Abolitionists served as ready scapegoats for those who sought simple and immediate remedies to the political crisis that had fostered economic panic.[9]

Compromise proposals came into Washington from all quarters of the North. Some were in the form of resolutions passed at procompromise Union meetings, some were the petitions of committees of industrialists, and some were the efforts of politicians wary of the

8. David M. Potter, *The Impending Crisis, 1848–1861* (New York, 1976), 524–28, 553; Kenneth M. Stampp, *And the War Came: The North and the Secession Crisis, 1860–1861* (Baton Rouge, 1950), 13–14; "The Late Election."

9. Quarles, *Douglass,* 168. On mob violence against abolitionists generally, see McPherson, *Struggle for Equality,* 40–45.

wrath of their constituents. All were the product of a fervor to preserve the Union and to sustain normal economic relations with the
South. The variety of schemes for sectional adjustment generally
took one of five forms: constitutional amendments that would give
additional guarantees to slavery; the repeal of personal liberty laws;
compensation to southerners who lost fugitive slaves; the admission
of New Mexico as a slave state; or the extension of the Missouri
compromise line to the Pacific. On December 18, 1860, John J. Crittenden of Kentucky introduced the most famous and comprehensive
of these initiatives, a series of constitutional amendments that
blanketed the range of conciliatory measures. The debate over the
Crittenden Compromise and others like it paralyzed Congress during
the entire interregnum.[10]

Attended by delegates from twenty-one states (although none from
the Deep South) and sponsored by the Virginia legislature, a peace
conference convened in Washington on February 4, 1861. After three
weeks of confusion and negotiation, the uninspired conference reported a compromise proposal nearly identical to that of Crittenden.
Although none of these measures ever passed the divided Congress,
week after week of wrangling gave evidence that most Democrats and
a handful of Republicans were willing to appease the South and extend the life of slavery in order to save the Union. That no compromise measure ever passed Congress was due largely to two factors:
one, secessionists in the Deep South had no interest in compromise
and judged every concession unacceptable; and two, most Republicans across the North had resolved to prevent any compromise.
Most legislatures also refused to support compromise; only New
Jersey formally endorsed the Crittenden measures. Indeed, Crittenden's plan was not a legitimate compromise at all, but rather a set
of one-sided concessions to the South. In the end, radical and moderate Republicans easily defeated all attempts at compromise.[11]

At least until late February, 1861, Douglass believed the possibility
of compromise to be real. At times, he did not seem to acknowledge
just how incompatible the Crittenden proposals were with the most
basic of Republican principles about slavery expansion. There was no
secrecy about Lincoln's own vehement opposition to compromise
and perhaps Douglass should have put more faith in Republican
steadfastness, but in the confused atmosphere of the secession crisis
his alarm over a potential settlement is understandable. Indeed,

10. Stampp, *And the War Came*, 21, 129–31.
11. *Ibid.*, 130–47; Potter, *Impending Crisis*, 529–35.

many abolitionists were apprehensive about concessions to the South that moderate Republicans might accept. Although it was often ill-defined, compromise sentiment was strong among the northern masses in the winter of 1860–61. Moreover, Lincoln had been elected by only small margins in many states. Democrats and Bell Unionists (supporters of Constitutional Union Party candidate John Bell) worked ardently for compromise. With the same disdain Douglass so frequently expressed, the radical Republican George W. Julian remarked that "to the very last the old medicine of compromise and conciliation seemed to be the sovereign hope of the people of the free states." To a black abolitionist whose political consciousness awakened with the Mexican War and the Compromise of 1850, who had seen the fate of the slaves bandied about in one political crisis after another, who had preserved hope of freedom and citizenship in the face of Chief Justice Taney's denial, a resolute stand by the North against southern secession could hardly have been a certainty. The best hopes of blacks had, after all, always been dashed by the "old medicine of compromise."[12] Why should it be any different this time?

Douglass observed the secession crisis with a combination of excitement and dismay. Deeply discouraged by the mob violence perpetrated against abolitionists, he complained that the state of the abolition cause was "somewhat gloomy and dark"; abolitionists had "plied the national heart and conscience with sound doctrine," but they seemed "as far from accomplishment of their work as during the proslavery mobs of twenty-five years ago." This widespread violence against abolitionists may account for some of the pessimism and bitterness in Douglass' rhetoric. In the early stage of the secession crisis, he felt fragmented, uncertain whom to trust or on whom to turn his anger. Although he shared the exhilaration that secession brought to many of his fellow abolitionists, he also felt an acute sense of powerlessness, and as the Union dissolved, he had to control his own distending rage against slaveholders, northern mobs, and compromisers. Douglass feared that secession would become a struggle only over the survival of the Union and not over slavery: "What disturbs, divides, and threatens to bring on civil war . . . and ruin this

12. Potter, *Impending Crisis*, 526, 528; McPherson, *Struggle for Equality*, 30–31; George W. Julian, *Political Recollections, 1840–1872* (Chicago, 1884), 186, quoted in Stampp, *And the War Came*, 131. Potter contends that with hindsight it is too easy to ignore the gravity and seriousness of the compromise movement during the secession crisis.

country," he declared in February, "but slavery." Only the "morally blind," he argued, could fail to see it.[13] Douglass wondered where to direct his moralism as the Deep South bolted the Union and the North weighed its options.

Douglass bristled at the prospect of concessions to the slaveholding states, and his editorials during the secession crisis were full of harangues against the "sneaking cowardice and pitiful imbecility" of northern compromisers. Repeatedly, he castigated northerners for their inability or unwillingness to see the crisis in abolitionists' terms. In Douglass' judgment, too many "whines of compromise" met the "arrogance and impudence" of southern secessionists: "robbed, plundered, insulted, spit upon, and defied," the United States government seemed only capable of responding with the "humble solicitation to be kicked again." He worried about the "Peace Congress" that convened in Washington in February and made special notice of the apparent backsliding of moderate Republicans like William H. Seward, who in a January 31 speech to Congress had expressed sympathy for compromise. By thundering against concessions to the South, Douglass was trying to reach an accessible audience among northerners. What he dreaded most was the idea that a great opportunity to strike a lasting blow for black freedom might be lost forever through the desire for peaceful reconstruction, so he braced for the worst and anxiously awaited the inauguration of Lincoln.[14]

With the hindsight that his 1881 autobiography provided, Douglass remembered the secession winter as a time ruled by fear. "Those who may wish to see to what depths of humility and self-abasement a noble people can be brought under the sentiment of fear," he wrote, "will find no chapter of history more instructive than that which treats the events in official circles in Washington during the space between the months of November, 1860, and March, 1861." Douglass did not expect most free-state politicians suddenly to convert to the idea of an organized war upon slaveholders, much less to the wisdom of abolition, but as always his editorials afforded him a way to preach his views, externalize his frustrations, provide a voice for blacks,

13. "Proslavery Mobs and Proslavery Ministry," *DM*, March, 1861; "The Union and How to Save It," 64.

14. "The Union and How to Save It," 62–63. For Douglass' concern over compromise, see the following editorials: "The Compromise Measures," "Reconstruction the New Danger," and "The Crisis in the U.S. Senate," all in *DM*, March, 1861; Stampp, *And the War Came*, 130–32.

reassure the converted, and feel that he was at least some small part of the national debate.[15]

By March, 1861, Douglass seemed well aware that his fondest hopes were at the mercy of events. He knew that the secession crisis was a test of power; whether it resulted in war depended upon the reaction of the Lincoln Administration. His hopes for the policies of the Republican government shifted constantly between confidence and uncertainty, and he looked to the inauguration of Lincoln as the "one ray of hope amid the darkness of the passing hour and the reign of doubt and distraction." The new president had made no promises to the cause of abolition, but the Republicans were committed to preserving the Union and stopping slavery's expansion. With uneasy expectation, Douglass aptly described the ideological and political predicament Lincoln faced: "What were small in Chicago [the Republican party's Chicago platform of 1860] will be found large at Washington, and what were moderate in the canvass, have become much augmented by the frowning difficulties since flung in the way of their accomplishment by the movement for disunion." Douglass yearned for a conflict he knew Republicans could not create alone. Although it seemed unrealistic before Fort Sumter, he wanted federal power marshalled for an organized war against the South and slavery. The necessity of a response to disunion, it seemed to him, might force Republicans into radical directions they would not take solely by their own accord.[16]

Douglass cautiously hoped that the Republicans would be true to their own ideology. Would "Mr. Lincoln boldly grapple with the monster of Disunion?" queried Douglass. He had no choice: "He must do this, or consent to be the despised representative of a defied and humbled Government. . . . He must do this, or compromise the fundamental principle upon which he was elected." A political crisis over the Union might yet be the wedge into a brighter future for black Americans. To "coerce" a confederacy of states led by slaveholders was to threaten slavery itself. As long as the Union was imperiled, a black abolitionist with limited audience and marginal influence could take heart that slavery was imperiled as well.[17]

However, Douglass was not confident that such coercion would occur, and he wondered whether even the firmest resolve on the part of the Republicans would carry the northern people with them. In the

---

15. Douglass, *Life and Times*, 332.
16. "The New President," *DM*, March, 1861, in Foner (ed.), *Life and Writings*, III, 67.
17. *Ibid.*

tense period between Lincoln's inauguration and the firing on Fort Sumter, he did not expect the North to fight to preserve the Union: "All talk of putting down treason and rebellion by force, by our demoralized Government and people," Douglass agonized, "are as impotent and worthless as the words of a drunken woman in a ditch." According to the frustrated editor, northerners had lost their "moral sense"; they had bravely elected Lincoln but were now about to "desert him, and leave him a potentate without power." Douglass decided that the southern perception of Yankees as "a miserable set of schemers, destitute of every element of honorable pride, . . . a nation of selfish, pinching shopkeepers" was tragically accurate. Impatient and angry, he recorded a litany of northern obeisance to proslavery interests: "History shows that the North has never been able to stand against the power and purposes of the South." One month after expressing sincere optimism in Lincoln's resolve, Douglass had seemingly given up on northerners. Peaceful disunion would continue, he contended, the independence of the slave states would soon be recognized by the Republicans, and the abolition movement in its present form was as good as dead.[18]

Douglass envisioned a future where abolitionists would attack slavery in a separate country and their work would take a revolutionary turn:

So much for the moral movement against slavery. Hereafter, opposition to slavery will naturally take a new form. The fire is kindled, and cannot be extinguished. The "irrepressible conflict" can never cease on this continent. It will change its methods and manifestations, but it will be nonetheless real for all that. Slaves will run away, and humane men and women will help them; slaves will plot and conspire, and wise and brave men will help them. Abolition may be postponed, but it cannot be prevented. If it comes not from enlightenment, moral conviction and civilization, it will come from the fears of tyrants no longer able to hold down their rising slaves.[19]

These sentiments are all the more interesting given the startling turn of events caused by the bombardment of one island fort in Charleston Harbor.

Douglass' ambivalence about the northern response to disunion reflects the emotion and extraordinary confusion caused by the secession crisis. Such anxiety prompted cynical attacks on northern opinion and, after the inauguration, on Lincoln himself. His diatribes against the North may also reflect his isolation from the Republican

18. *Ibid.*, 83; "The Future of the Abolition Cause," *DM*, April, 1861.
19. "Future of the Abolition Cause," 84.

mainstream. An earlier vague faith in Lincoln did not translate into confidence in the northern people.

Douglass even differed with many of his abolitionist colleagues who were willing to acquiesce in peaceful disunion. Widespread among abolitionists, especially Garrisonians, was the belief that disunion spelled the doom of slavery; letting the South go in peace, they contended, would lead inexorably to emancipation. "Disunion leaves God's natural laws to work their good results," declared Wendell Phillips. In Phillips' logic, the South's "declaration of independence" was "the jubilee of the slave."[20]

Douglass vehemently opposed such reasoning, seeing peaceable disunion as the abandonment of the slaves. To Phillips he answered: "The Union is gone but slavery remains; and we may well ask ourselves what will be the probable effect of the separation on the question of slavery. Will the South become less intensely slaveholding and the North more antislavery? We anticipate neither result." Instead, Douglass argued with William Goodell and a smaller group of abolitionists (including most black leaders) that southern secession and seizure of federal property had absolved the Republican party of its pledge of noninterference with slavery in the states. Hence, as Goodell contended in a position that would become very familiar during the war, the federal government had the constitutional "right to suppress rebellion and to abolish slavery, the cause of it." Although nearly all abolitionists welcomed disunion, few advocated war. Douglass, however, desired both.[21]

Interspersed with Douglass' denunciations of compromise and his advocacy of federal coercion was an interpretation of the idea of secession. He was not troubled at all by the doctrine of consent in his reaction to secession, since he had long ago adopted a selective outlook on the natural rights of slaveholders—they had few that abolitionists need respect. Governments may be formed by the consent of the governed, Douglass reasoned, but they endured by authority and the preservation of order. "Human governments are neither held together, nor broken up by such mild and gentle persuasives as are implied in the soft phrase—peaceful secession," he argued. "Theirs is

20. For Phillips' and the abolitionists' acceptance of peaceable disunion, see McPherson, *Struggle for Equality*, 34–37.

21. "Future of the Abolition Cause," 83. Goodell is quoted in McPherson, *Struggle for Equality*, 39. On the abolitionists' support for coercion, see Fredrickson, *Inner Civil War*, 59–61.

a voice of command, not of persuasion. They rest not upon paper, but upon power. They do not solicit obedience as a favor, but compel it as a duty."[22] If the Declaration of Independence meant what it said, Douglass had abandoned one of his own first principles. An ex-fugitive slave who rode Jim Crow cars and possessed no legal rights that the Supreme Court acknowledged was only too aware that governments rested on power and not on paper. But for Douglass the secession winter was no time for doctrinaire formulas. Secession had opened a door through which he had never peered. Held down by the power of government all his life, he now wished to see that same power wielded mercilessly against his oppressors. Through the open door of disunion, Douglass dreamed of witnessing the power of the federal government mobilized to crush slavery.

Some northern intellectuals were much more bothered by the doctrine of consent in the secession crisis. Horace Greeley, the antislavery editor of the New York *Tribune*, openly defended the South's right of secession. Moreover, some abolitionists opposed the use of force by the federal government to coerce the southern states back into the Union. Douglass was not troubled by these arguments. Any resolution to the secession crisis ultimately depended on military might: "The moorings that bind these states together," he warned, "can only be broken by opinion, backed up by force." He simply denied the right of secession, since the "right" of a southern state to secede depended on "her ability to do so and stay so." Douglass was willing to admit the abstract right of revolution, "but revolution in this country is rebellion, and rebellion is treason, and treason is levying war against the United States, with something more substantial than paper resolutions and windy declamations. There must be swords, guns, powder, balls, and men behind them to use them." These were ironic words for a man who yearned to share fully in America's revolutionary heritage, who claimed the right of revolution for his own people and viewed his own success as a direct result of exercising that principle. But Douglass was, of course, correct in his assertion that secession was ultimately a matter of force. Moreover, revolutions are never conducted by formal rules, nor are they sustained by reason alone. As George Fredrickson has suggested, what abolitionists like Douglass were really saying about secession is that there are two kinds of revolutions: good ones and bad ones. Early in the secession crisis,

22. "Dissolution of the Union," *DM*, January, 1861, in Foner (ed.), *Life and Writings*, III, 58.

Douglass hoped that the slaveholders' revolution would compel a wider antislavery revolution on the part of the northern people. In his response to secession, he was both wise and wishful.[23]

Like many northern intellectuals, Douglass carried his attack on secession into a defense of majority rule. By the end of February, he was concerned that the "victors" in the election of 1860 were about to be "conquered by the vanquished." Had the election gone the other way, he contended, the North would have submitted to "the Constitutional rule of the majority," but the South, facing the first election where not everything had gone its way, answered "by organizing and plotting Rebellion; by seizing arms, ammunition, forts and arsenals . . . by doing their utmost to break up the Government they could no longer rule." In this instance, Douglass' majoritarianism rested at least in part on his hatred of slavery. Secessionists were not only rebels against duly elected constitutional authority; they were "the slave-holding women-whipping rebels of Charleston." They were not only traitors; they had created a "treasonable, Slaveholding Confederacy."[24]

Well aware that southerners harkened to the Founding Fathers for their alleged right of secession, Douglass believed that in doing so they courted their own destruction, and he hoped that by invoking revolutionary ideology slaveholders had only made their position more vulnerable. Southerners, of course, saw no incompatibility between slavery and the ideals of the Founding Fathers in their defense of secession, but as an antislavery propagandist Douglass rarely missed an opportunity to exploit the inhumanity in proslavery ideology. "The slaveholder, kind or cruel, is a slaveholder still," Douglass had written in 1855, "the every hour violator of the just and inalienable rights of man. . . . He never lisps a syllable in commendation of the fathers of this republic, nor denounces any attempted oppression of himself, without inviting the knife to his own throat, and asserting

23. Fredrickson, *Inner Civil War*, 57–59, 62–64; "Dissolution of the Union," 59. In his second autobiography, *My Bondage and My Freedom*, 280, Douglass described his own discovery of the right of rebellion. Plotting an escape with fellow slaves, he imagined that "these meetings must have resembled, on a small scale, the meetings of revolutionary conspirators, in their primary condition. We were plotting against our (so called) lawful rulers; with this difference—that we sought our own good, and not the harm of our enemies. We did not seek to overthrow them, but to escape from them. . . . Liberty was our aim; and we had now come to think that we had a right to liberty, against every obstacle—even against the lives of our enslavers."

24. "The Victors Conquered By the Vanquished—The Minority Ruling the Majority," *DM*, March, 1861, in Foner (ed.), *Life and Writings*, III, 68, 59, 69; "Dissolution of the Union."

the rights of rebellion for his own slaves." To Douglass, there was no sovereign right of secession, especially when exercised by slaveholders. But he was glad they were trying.[25]

Secession and the coming of the war invoked Douglass' millennial nationalism and his apocalyptic view of history, and he tried to submerge his ambivalence about Lincoln and northern will in this long-term faith in the model republic yet to be redeemed. For Douglass, merging secular hopes in millennial symbolism was an ultimate way of making sense out of a season of fear and confusion. In disunion, he saw at least the possibility of a redefined federal republic. It might mean war and untold suffering, but a new government—a new Union—might emerge to replace the old one. This had long been Douglass' dream whenever he thought about the meaning of America and a sense of nationhood for blacks. He took every opportunity to invoke the principles of the Declaration of Independence and to claim a historical place for his people in America.[26]

But Americans had never welcomed blacks to the national family, not even by the back door. Slavery had shaped the past, corrupted the present, and denied blacks a secure future. Consistent with his apocalyptic outlook, Douglass yearned for events, however they might arise, that would stop time, overturn the past, and begin a new history. He wanted the old Union destroyed and a new Union re-created and rededicated. The old principles were fine, but a new history was necessary. These notions of overturning and rebirth were essential elements of nineteenth-century apocalypticism. In Douglass' view, the secession crisis brought together a collision of forces that might cause this break with the past.[27]

Throughout his life Douglass was acutely aware that one of the most important contributions he could make was to tell his own story. As the author of three autobiographies, he repeatedly re-created himself, linking the past with the present. But the autobiographies were more than attempts to preside over his biographers, to write his own personal history, and to search for his sense of self. They were a means to yoke the aspirations of his people—their future—with the model of his own past. He wanted to demonstrate that slavery could

---

25. Douglass, *Bondage and Freedom*, 269–70.
26. On millennialism and the coming of the Civil War, see Moorhead, "Between Progress and Apocalypse," 531–41; Moorhead, *American Apocalypse*, 42–81; Tuveson, *Redeemer Nation*, 137–86.
27. Moorhead, "Between Progress and Apocalypse," 634–39.

not break the will of a people to survive and flourish. How well Douglass may have done this is open to debate, but his attempt is nonetheless revealing. A people born into oppression must look forward; they must believe there can be a new history to replace and explain the old one. In an eloquent passage in the 1855 autobiography, Douglass stated his case: "The thought of only being a creature of the *present* and the *past* troubled me, and I longed to have a *future*—a future with hope in it. To be shut up entirely to the past and present is abhorrent to the human mind; it is to the soul—whose life and happiness is unceasing progress—what the prison is to the body; a blight, and mildew, a hell of horrors."[28] In disunion and the prospect of war, Douglass saw a glimmer of hope that a break might soon occur from the prison of the past. Douglass shared his generation's sentimental attachments to the past, to a sense of home and founding, but he also wanted to feel a part of America's historical continuum. He longed to understand his own origins as much as he "longed to have a future." Douglass seemed to take heart that, as long as America was young, it might still be malleable.

A comparison of two of Douglass' speeches a decade apart, one in 1852 and the other in 1862, reveals the significance of his millennial hope and the depth of his yearning to belong in America. Both speeches illuminate enduring impulses in his thought and help us understand his response to secession. In his celebrated Fourth of July address of 1852 in Rochester, Douglass had spoken of the meaning and freshness of America's founding: "I am glad . . . that your nation is so young," he lectured his white audience. He felt buoyed by the fact that America was "still in the impressible stage of her existence." "There is consolation in the thought that America is young," he continued. "Great streams are not easily turned from channels, worn deep in the course of ages. . . . As with rivers, so with nations." Doug-

---

28. On the nature and significance of Douglass' autobiographies, see Walker, *Moral Choices*, 209–28; Robert B. Stepto, "Narration, Authentication, and Authorial Control in Frederick Douglass' Narrative of 1845," in Dexter Fisher and Robert B. Stepto (eds.), *Afro-American Literature: The Reconstruction of Instruction* (New York, 1979), 178–91; and Henry-Louis Gates, Jr., "Binary Oppositions in Chapter One of Narrative of the Life of Frederick Douglass an American Slave Written by Himself," in *ibid.*, 212–32. Walker argues persuasively that Douglass' principal biographers, Quarles and Foner, have allowed the autobiographies to determine the nature of their work. Each has produced a "consistent" and "useful" Douglass. In the autobiographies, Douglass tried to present his life as a "pleasing progressive whole." In turn, his biographers have done the same. The complexity and conflict in Douglass' life and personality are, therefore, not confronted. Walker's analysis is also helpful in understanding Douglass' search for his "lost past," his efforts to create one and use it in the present. Douglass, *Bondage and Freedom*, 273.

lass urged his listeners to "cling" to the Fourth of July as the "first great fact of your nation's history—the very ringbolt in the chain of your yet undeveloped destiny." Implicit, and soon to be explicit, was his desire to break the chain of history, to preserve its founding principles and to frame a new nation.[29]

Then Douglass announced that the focus of his speech was not the past, but the present. "We have to do with the past only as we can make it useful to the present and to the future," he proclaimed. Again and again, he assured his audience of his admiration for the courage and wisdom of the "fathers" of American independence, but in every instance they were "your fathers." Douglass was not a member of the family; he did not share in the fathers' "rich inheritance." "The Fourth of July is *yours*, not *mine*," he admonished the crowd. "*You* may rejoice, *I* must mourn." In this moving speech Douglass took up the "plaintive lament of a . . . woe-smitten people" and converted it into an historic indictment of America's national crime. In this speech, as in others, Douglass illuminated his desire for a rending and a rebirth of the American nation.[30]

Defining the dilemma of what historian George Forgie has called the "postheroic generation," Douglass continued (in the sentimental language of his day): "Your fathers have lived, died, and have done their work, and have done much of it well. You live and must die, and you must do your work. You have no right to enjoy a child's share in the labor of your fathers, unless your children are to be blest by your labors. You have no right to wear out and waste the hard-earned fame of your fathers to cover your indolence." The sons of the Founding Fathers were charged not only with preserving the Republic and its principles but with performing "noble deeds" that would re-create the founding. Douglass dearly wanted to add black freedom to the burden of the "sons," just as he wished to play his own role in carrying that burden. To Douglass, as long as slavery existed, the "Union" was only half-born, incomplete, and threatened. The nation could only survive if the sons did their "work" as well as the fathers had done theirs. But the postheroic generation, it seemed to him, did not understand the challenge and was insufficiently aware of how endangered its Union really was. The nation needed awakening, which could

29. "The Meaning of July Fourth for the Negro," speech at Rochester, New York, July 5, 1852, in Foner (ed.), *Life and Writings*, II, 182–83, 185. On the significance of this speech, see Herbert J. Storing, "Frederick Douglass," in Morton J. Frisch and Richard G. Stevens (eds.), *American Political Thought: The Philosophic Dimension of American Statesmanship* (New York, 1971), 152–53.
30. "The Meaning of July Fourth for the Negro," 189.

only come through political and military conflict. "Argument" did not suffice; only "scorching irony" and "blasting reproach" could gain the "nation's ear." "For it is not light that is needed, but fire; it is not the gentle shower, but thunder," declared the bitter orator. "We need the storm, the whirlwind, and the earthquake. The feeling of the nation must be quickened; the conscience of the nation must be roused." Douglass' apocalypticism, one of the most consistent features in his thought over the next decade, was rarely in better form.[31]

Eight and one-half years later, Douglass not only welcomed disunion but saw in it the possible fulfillment of his own oft-repeated prophecy: slavery would one day destroy the Union and throw North and South into a war that would determine a new future for America. At the end of the 1852 speech, Douglass sounded the alarm: "Oh! be warned! be warned! a horrible reptile is coiled up in your nation's bosom"; "the venomous creature is nursing at the breast of your youthful republic; for the love of God, tear away, and fling from you the hideous monster, and let the weight of twenty millions crush and destroy it forever!" In Douglass' view, only such an expectation made life in America meaningful for blacks. When he spoke of the "twenty millions," he included the entire population. The whole nation would destroy the old and create the new, and the glory of the new founding would be shared by *all* the fathers, and the inheritance by *all* the sons.[32]

Exactly a decade later, in 1862 at Himrods Corners in Yates County, New York, Douglass delivered a second Fourth of July speech in which he addressed the same issues under very different circumstances. In "The Slaveholders' Rebellion," an oration that revealed much about his interpretation of the Civil War one year into the conflict, Douglass announced that the break with the past had come. "Our country is now on fire," he said; the prophecied "social earthquake" had occurred. The memory of the "fathers" had receded another decade into the past, but their significance remained the same.

31. George B. Forgie, *Patricide in a House Divided: A Psychological Interpretation of Lincoln and His Age* (New York, 1979), 3–53. Essentially, Forgie's theory is that those political and cultural leaders who came to maturity between the 1820s and the Civil War had been taught to revere the Founding Fathers, to acquire the virtues of George Washington, and to safeguard the Union. But the fame of the fathers curbed their own quest for immortality; their ambition was blunted and needed its own outlet. Hence, in the Civil War the "postheroic generation" found its moment to make history, both to preserve and to give the Republic, in Lincoln's words, a "new birth." "The Meaning of July Fourth for the Negro," 188, 192; Robert Penn Warren, *The Legacy of the Civil War* (Cambridge, Mass., 1983), 6.
32. "The Meaning of July Fourth," 201.

The only difference was that now Douglass felt more a part of the fathers' legacy. "The claim of our fathers upon our memory . . . ," he declared, "are founded in the fact that they wisely, and bravely, and successfully met the crisis of their day. And if the men of this generation would deserve well of posterity they must like their fathers, discharge the duties and responsibilities of their age." The past had truly become useful to the present. Perilous as the hour seemed, Douglass finally felt heir to the nation's inheritance and to the "responsibilities" of his generation. "Your fathers drew the sword for free and independent Government . . . ," he told his audience. "We are only continuing the tremendous struggle which your fathers and my fathers began eighty-six years ago." In 1852 Douglass had disclaimed any part of the fathers' inheritance and, although dearly wishing it were otherwise, felt no attachment to the Fourth of July. In 1862, however, in the midst of the sectional war he had hoped for, the revolutionary fathers had become his own, and the postheroic generation's self-imposed charge to preserve the work of the fathers while doing them one better had likewise become his own. Without disunion and war (especially a successful war that did, indeed, free the slaves), it is doubtful whether Douglass could ever have made this claim. It is equally doubtful whether he could have sustained hope in a future for blacks in America. If he could help it, he would not remain merely a "creature of the past and present."[33]

This was the central meaning of the secession crisis and the coming of the war for Douglass. It raised at least the possibility of "armed abolition," of mingling the cause of the slave with the life of the nation. "At last our proud Republic is overtaken," he wrote approvingly in April, 1861, after the attack on Fort Sumter. Although he predicted that the nation would suffer untold "desolations," the moment was "propitious" and the war welcomed. "Now is the time," wrote Douglass, "to change the cry of vengeance long sent up from the . . . toiling bondman into a grateful prayer for the peace and safety of the Government." He had rarely spoken of the United States government in such warm tones. This was possible because, for the moment, he beheld a crisis that "bound up the fate of the Republic and that of the slave in the same bundle."[34]

Whether disunion would lead to "armed abolition" under a new and regenerated federal government would not be known until well

33. "The Slaveholders' Rebellion," speech delivered on July 4, 1862, at Himrods Corners, Yates County, New York, in Foner (ed.), *Life and Writings*, III, 242–43.
34. "Nemesis," *DM*, May, 1861, in Foner (ed.), *Life and Writings*, III, 98–99.

beyond that first April of the Civil War. In an editorial entitled "Who Killed the American Eagle?" Douglass seemed certain at least that the old Union was dead. "The great American eagle is dead," he declared. "His power is gone forever." He then offered a metaphorical explanation of why the eagle had died: "By an old agreement . . . between Mr. South and Mr. North, the eagle was to be raffled off between the contracting parties every four years, and whichever got the highest number, was to take the bird for the next four years. For many years Mr. South had regularly won the eagle, and enjoyed its services. He had trained it to hunt slaves, to protect slave-traders, . . . to steal from Mexico, to tear the flesh of offensive strangers, to guard, protect and extend slavery." According to the imaginative editor, "Mr. North" had always coveted this bird of prey, and "he determined that if he should ever get possession of the eagle, he would teach him better manners, and train him to better habits." At last, in 1860, "Mr. North" won the eagle, but "before handing it over, as in honor bound, the treacherous Mr. South filled the unsuspecting bird with a heavy dose of secession powder so that our once majestic bird was as good as dead." Douglass reveals here his conception of the Union, a once-powerful republic hopelessly corrupted by slavery. Why had the eagle died? "The bird must die," Douglass argued, "and the verdict of the inquest must be that it died of poison, treacherously administered at the instigation of Mr. South by one James Buchanan." Douglass' use of the word *must* is suggestive of his interpretation of secession. Slaveholders, in association with their northern accomplices, had killed the old Union. They *must* kill it, Douglass reasoned, and it *must* die, for otherwise a new Union—a new nation with a new future—was not possible. This was not a contradiction of his belief that America was still young and malleable; it merely illustrates his faith in apocalyptic change. Thus, we can see even more fully why Douglass decried compromise in the secession winter. Concessions to the South only perpetuated the past and the irresolution of the present.[35]

During the final stage of the Fort Sumter crisis, Douglass was in Rochester preparing for a two-month trip to Haiti to investigate the prospects for black emigration to that island republic. He had become deeply discouraged with Lincoln during the month between Lincoln's inauguration (on March 4) and the early days of April. Lincoln's conciliatory First Inaugural Address had only perpetuated Douglass' "worst fears." Although he applauded Lincoln's condemnation of se-

---

35. "Who Killed the American Eagle," *DM*, April, 1861.

cession and his vow to preserve the Union, Douglass was enraged over the new president's promise not to interfere with slavery in the southern states and he condemned Lincoln's pledge to cooperate in the return of fugitive slaves. As a radical abolitionist and a black spokesman, Douglass was not very charitable toward Lincoln's delicate and unprecedented plight and found "no very hopeful impression" in Lincoln's address. The new president's disclaimers of any threat to slavery led Douglass to believe Lincoln had sunk to "the same moral level" as slaveholders.[36]

Douglass' angry editorial about the inaugural address reflected his psychological condition in the spring of 1861. The secession crisis had wrought five months of tension and frustration, and Douglass had allowed his own expectations to rise higher than any Republican president could have fulfilled. He was greatly disappointed that Lincoln did not deliver a much stronger statement against slavery (something even Douglass should have recognized as incompatible with an appeal for reconciliation), so he vented his frustration on the president, calling him "the most dangerous advocate of slave-hunting and slave-catching in the land." Douglass' mounting rage against slavery and the South had perhaps reached a stage where it could be absorbed only by war itself.[37]

Then came the news from Charleston Harbor on April 12. Lincoln had, after all, taken a stand against secession, and a state of war existed between the United States government and its slaveholding states. Douglass promptly cancelled his trip to Haiti and announced that he could not leave his post while a "tremendous revolution in all things pertaining to the possible future" of blacks ensued. Fort Sumter brought a "consummation" Douglass had long anticipated. The old Union was gone and the nation might now be forced to reinvent itself through a righteous war upon slaveholders.[38]

36. "A Trip to Haiti," DM, May, 1861, in Foner (ed.), Life and Writings, III, 85–88; "The Inaugural Address," DM, April, 1861, in ibid., III, 72–75, 79. For Lincoln's statements about slavery in the First Inaugural, see Roy P. Basler (ed.), The Collected Works of Abraham Lincoln (8 vols.; New Brunswick, N.J., 1953), IV, 262–64.

37. "The Inaugural Address," 76. For interesting speculation on the significance of "rage" in the 1850s and the secession crisis, see Charles B. Strozier, Lincoln's Quest for Union: Public and Private Meanings (New York, 1982), 201–202. See also Heinz Kohut, "Thoughts on Narcissism and Narcissistic Rage," in Paul H. Orenstein (ed.), The Search for the Self: Selected Writings of Heinz Kohut (2 vols.; New York, 1978), II, 615–58.

38. "A Trip to Haiti"; "The Fall of Fort Sumter," DM, May, 1861, in Foner (ed.), Life and Writings, III, 88–89.

4/CREATING THE HATED ENEMY: DOUGLASS, WAR PROPAGANDA, AND THE USES OF VIOLENCE

I think the lesson of the hour is insurrection. Insurrection of thought always precedes the insurrection of arms. The last twenty years have been an insurrection of thought.
—Wendell Phillips, "The Lesson of the Hour," lecture at Brooklyn, New York, November 1, 1859

I hated slavery, slaveholders, and all pertaining to them; and I did not fail to inspire others with the same feeling, wherever and whenever opportunity was presented.
—Frederick Douglass, *My Bondage and My Freedom*, 1855

BY THE SPRING OF 1861 FREDERICK DOUGLASS had long hoped that somehow, someday, war would be waged against American slaveholders. As a black abolitionist seeking immediate emancipation and as a former slave with personal motives, he lived for the day when slavery would be destroyed and slaveholders crushed. Where "arguments" had failed, he longed to see "events" prevail.[1] At least by the late 1850s, and perhaps as early as his break with the Garrisonians and his conversion to political antislavery (1847–52), Douglass had come to believe that American slavery would have a violent end, although he always wished that such violence be organized, official, and legal. He had long justified the slaves' right to rebel and kill their masters. As a youth, he himself had rebelled violently, and now, as a middle-aged reformer, he had lived to witness the United States government preparing to make war against slaveowners. How could a black editor best take advantage of these momentous events? All his life—in his writings as well as his oratory—Douglass had performed as an antislavery propagandist, and in this, one of the abolitionist's most important roles, he found his identity and vocation. After the firing on Fort Sumter, he did the natural and appropriate thing: he became a war propagandist.

Douglass' quest to create the hated enemy of the Union cause had deep personal roots. His various writings in the 1850s, especially the second autobiography, illustrate his enduring hatred of slaveholders as well as his desire for revenge against his former oppressors. Douglass' developing views on the uses of violence throughout his career as

---

1. "A Change of Attitude," *DM*, June, 1861.

an antislavery advocate provide many clues to understanding his wartime rhetoric.

Douglass rejoiced at the outbreak of hostilities in 1861. The northern response to Fort Sumter and Lincoln's call for seventy-five thousand volunteers seemed overwhelming. From April to mid-summer, he spoke nearly every Sunday at Zion Church in Rochester. On April 27 he told his audience that the preceding weeks had caused "thrilling excitement." "I have never spent days so restless and anxious," he claimed. "Our mornings and evenings have continually vacillated between the dim light of hope and the gloomy shadow of despair." The outbreak of the war brought a release from the anxiety of the secession crisis. In these heady days of patriotism, it seemed that history had made a turn and great events offered potential for great change. But Douglass also stressed caution in the midst of excitement and openly expressed his fears for what he affectionately called "our National Capital" and "our National Government." As four more southern states seceded from the Union and farmboys and mechanics all over the country began to imagine themselves soldiers, Douglass reminded the congregation at Zion Church that "we cannot see the end from the beginning."[2]

The outbreak of the Civil War came as a providential release to many former pacifist abolitionists like William Lloyd Garrison and John Greenleaf Whittier, who saw in it "the hands of God" and the divine "chastisement" of the nation for the sin of slaveholding. Douglass did not have pacifist principles to overcome, but he did see the conflict immediately, as did most abolitionists, as a "holy war" for black freedom. Abolitionists' hopes ascended to new heights in the wake of Fort Sumter; they joined the chorus of war fever and stood ready to usher slavery to an early death. After years of argument and prophecy, and after watching slavery dissolve America's political institutions, Douglass could hardly see the war in any other than abolitionists' terms. He was fully aware that the radical implications (emancipation) of a war to save the Union were not anticipated by most northerners, but as a minority agitator, a moralist preaching an unpopular politics, and a political activist arguing for a new morality, he strove to exploit the grand opportunity now open to all abolitionists.[3]

Although he welcomed the commencement of hostilities, Doug-

2. "Frederick Douglass on the Crisis," excerpts from two speeches at Zion Church, Rochester, April 27 and May 4, 1861, in *DM*, June, 1861.

3. On the abolitionists' response to the war, see McPherson, *Struggle for Equality*, 75–98; James Brewer Stewart, *Holy Warriors: The Abolitionists and American Slavery* (New York, 1976), 177–85. On Garrison, Whittier, and other abolitionists, as well as the

lass realized that the war fever sweeping the land was the result of southern action as much as northern will. He urged his readers to be wary that the spirit of compromise was still abroad in the free states, even though the South's attack on Fort Sumter had temporarily silenced its champions. The American people, declared Douglass, had been "many long and weary months . . . on the mountain with the wily tempter." Slavery had nearly received a new lease on life, he seemed to believe, from the various compromise efforts. True to their nature, though, the slaveholders had forced the issue; their "reckless impetuosity" had brought the crisis to military action. "Thank God!—the slaveholders themselves have saved our cause from ruin!" wrote Douglass. "They have exposed the throat of slavery to the keen knife of liberty."[4] Thus, immediately after Sumter, Douglass began his relentless crusade to focus northern attention on slaveholders themselves as the true enemies of the Union.

A "sudden revolution" seemed apparent in northern attitudes, and Douglass made the most of it. In words designed to whip up war fever, he joined the chorus of northern enthusiasm: "Never was a change so sudden, so universal, so portentous. The whole North . . . is in arms. Drums are beating, men are enlisting, companies forming, regiments marching, banners are flying, and money is pouring into the national treasury to put an end to the slaveholding rebellion." During the spring and summer of 1861, Douglass' rhetoric took on a character it would possess throughout the war. Like Lincoln, he refused to accept the legitimacy of the Confederate States of America, but a war waged by a legitimate government against treason and rebellion was official

---

reactions of conservative northern intellectuals, see Fredrickson, *Inner Civil War,* 61, 65–78. On the sudden popularity and increasing influence of abolitionists, see McPherson, *Struggle for Equality,* 78–90; Stewart, *Holy Warriors,* 182–85. Douglass' role as a war propagandist fits a larger pattern followed by abolitionists generally. The "Emancipation Leagues," organized first in Boston, were groups of influential abolitionists dedicated to propaganda campaigns that would move northern opinion in the direction of a war for emancipation. On the Emancipation Leagues, see McPherson, *Struggle for Equality,* 76–81.

4. "The Fall of Fort Sumter," 89–91. For Douglass' continued fears and warnings about "compromise," see "Antislavery in Rochester," *DM,* June, 1861; "Still in Danger of Compromise," *DM,* July, 1861; "The Lessons of the Hour," lecture at Zion Church, June 30, 1861, in Foner (ed.), *Life and Writings,* III, 139–40. With historical hindsight, one can see that Douglass' enduring fears about compromise were dubious at best. He seems to have equated the notion of "compromise" with the reluctance on the part of the Lincoln administration to wage war on slavery as well as the Confederate states. All of his concern about compromise seems to have served as a form of surrogate for his frustration with federal government policy, perhaps especially its refusal to accept the enlistment of black soldiers.

and legal violence. For the first time in his life, Douglass could do more than express sympathy with slave insurrections, the acts of desperation by oppressed peoples, and he felt released to advocate every form of violence against the South, to unleash a long-standing vengeance against his own former oppressors. "Let the grim visage of a northern army confront them [southern slaveholders] from one direction," he urged, "a furious slave insurrection meet them at another, and starvation threaten them from still another."[5]

Douglass reveled in the war psychology that seemed to be sweeping the North and with pen and voice did his best to help create it. "The cry now is for war, vigorous war, war to the bitter end," he proclaimed.[6] Every concerted war effort seems to necessitate a hated enemy, and Douglass took it upon himself to provide the Union cause with just such a creature. This was not a new role for the black abolitionist; it merely required a heightening of an old practice under new circumstances.

Douglass relished this aspect of his role as war propagandist. "We earnestly desire to see the South humbled," he wrote in a May, 1861, editorial. "The 'high looks' of the lordly Assyrians must be brought low." He considered himself an able commentator on the attributes of southern whites: "We know something by experience of the character of slaveholders." Indeed, Douglass did his utmost to keep the "character" of slaveholders before the eyes and ears of his audience. He wanted to cultivate the violent imagination of his readers and convert the old notion of the Slave Power (the object of abstract fear) into a hatred of slaveholders themselves. Wars must have justification, and the enemy must be rendered real, immediate, and threatening. Douglass gladly joined in one of the primary functions of the ancient art of war propaganda: the dehumanization of the enemy.[7]

Throughout 1861 Douglass attacked the character not only of planters but of all southern whites. In an assault that ran counter to most Republican and much abolitionist propaganda, Douglass portrayed nonslaveholding poor whites as mere "tools of the slave-

5. "Sudden Revolution in Northern Sentiment," *DM*, May, 1861, in Foner (ed.), *Life and Writings*, III, 92–93.
6. *Ibid.*, 93.
7. *Ibid.*, 102; "The Past and the Present," *DM*, May, 1861. For a helpful analysis of the dehumanization of enemies or victims, see Herbert C. Kelman, "Violence Without Moral Restraint: Reflections on the Dehumanization of Victims and Victimizers," in George M. Kren and Leon H. Rappoport (eds.), *Varieties of Psychohistory* (New York, 1976), 282–314, especially 310–11. Although much of this essay deals with the phenomenon of massacres, it is still informative in understanding the process of creating the hated enemy.

holders." They were "ignorant, besotted, and servile," possessing "no opinions of their own in political affairs." The power of the master class was absolute. "The slaveholders are the South . . . ," argued Douglass. "The six million of free nonslaveholding whites are but freight cars full of cattle, attached to the three hundred and fifty thousand slaveholding locomotives. Where the locomotives go, the train must follow."[8] In peace, the Slave Power was to be feared and opposed; in war, it must be destroyed.

In the May, 1861, issue of his paper, Douglass reprinted three pages of articles and letters describing lynchings, beatings, and other brutalities in the South. Duels (one over a mulatto girl), jailings for abolitionist sentiment, and one case after another of southern violence, intemperance, and intolerance were the subjects of these pieces taken from journals all over the country. Douglass' purpose was to offer "an illustration of the peculiar manners, temper, and morals of our slaveholding society." "Barbarous and bloody" was the nature of the South, the society upon which northerners were now asked to make war.[9]

The violent and aggressive nature of southern society had long been a favorite subject of abolitionists, but now it took on added significance because it could be linked to political and military aggression. In June, at one of his Sunday lectures at Zion Church in Rochester, Douglass demonstrated that the perfect enemy had been found. "What is a slaveholder but a rebel and a traitor?" he queried. "A man cannot be a slaveholder without being a traitor to humanity and a rebel against the law and government of the ever-living God." Douglass portrayed slaveholders as inherently depraved, natural criminals; he wanted his listeners to equate treason with slaveholding and thus fight to destroy both. He was calling forth the wrath of a people going to war, awaiting the first major clashes of the respective armies. Wartime requires unity of purpose; men must be convinced to act without moral ambiguity, and Douglass wanted his Rochester audience to make no distinctions about the enemy. "Southern men . . . ," he assured his listeners, "are all of the same species" and could understand "no law but the law of force." Douglass' wartime

8. "The Future of the Abolition Cause."
9. "The Reign of Ruffianism—The Brutal, Oppressive, and Blood-Stained South—Life in the Land of Chivalry," *DM*, May, 1861. Although these columns reflected a long tradition of antisouthern material in the abolitionist press, Douglass' choice of a title here is indicative of his newly adopted role as war propagandist.

speeches were deeply personal illustrations of his vision of the conflict—"I want to see the monster destroyed," he declared toward the end of his June lecture.[10] This was a war not only to abolish slavery, but to kill slaveholders as well.

Douglass frequently employed the old staple of political antislavery rhetoric—the theory of a Slave Power. Slavery evolved from and survived by a social philosophy, he argued. Those northerners who possessed no sympathy whatsoever for the slave might at least feel their own liberty threatened. "The slaveholder must be master of society," Douglass maintained, "otherwise he cannot long be master of his slaves." This threat alone, argued the impatient editor, should increase antislavery sentiment in the northern war effort.

By the end of the summer of 1861, though, Douglass was frustrated with northern opinion, the government's policy toward slavery, and military defeat. He was especially annoyed with federal insistence on returning fugitive slaves who had escaped to Union lines, and he hoped that the Union debacle at the first Battle of Bull Run would teach the North to better "distinguish between its friends and its foes at the South." This salutory reaction to Bull Run was common among abolitionists and conservative intellectuals alike. In defeat, Douglass wanted the North to learn the necessity of "effectively putting down the whole class of pestiferous slaveholders, so that the nation shall know them no more, except in history, to be execrated and loathed, with all other robbers and tyrants which have cursed and ruined human society."[11]

A hated enemy is often one of the tragic exigencies of war. Throughout the first two years of the Civil War, a constant theme in Douglass' rhetoric was the pressing need for northerners to learn to *hate* slaveholders. In his view, the North was insufficiently aware of the "exterminating vigor of a settled and deadly hate" with which southerners prosecuted the war; only when northerners felt the same "quenchless fire of a deadly hate," he wrote in an August, 1861, column, would they find the "secret" to military success. The South was in earnest and understood its cause, Douglass maintained, while the North did not. He equated earnestness with the willingness to

10. "The Decision of the Hour," lecture delivered at Zion Church, Rochester, June 16, 1861, in Foner (ed.), *Life and Writings*, III, 122–23.

11. *Ibid.*, 144; "Shall Slavery Survive the War?" *DM*, September, 1861; in Foner (ed.), *Life and Writings*, III, 129; "The War and Slavery," *DM*, August, 1861. On the reaction of northern conservatives to the first Battle of Bull Run, see Fredrickson, *Inner Civil War*, 73–76.

wage war on slavery as well as to preserve the Union. A slaveholders' rebellion, he continually argued, could only be suppressed by destroying slavery and slaveholders.[12]

Douglass would have to wait a year and a half before seeing such a reality, but in 1861, he seemed certain of his own duty: "The dangerous and demonical character of slavery . . . we have been endeavoring to expose," he wrote in October, "and to teach the nation they must hate and abolish, or be hated and abolished by it." By fall, Douglass was predicting that the war would be "long, revengeful, and desolating," and he urged his countrymen to prepare for such strife. In a view held widely among abolitionists in 1861, he believed that if the war lasted long enough slavery would crumble by "iron necessity," if not from moral idealism. Responding to a disheartened correspondent who challenged his optimism, he defended his sense of hope but warned that northerners had "not yet been sufficiently deluged with slaveholding contempt and scorn, nor drunk deep enough of the poisoned cup of slaveholding malignity." They had, in other words, not yet learned to hate the foe.[13] Douglass was determined to educate them.

Douglass made the most of every opportunity to exploit contempt for the South. When there were allegations of atrocities committed by Confederate soldiers, he reprinted and exploited the stories. In December, 1861, under a heading "Signs of Barbarism," he reported the claim that Virginians had produced candles made of tallow from dead Yankee soldiers. He also reprinted an account from the New York *Post* reporting the "distribution of the skin of old John Brown's son," who had been killed in battle. According to Douglass, these episodes demonstrated that if "left to themselves, the Southerners would wholly barbarize under the influence of slavery." What moral sense they did possess, he maintained, was due only to their "connection with the superior civilization of the North."[14]

In January, 1862, Douglass spoke at National Hall in Philadelphia.

12. "The Rebels, the Government, and the Difference Between Them," *DM*, August, 1861, in Foner (ed.), *Life and Writings*, III, 131–32.

13. "The Duty of the Abolitionists in the Present State of the Country," *DM*, October, 1861, in *ibid.*, III, 166; "Signs of the Times," *DM*, November, 1861, in *ibid.*, III, 171–73—a response to a letter from S. Dutton, Meredith, New York, October 14, 1861. On the abolitionists' belief that the war would force emancipation by "military necessity," see McPherson, *Struggle for Equality*, 90–93.

14. "Signs of Barbarism," *DM*, December, 1861. The authenticity of these reports about southern atrocity is questionable. I know of no verification for them. The propaganda uses of such stories, though, were not lost on abolitionist editors such as Douglass.

In an address on the meaning of the war, entitled "The Reasons for Our Troubles," he continued his attack on the character of slaveholders. All of the uncertainty, destruction, and suffering of the war he laid at the doorstep of the South, and he painted a "dismal and terrible" picture of the desolation the American people would yet have to suffer. "At this hour," Douglass declared, "there is everywhere at the South, nursed and cherished, the most deadly hate towards every man and woman of Northern birth." Northerners, he maintained, did not comprehend the "intensity of this slaveholding malice." To meet this challenge, Douglass offered only one harsh remedy: "we must meet them, defeat them, and conquer them."[15]

Although they seem vicious and sometimes simplistic, Douglass' appeals for hatred of the South fit his apocalyptic conception of the war. God's vengeance and retribution were at the center of millennial expectation in the nineteenth century. Evil was to be eradicated through great calamity; a new age of peace and justice would follow. But millennialism was an activist faith; the "overturning" of society depended greatly on human action. Thus hatred became a creative force, a necessary agent in an apocalyptic event. In a June, 1861, speech, Douglass likened the Civil War to the "apocalyptic vision" in the Book of Revelation. He described a cosmic battle between "good and evil, liberty and slavery." "Such is the struggle now going on in the United States," he declared. "The slaveholders had rather reign in hell than serve in heaven." Douglass envisioned a war that might be long and tragic, but also cleansing, and he portrayed slavery as an evil so comprehensive that it could only die in eschatological terms. Hatred of slaveholders, therefore, had great purgative power and an appointed role in America's Armageddon.[16]

Douglass' spiritual interpretation of the war will be analyzed at length in the next chapter, but his spiritual outlook is crucial as well in explaining his efforts as a war propagandist. He was demanding that Americans wage a total war to destroy what he considered a sick and tyrannical force within their midst. It was, therefore, a war for human progress and social revolution, a quest to preserve civilization and rekindle its best aspects while eradicating its worst. By 1862 Douglass portrayed slaveholders as nothing more than "barbarians

15. "The Reasons for Our Troubles," speech delivered at National Hall, Philadelphia, January 14, 1862, in Foner (ed.), *Life and Writings*, III, 198, 203.
16. "The Decision of the Hour," 119–20. On the role of vengeance and retribution in the apocalyptic conception of the Civil War, see Moorhead, *American Apocalypse*, 109–12; William A. Clebsch, "Christian Interpretations of the Civil War," *Church History*, XXX (June, 1961), 217–18; Fredrickson, *Inner Civil War*, 69.

making no pretensions to civilization." They and their system were the collective "monster" and their modes of warfare were "grim and hideous." "Digging up the bones of our dead soldiers slain in battle, making drinking vessels out of their skulls, drumsticks out of their arm bones, slaying our wounded soldiers on the field of carnage," and "firing upon unarmed men" were a few of the accusations Douglass flung at southerners. For the war to move in the direction he desired, Douglass had concluded that a "deadly hatred" for all things born of a slaveholding society would have to be engendered in the hearts and minds of northerners.[17]

Douglass' quest to create the hated enemy of the Union cause reflects a long-standing psychological need of his own. We must remember that he spent twenty-seven years of his life either as a slave or a fugitive slave; his sense of self-definition took its departure from his slave origins as the child of a black mother and her white master. He was both a reflection of the system into which he was born and its greatest contradiction. Slavery never received a more eloquent indictment than in Douglass' autobiographies, editorials, and speeches. He knew slavery as a system rooted in dehumanization and violence, and he knew from experience that slaves were both desired and despised. Slavery, in his view, required hatred and force in order to survive. It had taught him a great deal about the uses of violence, and it had taught him how to hate.

By 1861, Douglass had carried on a twenty-year discourse about the character of slaveholders. His first two autobiographies—the *Narrative* (1845) and *My Bondage and My Freedom* (1855)—were antislavery tracts as well as explorations of the self. Fraught with egotism and subject to the vicissitudes of memory, autobiography has limitations as a source of historical truth, but as an act of self-creation, it can vividly reveal the psychological and intellectual motivations of the author.[18] In Douglass' case, autobiography served well to create his own historical image: the fugitive slave who overcomes slavery,

17. "The Slaveholders' Rebellion," speech delivered at Himrods Corners, Yates County, New York, July 4, 1862, *DM*, August, 1862, in Foner (ed.), *Life and Writings*, III, 242, 244. For examples of Douglass' emphasis on the South's "hatred" of free institutions, see *ibid.*, 246; Douglass, *Life and Times*, 332. According to Douglass, southerners "had come to hate everything which had the prefix 'Free'—free soil, free states, free territories, free schools, free speech, and freedom generally, and they would have no more such prefixes."

18. On the nature and limitations of autobiography, see Elizabeth Bruss, *Autobiographical Acts* (Baltimore, 1976); Roy Pascal, *Design and Truth in Autobiography* (Cambridge, 1960). Bruss's work is an especially good analysis of the ideas of choice and

liberates himself through knowledge and will, and joins the public crusade to destroy the system that could not destroy him. But it also gave vent to symbolic, if not real, revenge against his former oppressors.

More than anything else, it is language that renders us human. Language not only carries the ability to know but, more important, the power of self-assertion. As literary critic Houston Baker, Jr., has demonstrated, language helped to "liberate" Frederick Douglass. As Douglass became a "public" man after his escape from slavery, his ability to speak and write not only allowed him to tell his story but gave meaning to his life.[19] By his own account it was literacy that opened Douglass' mind to the possibility of freedom. He learned his first letters from "Miss Sophia" (his mistress Sophia Auld, wife of his owner Hugh Auld) while an eight-year-old in Baltimore. Douglass' kind and loving mistress quickly ceased her teaching, however, when her husband raged with anger. A slave was not to be taught to read and write; it would "spoil the best nigger in the world," Douglass quoted his master as saying. Even if we concede that Douglass may have romanticized his discovery of literacy and used this episode of his life to fashion his autobiography as an antislavery polemic, knowledge and literacy did mean potential liberation to the young slave. Compared to most bondsmen, Douglass had a fortunate childhood. But it was through language that he learned of his own possibilities, about the concept of "abolition," and of the "free states" to the North. He learned that words could mean power and persuasion and alone could provide a sustenance to life, give it purpose, and offer hope.[20]

intention in autobiography. On black autobiography, see Stephen Butterfield, *Black Autobiography in America* (Amherst, 1974); John W. Blassingame, "Black Autobiographies as History and Literature," *Black Scholar*, V (1973–74), 2–9.

19. Houston A. Baker, Jr., *The Journey Back: Issues in Black Literature and Criticism* (Chicago, 1980), 33–46. Baker's chapter, "Autobiographical Acts and the Voice of the Southern Slave," is especially helpful in understanding the fugitive slave's use of autobiography (language itself) as a means of self liberation. Baker also argues that through the "act" of autobiography, Douglass inevitably lost some of his authentic black identity by creating a new public self that conformed to white Christian standards. This fact, however, does not prevent us from uncovering various aspects of character and motivation that Douglass revealed through his three autobiographies. On the significance of language in Douglass' autobiographies, see Robert B. Stepto, *From Behind the Veil: A Study of Afro-American Narrative* (Urbana, 1979), 16–26; Walker, *Moral Choices*, 209–28; Albert Stone, "Identity and Art in Frederick Douglass's Narrative," *CLA Journal*, XVII (1973), 192–213; H. Bruce Franklin, "Animal Farm Unbound," *New Letters*, XLIII (1977), 25–48.

20. Douglass, *Bondage and Freedom*, 141–47. On Douglass' discovery of literacy and special childhood, see Preston, *Young Frederick Douglass*, 93–104. On his discovery of the meaning of the word *abolition*, see his discussion of this in *Bondage and Freedom*, 165.

When Douglass was thirteen, he managed to purchase a copy of *The Columbian Orator*, a remarkable little book full of eloquent expressions of human liberty and dignity. Compiled in 1797 by the Massachusetts educator Caleb Bingham, *The Columbian Orator* was both a collection of patriotic speeches and a handbook on oratory. As Dickson Preston has pointed out, the book was a precious discovery for the young Douglass. With a dictionary in hand, he plowed through the book again and again. The speeches of Cato, Washington, Socrates, William Pitt the Elder, and others profoundly affected him. The book took on almost sacred qualities to the youthful slave, and he kept it as a model for the rest of his life. "The reading of these speeches . . . ," wrote Douglass, "enabled me to give tongue to many interesting thoughts, which had frequently flashed away for want of utterance." Now he could read words that condemned slavery and injustice, that justified a slave's right to rebel and run away, that extolled human liberty and freedom. The young Douglass was becoming aware that some part of the outside world cared, condemned slavery, and believed that persuasion could change people.[21]

At the very least, Douglass' literacy and his intense desire to learn afforded him new tools with which to thwart the oppression of slavery. This was true while he was still a slave, but also after his escape and emergence as a public man. Language (and the effective use of it as propaganda) afforded Douglass a means to vent his frustration and rage at the system of slavery and at its rulers. Thus the thread that ties together his autobiographies—his characterization and analysis of the nature of slavery and the slaveholder's mind—served a personal need for Douglass. Whether he was thirteen or forty-three, because he could speak and write and assemble words that could antagonize slaveholders, he could resist slavery and reaffirm his own existence.

The acquisition of literacy brought both bitter and sweet results. As his master had predicted (apparently in the presence of his slave), the more knowledge Douglass acquired, the more unhappy he became. Over time, knowledge of his lot made Douglass an angry slave, a rebellious and violent teenager who could be controlled only by brutality. Well before he escaped from slavery, Douglass harbored a rage that had to be released. Describing his reaction to the *Columbian Orator*, Douglass summed up his discovery: "The more I read, the more I was led to abhor and detest slavery, and my enslavers."[22] By

21. Douglass, *Bondage and Freedom*, 158. For an especially good portrayal of Douglass' purchase of the *Columbian Orator*, see Preston, *Young Frederick Douglass*, 98–100.
22. Douglass, *Bondage and Freedom*, 146, 159.

the time Douglass was able to unleash his rage against slaveholders in an officially sanctioned war (1861), he was well practiced in doing so—he had been creating the hated enemy for at least twenty years.

A conception of "enemy" can be abstract and rhetorical, or it can be literal and real. Douglass' view of slaveholders contained elements of both. As a slave he had learned to consider his various masters and overseers as immediate and daily foes. As an abolitionist in the North or traveling in England, the image he created of the slaveholder inevitably took on an abstract quality. But whether as an act of imagination or as a daily encounter governed by fear, Douglass perceived the slave-master relationship in the same manner. Even the affectionate Miss Sophia assumed in his eyes the status of enemy. When she vigorously obeyed her husband's orders forbidding young Frederick to learn to read or write, she became an abusive adversary. "Such is the relation of master and slave . . . ," wrote Douglass. "Nature made us *friends;* slavery made us *enemies.*"[23]

Perhaps Douglass survived as a slave, as psychologist Allison Davis argues, because he found ways to harness his hatred of slaveholders. The rage he harbored for his white father and his various owners, especially Thomas Auld who beat him mercilessly, could be subsumed in "fantasies of revenge." In the autobiographies, Douglass invented a heroic self-identity, a child and a man who resisted his oppressors, overcame them, and escaped their evil system. As an abolitionist, Douglass developed close associations with many caring white males, especially William Lloyd Garrison and Gerrit Smith, who blunted his distrust of whites and, according to Davis, began the "healing" of his hatred. He certainly became a more cultured and compassionate man in the twenty-three years after he escaped from slavery. His uncompromising aggression against slavery and racism had become largely verbal and literary. But the deeply personal tone of Douglass' wartime propaganda crusade indicates that his old hatred of slaveholders was not entirely healed by 1861. Only in the crucible of the Civil War did he manage to expunge at least part of his vengeance against slaveholders, although his postwar thought demonstrates that such vengeance was never fully exhausted during his lifetime.[24]

23. *Ibid.,* 161. On the role of anger and its control in black fiction (including slave narratives) see Raymond Hedin, "The Structuring of Emotion in Black American Fiction," *Novel,* XVI (Fall, 1982), 35–54.

24. Davis, *Leadership, Love, and Aggression,* 20, 23, 29, 35–37, 41, 52–53, 58, 74, 79. Davis' work is a psychobiographical treatment of four black leaders: Douglass, W. E. B. Du Bois, Richard Wright, and Martin Luther King, Jr. The interplay between compassion and hatred is a central theme in Davis' chapter on Douglass, and his

An inquiry into Douglass' role as a war propagandist would not be complete without examining his ideas on violence itself. Douglass' views on violence have been discussed by several historians and at least one political scientist. Ronald Takaki has argued that Douglass experienced deep personal ambivalence about violent means because of his mixed racial parentage and the kindness of Sophia Auld. For Douglass, argues Takaki, violence against southern whites meant warring against his own kinfolk. Takaki is correct in his assertion that Douglass possessed a white as well as a black consciousness, but this argument is unconvincing as an explanation of Douglass' dilemma over violence. It is true that he blamed the *system* more than individual masters for the oppression of slavery. He never lost his respect and sense of gratitude toward Sophia (who for a time was a surrogate mother), but she became a form of "enemy" just the same. Whether Douglass could actually have committed violence against her is unlikely, but to him she had become a "victim" of the system, part of it, and part of what must be resisted and destroyed. Douglass' masters had not been uniformly cruel by any means, and as we have seen before, his slave childhood was in many ways priviledged. This fact, however, did not blunt his hatred for slavery or of those responsible for it. For Douglass, the question of violence was always more a tactical than a moral problem. He did not relish the prospect, but morally he believed the slaves had the right to rise up and slay their masters.[25]

discussion of Douglass' enduring hatred of slaveholders corroborates much of my own analysis. We differ, however, in that Davis believes Douglass' "basic emotional conflicts were solved" (88), by 1860, and contends that Douglass was able to vent his "feelings of suicidal defiance" (77) through the surrogate of John Brown. But Davis ends his study in 1860 and fails to look at Douglass' continued vengeance toward slaveholders during and after the war. This aspect of Douglass' psyche was not healed by 1861. Davis is on the right track, though, when he says that Douglass had begun to suppress his fantasies of revenge by taking up the "sword of rhetoric" (79). On the development of Douglass' personality, especially his use of childhood fantasy, also see Stephen M. Weissman, "Frederick Douglass, Portrait of a Black Militant: A Study in the Family Romance," *Psychoanalytic Study of the Child*, XXV (1975), 725–51. On Douglass' creation of a heroic self-image, see Martin, *Mind*, 253–78.

25. On Douglass and violence, see Ronald T. Takaki, *Violence in the Black Imagination: Essays and Documents* (New York, 1972), 17–35; Leslie Friedman Goldstein, "Violence as an Instrument for Social Change: The Views of Frederick Douglass," *Journal of Negro History*, LXI (1976), 61–72; Martin, *Mind*, 24, 167–68; Willie Lee Rose, "Killing for Freedom," *New York Review of Books*, December 3, 1970, February 11, 1971; Jane H. Pease and William H. Pease, *They Who Would Be Free: Blacks' Search for Freedom, 1830–1861* (New York, 1974), 235–37, 242–43, 247–48. Takaki ends his essay "Not Afraid to Die" with the argument that Douglass' ambivalence over violence also stemmed from masculine and feminine influences. Because of the gentleness and

Douglass was never a genuine Garrisonian nonresistant. Technically, the term *nonresistant* meant a complete renunciation of all uses of physical force, a rigid brand of Christian pacifism given organizational form by William Lloyd Garrison and his followers in the New England Non-Resistant Society. Douglass never joined this organization and could never bring himself to live up to its principles; on more than one occasion he physically fought in self-defense with antiabolitionist mobs. But until his break with the Garrisonians, Douglass had embraced moral suasion as the means to destroy slavery, contending that the conscience of the world, including slaveholders, need only be bombarded sufficiently with moral argument and slavery would come crumbling down. These methods, however, only brought mounting intransigence from the South. The failure of moral suasion and an increasing sympathy for violence were, in part, caused by the Fugitive Slave Act of 1850 and the often violent resistance to it. The Kansas-Nebraska Act and subsequent armed conflict in Kansas, the oppressive implications of the Dred Scott decision, and, of course, John Brown's raid on Harpers Ferry in 1859, further rendered abolitionists more open to violent means.[26]

Douglass was profoundly influenced by all of these developments, and a brief look at his inreasing receptivity to violence in the 1850s is helpful to understanding his wartime rhetoric. By 1854 his earlier disdain for bloodshed had changed drastically in response to the

---

love he experienced from his Grandmother Bailey and Mistress Sophia, and the cruelty he encountered at the hands of southern men, Douglass came to view slavery, argues Takaki, as a system of white masculine oppression. Southern white males could only understand force, and this fact alone convinced Douglass that violence against slavery was inevitable. While this explanation is plausible, Douglass rarely made male or female distinctions in his voluminous rhetoric designed to expose the evil of slaveholders and to fashion them as the hated enemy. For an example of how Douglass placed blame on the "system" of slavery, see Douglass, *Life and Times*, 124; Douglass, *Bondage and Freedom*, 162.

26. See Goldstein, "Violence as an Instrument," 61–65. For the problems of defining *nonresistant*, see Carleton Mabee, *Black Freedom: The Non-Violent Abolitionists from 1830 Through the Civil War* (London, 1970). On Garrisonian nonresistance and the formation of the Non-Resistance Society, see Kraditor, *Means and Ends*, 86–90. Of Douglass' many encounters with mobs, probably his most famous came in Pendleton, Indiana, in 1843, where he was severely beaten; see Quarles, *Douglass*, 32–33. On the abolitionists' increasing receptivity of violence, see Friedman, *Gregarious Saints*, 202–13; Lawrence J. Friedman, "Antebellum American Abolitionism and the Problem of Violent Means," *Psychohistory Review*, IX (1980), 26–32; Jane H. Pease and William H. Pease, "Confrontation and Abolition in the 1850s," *Journal of American History*, XLVIII (March, 1972), 923–37; John Demos, "The Antislavery Movement and the Problem of Violent Means," *New England Quarterly*, XXXVII (December, 1964), 501–26.

Fugitive Slave Act. In a column entitled "Is It Right and Wise to Kill a Kidnapper?" (inspired by the attempted rescue of the fugitive Anthony Burns in Boston) he not only justified violence in self-defense against slave-catchers, but celebrated it. The "slaughter" of a slave-catcher, wrote Douglass, "was as innocent, in the sight of God, as would be the slaughter of a ravenous wolf in the act of throttling an infant." By definition, a slave-catcher had "forfeited his right to live." Opposition to the Fugitive Slave law involved individual acts of courage and violence, and Douglass himself participated in active resistance to it. In 1851 he harbored the three black fugitives who had fought off their pursuers, killing one, at Christiana, Pennsylvania. By rail, they fled to Douglass' home in Rochester. He fed and sheltered them, then, with Julia Griffiths' assistance, drove them in his carriage to the Genessee River, where they boarded a steamer to Toronto. To Douglass, the Christiana fugitives were "heroic defenders of the just rights of man against manstealers and murderers." On the deck of the ship, just before their departure to safety in Canada, one of the fugitives gave Douglass a revolver as a token of gratitude. He cherished this memento; it had been taken from the hand of the dead slave-catcher in Christiana.[27]

Increasingly during the 1850s, Douglass turned his attention to the prospect of slave insurrection in the South. In 1856, in the midst of the Kansas controversy, he declared that the "slave's right to revolt is perfect." He shuddered at the horrors slave insurrection would bring, but "terrible as it will be, we accept and hope for it." "The slaveholder has been tried and sentenced," Douglass continued, "his execution only awaits the finish to the training of his executioners." In the despair following the Dred Scott decision, Douglass saw slave rebellion as offering at least one path to black liberation. With fearful anticipation, he predicted that "in an awful moment of depression and desperation, the bondman and bondwoman at the South may rush to one wild and deadly struggle for freedom," and announced that he was in "no frame of mind" to see this prospect "long deferred." Although Douglass never called for slave insurrection in quite the same overt manner as did David Walker in 1829 or Henry Highland Garnet in 1843, he came very close to their appeals. Continuing his rhetoric of violence in the summer of 1859, he suggested that a "day

27. "Is It Right and Wise to Kill a Kidnapper," *FDP*, June 2, 1854, in Foner (ed.), *Life and Writings*, II, 287. On Douglass' response to the Fugitive Slave Act, also see Goldstein, "Violence as an Instrument," 66–67. On the Christiana episode, see Douglass, *Life and Times*, 280–82; *FDP*, September 25, 1851.

of reckoning" was at hand and called upon the "black armies of the South" to rise and "be the instruments of their own deliverance from bondage." America's contempt for blacks, he wrote, would only be washed away with "a little St. Domingo put into the coffee of our Georgia slaveholders."[28]

Douglass' advocacy of slave revolt was a view shared much more widely among black than among white abolitionists. In 1856, Lewis Tappan became alarmed at Douglass' "vengeance is mine" attitude toward slaveholders. "In your speeches and in your paper," Tappan complained, "you advocate the slaughter of slaveholders. I cannot go with you." He accused the black leader of "scattering firebrands, arrows, and death." Tappan was still a strong adherent of nonviolence and his shock at Douglass' rhetoric is understandable. His reaction, though, serves as a good measure of Douglass' changing thought on slave insurrection. Douglass never encouraged slave revolts with relish, but by the time of John Brown's raid in 1859 he was prepared to accept and make the most of what appeared inevitable.[29]

Douglass first met John Brown in November, 1847, in Springfield, Connecticut, while on a speaking tour. The eccentric Brown and the young black orator, recently returned from England, had a lasting impact on each other. There can be little doubt that through the course of the 1850s, Douglass' acquaintance with Brown quickened his receptivity to violence, but, as Leslie Goldstein has argued, Douglass' proclivity to accept violent means was already established before 1847. On several occasions between 1847 and 1859, Douglass and Brown shared each other's company. Douglass claimed that Brown laid out the skeleton of his ultimate Harpers Ferry plan in their very first meeting, and during his clandestine travels of 1857 Brown lived for nearly one month in the editor's Rochester home. Few prominent abolitionists were as enmeshed in Brown's Harpers Ferry conspiracy as Douglass, but in their famous final meeting at the stone quarry in Chambersburg, Pennsylvania, in August, 1859, Douglass counseled against the raid the old rebel was about to launch. Indeed, Douglass never actively participated in nor organized any actual slave revolt, either before or during the Civil War. He did not lack physical cour-

---

28. *FDP*, November 28, 1856, quoted in William Chambers, *American Slavery and Colour* (New York, 1857), 174; Lewis Tappan to Douglass, Brooklyn, New York, December 19, 1856, in FD Papers (LC); "The Dred Scott Decision," in *ibid.*; *DM*, August, 1859. See David Walker, *Walker's Appeal in Four Articles* (1830; rpr. New York, 1969); Henry Highland Garnet, *An Address to the Slaves of the United States of America* [delivered 1843] (1848; rpr. New York, 1969).

29. Lewis Tappan to Douglass, December 19, 1856, in FD Papers (LC).

age; he was simply too much of a realist to join the Harpers Ferry raid. Douglass was also wise enough to know that rhetoric was his best weapon. Brown could take insurrection "into Africa"; Douglass would remain a source for insurrectionary thought.[30]

John Brown's raid fueled the sectional conflict like few events before it, and its aftermath offered Douglass his best "use" of violence. For Douglass, the distance between antislavery propaganda and war propaganda (designed to promote actual warfare against the South) had shortened in the several years preceding Harpers Ferry, and at times during the period from fall 1859 to summer 1861 these two purposes became almost indistinguishable in his rhetoric. His wartime role as a war propagandist drew heavily on his earlier reflections about violence and his contributions to the canonization of John Brown. More so than most abolitionists, Douglass was predisposed to make the fullest use of the idea of violence.

Although his association with the leader of the Harpers Ferry raid forced him into six months of exile in England, Douglass found an effective weapon in Brown's martyrdom. Fanaticism can cut two ways: it can help or hinder a moral or political cause. Ironically, what he had discouraged Brown from doing now served the cause in unanticipated ways. The encouragement of slave insurrection served several objectives, but none in Douglass' mind was more important than the *fear* it instilled in slaveholders. His first response to the alarm Brown had caused in the South was one of elation. The "terror-stricken slaveholders at Harpers Ferry" were just what Douglass wanted to see. In June, 1860, he declared that he had "little hope of the freedom of the slave by peaceful means." "The only penetrable point of a tyrant," wrote Douglass, "is the *fear of death*. The outcry that they make, as to the danger of having their *throats cut* is because they deserve to have them *cut*."[31]

30. On Douglass' relationship with John Brown, see Quarles, *Douglass,* 169–85; Benjamin Quarles, *Allies for Freedom: Blacks and John Brown* (New York, 1974), 19–21, 38–39, 60–61, 76–79, 114–16; Goldstein, "Violence as an Instrument," 61–62; Stephen B. Oates, *To Purge This Land with Blood* (New York, 1970), 62–63, 224–25, 282–83. For the "into Africa" quote, see Oates, *To Purge,* 171. While standing with his son Jason watching the town of Osawatomie burn in Kansas in 1856, Brown is believed to have said, "There will be no more peace in this land until slavery is done for. I will give them something else to do than to extend slave territory. I will carry this war into Africa."

31. Douglass to the Rochester *Democrat and American,* Canada West, October 31, 1859, in Foner (ed.), *Life and Writings,* II, 461. Douglass' hasty flight should not negate the fact that his speaking and fund-raising tour of England had been planned in advance of Brown's raid. On the notion of "fear" and the uses of violence in Douglass' rhetoric, see Goldstein, "Violence as an Instrument," 70. The fear caused by John Brown's raid in

In a speech at Newcastle-upon-Tyne in February, 1860, Douglass defended Brown against charges of criminality. "Slaveholders," he argued, "could not constitute a peaceable neighborhood"; the old warrior had "entered a community already at war—a war of oppression on the one part and of rebellion on the other." This "state of war" perspective on slavery is a position Douglass had increasingly embraced over the 1850s, but he had never possessed such an opportunity to exploit it. In August, 1860, in a lament about the failure of moral suasion, he further expounded his theory of black liberation by violence: "The motive power which shall liberate the slave," he contended, "must be generated in the bosom of the bondman." In the summer after Harpers Ferry, moral suasion alone no longer seemed a tenable position. "Outside philanthropy never disenthralled any people," wrote Douglass. "It required a Spartacus . . . to arouse the servile population of Italy, and defeat some of the most powerful armies of Rome, at the head of an army of slaves; and the slaves of America await the advent of an African Spartacus." But it was one thing to call for insurrection and quite another to lead one. By 1860–61, Douglass was convinced that the ultimate answer to black hopelessness in America would be rebellion, although about the time and form of that rebellion he could only speculate. Ultimately he would work tirelessly to recruit an "army of slaves," but he would never personally lead one. He believed that slaves must either "suffer or rebel," and he called for insurrection in all its chaotic horror. But Douglass fashioned himself more of a Cicero than a Spartacus.[32]

If he was to affect history as he wished, Douglass knew what role he could best play. Defending himself against the accusation of complicity with John Brown, Douglass vehemently denied that he had ever encouraged the raid or promised to participate; nevertheless, he wanted to be recognized as a willing conspirator against slavery. Thus, he announced himself "ready to write, speak, publish,

---

the South is also a central theme in Stephen Channing, *Crisis of Fear: Secession in South Carolina* (New York, 1970), 17–57. Douglass to James Redpath, Rochester, June 29, 1860, in Foner (ed.), *Life and Writings*, II, 487.

32. Speech delivered at Newcastle-upon-Tyne, reported in Newcastle *Daily Express*, February 21, 1860, in *DM*, April, 1860. In a speech he delivered numerous times after the Civil War, Douglass summed up his sense of Brown's primary significance to the abolition cause: "The opportunity was great and the man was great," he proclaimed. "With the Allegheny mountains for his pulpit, the country for his church, and the whole civilized world for his audience, John Brown was a thousand times more powerful as a preacher than as a warrior" ("A Lecture on John Brown," FD Papers [LC], reel 14, p. 19). Douglass perceived his own role with violent action in much the same manner—more "preacher" than "warrior" ("The Prospect in the Future," 496–97).

organize, combine, and even to conspire against slavery, where there is a reasonable hope for success." With the same adaptability with which he approached political parties, Douglass gave violence its place among antislavery weapons. As to why he had not joined the Harpers Ferry raid, Douglass had a ready reply: "The tools to those that can use them. Let every man work for the abolition of slavery in his own way. I would help all, and hinder none." This *rhetoric* of violence was an outlook Douglass shared with most other black abolitionists from the mid-1850s into the first year of the Civil War. As Lawrence Friedman has suggested for white abolitionists ("immediatists" who had long held to pacifism and moral suasion), the acceptance of violent means could have a revitalizing and curative effect. For frustrated abolitionists in the late 1850s, aggression, whether physical or rhetorical, reinvigorated their flagging missionary zeal. John Brown's raid came at a propitious moment. Violence, if "righteous," could be not only useful but just.[33]

As Douglass illustrated, violent language could serve emotional needs in ways just as important as violent action. Clearly, he did reap such a benefit, feeling revitalized by the prospect of slave revolts, especially in the wake of Harpers Ferry. "One of the most hopeful indications" for the "speedy fall" of slavery, he declared in September, 1860, was to be found in the "desperate insurrectionary movements of slaves." Douglass firmly believed in the slaves' right to rebel, but revolutionary—"desperate"—violence troubled him. Black bondsmen had been a majority in Santo Domingo, but they would never possess such an advantage in America. He had ample reason for viewing slave uprisings with fear and ambivalence, since widespread insurrection could have defeated his dream of black liberation through the agency of the federal government, with its resultant citizenship and equality. Thus, the rub came for Douglass in the ends as well as the means. If widespread insurrection succeeded in bringing slavery down in America, what place would black freedpeople have in the society to follow? In the wake of a southern "race war," how would blacks be assimilated into the new order? These were troublesome questions for Douglass. His rhetoric of violence notwithstanding, he clearly preferred the day of jubilee to come by constitutional means. Even after the outbreak of war, certain conditions had to be met before Douglass would join a "John Brown movement." "When I join any movement such as I suppose contemplated," he told Samuel May

33. See Pease and Pease, *They Who Would Be Free*, 233–50. Friedman, in *Gregarious Saints*, 196–222, places great emphasis on the concept of "righteous" violence.

in August, 1861, "I must have a country or the hope of a country under me—a government around me—and some flag of a Northern or Southern nation floating over me." Douglass argued that blacks could not fight two enemies at once—northern racism and southern slaveholders—and he insisted on a legitimate role for them in their own liberation. "Nothing short of an open recognition of the Negro's manhood," he argued, "his rights as such to have a country equally with others would induce me to join the army in any capacity."[34]

Once the Civil War had commenced, Douglass saw greater ends in violence than cathartic effects. He wanted for all black people what he had always desired for himself: the recognition of his manhood and full acceptance into the family of American citizens. The "hope of a country" had taken an important turn in 1861, but much still had to be done to convince America of what it meant. The country had to be persuaded to fight the right kind of war. With armies in the field contending over the future of the Union, slavery had never seemed so vulnerable. Using the weapons he understood best, Douglass could now crusade for righteous violence against slaveholders, waged by the United States government. Once again, through language, Douglass could blend reality with inner and symbolic purposes. Words and action had never seemed in such close relationship. As a war propagandist, Douglass found his own mixture of rhetorical and actual violence.

Douglass understood the meaning of vengeance to the oppressed as well as the revitalizing effects of violent self-defense. He had, after all, verbally and even physically assaulted slaveholders for twenty years before taking on the role of war propagandist in 1861. In his celebrated fight with the overseer Edward Covey while a sixteen-year-old slave nearly broken in spirit, Douglass experienced what he later called a "resurrection . . . an attitude of manly independence," in which he "was *not afraid to die.*" His violent resistance had revived his "crushed self-respect," Douglass wrote, and taught him that "a man without force is without the essential dignity of humanity." Douglass assured his readers that he relished subsequent opportunities "to provoke him [Covey] to an attack," since his "natural temper" predisposed him to inflict "serious damage" should the over-

---

34. "Insurrectionary Movements in Texas," *DM*, September, 1860; Douglass to Samuel J. May, Rochester, August 30, 1861, in Foner (ed.), *Life and Writings*, III, 158–59. It is also interesting to note that during the summer and fall months of 1861, Douglass ran a series of articles in his paper on the prior slave insurrections led by Denmark Vesey in 1822 and by Nat Turner in 1831. See *DM*, August, September, October, November, 1861.

seer ever attempt another beating.[35] Slavery had taught the young slave a sense of revenge and the meaning of personal violence. In Douglass' view, slaveholders deserved their fate, whether at the hands of a single teenage slave, a Nat Turner, or the Union armies.

It is interesting to speculate on what might have happened to Douglass' outlook on violence had the Civil War not occurred when it did. Had the sectional crisis not resulted in war in 1861, followed by emancipation two years later, Douglass might not have held out as a preacher of merely rhetorical violence, and might instead have become an even stronger advocate of insurrection. There is ample evidence to show his sympathy with and expectation of slave rebellion. Much has been made of the fact, however, that Douglass never actually joined an insurrectionary movement.[36] Perhaps the timing of the Civil War in his life and his developing thought can help explain this phenomenon. But the problem, once again, was one of tactics and practicality—organizing slave rebellions in the South was simply too dangerous. Moreover, as the political crisis over slavery deepened in the late 1850s, and with the rise of the Republican party in which Douglass vested sincere hope, a revolutionary turn in his approach to violence was averted. Indeed, one might argue that for a black abolitionist like Douglass, who eschewed emigration, the Republican party provided a viable alternative to violence. As it helped cause the disruption of the Union on the one hand, the antislavery political party may have served to blunt the further radicalization of black abolitionists on the other.

The fact is, of course, that the war did come in 1861. Secession and Fort Sumter prevented any further revolutionary turn in Douglass' thinking and, concurrently, gave new meaning to his rhetoric of violence. He was unleashed from the shackles of his own sense of realism, from his fears of the outcome of unrestrained violence against slaveholders, from his restraint born of the caution of slaves themselves. His own sense of revenge against slaveholders was also released, and he was freed to advocate the death of every Covey in the South. His hopes for righteous violence in the cause of abolition were given vent. Potentially, all of Douglass' ends could be served; as a writer and an orator, he could symbolically kill slaveholders in the midst of an organized war against the South. In 1861, Douglass was excited and frustrated; he quickly learned that there was much to do if the northerners were to be convinced that theirs was a holy war for black freedom.

35. Douglass, *Bondage and Freedom*, 246–49.
36. See Goldstein, "Violence as an Instrument," 71; Rose, "Killing for Freedom."

5/FREDERICK DOUGLASS AND THE AMERICAN APOCALYPSE

We can yet see in the Civil War an image of the powerful, painful, grinding process by which an ideal emerges out of history. That should teach us humility beyond the Great Alibi and the Treasury of Virtue, but at the same time it draws us to the glory of the human effort to win meaning from the complex and confused motives of men and the blind ruck of event.
    —Robert Penn Warren, *The Legacy of the Civil War,* 1961

Zion shall be redeemed with judgment, and her converts with righteousness.
    —Isaiah 1:27

To most of the four million black folk emancipated by civil war, God was real. They knew him. . . . To these black folk it was the Apocalypse. The magnificent trumpet tones of Hebrew Scripture, transmuted and oddly changed, became a strange new gospel. All that was Beauty, all that was Love, all that was Truth, stood on the top of these mad mornings and sang with the stars. A great human sob shrieked in the wind, and tossed its tears upon the sea,—free, free, free.
    —W. E. B. Du Bois, *Black Reconstruction,* 1935

IN 1862–63, THE PROSPECT of emancipation gave a new purpose to the Civil War and a new meaning to American history. For the slaves themselves and for abolitionists both black and white, emancipation was initially something more easily felt than explained. For Frederick Douglass, a most important moment had been reached in a long struggle. One year into the conflict, Douglass spoke of the inexorable way emancipation had become its central question: "It is really wonderful . . . how all efforts to evade, postpone, and prevent its coming, have been mocked and defied by the stupendous sweep of events."[1] Douglass searched for ways to understand and affect the turn of events. In large measure his wartime thought reflects a spiritual interpretation of the war that fits squarely into several intellectual and theological traditions: millennialism, apocalypticism, civil religion, the providential view of history, and the jeremiad. In his search for the meaning of the Civil War, Douglass forged a significant place for himself in these traditions.

For Douglass and many of his contemporaries, God's presence in the crucible of the Civil War was an irresistible notion; the desperate

1. "The War and How to End It," speech by Douglass at Corinthian Hall, Rochester, March 25, 1862, *DM,* April, 1862.

nature of the conflict and the totality of its aims invoked the spiritual side of the American character. In Protestant America, North and South seemed to be contending for the future beyond the Apocalypse. Examples of the millennialist response to the Civil War abound. Abraham Lincoln's "Second Inaugural Address" provides a famous illustration. Searching for the meaning of emancipation, Lincoln declared that the "Almighty has his own purposes" and gave the country "this terrible war, as the woe due to those by whom the offence came." But perhaps the clearest apocalyptic statement about the Civil War resounded from Julia Ward Howe's "The Battle Hymn of the Republic." Howe captured in poetry one of the central ideological and spiritual traditions of her age. In her opening line— "Mine eyes have seen the glory of the coming of the Lord"—Howe struck the essential chord of millennialism (God's Second Coming). She envisioned God's presence in the soldiers' "watchfires" and His imminent judgment by a "terrible swift sword." Written in 1862, the "Battle Hymn" was a millennialist paean, which for many northern Protestants expressed the meaning of the Civil War.[2]

In nineteenth-century America, millennialism was a cluster of religious and secular ideas inherited from the Puritans, refashioned through the Revolutionary era, nurtured through numerous waves of revivalism, and forged into a national creed during the antebellum period. It taught that Christ would have a Second Coming in the "new Israel" of America. Moreover, millennialism helped foster an American sense of mission, a belief that the United States was the "redeemer nation" destined to perform a special role in history. Since John Winthrop's vision of a "city upon a hill," Americans had believed that their new world—and later their new nation—was a place where mankind had been offered a second chance. A "new Adam" could flourish in a new garden full of hope. A nation of Protestants came to interpret events, at least in part, as steps in their providential destiny. But nations, like individuals, it was believed, must suffer and be tested before they could fulfill their appointed destiny. Following biblical prophecy of the Apocalypse, many northern Protestants had come to believe by the 1850s that their country was on the brink of such a rending, an apocalyptic war that would usher in a new era of peace and freedom. Hence, as the war came and as the level of death and suffering reached shocking proportions, Douglass joined the

2. Basler (ed.), *Collected Works of Lincoln*, VII, 332–33. For an analysis of Howe's "Battle Hymn," see Wilson, *Patriotic Gore*, 92–97; Tuveson, *Redeemer Nation*, 197–202; Moorhead, *American Apocalypse*, 79–80.

many Americans who believed they were in the midst of a conflict for God's purposes.[3]

Millennialism has always been a concept fraught with ambiguity, and Douglass' espousal of this tradition is no exception. The millennialist vision seems never to be without eschatological symbolism, whether in a purely religious or secular context, yet it also represents a hope of a better world without which some people have not seemed capable of living. Hence, the paradox and vagueness of the belief in millennialism, which can be viewed as dreadful calamity, as it is in many biblical uses of the concept, or can reflect an optimistic, perfectionist view of history. But the distinctions between an activist (as used by hopeful reformers) and a pessimistic millennialism must not be too rigidly drawn. For mid-nineteenth-century American Protestants, both positions combined to form an apocalyptic outlook, the expectation of God's extraordinary intervention in history to destroy an evil age and replace it with a new, eternal creation. The only certainty in millennial thought seems to have been its capacity to sustain dichotomies of belief and emotion. Prophecies of gloom and doom coexisted with ideas of national mission; unbounded promise mixed with dreadful threat; anxiety marched with hope. So when we find ambiguity in the spiritual perception of the Civil War held by a Frederick Douglass, or anyone else, we should not be surprised— such ambiguity had always characterized millennialism and apocalypticism, and helped them flourish in America. Indeed, apocalypticism was often a response to or an escape from the ambiguity in millennial expectation. The reaction to the outbreak of the Civil War among northern Protestants illustrates this fact. Apocalypticism had always reflected the special hope of the persecuted, the dispossessed,

---

3. The literature on millennialism is extensive. Most helpful to me have been Moorhead, "Between Progress and Apocalypse"; Moorhead, *American Apocalypse*, 1–128; Tuveson, *Redeemer Nation*, 1–90, 187–214; Brown, "Watchers for the Second Coming"; Smith, "Millennarian Scholarship in America"; Conrad Cherry (comp.), *God's New Israel: Religious Interpretations of American Destiny* (Englewood Cliffs, N.J., 1971); Rush Welter, *The Mind of America, 1810–1860* (New York, 1975), 19–21, 260–61; J. F. Maclear, "The Republic and the Millennium"; Fredrickson, *Inner Civil War*, 7, 68–69, 118–19; Nathan O. Hatch, *The Sacred Cause of Liberty: Republican Thought and the Millennium in Revolutionary New England* (New Haven, 1977), 21–54, 139–75; and Wilson, *Patriotic Gore*, 91–106. On the impending apocalyptic war, see R. W. B. Lewis, *The American Adam: Innocence, Tragedy, and Tradition in the Nineteenth Century* (Chicago, 1955). For a discussion of the idea of America on the brink of disaster in the 1850s, see Moorhead, *American Apocalypse*, 18–22. For the "millennial tone" of rhetoric by clergy and laymen alike on the eve of the American Revolution, see Gordon Wood, *The Creation of the American Republic, 1776–1787* (New York, 1969), 117.

or the enslaved; it could be cathartic, and it had always been the child of crisis.[4]

Douglass' spiritual interpretation of the Civil War must also be assessed as part of the tradition of civil religion. Although the term hardly caught on in the mid-nineteenth century, the influence of the ideas it represented did. The contours of America's civil religion were forged by the actions and rhetoric of the Founding Fathers during the Revolutionary era. America's mission as a chosen people formed the core idea of a national faith; indeed, this concept of mission became the central unifying myth of nineteenth-century America. Politi-

---

4. For biblical references to millennialism, see, for example, Amos 5:18; Isaiah 1–2; and Revelation 19:11–21. On American millennialism, see Moorhead, *American Apocalypse*, 9–10; George M. Marsden, *The Evangelical Mind and the New School Presbyterian Experience: A Case Study of Thought and Theology in Nineteenth-Century America* (New Haven, 1970), 197. In antebellum America, a distinction arose between pre- and postmillennialism. Premillenialists held to the traditional notion that Christ must return to earth in the flesh *before* the new kingdom could occur. The evils of the present day, premillennialists maintained, betokened God's imminent decision to impose His judgment on the world. By far the more prevalent position in America, though, was postmillennialism, which held that Christ would return to earth *after* the millennium. Postmillennialists believed they already lived in the millennial age; their world already exhibited triumphs of reform, progress, and human potential. For the differences between the two positions and the problems of ambiguity, see Moorhead, *American Apocalypse*, 6–41; Moorhead, "Between Progress and Apocalypse," 528–58; Lewis Perry, *Radical Abolitionism: Anarchy and the Government of God in Antislavery Thought* (Ithaca, 1973), 37–46; Welter, *Mind of America*, 19–21, 260–61.

As the companion concept to millennialism, and frequently considered synonomous, apocalypticism commands a careful definition as well. For my working definition, I have relied upon George A. Buttrick (ed.), *The Interpreter's Dictionary of the Bible* (4 vols.; Nashville, 1957), I, 157–61; and Martin Rist, "Revelation," in *ibid.*, IV, 347–51. Rist defines *apocalypticism* as follows: "the eschatological belief that the power of evil (Satan), who is now in control of this temporal and hopelessly evil age of human history in which the righteous are afflicted by his demonic and human agents, is soon to be overcome and his evil rule ended by the direct intervention of God, who is the power of good, and who thereupon will create an entirely new, perfect, and eternal age under his immediate control for the everlasting enjoyment of his righteous followers from among the living and the resurrected dead" (347). On the hold that the apocalyptic outlook had on the northern mind at the time of the Civil War, see Wilson, *Patriotic Gore*, 91, 106. This "vision of judgment," writes Wilson, was the myth that "possessed the minds of the publicists, the soldiers and the politicians to an extent of which the talk about 'Armageddon' at the time of the first World War can give only a feeble idea, and the literature of the time was full of it" (91). Also see Moorhead, "Between Progress and Apocalypse," 524–42; Robert M. Albrecht, "The Theological Response of the Transcendentalists to the Civl War," *New England Quarterly*, XXXVIII (March, 1965), 21–34. On the relationship between apocalypticism and millennialism, see Moorhead, *American Apocalypse*, 82–83; Tuveson, *Redeemer Nation*, especially 187–214. On the reaction to the Civil War among northern Protestants, see Sydney Ahlstrom, *A Religious History of the American People* (New Haven, 1972), 670–97; Clebsch, "Christian Interpretations."

cians and the clergy found a common creed to share. In the Revolution, Americans experienced their "exodus"; in the Declaration of Independence, they possessed "sacred scriptures"; in Washington they found a Moses, and in Jefferson, a high priest. But like the children of Israel, the Americans had to be tested. Answers to the deepest questions about national meaning and self-definition awaited the Civil War, a conflict in which the sacred trust of the founders would be challenged and reborn. These were the myths essential to a civil religion.[5]

The literary and oratorical tradition of the jeremiad is one of the oldest in American thought. No longer considered simply a form of lamentation about waning zeal, recent studies have deepened our understanding and broadened the definition of the jeremiad. It is a national ritual not only of self-condemnation, but also an appeal to the most optimistic aspects of the American mythology of mission. The Civil War reinvigorated the jeremiad, and Douglass made prolific use of it in ways unique to black intellectuals.[6]

Although he came by his education in a much less formal way than most of his abolitionist peers, Douglass shared with them the inheritance of each of the religious and ideological traditions previously

5. Robert N. Bellah, "Civil Religion in America," *Daedalus* (Winter, 1969), 1–21. An excellent collection of the writings on civil religion is Russell E. Richey and Donald G. Jones (eds.), *American Civil Religion* (New York, 1974). Also helpful in understanding the varied sources and uses of civil religion are Tuveson, *Redeemer Nation;* Cherry (comp.), *God's New Israel,* 8–21; Nathan O. Hatch, "The Origins of Civil Millennialism in America: New England Clergymen, the War with France, and the Revolution," *William and Mary Quarterly,* XXXI (July, 1974), 407–30. Numerous scholars have analyzed the role of myth in American cultural and political history, but none more succinctly than Sacvan Bercovitch, when he wrote that "myth may clothe history as fiction, but it persuades in proportion to its capacity to help people act in history," in *The American Jeremiad* (Madison, 1978), xi. Civil religion has served precisely this function.

6. Perry Miller first analyzed this rhetorical device as the earliest American genre of literature. The seventeenth-century New England clergy vented their outrage over the waning zeal of their parishioners, chastising them in an "unending, monotonous wail" for their part in the failure of the Puritan "errand." See Perry Miller, *Errand into the Wilderness* (Cambridge, Mass.; 1958), 8; Perry Miller, *The New England Mind: From Colony to Province* (Boston, 1961), 27–39. Sacvan Bercovitch has broadened the definition of the jeremiad, emphasizing especially the optimistic aspects of the American sense of mission. For his analysis of the nineteenth century, see Bercovitch, *American Jeremiad,* 148–210. James Moorhead has followed Miller's model in characterizing the jeremiad for the nineteenth century as a "theological rationale for the sufferings of a chosen people," and demonstrated how the Civil War reinvigorated its use. See Moorhead, *American Apocalypse,* 43–49. Also see David Howard-Pitney, "The Enduring Black Jeremiad: The American Jeremiad in Black Protest Rhetoric, from Frederick Douglass to W. E. B. Du Bois, 1841–1919," *American Quarterly,* XXXVIII (Fall, 1986), 481–92.

mentioned. Although not a strong adherent of organized religion and openly contemptuous of the clergy through much of his life, Douglass nevertheless accepted and contributed to the Christian interpretation of the Civil War. His spiritual outlook shaped his conception of the war; he found in the conflict the fulfillment of prophecy, both biblical and his own.

On emancipation day, January 1, 1863, Douglass was in Boston to participate in what was expected to be a massive celebration at Tremont Temple. Speech followed speech throughout the day and into the evening, with Douglass providing his usual share of the oratory. Tension mounted as the large gathering waited impatiently for the news of Lincoln's Proclamation. When the news finally arrived, great jubilation engulfed the crowd. Not surprisingly, this celebration was a deeply spiritual response to a most important moment in the history of black Americans. When a semblance of order was restored following the initial tears and shouting, Douglass led the throng in a chorus of his favorite hymn, "Blow ye the Trumpet Blow." Next, an old black preacher named Rue led the group in "Sound the loud timbel o'er Egypt's dark sea, Jehovah has triumphed, his people are free!" Eighteen years later, while writing his third autobiography, Douglass captured the meaning of that day for his people in words that more generally reflect his vision of the war: "It was not logic, but the trump of jubilee, which everybody wanted to hear. We were waiting and listening as for a bolt from the sky, which should rend the fetters of four millions of slaves; we were watching as it were, by the dim light of stars, for the dawn of a new day; we were longing for the answer to the agonizing prayers of centuries. Remembering those in bonds as bound with them, we wanted to join in the shout for freedom, and in the anthem of the redeemed." The cruel and apocalyptic war had become holy.[7]

Douglass' God was a God of action who would act "in His own good time," as the old slave Uncle Lawson had taught the impatient slave boy. Just as there were turning points in his own life that he could not fully explain in rational terms, Douglass came to see history in the same way. The message of a "better day coming"—the millennial tone so prevalent in mid-nineteenth-century black thought—found

---

7. On the Boston jubilee meeting, see Douglass, *Life and Times*, 351–54; Quarles, *Douglass*, 199–202; Benjamin Quarles, *Lincoln and the Negro* (New York, 1962), 143–46. For a thorough reporting of the jubilee meetings held all over the North, see *DM*, February, 1863. On emancipation celebrations generally, see William H. Wiggins, Jr., *O Freedom! Afro-American Emancipation Celebrations* (Knoxville, 1987). On Douglass' millennialism, see Martin, *Mind*, 173–74.

one of its greatest exhorters in Douglass. This was, of course, a message of hope for an oppressed people and therefore a struggle to sustain. By 1861, Douglass was well conditioned to its burdens and well practiced in capitalizing on the spiritual potential of major events.[8]

The belief that history is governed by a "divine providence" can be expressed in many forms: in allusions to natural law, through faith in the doctrine of progress, and in various other modes of moral determinism. Douglass often expressed it effectively in metaphor, and the Civil War especially brought out this aspect of his thought. In a speech at Cooper Institute in New York in February, 1863, he declared not only his faith in progress but his belief that southerners were destined to fail because their cause violated natural law. Douglass used the phrases "laws of God" and "laws of nature" interchangeably to define history. "The world," he announced, "like the fish preached to in the stream, moves on in obedience to the laws of its being, bearing away all excrescences and imperfections in its progress. It has its periods of illumination as well as of darkness, and often bounds forward a greater distance in a single year than in an age before."[9] This view of history "bounding forward" exhibits Douglass' state of mind in the wake of emancipation. It also illuminates an essential element in the apocalyptic mentality: God was the engine of history, and his interventions kept it on a course of progress.

One of the most common ways in which Douglass expressed his providential view of history was in the phrase *the logic of events*. A reformer's cause is always to some extent at the mercy of events, but Douglass often imbued this notion with a spiritual meaning. Suffering from impatience with the Union war effort in the summer of 1861, Douglass stated in a letter to Samuel J. May that his confidence rested more in the "stern of logic of events" than in the "disposition of the Federal army." As had long been his habit, Douglass' disposition fluctuated between hope and despair. In the fall of 1861, in response to a "sick and disheartened" correspondent who had challenged the black editor's optimism, Douglass argued that the prospects for emancipation did not lie in the government at Washington: "There are powers above those of the Government and the army—a power behind the throne, greater than the throne itself." In time, the government would be "borne along on the broad current of events," Doug-

8. Douglass, *Bondage and Freedom*, 169.
9. "The Proclamation and the Negro Army," speech at Cooper Institute, New York, February, 1863, DM, March, 1863, in Foner (ed.), *Life and Writings*, III, 326. For another of Douglass' comparisons of history to the "changeless laws of the universe," see "The War and How to End It."

lass told his correspondent. Though seemingly vague, Douglass rooted this hope in the long-war theory: if the war lasted long enough and became desperate enough, he maintained, emancipation would become an "iron necessity" of the Union cause. Keeping faith in jubilee, Douglass seemed to be telling his frustrated friend, required constant vigilance—"keep pounding on the rock," he urged—but also the belief that history was a "mighty current" driven by necessity and divine power.[10]

By spring, 1862, Douglass was convinced at least for the time being that "events steadily conspire to make the cause of the slave and the cause of the country identical." In March, Congress abolished slavery in the District of Columbia. "I trust I am not dreaming," Douglass wrote to Charles Sumner, "but the events taking place seem like a dream." At times in his life, Douglass had seriously doubted that he would ever live to see the United States Congress liberate slaves anywhere. Somehow, this war gave reality to dreams that decades of agitation could not accomplish. Abraham Lincoln's preliminary Emancipation Proclamation of September 22, 1862, elicited from Douglass a grudging but sincere faith in the president's resolve. But even if Lincoln's character turned out to be untrustworthy, reasoned Douglass, "events greater than the President, events which have slowly wrung this proclamation from him may be relied on to carry him forward in the same direction." Douglass waited for emancipation day with great anxiety, but to him, it was not Lincoln's moment, not the work of "individual design." Lincoln, imagined Douglass, was "but the hands of the clock." On January first, he claimed, the "national ship" would swing around and be wafted off by the "trade winds of the Almighty." Douglass' view of emancipation (in its various stages and meanings) was seldom without this spiritual, millennial component.[11]

10. Douglass to Samuel J. May, Rochester, August 30, 1861, in Foner (ed.), *Life and Writings*, III, 159; "Signs of the Times," 170–73. Douglass' discussion of the importance of events was varied and frequent. In a November, 1861, editorial on the Frémont affair (Gen. John C. Frémont's attempt to free slaves in Missouri and Lincoln's controversial overturning of the order), in which Douglass used such terms as the "voice of history" to describe the significance of Frémont's actions, he contended that "truth consults no man's taste, and events enter without begging any man's permission." See "Frémont and Freedom—Lincoln and Slavery," *DM*, November, 1861, in Foner (ed.), *Life and Writings*, III, 174–75.

11. "The War and How to End It"; Douglass to Charles Sumner, April 8, 1862, in Foner (ed.), *Life and Writings*, III, 233; "A Change of Attitude," where Douglass wrote that "events are more potent than arguments"; "Emancipation Proclaimed," *DM*, October, 1862, in Foner (ed.), *Life and Writings*, III, 274; "January First, 1863," *DM*, January, 1863, in *ibid.*, III, 306.

The Civil War provided the central event in Douglass' life that reinforced his providential view of history. The war justified and actualized his faith in both reason and revelation, and it forged reality and meaning out of strained hope. In a speech on John Brown, first delivered in 1860 but repeated numerous times throughout the rest of his life, Douglass summed up this providential outlook: "There is in the moral world a force, a principle, a law, call it by what name you will, retributive justice, logic of events, revenge of time, or judgments of God, which has asserted itself all along the sweep of history, and the instruments employed in its enforcement, whether dying on the gallows, on the cross or at the stake, have compelled the world to recognize them as its heroes, martyrs, and saviors." Douglass was not always doctrinaire in determining the source of this control over history. He was certain, though, that the Civil War, as he wrote in December, 1861, was "too momentous an affair to be accidental."[12]

Apocalyptic tradition found common ground in religion, but even more so in language. Douglass had discovered his sense of self and, indeed, a portion of his personal freedom through language. Through the discovery of literacy while a slave and the exercise of autobiography while free, Douglass had found ways to liberate himself while still living within the racist constrictions of American society. By the same mode, he searched for the meaning of the Civil War. Apocalyptic language runs throughout Douglass' Civil War era rhetoric. Sometimes it took the form of biblical themes and imagery. For example, in the summer of 1857, at a time when black optimism was sparse, Douglass spoke at a commemoration of the twenty-third anniversary of West Indian emancipation. British emancipation, declared the orator, served "as a city upon a hill" for black Americans. It had been a "bolt from the moral sky . . . something Godlike . . . commanding the devil of slavery to go out of the British West Indies." Douglass announced on that occasion that he had seen the "apocalyptic vision" and only wished that more Americans could see it with him. Apocalyptic imagery simplified historical complexity and served the nineteenth-century orator well. In times of crisis or despair (such as the aftermath of the Dred Scott decision in 1857), these appeals fell on welcome ears in abolitionist audiences. The cause was not dead while

12. "A Lecture on John Brown," in FD Papers (LC), reel 14, p. 6. The finding aid for the FD Papers at the Library of Congress dates this speech as 1860. It was first delivered in 1860, but the collection's version must be dated from at least 1880. On page 11, Douglass stated that "more than 20 years have passed" since Brown's Harpers Ferry raid. "Frémont and His Proclamation," DM, December, 1861, in Foner (ed.), Life and Writings, III, 182–83.

it was still God's cause, and if an apocalyptic God could change history abruptly in the British empire (even bloodlessly), why not in America too?[13]

When the war came in 1861, Douglass used apocalyptic language with more aplomb. In April, he refused to deny the charge that James Redpath's Haitian emigration scheme was really a cover for the recruitment of a black army to invade the South (though it was certainly untrue). Instead, he preferred to goad the slaveholders' fears. "Wrapped up" in this claim, he contended, was "the prophecy of the final reign of justice and liberty among men. It is the flaming sword of heaven, bidding the oppressor beware!" At one of his Sunday lectures at Zion Church in Rochester, June 16, 1861, Douglass' apocalypticism was in perfect form: "Only mighty forces, resting deep down among the foundations of nature and life, can lash the deep and tranquil sea of humanity into a storm, like that which the world is now witnessing." Douglass was calling his flock to witness the special historical moment that seemed to be dawning. Cosmic dualism—the eternal conflict between good and evil—an essential element in the apocalyptic tradition, had never appeared so relevant: "Men have their choice in this world," Douglass said. "They can be angels, or they may be demons. In the apocalyptic vision, John describes a war in heaven. You have only to strip that vision of its gorgeous Oriental drapery, divest it of its shining and celestial ornaments, clothe it in the simple and familiar language of common sense, and you will have before you the eternal conflict between right and wrong, good and evil, liberty and slavery, truth and falsehood." It is difficult to measure how literally Douglass took his own apocalypticism, especially in its purely religious form, but the frequency with which he appealed to apocalyptic imagery, the seriousness with which he preached it, and the general millennial tone of his wartime rhetoric suggest that his interpretation of the Civil War rested squarely on this Christian tradition.[14]

Douglass put apocalyptic imagery to many uses during the war. In May, 1862, he urged abolitionists to take heart because abolition was slowly becoming the policy of the government; southerners would

13. For the way in which diverse northern intellectuals shared in this millennial enthusiasm and used its language, see Fredrickson, *Inner Civil War,* 118–19; Tuveson, *Redeemer Nation,* 187–214; Moorhead, *American Apocalypse,* 23–104. "West Indian Emancipation," in FD Papers (LC). On Douglass' liberation through language—his "quest for being" through autobiography—see Baker, *Journey Back,* 32–46.

14. "The Wicked Flee When No Man Pursueth," *DM,* April, 1861; "Decision of the Hour," 119.

see to it, for they had sown the seeds of their own doom. "Pride goeth before the fall," wrote Douglass, "whom the gods would destroy they first make mad." When the war was over, Douglass joined his countrymen in trying to understand the assassination of Abraham Lincoln in apocalyptic terms: "It was as if some grand convulsion in nature had occurred," Douglass declared in a speech in December, 1865, "for had the solid earth opened and swallowed up one of our chief towns or cities, had the tombs burst beneath our feet . . . the sensation of horror could not have been more profound." Lincoln's untimely death, like the cruel war before it, had caused deep spiritual contemplation. When Lincoln was murdered, "a hush fell upon the land," said Douglass, "as though each man in it heard a voice from heaven . . . and paused to learn its meaning." To a millennialist, God seemed to have one final agonizing judgment to cast over the guilty land.[15]

Douglass' apocalyptic interpretation of the Civil War must also be understood in the context of his growing sense of American nationalism. In this, he shared a central belief with his generation of northern intellectuals. America's millennial nationalism—the belief in the American republic as a chosen nation—was pervasive by the mid-nineteenth century and rendered even more so by the Civil War. Even Herman Melville, who could not be accused of unbridled optimism, voiced this mythology of mission. "We Americans are the peculiar, chosen people," wrote Melville, "the Israel of our time, we bear the ark of the liberties of the world." The United States was seen as God's redemptive instrument in history, and with providential appointments went burdens of world significance. The notion of an elected nation included both promise and threat. How could the model republic, called to nationality by the Founding Fathers, endure its own tragic flaws? The Civil War became the crucible in which the nature and existence of that nationalism would be either preserved and redefined, or lost forever.[16]

Douglass embraced virtually every aspect of America's mythology of mission—he believed the very idea of a republic was being tested in

15. "Of the War," and "A Report of Progress," *DM,* May, 1862; "Abraham Lincoln—A Speech," FD Papers (LC), reel 14, p. 2.

16. Melville is quoted in Moorhead, *American Apocalypse,* 44. On millennial nationalism, see Clebsch, "Christian Interpretations," 216–17; Moorhead, *American Apocalypse,* 14–18; Fredrickson, *Inner Civil War,* 184–89; Tuveson, *Redeemer Nation,* chaps. 4–5; Paul C. Nagel, *One Nation Indivisible: The Union in American Thought, 1776–1861* (New York, 1964), 147–76; Maclear, "The Republic and the Millennium," 203–205.

the Civil War, he believed the world was watching, and he staked his own future on the outcome. Nothing else in his life stimulated such an outpouring of his own brand of American nationalism as the crisis of the Union. To the oft-repeated assertion by American millennialists that the Civil War was "a crisis in the world's history," as the New York *Independent* put it in 1861, Douglass added his own claims of world significance. As consolation for all the war's suffering, Douglass advocated looking to the "vastness and grandeur of its mission." In a speech he gave all over the North in the fall and winter of 1863–64, Douglass maintained that "the world has not seen a nobler and grander war than that which the loyal people of this country are now waging . . . not merely to free a country or a continent—but the whole world from slavery." Douglass urged his auditors to mourn the dead but not to mourn their "mission." "We should . . . stand in our appointed place," he challenged, "and do this great service for mankind."[17]

It is true that Douglass did not make such statements quite so zealously before emancipation, but his vision of the chosen republic under divine judgment was prevalent in his rhetoric throughout the war. In January, 1862, in language which was both nationalistic and apocalyptic, Douglass described the Armageddon of the model republic: "The fate of the greatest of all Modern Republics trembles in the balance," Douglass contended. "The lesson of the hour is written down in the characters of blood and fire. We are taught as with the emphasis of an earthquake, that nations, not less than individuals, are subjects of the moral government of the universe, and that . . . persistent transgressions of the laws of this Divine government will certainly bring national sorrow, shame, suffering and death. Of all the nations of the world, we seem most in need of this solemn lesson." Only in the survival of an American nation, reborn and redefined, could Douglass' nationalism find a true home. Although his confidence needed bolstering in early 1863, there was the assurance that an "earthquake" could radically alter the landscape.[18]

Americans had long invested the Union with sacred qualities, but as disunion in 1861 demonstrated, this sacred trust had always been at best inchoate; the United States was a nation full of promise, but

17. New York *Independent*, August 22, 1861, quoted in Moorhead, *American Apocalypse*, 40; "The Mission of the War," in Foner (ed.), *Life and Writings*, III, 390. On the notion of world significance, see Moorhead, *American Apocalypse*, 36–41, 56–65.
18. "The Reasons for Our Troubles," speech delivered in National Hall, Philadelphia, January 14, 1862, in Foner (ed.), *Life and Writings*, III, 197.

also of paradox. Douglass preached a message similar to that of the theologian Horace Bushnell, who believed governments were conceived by God and put into the world through human agents. Nations, like individual sinners, had to experience suffering in order to fulfill their destiny. The nation needed "reverses and losses, and times of deep concern," Bushnell declared in a famous sermon on the Sunday after First Bull Run; otherwise, the American republic was merely a fiction until tested. As in the theological concept of individual atonement, nations had to endure the same process. It could not occur, said Bushnell, "without the shedding of blood."[19]

Douglass returned again and again to the analogy of nations to individuals. In an appeal to the British not to intervene on behalf of the Confederacy, written in November, 1862, and published in *The Independent,* he was explicit: "There is no more exemption for nations than for individuals," he argued, "from the just retribution due to flagrant and persistent transgression. For the time being, America is the blazing illustration of this solemn truth."[20] Douglass frequently gave the nation personal qualities in his effort to describe the peril of the war. In January, 1862, he described the American republic as but a "young nation" still standing "within the inner circle of childhood." But the youthful nation had lost its way, its "character" had been corrupted, its loyal citizens "sicklied over with a pale cast of thought." A national time of troubles would naturally evoke such lamentations. But Douglass would not let up. "It would seem, in the language of Isaiah," he exclaimed, "that the whole head is sick, and the whole heart is faint." The nation, Douglass seemed to be saying, had a sick soul.[21]

19. Horace Bushnell, "Reverses Needed: A Discourse Delivered on the Sunday After the Disaster of Bull Run," quoted in Moorhead, *American Apocalypse,* 139–41. No American thinker exemplified this strain of thought better than Bushnell. "We are born into government as we are into the atmosphere," he contended. Men could not make governments, they only "sketched them," he argued, "and God put them in us to be sketched." On Bushnell, also see Clebsch, "Christian Interpretations," 215–18; Maclear, "The Republic and the Millennium," 203–205; and Lewis, *American Adam,* 66–73.

20. "The Slaves Appeal to Great Britain," New York *Independent,* November 20, 1862, in Foner (ed.), *Life and Writings,* III, 301. There are many examples of Douglass' use of the "nations and individuals" analogy. See especially Douglass to *Beacon of the Loire,* November, 1865, in Frederick Douglass Collection, Moorland-Spingarn Research Center, Howard University, Washington, D.C.

21. "The Reasons for Our Troubles," 197–99. Douglass frequently discussed the notion of a national *soul.* The following is typical of these expressions: "It is the *soul* that makes the nation great or small, noble or ignoble, weak or strong. It is the Soul that exalts it to happiness or sinks it to misery." See *Quotations and Acrostics from Speeches by Frederick Douglass,* a collection begun by Douglass' daughter, Rosetta

The above remarks came in a speech entitled "The Reasons for Our Troubles" in January, 1862—well before emancipation became the official policy of the Union war effort, and during a period of some of Douglass' bitterest harangues against the Lincoln administration. But the theme of a national soul persisted in his rhetoric well after emancipation. In April, 1863, in the midst of his campaign to recruit black soldiers, Douglass stated that his faith did not ultimately rest in armies and munitions, but in the "reform of the national heart." What was at stake in the contest, he contended, was "the soul of the nation."[22] Douglass sought the meaning of the nation's suffering, at least in part, in the doctrine of atonement. If a Christian nation, like an individual, could realize its worst sins and face the consequences of divine retribution, then perhaps a new nation could be born. To Douglass, the prospect of black freedom gathered hope from the nation's woes.

The religious historian William Clebsch has identified the notion of a "cleansing tragedy" as one of the central themes in the Christian interpretation of the Civil War. The tragic sense ran deep in the mid-nineteenth-century American mind. A sentimental age demanded meaning out of death, especially when experienced by thousands in a catastrophic civil war, and many humanitarian abolitionists could condone the horrors of the war only when they convinced themselves that such a war represented divine and regenerative chastisements on the American people. Once persuaded, many millennial nationalists unabashedly called for the righteous shedding of blood. Henry Ward Beecher, on the day after the surrender of Fort Sumter, said: "Give me war redder than blood and fiercer than fire; if this terrific infliction is necessary that I may maintain my faith . . . in this land as the appointed abode and chosen refuge of liberty for all the earth."[23]

Douglass Sprague, and completed by her daughters, in Douglass Collection (Howard). Douglass' biblical reference here is Isaiah 1:5. His conception of the war as a rite of passage for the youthful nation is very similar to numerous other northern intellectuals. Emerson, for example, believed the war meant that America was "just passing through a great crisis in its history, as necessary as . . . puberty to the human individual . . . settling for ourselves and our descendents questions which . . . will make the peace and prosperity or the calamity of the next ages." Quoted in Bercovitch, *American Jeremiad*, 201.

22. "Do Not Forget Truth and Justice," *DM*, April, 1863, in Foner (ed.), *Life and Writings*, III, 338–39.

23. Clebsch, "Christian Interpretations," 218. See Beecher's sermon, "The Battle Set in Array," April 14, 1861, Plymouth Church, Brooklyn, New York, in Cherry (comp.), *God's New Israel*, 172–73. An excellent example from the end of the war is Horace Bushnell, "Our Obligations to the Dead," commencement address, Yale College, July 26, 1865, in *ibid.*, 199. On this question generally, also see Fredrickson, *Inner Civil War*, 82–83. Much of Douglass' rhetoric was in this same style.

Although he could not match theologians like Bushnell or Beecher in purely religious nationalism (nor did he share Bushnell's conservatism), Douglass certainly contributed to the theme of a cleansing tragedy. Just before Antietam and the preliminary emancipation proclamation, he urged his readers not to despair about abolition. "A few weeks more of sufferings, disasters, defeats, and . . . the slaughter of our country's first born," he argued, would force the nation to free the slaves. Douglass' language was strikingly similar to that in Bushnell's famous "Reverses Needed" sermon preached more than a year earlier. "We are saved as by fire," he asserted in words more fitting the pulpit than the editorial page; "we grieve with the sorrow-stricken families all over the North, but their terrible afflictions and heavy sorrows are their educators." This classic Christian notion that people must suffer and repent in order to reform seemed to run deep in Douglass' consciousness, and his writings reflect a sense of authentic tragedy. A holy cause could justify almost any level of suffering; indeed, it seemed to necessitate it. "The tears and blood we are now pouring out may at last bring us to our senses," Douglass claimed with some certainty.[24] If through suffering and tragedy individuals found rebirth, then why not nations as well? To Douglass the Civil War was just such an authentic and collective tragedy. He wanted all northerners to see the conflict as he did—as a moral crusade for black freedom in which the American republic would experience reformation through the fiery trial of war.

Douglass' mixture of nationalism and apocalypticism was never so bold as when describing the regenerative nature of the Civil War. The Emancipation Proclamation had invested the war with "sanctity," he told a British audience in November, 1862; "it will make justice, liberty, and humanity permanently possible in this country." In a flourish of idealism, Douglass claimed that the war's regenerative power applied to everyone, black and white. "We are all liberated by this proclamation," he asserted in February, 1863. "It is a mighty event for the bondman, but it is a still mightier event for the nation at large." Douglass thus merged his American nationalism with his own brand of black nationalism. As the historian Wilson Moses had demonstrated, Douglass had always been aware of the peculiar place of black people as a nation within a nation. He had long been an active proponent of black self-help programs and assimilationism, while denouncing virtually all schemes of emigration. But this did not

24. "Antislavery Progress,"*DM*, September, 1862, in Foner (ed.), *Life and Writings*, III, 271. For strikingly similar expressions of this idea, see Bushnell, "Our Obligations to the Dead," 201.

make him any less of a black nationalist, or lessen his sense of the separate cultural identity of his people. The Civil War thrust these two forms of nationalism into vivid juxtaposition and allowed Douglass to dream that there might one day be only one. If the Union's survival and black freedom could become one cause, then perhaps a truly new nation would emerge.[25]

Like many other millennialists, Douglass believed that the antebellum American republic had been inchoate and temporary. The nation needed to experience a "new birth," as Lincoln put it in the Gettysburg Address, in order to survive. Or, as William Clebsch has put it, the Civil War provided the "anvil of suffering" out of which the nation could finally be "actualized." Douglass delivered a similar message at the thirteenth anniversary celebration of the founding of the American Antislavery Society in December, 1863. The "old Union" was "dead," he pronounced, its "bones quietly inurned under the shattered walls of Sumter." Northerners were fighting for a new Union, Douglass contended, one in which there would be "no North, no South . . . no black, no white, but a solidarity of nation, making every slave free, and every free man a voter." This concluding flourish, to a speech that contained numerous allusions to the honesty and wisdom of Abraham Lincoln, was in many ways similar to the brief remarks the president had delivered just two weeks earlier at a cemetery in Gettysburg.[26]

Douglass' analysis of the Civil War as a national regeneration thus illustrates the two central tenets of apocalypticism: the cosmic conflict between good and evil, and the historical, divinely rendered break between two distinct ages. The old Union had represented the dismal, irredeemable first age, and the war had ushered in the beginning of the new one. Douglass may have expressed this best in a recruiting speech to potential black soldiers in Philadelphia on July 6,

25. "The Slaves' Appeal to Great Britain," 301; "The Proclamation and the Negro Army," 322; Wilson Jeremiah Moses, *The Golden Age of Black Nationalism* (Hamden, Conn., 1978), 38–44, 46, 50–55. With insight, Moses argues that Douglass "belonged to that tradition of black nationalists who militantly asserted their right to American citizenship." A rigid distinction between nationalism and emigrationism is not very useful in understanding black nationalism in the Civil War era. We can best understand Douglass' black nationalism as a mixture of assimilationism and pragmatic separatism. On the nature of mid-nineteenth-century black nationalism as a direct product of American "civil religion," see Wilson Jeremiah Moses, *Black Messiahs and Uncle Toms: Social and Literary Manipulations of a Religious Myth* (University Park, Pa., 1982), 28–29; Sweet, *Black Images of America*, 5.

26. Clebsch, "Christian Interpretations," 216–17; "Our Work Is Not Done," speech at thirtieth anniversary celebration of the American Antislavery Society, Philadelphia, December 3, 1863, in Foner (ed.), *Life and Writings*, III, 385–86.

1863. He urged his listeners not to be discouraged by the legacy of slavery and discrimination under which all blacks labored, and asked them to try to forget their history down to the dawn of emancipation. "These were all dark and terrible days of the republic," Douglass admitted. "I do not bring you the dead past," challenged the orator. "I bring you the living present. Events more mighty than men, eternal Providence, all-wise and all-controlling, have placed us in new relations to the Government and the Government to us." The Battle of Gettysburg had ended just three days prior to this speech, but the news of its horrible casualties must have reached Douglass' audience before he spoke. How could he assuage the fears of these black recruits? How else but by an appeal to their sense of manhood, to their hopes for dignity and citizenship, and by a spiritual invitation to participate in America's millennial future.[27]

In Douglass' millennial nationalism during the Civil War era, we find his frequent use of the jeremiad. Wilson Moses is the first historian to analyze the *black* jeremiad extensively. His working definition is very useful: the "constant warnings" issued to white audiences by black intellectuals "concerning the judgment that was to come for the sin of slavery." Since his earliest days as an abolitionist, Douglass had lent his voice to this ritual; indeed, by the late 1850s and especially during the Civil War, he was the principal black Jeremiah. He reached larger white audiences and preached the message of interracial nationalism more than any other black spokesman. This does not necessarily mean that his influence on white America was profound, but on its own terms, the black jeremiad had no more eloquent nor constant voice than that of Douglass.[28]

Douglass' jeremiads took many forms. He directed his "warnings" at the nation as a whole, at white abolitionists, and at his fellow blacks. The immediate prewar years stimulated an almost constant wail from Douglass, whether attacking presidents, slaveholders, or abolitionists. In a January, 1859, editorial, he lamented the "heart-

27. "Address for the Promotion of Colored Enlistments," Philadelphia, July 6, 1863, in Foner (ed.), *Life and Writings*, III, 364.
28. Moses, *Black Messiahs and Uncle Toms*, 30–31. But also see the whole of chapter 3, which concentrates on the thought of David Walker. Surprisingly, Moses does not include Douglass in his analysis, and considers the black jeremiad largely a pre–Civil War phenomenon. But in words that could accurately describe Douglass' use of the jeremiad, Moses argues that the black adaptation of this tradition "revealed a conception of themselves as a chosen people, but it also showed a clever ability to play on the belief that America as a whole was a chosen nation with a covenantal duty to deal justly with the blacks." One of my goals in this study has been to place Douglass at the head of the black adaptation of this tradition in the nineteenth century.

lessness . . . and stone-dead indifference" toward the slavery issue of some of the antislavery press and the nation generally. The same month he bitterly attacked President Buchanan's handling of the Kansas question, but true to the jeremiadic tradition, turned his lament into a cry for hope: "Go on, sir; let the nation go on, sir. The end is at hand. The haughty Assyrians will yet be brought low—the ire of offended justice will yet flash upon your soul, and burn up your heart strings with unquenchable fire." Warnings of impending doom went hand in hand with attacks on religious hypocrisy and national declension. In July, 1859, Douglass complained that too much of American Christianity had become "emasculated, corrupt, torpid, lifeless, a minister of moral death." The decay of what he liked to call the "national heart" was a constant theme in Douglass' prewar rhetoric.[29]

When the war came, millennialists like Douglass responded in their familiar way, interpreting the conflict as both tragedy and prophetic opportunity. In May, 1861, Douglass gave his readers a classic jeremiad wrapped in apocalyptic language. "We have sown the wind, only to reap the whirlwind," he charged. "The Republic has put one end of the chain upon the ankle of the bondman, and the other end about its own neck." A chosen but sinful people were about to reap the harvest of their own iniquity: "The land is now to weep and howl, amid ten thousand desolations brought upon it by the sins of two centuries. . . . Could we write as with lightning, and speak as with the voice of thunder, we should . . . cry to the nation, Repent, Break Every Yoke, let the Oppressed Go Free for Herein alone is deliverance and safety!" But it was not too late, Douglass claimed, if the slaves' "cry of vengeance" could be merged with the cry to save the Union. The moment of truth in the nation's life had been reached.[30]

The familiar mode of the jeremiad served Douglass well in responding to national days of fasting. Early in the conflict, President Lincoln declared September 26, 1861, a national day of fasting and prayer. Douglass answered the call with an appeal for prayer and reflection, but also with an attack on the lack of abolitionism in the Lincoln administration. "Our Government no where confesses that slavery is our national sin, nor exhorts to repentance of it," he charged. In a deeply religious editorial, Douglass quoted at length from the first

29. "The True Issue," *DM*, January, 1859; "The President's Address," *DM*, July, 1859. For one of Douglass' bitterest attacks on America, see "American Civilization," *DM*, October, 1859. For good examples of how Douglass' jeremiads took aim at the indifference (declension) of his own people, see *DM*, May, 1859.

30. "Nemesis," 98–99.

chapter of Isaiah, where the prophet warns the nation of Israel of God's displeasure with its sacrifices and burnt offerings, and of His impending judgment. God was not impressed by the entreaties of His sinful people: "I will hide mine eyes from you: yea, when ye make many prayers, I will not hear: your hands are full of blood." Isaiah's Old Testament rebuke of the nation of Israel formed the perfect model for Douglass' warnings to the new Israel. Isaiah calls God's people a "sinful nation . . . gone away backward." Their "whole head is sick, and the whole heart faint"; their country is "desolate," and their cities "burned with fire." The imagery and the message were perfectly suited to Douglass' purposes. Again and again, the black orator invoked the same language and the same themes to explain the calamity of the Civil War. A chosen but guilty people had to repent, suffer, and reform, or lose its destiny altogether. In this crisis, perhaps the best option for a black editor-orator was to stand with Isaiah and Jeremiah and issue the warnings; God's people might be listening as never before.[31]

Douglass used the jeremiad as yet another means to express his understanding of the Civil War. The war was the long-awaited calamity in which America's great paradox might be resolved, the wedge through which blacks might enter the family of the American nation. This was a moment when Afro-Americans might wrest a new definition out of the terrible duality of their lives. America's first principles could be appealed to, not only to free the slaves but to save the nation. Both causes possessed a sacred quality, and they might be mingled in one holy war. The war represented, therefore, the act of creation as well as preservation. These were the best hopes of a black abolitionist. The nation, however, had to be awakened to its mission.

The jeremiad provided a means for a black intellectual like Douglass to vent his frustration and rage while still preserving his hope, attack the United States government while at the same time demanding a place in its future. Black Jeremiahs, like their white counterparts in historian Sacvan Bercovitch's analysis, lamented declension but "simultaneously . . . celebrat[ed] a national dream." The jeremiad allowed them to express their assimilationist desire and still advocate the distinct purpose of blacks; it was a way to be both black and American, to demonstrate loyalty to the Union and to the slave. This combination had been much more difficult before Fort Sumter. Black spokesmen like Douglass seemed to be saying that blacks were not only a nation within a nation but a chosen people within a chosen

31. "Our National Fast," *DM,* October, 1861; Isaiah 1:4–5.

people. If America did not have a special destiny that it must be called back to—or forced to fulfill through a cruel war—then what was to be made of its enslaved race? A powerful sense of mission thrived in nineteenth-century America, fed by republican ideology, boundless land, and evangelical Christianity. If blacks were to stay in America and not resort to wholesale insurrection, Douglass believed they had to share in that mission. Without the mythology of mission, it is difficult to imagine how he could have sustained his hopes for black freedom in America.[32]

Millennial hopes had always been difficult to sustain, though impossible to suppress. For Douglass, moreover, the struggle to keep faith in jubilee had been too overwhelming by temporal means alone. Although always dissatisfied with organized religion, he could neither understand his own life nor express the aspirations of his people apart from spiritual considerations. "When all our earthly helps and hopes break down . . . ," he wrote in autumn, 1861, "the soul goes up to the eternal and invisible for help." Although he preferred reason, he never gave up on revelation.[33]

Undoubtedly Douglass used apocalypticism and jeremiads as effective rhetorical devices. Appealing to white Christian, nationalistic audiences, Douglass knew the power of his apocalyptic imagery. But we must not mistake belief for expediency in this instance. Douglass believed what he preached. He believed in American mission, in a providential God who shaped history, in history that could reshape nations in a few calamitous years. Douglass' millennialism was real.

Thus, it was through the idea of national regeneration that Douglass envisioned the purpose of the Civil War. After ceasing publication of his newspaper in August, 1863, he wrote a speech entitled "The Mission of the War," which he delivered in city after city across the North well into 1864. It is impossible to determine how many people heard this address, but the total would number in the thousands. The speech was, in part, a series of warnings against backsliding on emancipation, against the racism of the Democratic party and its political threat in 1864, and against the weariness caused by the horrible human costs of the war. But the speech was also a clear and eloquent statement of Douglass' interpretation of the American Apocalypse. "You and I know that the mission of this war is National regeneration," he bluntly declared. He invoked the mythology of mission in some of its most widely understood language: "I do believe

32. Bercovitch, *American Jeremiad*, 180.
33. "Our National Fast."

that it is the manifest destiny of this war to unify and reorganize the institutions of the country—and that herein is the secret of the strength, the fortitude, the persistent energy, in a word, the sacred significance of this war." Douglass never expressed the notion of holy war in clearer terms. We might best know the significance of the Civil War in Douglass' life by understanding his own conception of the "sacred significance" of the conflict. Throughout the war, like the apocalyptic trumpet in Julia Ward Howe's vision, Douglass spoke with a voice that could never call retreat.[34]

34. "The Mission of the War," 397, 399–401.

6/THE BUGBEAR OF COLONIZATION

The highest interests of the white race, whether Anglo-Saxon, Celt, or Scandinavian, require that the whole country should be held and occupied by these races alone . . . ; The Anglo-American looks upon every acre of our present domain as intended for him and not for the Negro.
—U.S. House of Representatives, *Report on Emancipation and Colonization*, 1862

But why, oh why! may not men of different races inhabit in peace and happiness this vast and wealthy country? Different races have lived in it very comfortably, and with one exception do now manage so to live.—What is it in the American branch of the Anglo-Saxon race which renders it incapable of tolerating the presence of any people in the country different from themselves? Are not Americans themselves a composite race? Why may not men of different colors as well as men of different religions live civilly together under the same Government?
—Frederick Douglass, September 16, 1862

WHEN FREDERICK DOUGLASS SPOKE of national regeneration in the midst of the Civil War, he expressed the yearnings of blacks to belong in America. To Douglass, national regeneration meant a spiritual and political rebirth for the United States; it meant the achievement of full citizenship as well as civil and political equality for blacks, and the beginning of the acceptance of black people into the national family. Moreover, national regeneration meant a reaffirmation of America's creeds. Douglass imagined a nation in which race would have no distinction before the law.

But for blacks to "belong" in America they had to stay within its borders. In order to achieve black freedom, and in order for America to fulfill its destiny as Douglass envisioned it, one of the oldest schemes in American race relations had finally to be put to rest. Colonization—the relocation of blacks in foreign places—had long held the American imagination. Its motives throughout the nineteenth century had been as disparate as its adherents. Since the Revolution, and especially after the War of 1812, whenever Americans had faced the prospect of a rising population of free blacks, schemes of colonization had emerged.

The most effective procolonization agency of the prewar years was the American Colonization Society, founded in 1816. During the 1820s and 1830s the society had been successful in establishing the colony of Liberia and in relocating some 4,571 black Americans in that West African country. By the 1840s the Colonization Society had fallen on hard times: mortality rates of over 50 percent among the settler population, internal strife among the leaders of the parent organization in America, increasing abolitionist hostility, an unwilling black populace, and the overwhelming logistical and financial burden of any African colonization scheme doomed the society to failure. But its theoretical basis never lost popularity nor famous advocates. As its chief historian has demonstrated, the great irony of the American Colonization Society was that "the idea of colonization as a solution to the race question was still popular," even when the society was not.[1]

A revival of colonizationist fervor occurred in the 1850s and accelerated after the outbreak of the Civil War. Whether by private or state sponsorship, colonization as actual policy or ideology represented a serious threat to Douglass' vision of Afro-American destiny, and during the war this issue animated the black editor and stimulated some of his most embittered criticism of American racism. His wartime writings reveal a thoroughgoing critique of colonizationist plans and ideology, as well as a contentious relationship with the Lincoln administration on this issue. An examination of Douglass' response to colonization further illuminates his conception of the meaning of the Civil War for blacks. The colonizationist premise that blacks could never live and compete effectively with whites as social and political equals—a belief shared by most white Americans as late as the 1860s—remained one of the greatest obstacles to overcome once the war was won. Colonization threatened to explode the dreams blacks now found attainable in the midst of a calamitous war. Its many impracticalities notwithstanding, colonizationist ideology seemed to be white America's last resort in order to preserve white supremacy.

Douglass hoped that emancipation and black military participa-

1. P. J. Staudenraus, *The African Colonization Movement, 1816–1865* (New York, 1961), 239. On numbers and welfare of Afro-Americans transported to Liberia, see Tom W. Shick, *Behold the Promised Land: A History of Afro-American Settler Society in Nineteenth-Century Liberia* (Baltimore, 1977), 27; Tom W. Shick, "A Quantitative Analysis of Liberian Colonization from 1820 to 1843 with Special Reference to Mortality," *Journal of African History*, XII (1971), 45–59. On differences in colonizationist sentiment between the late eighteenth and early nineteenth centuries, see Jordan, *White Over Black*, 566–69. Jordan shows how colonization could be both "so persistent" and so "preposterously utopian" to American thinkers. His notion that colonization was a "compelling fantasy" that, for many Americans, never lost its "elements of realism" suggests the way the idea endured down to the Civil War.

tion would eliminate the issue of colonization once and for all. In a recruiting speech in New York City in April, 1863, he expressed his hope that black valor on the battlefield might finally destroy "the bugbear 'colonization' which has so troubled the American people."[2] But the "bugbear" of colonization died hard, and in the midst of the Civil War it remained a half-illusory, half-real prospect that large numbers of the five million free blacks might be expatriated to foreign lands. Douglass considered the threat serious enough to condemn it at every opportunity.

In a May, 1863, speech about the future of blacks in America, Douglass identified the most important question before the nation: "The destiny of the nation has the Negro for its pivot," he claimed, "and turns upon the question as to what shall be done with him." He outlined several possible answers to this question, and in so doing suggested the possible outcomes of the Civil War. They included Confederate military victory and the persistence of slavery in America; a race war where whites from both sections might combine to "exterminate the black race entirely"; a war that might abolish slavery only to replace it with a racial caste system; and what Douglass considered a colonizationist war. He called colonization the "best defined solution of our difficulties about the Negro" and reasoned that to many Americans it formed "a singularly pleasing dream." In calling it the "best defined" solution, Douglass recognized colonization's appeal among whites as a blueprint for America's racial future. In the context of the war, he dismissed colonization as financially and physically impractical, but it is instructive that he nevertheless included it in his conception of the possible outcomes of the war. Even from the vantage point of the spring of 1863 (after the Emancipation Proclamation and while the recruiting of black soldiers was underway), Douglass took the colonizationist threat seriously. Douglass' own preferred outcome was, of course, an "abolition war" that would preserve the Union, emancipate the slaves, and initiate full civil and political equality for all blacks, but in early 1863 the outcome of the war was still in doubt. Of one thing Douglass was certain, however: the destiny of black Americans lay in the land of their birth.[3]

Douglass' speculations on the possible outcomes of the war had one common theme: his condemnation of white supremacy and

2. Speech at Shiloh Church, New York, April 30, 1863, in *DM*, June, 1863.
3. "The Present and Future of the Colored Race in America," speech at Church of the Puritans, New York, May, 1863, *DM*, June, 1863, in Foner (ed.), *Life and Writings*, III, 348–51.

therefore of the desire among whites to colonize blacks. Now that emancipation was official policy of the Union government, something indeed would have to be "done with the Negro," and each outcome Douglass suggested, except abolition followed by legal black equality, contained some degree of elimination or circumscription for blacks. More than anything else, he wanted both the humanity and the citizenship of blacks recognized, but before that was possible, he seemed fully aware that Americans had to be convinced that blacks and whites could live together in what he called a "common nationality." Douglass attacked colonization not because he considered it the most likely outcome of the war, but because he considered it possible and believed that as long as colonizationist thinking persisted, blacks could never secure equality in America.[4]

In order to understand Douglass' wartime antipathy to colonization, we must look at his prewar response to the issue. His views on colonization were well rehearsed before the crises of the 1850s and the war fostered a revival of the controversy. He first entered the debate over colonization in 1849 with arguments he would consistently use for the rest of his life. Responding to a revival of the issue in the United States Senate (the ACS had frequently lobbied Congress for government sanction and financial support), Douglass charged that "the slaveholding *charmers* have conjured up their old *familiar spirits* of colonization." Although he called the latest revival a "ruse to divert attention" from the more immediate issue of slavery in the territories, it is clear that he never considered colonization as a mere ploy to achieve other ends. He always interpreted proposals for colonization as an insult to black people, and the suggestion that blacks should leave America because an integrated society seemed inconceivable to whites only prompted him aggressively to claim his birthright as an American citizen. In his first editorial on the subject, he tried to speak plainly: "We live here—have lived here—have a right to live here, and mean to live here."[5]

In a speech in Boston's Faneuil Hall in May, 1849, Douglass narrowed his hostility to the American Colonization Society to the sin-

4. *Ibid.*, 352. On the colonizationist image of blacks held by whites, and black intellectual resistance to the idea, see Sweet, *Black Images of America*, 35–68. On the black abolitionist response to colonization, see Blackett, *Building an Antislavery Wall*, 47–78.

5. "Colonization," *North Star*, January 26, 1849, in Foner (ed.), *Life and Writings*, I, 351–52. On the revival of colonization in the 1850s, see Fredrickson, *Black Image in the White Mind*, 115–17, 147–49.

gle fact that it fostered a "feeling of hatred against the black man." In this, his first public lecture devoted exclusively to the issue of colonization, the black orator did not focus on the feasibility of relocating millions of people in Africa; instead, he attacked the notion that racial prejudice could not be overcome in America. Racial prejudice *could* be vanquished, Douglass asserted. "I will tell you how to get rid of it," he challenged his listeners. "Commence to do something to elevate and improve . . . the colored man, and your prejudice will begin to vanish. The more you try to make a man of the black man, the more you will begin to think him a man." To Douglass, colonization was always a debate over human dignity. As he had already discovered many times in his own life, especially during his travels in the British Isles, experience could erode prejudice. But at a time when proslavery ideology and racism were becoming more aggressive and articulate, Douglass' racial egalitarianism was a beleaguered creed.[6]

To the extent that their goal was the improvement of the lot of black people, Douglass occasionally acknowledged the good intentions of colonizationists, yet whatever benevolent features colonization represented could not mask what he saw as the central problem—racial prejudice. "The secret of the colonization scheme," Douglass declared in 1853, was the presence of an increasing free black population. "It is easily seen," he told an all-white gathering of the American and Foreign Antislavery Society, "that just in proportion to the intelligence and respectability of the free colored race at the North is their power to endanger the stability of slavery. Hence the desire to get rid of us." Douglass was discouraged by all the talk of colonization during the 1850s and wanted to alter the nature of the issue by changing the assumptions upon which the debate turned. He struggled to replace the colonizationist view of American race relations with an assimilationist view. But this was a prospect that would have to await the revolutionary situation of the next decade. As a spokesman for that free black population that continued to inspire revivals of colonizationist thinking, Douglass simply urged his people to take heart and resist. "Remember that a home, a country, a nationality," he asserted, "are all attainable this side of Liberia."[7]

6. "The American Colonization Society," speech in Faneuil Hall, Boston, May 31, 1849, in Foner (ed.), *Life and Writings*, I, 394–96. On the rise of aggressive racism and its significance in colonizationist thought, see Fredrickson, *Black Image in the White Mind*, 1–42.

7. "The Present Condition and Future Prospects of the Negro People," 252–53. On the benevolent side to colonization, see Douglass to Smith, August 4, 1851, in Gerrit Smith Papers, where Douglass describes a call from a Professor Upshaw of Bowdoin

In 1856 Douglass summarized his opposition to colonization in a letter to the Philadelphia Quaker businessman and philanthropist Benjamin Coates. His arguments can be combined into three essential points. First, colonization diverted national attention from abolition and served to "deaden the national conscience when it needed quickening." Moreover, colonizationist ideology furnished an apology for delaying emancipation, "thus interposing a physical impossibility between the slave and his deliverance." Second, Douglass despised colonization because it broke the hopes of the free black man in America; it "robs his future . . . ," he charged, "of all that can gladden his heart." And third, Douglass again cited the power of colonizationist thinking "to confirm existing prejudice as a thing natural and unsurmountable."[8] Hence, whatever the motives, Douglass believed that the colonization debate ultimately served the ends of white supremacy: to postpone emancipation and to deny blacks any claim to American nationality. He simply did not consider credible the belief held by some colonizationists that their plans would hasten emancipation by making it safe. Colonizationists considered racial prejudice permanent and racial equality impossible; Douglass accepted neither premise and offered himself as an example to overcome both ideas. Even if emancipation could have been hastened by colonizationist schemes, to Douglass it was an unacceptable price for his people to pay for their freedom.

Throughout the 1850s the enduring colonization issue paralleled the emergence of black emigrationism and in some ways was the most vexing aspect of the lives of free blacks on the eve of the Civil War. Could they survive and prosper in a land where slavery might endure? Could they envision a secure future in a society that showed few signs of movement toward racial equality? Frederick Douglass led the opposition to black emigration schemes, sometimes by ignoring them but more often by engaging his fellow black intellectuals in heated debate. This controversy over the Afro-American search for a place characterized the early development of black nationalism in America before the Civil War and tells us much about the black

---

College. "Full two hours did he labor with me in favor of colonization," complained Douglass. "The dear man thinks he is doing God service by advocating that man-hating scheme." For colonization as a philanthropic movement, see Staudenraus, *African Colonization Movement*, 12–22.

8. Douglass to Benjamin Coates, April 17, 1856, in Foner (ed.), *Life and Writings*, II, 387–88. On Douglass' sense of attachment to his native land, also see Preston, *Young Frederick Douglass*, 159–62. In his first return to his native state in November, 1864, Douglass spoke lovingly of Maryland.

intellectual's search for self-definition as well as the nature and limits of black leadership in the 1850s. Douglass has often been portrayed
as the chief spokesman of anti-emigrationism, and indeed he was, but
as I have tried to demonstrate, his assimilationism made him no less
of a black nationalist. He did not reject voluntary expatriation without sympathy and understanding for some of its motives.[9]

Three major movements of black emigrationism emerged in the
1850s. The first, beginning in 1852, was led by Martin R. Delany, a
physician and antislavery editor from Pittsburgh who had assisted
Douglass in founding the *North Star.* In 1854 Delany wielded great
influence over the National Emigration Convention held in Cleveland, denouncing all cooperation with white colonizationists and
advocating mass emigration to the Caribbean or South America. By
1859 Delany shifted his interest to Africa. He made friendly over-
tures to Liberia, sought money from white colonizationists, and led
the celebrated Niger Valley Exploring Party into West Africa. A second movement emerged with the African Civilization Society,
founded in 1858 and led by the well-traveled black minister Henry
Highland Garnet. As early as 1850 Garnet developed ties to the English free-produce movement; he modeled his own organization on
the plan to develop West Africa's economic potential, especially
through cotton production. Garnet's African Civilization Society
was biracial, closely linked to philanthropists in the American Colonization Society, and very controversial among free blacks. Beginning in 1859, the third phase of emigrationism focused on Haiti.
With Christian missionary zeal, the Haytian Emigration Bureau was
led by the black Episcopalian James T. Holly of New Haven, Connecticut, and the Scottish-born journalist and abolitionist from
Boston, James Redpath. In 1860–61, the bureau had several agents
working in cities across the North, published its own newspaper, the
Pine and Palm, and stirred considerable interest among free blacks.
Emigration schemes caused great rancor among black leadership on
the eve of the Civil War. Garnet's organization was especially di-
visive; indeed, the majority of black leaders, Douglass most vehemently, fought the African Civilization Society. Opposition meetings were held all over the North in 1859–60, some collapsing into
bitter exchanges and fist-fights.[10]

9. On Douglass' black nationalism as well as his thought about emigrationism, see
Moses, *Golden Age,* 38–41, 83–90.
10. Martin R. Delany, *The Condition, Elevation, Emigration, and Destiny of the
Colored People of the United States* (1852; rpr. New York, 1968), 178–88. On Delany's

The bitterness of the debate over emigration was a measure of the importance of the issue as well as the deep frustration blacks felt in America in the late 1850s. No one was more aware than Douglass of the sense of desperation that permeated black thinking in the 1850s. The message of the Fugitive Slave Act of 1850, its widespread resistance, and the nearly twenty thousand fugitives who stole away to Canada (many with Douglass' personal assistance) formed the context in which many blacks lost faith in America. The despair that blacks felt in the wake of the Dred Scott decision in 1857 only made the last years of the decade more fertile for the growth of emigrationism. Except for the abolitionist tradition, which was entering new political paths, the country seemed to be telling black leaders to take their hopes elsewhere.

Although Douglass rarely gave in to emigrationist arguments, he feared that other black leaders might. As early as 1851, he wrote to Gerrit Smith of his "fear that some whose presence in this country is necessary to the elevation of the colored people will leave us." Although they might not lead resettlement expeditions, Douglass knew that some black intellectuals could find life more fulfilling in the

---

life, see Dorothy Sterling, *The Making of an Afro-American: Martin Robison Delany, 1812–1885* (Garden City, N.Y., 1971). On Delany as black nationalist and emigrationist, see Cyril E. Griffith, *The African Dream: Martin R. Delany and the Emergence of Pan-African Thought* (University Park, Pa., 1975); Floyd J. Miller, *The Search for a Black Nationality: Black Emigration and Colonization, 1787–1863* (Urbana, 1975), 115–33; Floyd J. Miller, "The Father of Black Nationalism: Another Contender," *Civil War History*, XVII (December, 1971), 310–19. For a sympathetic analysis of the National Emigration conventions and on the Niger Valley Party, see Miller, *Search for a Black Nationality*, 137–57, 173–83, 198–216. For a more critical analysis of the same, see Moses, *Golden Age*, 35–37, 46; Pease and Pease, *They Who Would Be Free*, 260–65. On Garnet and the African Civilization Society, see Pease and Pease, *They Who Would Be Free*, 267–72; Miller, *Search for a Black Nationality*, 192–93, 228–31. Garnet favored a selective, carefully planned, and well-financed emigration to Africa. His connections with the English African Aid Society and his three-year residence in Jamaica were profound influences on Garnet's emigrationist outlook. On Holly and the Haytian Emigration Bureau, see Miller, *Search for a Black Nationality*, 232–49. On Redpath, also see Willis D. Boyd, "James Redpath and American Negro Colonization in Haiti, 1860–1862," *Americas*, XII (October, 1955), 169–78. The Haytian Emigration Bureau's agents included H. Ford Douglass in Chicago, William Wells Brown in Canada, and Garnet in New York. By one count, nearly nine hundred blacks, many from Canada, emigrated to Haiti in 1861. High rates of death and disease among the first settlers, however, and the widespread reports of this suffering back in the United States, devastated the ill-fated movement. There were some exceptions to the stories of suffering and death in Haiti. Douglass received a letter from a group of thirty emigrants sometime before July, 1862, reporting that all was going well for them. They were very complimentary of the Haitian government and confident about their new status. See *DM*, July, 1862.

British Isles or elsewhere. In an appeal on behalf of the Rochester Colored National Convention of 1853, Douglass stated the plight of the antebellum black intellectual: "It would seem that education and emigration go together with us," he lamented, "for as soon as a man rises among us, capable by his genius and learning, to do us great service, just so soon he finds that he can serve himself better by going elsewhere." Many black intellectuals, he argued, were overeducated for the racial atmosphere of American society: "The Russwurms— the Garnets—the Wards—the Crummells and others," he complained, "having no taste to continue a contest against such odds, . . . have sought more congenial climes." Douglass deeply regretted this personal form of emigration; every model of black achievement was sorely needed in America. "But," he admitted, "I cannot blame them, for with an equal amount of education, and the hard lot which was theirs, I might follow their example."[11]

As debate ensued over Haiti and the African Civilization Society in 1859, Douglass seemed even more understanding of the desire for expatriation among black individuals. In April a young black named Mifflin G. Gibbs stopped at Douglass' office in Rochester to discuss his decision to move to Vancouver, Canada. Douglass admitted to no quarrel with the personal motives of the young man, who simply could not "stand the pressure of the States," but he lamented this loss of potential black leadership from America. "We shall not be deemed selfish," he hoped, "if we refuse to encourage this drain upon our best blood." Douglass believed that blacks had been "mercilously bled" of leadership by the attractions of other lands.[12]

In 1859–60, Douglass and Garnet engaged in a bitter exchange over the efforts of the African Civilization Society. Douglass characterized the stark differences between himself and Garnet: "We prefer to remain in America, and we do insist upon it in the very face of our respected friend . . . *you* go there, *we* stay here, is just the difference between us." Douglass replied to Garnet's entreaties with a long and angry diatribe against emigrationist ideas. He condemned the Civilization Society's economic plans, arguing that cotton producers in America had nothing to fear from African cotton, and declared Garnet's organization no different from the American Colonization

11. Douglass to Smith, January 31, 1851, in Gerrit Smith Papers; Douglass to Harriet Beecher Stowe, *Proceedings of the Colored National Convention*, Rochester, July 6–8, 1853, in Foner (ed.), *Life and Writings*, II, 231. The four black leaders Douglass refers to here are John Brown Russwurm, Henry Highland Garnet, Samuel Ringgold Ward, and Alexander Crummell.

12. *DM*, May, 1859.

Society, for it based its efforts "upon the lying assumption that white and black people can never live in the same land on terms of equality." The work of black leaders was in America, he contended, where they could speak for the slaves. He urged Garnet to leave the black masses alone to work out their destiny in their native land. "We are perpetually kept, with wandering eyes and open mouths," wrote Douglass, "looking out for some mighty revolution in our affairs here, which is to remove us from this country." Douglass could countenance emigrationist feelings among some of his fellow black intellectuals because he shared their frustrations and understood their desires for greater fulfillment. But he would not support any plan that called upon blacks as a group to renounce their American identity and embark on wholesale emigration.[13]

Douglass' hostile reactions to African emigration included some stereotypical anti-African images. He rejected the pan-African vision held by some of his black contemporaries: "A few shiploads of colored people from the United States," he argued in 1858, could not "solve the problem of the redemption of Africa." Douglass' rather unsophisticated, Eurocentric view of Africa rendered him uninterested in the missionary impulse of Garnet's African Civilization Society. Parts of Africa, he asserted, were in "a deplorable condition . . . floundering in the depths of barbarism." Douglass declared himself just as wary of the "ignorance and savage selfishness" of African chieftains as he was of Maryland slave-traders.[14]

Douglass was kinder to the Haitian emigration scheme. In May, 1859, he conceded that Haitian emigration made more sense than going to Africa, but he seemed almost embarrassed by the emigrationist fervor among blacks. He wished that the Haitian movement could be organized without publicity and advertisement: "If we are going away," he urged his Chicago readers, "let us go without noise, and be done with it." Douglass was convinced that whenever blacks debated, much less endorsed, emigrationism they gladdened "the hearts of our enemies who wish to get rid of us." Although he wanted blacks to be free to assert one of the most basic forms of liberty—the right to emigrate—he wished that they could do so without affirming

13. "African Civilization Society," *DM*, February, 1859. On the Douglass-Garnet conflict, see Joel Schor, "The Rivalry Between Frederick Douglass and Henry Highland Garnet," *Journal of Negro History*, LXIV (Winter, 1969), 30–38.

14. "The Letter of Benjamin Coates, Esq.," *FDP*, September 17, 1858, in Foner (ed.), *Life and Writings*, V, 413–14; "African Civilization Society." On Douglass' anti-African views, which became even more pronounced after the Civil War, see Martin, *Mind*, 202–13.

white America's perception of them. In his view, most black emigration schemes gave credence to the belief that whites and blacks could not coexist in America, and the white colonizationist image of blacks, he felt, needed no reinforcement.[15]

For a time between November, 1860, and April, 1861, Douglass gave qualified support to the Haitian movement. Beginning in January, 1861, he printed advertisements and addresses for Redpath's Haytian Emigration Bureau in every issue of the *Douglass Monthly,* and in an editorial published at roughly the same time South Carolina seceded from the Union, he endorsed the Haitian scheme. Amidst the uncertainty and racial demogoguery of the secession winter, suggested the editor, emigrationist feeling had become stronger than ever. As reasons for his own shift in attitude, he cited the "generous inducements" of the Haitian government as well as the island's close proximity to the North American mainland. "If we go anywhere, let us go to Hayti," wrote Douglass; "let us go where we are still within hearing distance of the wails of our brothers and sisters in bonds." Haitian emigration also appealed to Douglass, because it was within the hemisphere, because it was in cooperation with a black republic that stood symbolically for abolition, and because it was selective (an option for individuals and families). Many of his "old objections" to African colonization did not apply in the Haitian situation, and he could advocate removal to Haiti without "conceding that Africa is our only home, and that we have no right to remain in America." He also claimed that he could support the Haitian plan without "appealing to our enemies for the means of getting out of the way of their hatred." But Douglass' reasoning was selective and inconsistent, and he admitted that the real reasons for emigration were that blacks faced an apparently bleak future in America. As previously indicated, the secession winter was a time of pessimism and confusion for Douglass. In December, 1860, he was still reeling from the defeat of black suffrage in New York and the attack of a white mob in Boston; moreover, he felt genuinely uncertain about the meaning of the Republican triumph and imminent southern secession. Economic prospects for blacks in America were "becoming more and more limited," so he could not oppose "a measure which may prove highly advantageous to many families."[16]

15. "All Going to Hayti," *DM*, May, 1859.
16. "Emigration to Hayti," *DM*, January, 1861. At this point, Douglass was also concerned about the possible repeal of personal liberty laws by northern legislatures and therefore expected increased problems for fugitive slaves. For further comment on Douglass' doubts and lost hopes during the period after Lincoln's election, see P. Foner, *Frederick Douglass,* 189.

Douglass' endorsement of the Haitian movement was an assertion of the individual's right to emigrate, made in the context of political crisis and personal frustration. "Emigration to Hayti is wise or foolish . . . ," he contended in March, 1861, "according to the circumstances of the emigrant himself." Those who were economically dispossessed should go, but they should go as a matter of individual choice, not because of "inability to live among white people, or for the charms of a Colored Nationality." Expatriation to a Caribbean nation created and ruled by blacks was acceptable, even attractive, to Douglass if done simply for human needs.[17]

For a brief time in the spring of 1861, Douglass caved in to emigrationism and planned a ten-week trip to Haiti to investigate the island for himself. In the May issue of his paper he wrote very affectionately of Haiti, calling it a "refutation of the slanders and disparagements of our race." Haiti's symbolism was irresistible to Douglass. Americans, he maintained, had made it "the bugbear and scare-crow of the cause of freedom," but for those blacks "looking out into the world for a place to retreat, an asylum from the apprehended storm," Haiti offered refuge. These were no longer the words of the ardent anti-emigrationist. Although he would not move permanently himself, Douglass was willing to spend part of his summer investigating the prospects for those more willing to go.[18]

There is every reason to believe that had the war not started when it did, Douglass would have even more warmly supported Haitian emigration as one option for his people. It is also interesting to speculate on the rhetorical uses to which he put the Haitian question. Haiti, said Douglass, was a "modern land of Canaan, where so many of our people are journeying from the rigorous bondage and oppression of our modern Egypt." From 1859, when he wished that blacks would only discuss it quietly, to the eve of Fort Sumter when he allowed himself rather heady expressions of Caribbean black nationalism, Douglass seems to have converted the issue of Haitian emigration into yet another source of millennial hope in troubled times and yet another way for him to express the anger and frustration blacks then felt. He seems to have enjoyed raising the "bugbear" of Haiti in order to thwart the spirit of the older "bugbear" of colonization.[19]

Douglass abandoned his trip to Haiti almost as soon as he had announced it. The beginning of the war caused a rapid reversal of

17. "Haytian Emigration," *DM*, March, 1861. On Haitian emigration, also see McPherson (ed.), *The Negro's Civil War*, 178–89.
18. "A Trip to Hayti," 86–88.
19. *Ibid.*

Douglass' support of the Haitian scheme, just as similar rapid reversals on emigration occurred to many black intellectuals, such as Delany, Garnet, H. Ford Douglass, and William Wells Brown. Two months after Fort Sumter, Douglass again chastised "wholesale schemes" of emigration for their power to awaken and confirm popular prejudice. The Haitian movement had lost him, Douglass now maintained, the "moment it began to theorize" and represent a "creed" that only enhanced white hatred of blacks.[20]

It is hardly surprising that at the very time Douglass realized his hope of an organized war against the South he lost interest in black expatriation, but this is all the more reason to underscore the importance of the Civil War in his life and thought. Had the war not come when it did, his emigrationism would never have dissipated so quickly. Perhaps the kind of assimilationist ideology Douglass advanced could not have survived another decade in America, and the process of expended alternatives might have forced even him to consider expatriation. The outbreak of the war, however, with its revolutionary potential to destroy slavery in America, brought an abrupt change in the prospects of Afro-Americans. The future seemed charged with excitement instead of despair. A generation of black leadership was about to cease its internal debate over emigration, but the divided nation, warring over questions of national existence, had not finished with its long struggle over the expatriation of black people. The colonization controversy was about to be rekindled, fueled by the prospect of widespread emancipation.

Driven by what the historian George Fredrickson has called a "conservative fatalism" about American race relations rather than by Negrophobia, the Lincoln administration gave Douglass and others much to think about regarding colonization during the first two years of the Civil War. Lincoln had long opposed slavery on political and moral grounds and he recognized the humanity and natural rights of blacks, but until the last two years of the Civil War he maintained a rigid distinction between slavery and racial equality. Typical of his age, Lincoln believed that white prejudice was unconquerable. Through the crucible of the Civil War, however, his views of black destiny changed, and it is hard to escape the conclusion that by the end of the war Lincoln, forced by events and driven by his own mixture of pragmatism and idealism, had risen above the racism of his

20. "The Haytian Emigration Movement," *DM*, July, 1861.

time. But Lincoln was slow to relinquish his preferred plan of compensated emancipation coupled with colonization. The president had long viewed colonization as the ultimate solution to America's race problem, and throughout the 1850s he had combined his goal of putting slavery on a course of "ultimate extinction" with the promotion of voluntary colonization by blacks emigrating to their "natural" tropical habitat. Although he espoused voluntary colonization only, Lincoln was unmistakably committed to black removal.[21]

Lincoln very early set in motion a multilayered effort to colonize free blacks. His newly appointed minister-resident to Guatemala, Elisha Oscar Crosby, received instructions in March, 1861, to seek a place for black colonists in Central America. The attack on Fort Sumter occurred before Crosby reached his post, thus dashing any

21. George M. Fredrickson, "A Man But Not a Brother: Abraham Lincoln and Racial Equality," *Journal of Southern History*, XLI (February, 1975), 56. Lincoln stated his position most effectively in his sixth debate with Stephen A. Douglas, at Quincy, Illinois, October 13, 1858. See Basler (ed.), *Collected Works of Lincoln*, III, 16, 248–49.

For the extremes in the opposing views on Lincoln and race, see Lerone Bennett, Jr., "Was Abe Lincoln a White Supremacist?" *Ebony*, XXIII (February, 1968), 35–38, 40, 42; Herbert Mitgang, "Was Lincoln Just a Honkie?" *New York Times Magazine*, February 11, 1968, pp. 34–35, 100–107. The scholarly discussion of this question has been immense. See Arvarh E. Strickland, "The Illinois Background of Lincoln's Attitude Toward Slavery and the Negro," *Illinois State Historical Society Journal*, LVI (Autumn, 1963), 474–94; Quarles, *Lincoln and the Negro*; Fredrickson, "A Man But Not a Brother"; Don E. Fehrenbacher, "Only His Stepchildren: Lincoln and the Negro," *Civil War History*, XX (December, 1974), 293–310; G. S. Boritt, "The Voyage to the Colony of Linconia: The Sixteenth President, Black Colonization, and the Defense Mechanism of Avoidance," *Historian*, XXXVII (August, 1975), 619–33; Mark E. Neely, Jr., "Abraham Lincoln and Black Colonization: Benjamin Butler's Spurious Testimony," *Civil War History*, XXV (January, 1979), 77–83; LaWanda Cox, *Lincoln and Black Freedom: A Study in Presidential Leadership* (Columbia, S.C., 1981), 3–43; and V. Jacque Voegeli, *Free But Not Equal: The Midwest and the Negro During the Civil War* (Chicago, 1967), 39, 43–45, 66–67. This question of Lincoln's racial views and their impact on his policies has caused a complex and at times angry debate among historians. One problem appears to be settled: Neely has convincingly shown that Gen. Benjamin F. Butler's 1865 allegations that Lincoln still openly hoped for colonization in the last months of the war were fabricated and false. This makes Fredrickson's conclusion—that Lincoln's racial views did not substantively change in the final two years of the war—less weighty, as it was based in part on the Butler testimony. Fehrenbacher argues that Lincoln's colonization may have been a great *political* achievement, in that his primary motive all along may have been to ease tensions and condition public opinion for eventual universal emancipation. This conclusion is helpful but not entirely convincing. Fehrenbacher himself acknowledges that the quest for colonization was "the strangest feature of Lincoln's presidential career." As many scholars have noted, this subject requires a concern for fairness toward Lincoln, an effort not to make him say what we would have him say. Such has been the tendency toward America's most mythic character. All scholars who have approached the subject of Lincoln and race seem aware that much is left to speculation. For Lincoln's early colonizationist thought, see Basler (ed.), *Collected Works of Lincoln*, II, 132, 255, 298–99, 409–10.

hopes that this original initiative might help ease tensions in the secession crisis, but Crosby continued to send dispatches of encouragement about potential colonization in Central America throughout 1861, despite the fact that the Honduran and Guatemalan governments were opposed to the idea. Also in 1861, the Lincoln administration supported the Chiriqui Improvement Company, under the leadership of a wealthy Philadelphia shipbuilder named Ambrose W. Thompson. Thompson controlled several hundred thousand acres of land in Panama and since 1855 had attempted to obtain government support for coal mining and a transisthmian railroad in the region. After considerable negotiation throughout the summer and fall of 1861 involving the Missourian Francis P. Blair, Sr., Lincoln's brother-in-law Ninian W. Edwards, and Secretary of the Interior Caleb B. Smith, Lincoln authorized a contract with the Chiriqui Company and ordered the outfitting of an expedition to investigate the region.[22]

Douglass could have known little if anything of these machinations, so he probably became aware of the colonization plans of the Lincoln administration in December, 1861. In Lincoln's first annual message to Congress, he urged the colonization of ex-slaves and free blacks to "some place, or places, in a climate congenial to them." Lincoln did not specifically reveal the efforts already underway, but he made it clear that colonization of blacks was important to his overriding desire that the war not "degenerate into a violent and remorseless revolutionary struggle."[23] Although by 1864–65 they would come surprisingly close to each other in their vision of the war's purpose, Douglass' and Lincoln's conflicting war aims at this early stage are clear. Douglass wanted precisely what Lincoln did not: a "revolutionary struggle" that would make black freedom in America indispensable to the Union cause.

The year 1862 proved to be decisive in the Civil War, not only on the battlefield but for the Lincoln administration's racial policy as well.

22. On the Crosby instructions, see Walter A. Payne, "Lincoln's Caribbean Colonization Plan," *Pacific Historian*, VII (May, 1963), 67–68. On the Chiriqui initiative, see Warren A. Beck, "Lincoln and Negro Colonization in Central America," *Abraham Lincoln Quarterly* (September, 1950), 166–69; Paul J. Sheips, "Lincoln and the Chiriqui Colonization Project," *Journal of Negro History*, XXXVII (October, 1952), 419–21. Also see Charles H. Wesley, "Lincoln's Plan for Colonizing the Emancipated Negroes," *Journal of Negro History*, IV (January, 1919), 7–21.

23. Basler (ed.), *Collected Works of Lincoln*, V, 48–49. Lincoln urged that "steps be taken for colonizing" those slaves freed as confiscated enemy "property." Moreover, the president suggested that "it might be well to consider . . . whether the free colored people already in the United States could not, so far as individuals may desire, be included in such colonization."

In April, Congress abolished slavery in the District of Columbia and authorized $600,000 for the colonization of free blacks to Liberia, Haiti, or elsewhere. On July 17, 1862, Congress passed the Second Confiscation Act, freeing virtually all slaves liberated by Union forces and empowering the president to enlist black soldiers. The bill also authorized the president to provide for the "transportation, colonization, and settlement in some tropical country . . . of such persons of the African race . . . as may be willing to emigrate." From April through August, Lincoln received a great deal of advice regarding black colonization, most of it encouraging him to proceed with the Chiriqui operation or some other plan. Moreover, serious interest in black emigration came from the British West Indies and the Danish island of St. Croix. The British islands had been experiencing labor shortages for three decades. Led by Jamaica, several British colonies submitted detailed proposals to the Colonial Office in London, requesting help in procuring black settlers presumed to be available because of the American war, and by the end of August, 1862, agents from several West Indian colonies were on their way to Washington. But because of the delicate diplomatic relationship between the United States and Great Britain as well as opposition to colonization within the Lincoln administration, this West Indian initiative never came to fruition.[24]

At this crucial juncture, with the war raging in central Virginia and soon to be thrust into Maryland, Lincoln met a delegation of five blacks at the White House on August 14, 1862, to discuss coloniza-

24. *Statutes At Large of the United States of America, 1789–1873* (17 vols.; Boston, 1850–73), XII, 582. On Congress' actions, see Sheips, "Lincoln and the Chiriqui Colonization Project," 422–24; Beck, "Lincoln and Negro Colonization," 170–73; Voegeli, *Free But Not Equal*, 24–29.

On the advice to Lincoln, see Sheips, "Lincoln and the Chiriqui Colonization Project," 424–27; and Beck, "Lincoln and Negro Colonization," 171–73. "Correspondence Respecting the Emigration of Free Negroes from the United States to the West Indies," CO 884/2, June 19, 1863, Confidential Print, Public Record Office, London, England. On the British West Indian initiative, see Shick, *Behold the Promised Land*, 124–29. From reading the correspondence in the PRO, one gains a sense of how deeply involved Lincoln administration officials were in colonization schemes. In Lincoln's cabinet, Attorney General Edward Bates, Postmaster General Montgomery Blair, and Secretary of the Interior Caleb B. Smith favored colonization, while Secretary of State William H. Seward, Secretary of the Treasury Salmon P. Chase, and Secretary of the Navy Gideon Welles opposed it. Support followed Lincoln's voluntary plan, although Bates favored compulsory removal if blacks did not cooperate. On Chase's opposition, see David Donald (ed.), *Inside Lincoln's Cabinet: The Civil War Diaries of Salmon P. Chase* (New York, 1954), 112; and on Welles's opposition, see Howard K. Beale (ed.), *Diary of Gideon Welles, Secretary of the Navy Under Lincoln and Johnson,* (3 vols.; New York, 1960), II, 150–53. In the spring of 1862, Lincoln also launched his abortive attempt to convince the border slave states to accept a gradual and compensated emancipation plan coupled with colonization.

tion. The group was led by Edward M. Thomas of Washington, D.C., president of the Anglo-African Institute for the Encouragement of Industry and Art. In this first formal meeting of a president with blacks, Lincoln gave his fullest expression of colonizationist ideology. Although it was a congenial meeting, Lincoln's widely publicized statement could not have been better calculated to raise black indignation. "You and we are different races," said Lincoln. "We have between us a broader difference than exists between almost any other two races. . . . I think your race suffer very greatly, many of them living among us, while ours suffer from your presence." For this reason and others, Lincoln concluded, "we should be separated." The president acknowledged that blacks were suffering "the greatest wrong inflicted on any people," but racial equality, in his view, was impossible in America. "I cannot alter it if I would," Lincoln claimed, "it is a fact about which we all think and feel alike, I and you."[25] No matter how deeply felt, these were harsh and insensitive assertions for the President of the United States to make to the faces of free blacks. He was bluntly denying perhaps their fondest hope; certainly this was the case for Douglass as he read the text of Lincoln's speech back in Rochester.

Lincoln blamed the war on the presence of blacks: "But for your race among us there could not be war, although many men engaged on either side do not care for you one way or the other." The president urged his black visitors to take the lead, to avoid a "selfish view of the case," and to organize expatriation for the good of their race. "It is exceedingly important that we have men at the beginning capable of thinking as white men," he urged, "and not those who have been systematically oppressed." This might reflect Lincoln's awareness that wholesale expatriation of the freedmen would never be possible, but initial successes with groups of prosperous free blacks might sufficiently ease the awful upheaval he anticipated with emancipation. But even to those most amenable to emigration, it must have been painful to be told that they must do so by "thinking like white men." Lincoln concluded his remarks by putting the best possible face on Central America as the site of his colonization project. He told the delegation that he would do everything in his power to make them "equals" to each other in their new land.[26] As always, the de-

25. On the circumstances of the meeting, see Quarles, *Lincoln and the Negro*, 115–16; McPherson (ed.), *Negro's Civil War*, 89–90; Basler (ed.), *Collected Works of Lincoln*, V, 370–72.

26. Basler (ed.), *Collected Works of Lincoln*, V, 372–75.

bate over colonization turned on two very different conceptions of the future of black Americans. To Lincoln, a biracial democracy in America would never be possible. On the other hand, most black intellectuals were flushed with new hopes about a future precisely opposite from that outlined in Lincoln's colonizationist appeal—a future that Lincoln bluntly denied them.

Douglass was outraged at Lincoln's address to the black delegation. In September he reprinted Lincoln's remarks in full and then penned the harshest criticism he ever levied at the president. "Mr. Lincoln assumes the language and arguments of an itinerant Colonization lecturer," charged Douglass, "showing all his inconsistencies, his pride of race and blood, his contempt for Negroes and his canting hypocrisy. How an honest man could creep into such a character as that implied by this address we are not required to show." The black editor repeatedly stressed the "unfairness" of Lincoln's claim that the "mere presence" of blacks had caused the war, and he likened Lincoln's logic to "a horse thief pleading that the existence of the horse is the apology for his theft or a highway man contending that the money in the traveler's pocket is the sole first cause of his robbery." The presence of blacks had not caused the war, contended Douglass; it came of the "cruel and brutal cupidity of those who wish to possess horses, money, and Negroes by means of theft, robbery, and rebellion." Douglass pointed to Lincoln's affirmation of white supremacy, calling him "a genuine representative of American prejudice and Negro hatred." As one who had openly supported the Republican party in 1860, Douglass felt betrayed by Lincoln's stark appeal for colonization. This deep sense of hurt is best illustrated in his reaction to the tone and style of Lincoln's address: "The tone of frankness and benevolence which he assumes in his speech to the colored committee," Douglass contended, "is too thin a mask not to be seen through. The genuine spark of humanity is missing in it, no sincere wish to improve the condition of the oppressed has dictated it. It expresses merely the desire to get rid of them, and reminds one of the politeness with which a man might try to bow out of his house some troublesome creditor or the witness of some old guilt." An angry Douglass now feared that a colonizationist outcome to the war was a real possibility.[27]

27. "The President and His Speeches," DM, September, 1862, in Foner (ed.), Life and Writings, III, 267–70. For a discussion of the developing relationship between Lincoln and Douglass, see Christopher Breiseth, "Lincoln and Frederick Douglass: Another Debate," Illinois State Historical Society Journal, LXVIII (1975), 9–26.

Reaction to Lincoln's colonization address among blacks generally was hostile, and protest meetings were held in several cities across the North. In language rich with patriotism and resolve, a Queens County, New York, gathering lectured Lincoln: "This is our native country; we have as strong attachment naturally to our native hills, valleys, plains, luxuriant forests . . . mighty rivers, and lofty mountains, as any other people." A Philadelphia meeting of blacks assured the president that they still had faith in him but denounced his colonization plan and the country's racial prejudice. The Philadelphians pointed to their own economic and social progress as evidence that white supremacy could be thwarted. "Shall we sacrifice this, leave our homes, forsake our birthplace, and flee to a strange land," they asked, "to appease the anger and prejudice of the traitors now in arms against the Government?" A. P. Smith of Saddle River, New Jersey, wrote an angry reply to Lincoln in which he wondered that even if racial prejudice was as powerful as the president indicated, "must I crush out my cherished hopes and aspirations, abandon my home, and become a pauper to the mean and selfish spirit that oppresses me?" No matter how vast the prejudice or how daunting the prospect of defeating it, many blacks felt deeply wronged by the assumption that their color alone required their removal from America. The debate over colonization always came back to its root: the peculiar American struggle over white supremacy.[28]

Although a diminishing minority, some blacks responded favorably to Lincoln's colonization proposals. What some called "Haitian fever"—a proclivity to leave America for a better chance and a freer atmosphere elsewhere—always survived under the surface of black opinion. By October, 1862, Kansas Senator Samuel Pomeroy, the administration's chief promoter of colonization schemes, claimed he had received 13,700 applications from potential black emigrants. Two months earlier, Pomeroy had issued a widely published appeal, "To the Free Colored People of the United States," describing the advantages and noble purpose of the Chiriqui scheme. The administration's sincere efforts notwithstanding, its Central American colonization

28. The resolutions of the New York and Philadelphia meetings are in Herbert Aptheker (ed.), *A Documentary History of the Negro People in the United States*, (3 vols.; New York, 1968), I, 472–74. Smith's letter is in *DM*, October, 1862. For further black reaction to Lincoln's proposal, see Robert Purvis to Samuel C. Pomeroy, August 28, 1862, in New York *Tribune*, September 20, 1862; George B. Vashon to Abraham Lincoln, reprinted in *DM*, October, 1862. On black reaction generally, see Quarles, *Lincoln and the Negro*, 117–19; James M. McPherson, "Abolitionists and Negro Opposition to Colonization During the Civil War," *Phylon*, XXVI (1965), 395–96.

project crumbled in the fall of 1862. Clearly, some free blacks were anxious to emigrate, but it is not likely that black interest was as substantial as Pomeroy's statistics may indicate.[29]

The resurgence of the colonization issue afforded Douglass the opportunity to discuss racial theory. In essence, his response to the Lincoln proposals of the summer of 1862 was an analysis of American racism. Douglass knew that the colonizationist threat rested on certain assumptions: that white prejudice was unconquerable; that blacks naturally gravitated toward tropical climates and, indeed, might become extinct if they did not; that color was a natural barrier to racial intermarriage; that race determined physical and intellectual aptitude; and that the "character" of the black and white races had determined that they must separate. To Douglass, the debate over colonization was a struggle to refute this scheme of racial determinism.[30]

In September, 1862, Douglass launched a counterattack, insisting that Negro-hating mobs and colonization agents were united by what he called the "satanic spirit of colonization." United by racial theory, mobs provided the "brickbats and pistols," while colonizationists furnished the "arguments and piety." Douglass felt compelled to resist what he called the "miserable philosophy" of the latest colonizationist threat. To the claim that the black man's "nature" had inclined him to servility and hence rendered him unready to compete in a free society, Douglass charged that it was his "color" and not his nature that so troubled colonizationists. He reaffirmed his belief in "a common human nature for all men" and asserted that racial prejudice was just "another proof of man's perverse proclivity to create the causes of his own misery." Climatic racial theory did not impress him either. If colonizationists considered their mission to be a climatic

29. On Pomeroy and black interest, see S. C. Pomeroy to Doolittle, October 20, 1862, in James R. Doolittle Papers, State Historical Society of Wisconsin, Madison, Wisc. (this letter is also a good measure of the depth of Pomeroy's commitment to the project); Quarles, *Lincoln and the Negro*, 122–23; Sheips, "Lincoln and the Chiriqui Colonization Project," 436–38; Beck, "Lincoln and Negro Colonization," 176–78. Douglass reported that a group of blacks in Washington, D.C., had petitioned the government to be colonized in Africa (*DM*, May, 1862). He also received letters from a W. W. Tate, who challenged the editor's position on colonization and argued that it was the best option for blacks (*DM*, July, 1862), and from a John W. Menard of Washington, D.C., who argued that the idea of a "white nationality" could never be overcome in America (*DM*, April, 1863). On positive black response, see Quarles, *Lincoln and the Negro*, 121–23; *DM*, May, 1862.

30. See Fredrickson, *Black Image in the White Mind*, 71–129, 145–52. Some of this reflects an unsophisticated Negrophobia, some of it scientific racism, and some what Fredrickson has called "romantic racialism."

redistribution of the races, Douglass demanded that Caucasians who had emigrated to every continent of the earth be sent back to Europe. To the colonizationists' belief that a "ban of nature" prevented inter-marriage between the races, he pointed to the large mulatto popula-tion in America. "Public opinion, prejudice, condition may prevent intermarriages," he acknowledged, "but the ban of nature does just no such thing." As a mulatto himself, Douglass had spent a good deal of psychological energy seeking his own identity as half-black/half-white, former slave, and American, and he tired easily of the old white fear of "amalgamation." To him, fear of miscegenation always reflected a larger purpose: "Whenever any new villainy is to be perpe-trated," he contended, "or any old one against the Negro perpetuated, the popular prejudice is rallied by a denunciation of amalgamation." Douglass rarely missed an opportunity to ridicule the most vulnera-ble and pernicious aspects of racism. Finally, he responded to the colonizationists' disclaimer of future racial equality by casting the issue in global terms: "If men may not live peaceably together . . . in the same land, they cannot so live on the same continent, and ulti-mately in the same world." If racial heterogeneity could not work in America, where could it? "If the black man cannot find peace from the aggressions of the white race on this continent," Douglass rea-soned, "he will not be likely to find it permanently on any part of the habitable globe. The same base and selfish lust for dominion which would drive us from this country would hunt us from the world."[31]

The analysis of white racial theory was one of the most prevalent themes in Douglass' thought throughout his life. Since at least 1854, he had taken a formal interest in ethnology, the nineteenth-century study of the origins of race. Douglass made strong claims for mono-genesis, the humanity of blacks, and for human equality, and his defense of a single human origin buttressed his moral and optimis-tic view of human nature. It also reinforced his assimilationism and American nationalism. He never wavered in his cardinal be-lief in "the instinctive consciousness of the common brotherhood of man."[32]

31. "The Spirit of Colonization," *DM*, September, 1862, in Foner (ed.), *Life and Writings*, III, 261–65.

32. "The Claims of the Negro Ethnologically Considered," address delivered at Western Reserve College, July 12, 1854, in Foner (ed.), *Life and Writings*, II, 295. In the 1850s Douglass immersed himself in the ethnological origins debate. In the idea of monogenesis—the single origin of humanity—Douglass was defending an unpopular and embattled position. For another illustration of Douglass' ethnological theory, see his speech "The Races," in FD Papers (LC). On Douglass' lifelong critique of white supremacy, as well as his ethnology, see Martin, *Mind*, 109–35, 225–50.

The possibility of a biracial society of equals was a principle Douglass could never concede. If he had, the meaning and purpose of his public life would have been compromised. Instead, he asserted his people's claim to equality in the national as well as the human family. Douglass' response to the colonizationist threat reflected his keen awareness that he faced a powerful form of racial determinism girded by respected scientific theory. The roots of white supremacy ran deep in America, but confident of his own ethnological views and relying on millennial faith and human reason, Douglass believed that the cruel war could tear out those roots.[33]

In September, 1862, through Postmaster General Montgomery Blair, the Lincoln administration tried officially to enlist Douglass' aid in its colonization scheme. Douglass had written a letter of protest to Senator Pomeroy, and Blair sought to demonstrate the black editor's "misapprehension" of the enterprise. Blair assured Douglass that there was "no question of superiority or inferiority involved in the proposed removal." He invoked the reputation of Thomas Jefferson to underscore the idea of racial separation. The minority race, argued Blair, must go elsewhere to imitate the civilization established by the majority race; the propriety of colonization stemmed from "the differences between them . . . , and it seems as obvious to me as it was to . . . the mind of Jefferson that the opinion against which you protest, is the necessary result of indelible differences thus made by the Almighty."[34] Here it was again: colonization theory, gilded by the image of Jefferson, determined by God, driven by white supremacy while claiming otherwise, and callously argued by a member of Lincoln's cabinet.

In his reply, Douglass thanked Blair for the opportunity to assess the colonization issue "more fully than I have yet done." As evidence to refute the climatic theory—that each race had its natural habitat on earth—Douglass pointed to nearly two hundred and fifty years of

33. See Fredrickson, Black Image in the White Mind, 130–64. Douglass never stopped contending that racial prejudice could be conquered. For one of the best wartime examples of this aspect of his thought, see "The Present and Future of the Colored Race in America," 354–55. The claim of multiple racial origins and, therefore, black inferiority, Douglass argued, was merely "the philosophical and ethnological apology for all the hell-black crimes ever committed by the white race against the blacks."

34. The letter to Pomeroy does not survive. Aside from the protest, Douglass had written a letter of introduction to Pomeroy for his son Lewis, who had applied for the emigration project. In what must have been a painful statement, Douglass acknowledged his son's right to "natural, self-moved, spontaneous emigration." Lewis later joined the Union army with the 54th Massachusetts in 1863. See Montgomery Blair to Douglass, September 11, 1862, in Foner (ed.), Life and Writings, III, 281–83.

black residence on North American soil. Blacks had withstood all the rigors of the temperate zone and rapidly increased as a race. "If any people can ever become acclimatized," he declared, "I think the Negro can claim to be so in this country." The theory of racial climatic zones had gained wide acceptance in antebellum America, especially from the work of the great Harvard biologist Louis Agassiz, and application of Agassiz's notion of "zoological provinces" for animal and plant life to the races of man gained almost universal support. Hence, colonizationists found much scientific support for their vision of North America as a Caucasian preserve. To Douglass, scientific racial theory never lacked political content, and he considered all discussion of "confining different varieties of men to different belts of the earth's surface" to be "chimerical in the extreme."[35]

To Blair's assertions that "differences" between the races determined that they could not live peacefully in the same society, Douglass reminded him that it was whites who wished so vehemently to get rid of blacks and not the reverse. Douglass again laid claim for blacks to American nationality and in so doing struck another of the deepest chords in colonizationist thinking. As George Fredrickson has shown, the Civil War brought a new urgency to the idea of American nationality. What Fredrickson calls a "militant racial nationalism" was strongly reasserted during the sectional crisis by Negrophobes and Republican Free-Soilers alike. No less a Republican stalwart than William H. Seward had expressed this racial vision of American nationality in 1860: "The great fact is now fully realized that the African race here is a foreign and feeble element, . . . incapable of assimilation . . . and it is a pitiful exotic unnecessarily transplanted into our fields, and which it is unprofitable to cultivate at the cost of the desolation of the native vineyard." Although some Republicans resorted to this kind of rhetoric under proddings from Democrats and southerners who accused them of favoring racial equality, there is also no doubt that it represented a genuine strain in their ideology. The American republic, most whites believed, would remain a white man's domain.[36]

Douglass challenged this white nationalism. In his view, to reject colonization was to embrace American nationality, and he insisted to

35. Douglass to Montgomery Blair, September 16, 1862, in *ibid.*, 283, 285. On Agassiz and the theory of climatic zones, see Fredrickson, *Black Image in the White Mind*, 137–45.

36. Seward's campaign speech was in Detroit, September, 1860, quoted in Fredrickson, *Black Image in the White Mind*, 141. On Republican attitudes toward race and colonization, see Sewell, *Ballots for Freedom*, 321–36; E. Foner, *Free Soil*, 261–300.

Blair that blacks and whites could live "under the same government." "We have readily adapted ourselves to your civilization," he continued. "We are Americans by birth and education, and have a preference for American institutions as against those of any other country. That we should wish to remain here is natural to us and creditable to you." Douglass and the Republicans came to a similar view of the future of slavery in America. But on the future racial character of an American nation, they were as yet far apart.[37]

Douglass' final objections to Blair's entreaty related to the effects of colonization. Colonizationist ideology, he claimed, was too easily proslavery theory in disguise. "The argument that makes it necessary for the black man to go away when he is free," wrote Douglass, "equally makes it necessary for him to be a slave while he remains here." Although this connection may not have been entirely fair to the Republicans, it reflects Douglass' broadest sense of the impact of colonizationist thinking. "Slavery has a lease on life given it by colonization," he maintained. "The whole scheme becomes an opiate to the troubled conscience of the nation and barricades . . . the natural course of freedom to the slave." Douglass insisted that slavery, racism, and future black equality be discussed as a single question, to be settled on American soil within American institutions. He ended his letter to Blair with the theme of national regeneration, claiming confidently that out of "this terrible baptism of blood and fire through which our nation is passing and into which it has been plunged, not as has been most cruelly affirmed, because of the presence of men of color in the land, but by malignant . . . vices, nursed into power . . . at the poisoned breast of slavery, it will come at last, renewed in its health, purified in its spirit freed from slavery, vastly greater and higher than it ever was before in all the elements of advancing civilization."[38]

Douglass' best answer to colonization was to reassert his people's claim to American nationality. For forty years before the war, blacks and abolitionists had engaged white colonizationists on a significant but often symbolic level. Colonizationists—despite the obvious reality of the Liberian experiment—often treated blacks as a symbolic presence in America, a subject of social criticism that might be wished away in conventions or by fund-raising.[39] But in 1862 all

37. Douglass to Montgomery Blair, September 16, 1862, in Foner (ed.), *Life and Writings*, III, 286.
38. *Ibid.*, 288–90.
39. On the way benevolent reformers saw blacks as symbols, see Fredrickson, *Black Image in the White Mind*, 109.

discussion of colonization took place in an urgent, almost desperate atmosphere. For blacks themselves, the forty-year confrontation with colonization had served by and large to unify them and force a realization of their dual identity as blacks and Americans. The long debate over expatriation was a struggle by blacks to preserve an autonomous self-image while resisting the white colonizationist image of them, to define themselves not as white Americans defined them. In the midst of the Civil War, Douglass led this struggle against the last hurrah of colonizationist ideas.

In his second annual message to Congress on December 1, 1862, Lincoln reaffirmed his commitment to voluntary black expatriation, but he did so in a new tone. Whether colonization plans worked or not, Lincoln urged his countrymen to prepare for the continued presence of the free black population. He denied that the freedmen threatened white labor or that they would swarm out of the South into northern communities. Clearly, Lincoln still hoped that "deportation" would be part of the process, but the second annual message was primarily his attempt to prepare the way for the universal emancipation policy he was about to adopt. He seemed acutely aware that he was helping to usher in the "revolutionary" result he had sought to avoid.[40]

Largely because of the opposition of Central American governments, but also because of emancipation and the enlistment of black soldiers, the Lincoln administration's colonization schemes ground to a halt by early 1863. This abandonment of colonization did not occur, though, before Lincoln approved the ill-fated Ile-à-Vache project, an attempt to colonize blacks on an island off the south coast of Haiti. Of 453 black emigrants landed on the island by April, 1863, nearly 100 would die of starvation and disease in less than one year. Lincoln was compelled to dispatch a transport in February, 1864, to bring back the survivors.[41]

That after 1862 a racial *modus vivendi* would be forged by means other than colonization does not obviate the fact that it was the desired policy of Lincoln and the North. Because it was unrealistic

---

40. Basler (ed.), *Collected Works of Lincoln*, V, 534–37.

41. Beck, "Lincoln and Negro Colonization," 178–83; Sheips, "Lincoln and the Chiriqui Colonization Project," 441–45, 450–52; Payne, "Lincoln's Caribbean Colonization Plan," 65–67. The Chiriqui project had been abandoned in October, 1862. Costa Rica, San Salvador, Honduras, and Guatemala had strenuously objected to the idea of a U.S. colony on their soil, inhabited by thousands of freed slaves. On the Ile-à-Vache project, see McPherson (ed.), *Negro's Civil War*, 96–97; Shick, *Behold the Promised Land*, 130–31; Voegeli, *Free But Not Equal*, 97–98.

and disastrous in practice makes the enduring nature of colonizationist ideology all the more remarkable. Its impracticality in no way changed the moral message or the psychological impact for blacks, and even if we concede historian Don Fehrenbacher's argument that Lincoln used colonization as a means of "conditioning the public mind for the day of jubilee," it does not alter the message sent to blacks. Free black leaders like Douglass could hardly avoid the conclusion that even if the colonization schemes were not realistic, a "safety valve . . . for white racism" had been purchased with the dignity and hopes of black people.[42]

To understand fully the importance of colonization during the Civil War we must look at the nature of the black reaction and not merely at the motives of Lincoln and his associates. The complexity of that reaction surpassed the understanding of the beleaguered president and most of his generation. White leaders would not easily give up their preferred solution to America's racial dilemma; led by Douglass, black leaders would not give in to a solution that denied their identity and robbed their future. Events larger than both would settle this question for them and render a colonizationist war impossible.

42. Fredrickson, *Black Image in the White Mind*, 151; Shick, *Behold the Promised Land*, 128–30; Fehrenbacher, "Only His Stepchildren," 308.

7/DOUGLASS AND THE MEANING OF THE BLACK SOLDIER

All this is the universal Southern panorama; but five minutes walk beyond the hovels and the live oaks will bring one to something so un-Southern that the whole Southern coast at this moment trembles at the suggestion of such a thing,—the camp of a regiment of freed slaves.
—Thomas Wentworth Higginson, near Beaufort, South Carolina, November 27, 1862

NOTHING SO TYPIFIED the antislavery character of the Civil War as the black soldier. In the last two years of the war 179,000 blacks joined the Federal army and navy, providing 10 percent of all who served the Union cause. Indeed, the participation of the black soldier was perhaps the most revolutionary feature of the Civil War. Thousands of ex-slaves strutting down southern roads to do battle with their former masters was a sight that at the outset of the war few Americans expected to see, nor did many expect to witness a crack black regiment, recruited in northern communities by abolitionists, march through Boston Common to the cheers of twenty thousand onlookers. By 1863 the war to save the Union had irrevocably become as well the war to free the slaves, and black soldiers came to symbolize their people's struggle for freedom, a recognition of their humanity, the rights of citizenship, and a sense of belonging in a new nation.

From the very beginning of the conflict, Frederick Douglass argued for black military participation. An "abolition war" awaited only the will on the part of the northern people to destroy slavery and put blacks in uniform. As agitator, recruiter, and spokesman, Douglass gave the black soldier immense significance. The service of blacks in the Union forces came to represent both public and private meanings in Douglass' wartime thought.

Immediately following Abraham Lincoln's call for volunteers in April, 1861, blacks in cities across the North began to mobilize militia units, and thousands of black men demonstrated their readiness if the government would have them. From his editor's desk in Rochester, Douglass joined the chorus calling for black enlistment. He urged his people "to drink as deeply into the martial spirit of the times as possible; organize . . . companies, purchase arms . . . and learn how to use them." Douglass scoffed at Lincoln's assurances to the South that the war would not threaten slavery; he saw the conflict immediately as a struggle over slavery and insisted on two radical propositions: emancipation and black enlistment. "Let the slaves and free colored people be called into service," Douglass declared, "and formed into a liberating army, to march into the South and raise the banner of Emancipation." Douglass claimed that ten thousand black recruits could be raised in thirty days. He also recognized the symbolic importance of black regiments for his people: "The slaves would learn more as to the nature of the conflict from . . . one such regiment," he argued, "than from a thousand preachers."[1]

But black soldiers were officially excluded from Union forces for at least the first year and one-half of the war, and by September, 1861, Douglass was furious over the exclusion policy. He called it a "spectacle of blind, unreasoning prejudice" and accused the Lincoln administration of fighting with its "white hand" while allowing its "black hand to remain tied." The optimism with which many blacks met the outbreak of the Civil War ripened them for great disappointment over the denial of black enlistment. Most northern whites did not accept the idea of black soldiers until the preservation of the Union required an assault on slavery itself, and, the impatience of abolitionists and the bitterness of black leaders notwithstanding, this would not occur until well into the second year of the war.[2]

Not all blacks responded to the war with unqualified enthusiasm. The *Christian Recorder*, the African Methodist Episcopal Church newspaper in Philadelphia, dissented from Douglass' call for black troops. "To offer ourselves now," wrote its editor Elisha Weaver, "is to abandon *self-respect* and invite insult." Blacks should not fight, Weaver contended, in a war where "not only our citizenship, but our common humanity is denied." The *Christian Recorder* interpreted the war as a crisis among conflicting factions of white men and therefore not a black man's struggle. In the *Anglo-African*, a black signing himself "R. H. V." denounced the call to arms: "No regiments of black troops should leave their bodies to rot upon the battlefield beneath a Southern sun," he argued, "to conquer a peace based upon the perpetuity of human bondage." Distrust for the motives of the

1. "Black Regiments Proposed," *DM*, May, 1861, in Foner (ed.), *Life and Writings*, III, 97. "How to End the War," in *ibid.*, III, 94–95. On initial black response to the war and the prospect of volunteering, see Benjamin Quarles, *The Negro in the Civil War* (New York, 1953), 24–29; Dudley T. Cornish, *The Sable Arm: Negro Troops in the Union Army, 1861–1865* (New York, 1956), 2–3, 6–7; McPherson, *Struggle for Equality*, 192–93.

2. "How to End the War"; "Fighting Rebels with Only One Hand," *DM*, September, 1861, in Foner (ed.), *Life and Writings*, III, 152–53.

Union war effort marked these and other negative reactions to black enlistment. Although this early resistance to soldiering among blacks was more the exception than the rule, it reflected a lack of confidence that the war enveloping the country in 1861 could be transformed into an abolitionist crusade. Some blacks felt no deep attachment to the Union; some simply required more certainty before offering to serve. Most probably were both optimistic and cautious.[3]

In the North, free blacks lived circumscribed lives; they worked primarily as menial laborers and in most states were denied all political and legal rights. Black exclusion laws passed by the federal and state governments during the early national period included a federal law dating from 1792 restricting militia participation to white male citizens. As late as 1859 Massachusetts Governor Nathaniel P. Banks vetoed a law that would have included blacks in that state's militia. A society that systematically denied racial equality was not about to convert overnight to allow blacks to bear arms for the government. But part of the irony of America's racial history was that blacks had fought in all of this country's major wars. Abolitionists of both colors continually emphasized the black role in the American Revolution, the War of 1812, and the Mexican War.[4]

Until late 1862 the prospect of black enlistment was linked to an evolving policy of emancipation. Repeatedly in 1861 the Lincoln administration sought to avoid war measures that would lead to wholesale emancipation. Ever sensitive to keeping the four border slave states in the Union, Lincoln renewed his pledge not to interfere with slavery in his July 4 message to Congress. On August 30, General John C. Frémont, acting without authorization from the government but with tumultuous approval among abolitionists, proclaimed emancipation for the state of Missouri. Lincoln promptly revoked it. A

---

3. *Christian Recorder*, April 20, 27, 1861; *Anglo-African Magazine*, August 24, 1861, September 28, 1861. For further expressions of distrust, see *Christian Recorder*, October 12, 1861, July 26, 1862, February 14, 1863. On the *Recorder's* rejection of black enlistment, see Clarence E. Walker, *A Rock in a Weary Land: The African Methodist Episcopal Church During the Civil War and Reconstruction* (Baton Rouge, 1982), 31–35. For numerous expressions of sentiment for and against black enlistment in 1861, see McPherson (ed.), *Negro's Civil War*, 29–36.

4. Litwack, *North of Slavery*, 31–32, 64–186; Ira Berlin (ed.), *Freedom: A Documentary History of Emancipation, 1861–1867*, Series 2, *The Black Military Experience* (New York, 1982), 5–6; Mary Frances Berry, *Military Necessity and Civil Rights Policy: Black Citizenship and the Constitution, 1861–1868* (Port Washington, N.Y., 1977), 19–28; McPherson, *Struggle for Equality*, 193.

certain inevitability, though, moved the issue of emancipation forward. At Fortress Monroe, Virginia, in May, 1861, the ambitious politician-general Benjamin F. Butler declared the slaves who entered his lines "contraband of war." The idea of slaves as confiscated enemy property caught on. In early August, striking a balance between legality and military necessity, Congress passed the First Confiscation Act, allowing for the seizure of all Confederate property used to aid the war effort. Although not technically freed by this law, the slaves of rebel masters came under its purview, and thus a process toward black freedom as a military necessity took root. In Virginia, the Mississippi Valley, and along the coast of the Carolinas, wherever Union armies gained ground, the institution of slavery began to crumble. Initial consideration of blacks as soldiers must be seen in this context: a war that, if waged long enough, would have to crush southern society in order to preserve the Union.[5]

The refusal to use black troops and the lack of hostility to slavery discouraged those who saw the coming of the day of jubilee in the guns of 1861. Like other abolitionists, Douglass denounced Lincoln's revocation of Frémont's proclamation. In an editorial, "Frémont and Freedom—Lincoln and Slavery," Douglass argued that the general had been deliberately sacrificed to appease the proslavery sentiment of the border states. At least in his rhetoric, Douglass never seemed fully to appreciate the political importance of the border states, and he was untrammeled by Lincoln's concern over them. He called them the "mill-stone about the neck of the Government, . . . their so-called loyalty . . . the very best shield to the treason of the cotton states." Throughout the autumn of 1861 he urged his readers to keep faith, and he made a heroic figure of Frémont and an abolitionist symbol of the general's emancipation decree. By the end of the year, though, his confidence in the Union government waned: "Up to this hour," he declared, "nothing of a straightforward, tangible and substantial indication of the abolition of slavery has come from Congress, Cabinet, or Camp." He counseled hope in the "powers above" and "events greater" than the government. His firmest hope, he continually reminded his readers, was that "necessity is master of all."

5. Basler (ed.), *Collected Works of Lincoln*, IV, 439. On the abolitionists' reaction to Frémont, see McPherson, *Struggle for Equality*, 72–74. On Butler and the evolution of emancipation as a "military necessity," see Louis S. Gerteis, *From Contraband to Freedman: Federal Policy Toward Southern Blacks, 1861–1865* (Westport, Conn., 1973), 11–32.

During the months in which emancipation evolved haltingly into a war necessity, Douglass waited impatiently and worked for the same result.[6]

Douglass was not quite accurate in his claim that nothing had been done toward the abolition of slavery by Lincoln's cabinet. In December, 1861, Secretary of War Simon Cameron recommended to Congress that the slaves of rebel masters not only be freed but armed when they entered Union lines. President Lincoln rescinded Cameron's recommendation, but not before it reached the press and public. As the numbers of "contrabands" grew nearly out of control and as the war itself intensified in the spring of 1862, interest in black enlistment reached new levels. In May, in the Sea Islands of South Carolina, General David Hunter made the first attempt to organize a black regiment. As commander of the Union occupation forces in the Sea Islands, Hunter had been empowered in vague terms to organize the large slave population, so he boldly issued a short proclamation declaring all slaves in South Carolina, Georgia, and Florida free. He also ordered all able-bodied black males between the ages of eighteen and forty-five to report to his headquarters on Hilton Head Island for enlistment in the army. Suspicious of their would-be liberators and ever-mindful of their old masters' warnings of Yankee intentions to deport them to Cuba, most blacks refused Hunter's order, and the general quickly responded with an impressment policy that forced five hundred men in one day to leave their wives and families, many at the point of bayonet. The abolitionist missionaries and teachers who had come to help the Sea Island blacks' transition from slavery to freedom were outraged at Hunter's tactics. The federal government neither disbanded nor recognized this first black regiment. Hunter kept it in training until early August, 1862, but after repeated failures to obtain pay and supplies from the War Department, he abandoned all but one company. The first attempt to enlist black soldiers ended in failure and distrust, but the ill-advised methods of an antislavery general notwithstanding, the groundwork had been laid for larger efforts.[7]

Throughout the summer of 1862, events rapidly made northern

6. "Frémont and Freedom—Lincoln and Slavery"; "General Frémont's Proclamation to the Rebels of Missouri," *DM*, October, 1861; "The Slave Power Still Omnipotent at Washington," *DM*, January, 1862; "Signs of the Times," all in Foner (ed.), *Life and Writings*, III, 174–76, 161, 185, 171, respectively.

7. McPherson, *Struggle for Equality*, 194–96; Willie Lee Rose, *Rehearsal for Reconstruction: The Port Royal Experiment* (New York, 1964), 144–48, 187–90; Cornish, *Sable Arm*, 40–53.

public opinion more favorable to the use of black troops. In the wake of General George B. McClellan's unsuccessful Peninsular Campaign, Congress acted in July to authorize black enlistment. The Second Confiscation Act empowered Lincoln to "employ . . . persons of African descent . . . for the suppression of the rebellion," and another enactment repealed the 1792 law barring blacks from militia service. War weariness, declining white manpower, and the military situation caused the Lincoln administration to change its course on black enlistment. On August 25, Secretary of War Edwin Stanton authorized General Rufus Saxton, military governor of the South Carolina Sea Islands, to raise five regiments of black infantry. In November, the brilliant Massachusetts abolitionist Thomas Wentworth Higginson went to the Sea Islands as the commander of the officially sanctioned and much-heralded First South Carolina Volunteers. In 1863, Higginson's famous regiment would play an important role in military actions along the Carolina coast, as well as in the growing acceptance of a revolutionary idea: ex-slaves fighting in the United States Army to conquer the lands of their former masters.[8]

Douglass was an intensely interested observer of this evolving policy toward black troops, and he combined his agitation for black enlistment with a wide-ranging discussion of the *loyalty* of his people. He made effective use of the idea of black loyalty, whether speaking in his role as a black abolitionist or that of a war propagandist. "I believe up to this time," Douglass told a Philadelphia audience in January, 1862, "no man . . . has been able to cast the shadow of a doubt upon the loyalty and patriotism of the free colored people in this the hour of the nation's trial and danger." But he was bitter that the government had spurned the services of black loyalists at this early stage in the war: "The Washington Government wants men for its army," he said, "but thus far, it has not had the boldness to recognize the manhood of the race to which I belong." Loyal sentiment rapidly turned sour when the right to fight was denied. "I do not wish to say ought against our Government . . . ," Douglass proclaimed, "but I owe it to my race, in view of the cruel aspersions cast upon it, to affirm that, in denying them the privileges to fight for their country, they have been most deeply and grievously wronged."[9] Douglass insisted on full acceptance of black patriotism.

8. *Statutes At Large of the United States of America*, XII, 589–92, 597–600. On the recruitment of the first regiments in South Carolina, see Berlin (ed.), *Freedom*, Ser. 2, pp. 5–7; Thomas Wentworth Higginson, *Army Life in a Black Regiment* (New York, 1969), 32–77.
9. "The Reasons for Our Troubles," 196, 204–205.

A month later in a speech in Boston, Douglass tried to express the extent of his own loyalty. "I allow no man to exceed me in the desire for the safety and welfare of this country," he told the Emancipation League. Again, he linked loyalty with the blacks' desire for military service. Ignoring the opposition to enlistment among some blacks, Douglass boasted that he and his people had exhibited more than their share of patriotism, but their "most ardent desire to serve the cause" had been ignored. "Colored men were good enough to fight under Washington," complained the orator. "They are not good enough to fight under McClellan."[10] The best way Douglass knew to agitate for black enlistment was to assert the loyalty of potential black soldiers.

Douglass was fond of stressing the perseverance of black loyalty. "The Negro is the veritable Mark Tapley of this country," declared the editor in July, 1862, referring to the amiable character in Charles Dickens' *Martin Chuzzlewit*. Despite "every possible discouragement," argued Douglass, blacks remained patriotic. "Repelled with insult," they remained determined to serve. Rhetorically, Douglass made much of the heroic southern slave who spied on the enemy, entered Union lines with valuable information, and led daring raids and escapes. When the history of the war was written, he declared, it would show that "the loyal army found no friends at the South so faithful, active, and daring in their efforts to sustain the Government as the Negroes." He cheered the heroics of Robert Smalls, the black South Carolina sea pilot who spirited the Confederate steamer *Planter* out of Charleston harbor to the safety of a Federal fleet, and he hailed the first black troops organized in South Carolina and Louisiana. Blacks in North and South, he maintained, "seem determined to deserve credit whether they get it or not." Douglass spoke for a people he believed ready to serve in any capacity: "with a pickaxe if he cannot with a pistol, a spade if he cannot with a sword."[11] Douglass knew that little satisfaction would come from wielding spades instead of swords, but the idea of the black soldier in full uniform with musket in hand was kept alive through a combination of humility and persistence.

Loyalty is a tortured concept in time of war. It often serves the ends of conservative nationalism while causing inherent conflict over dis-

10. "The Future of the Negro People of the Slave States," speech delivered before the Emancipation League, Boston, February 12, 1862, *DM*, March, 1862, in Foner (ed.), *Life and Writings*, III, 213.

11. "Services of Colored Men," *DM*, July, 1862, in *ibid.*, 234–35.

sent and individual liberty.[12] For Douglass, loyalty was both an ideal and a pragmatic device. The Civil War, which offered the first opportunity for blacks to demonstrate their birthright and their American nationalism, provided an opening wedge through which he might realistically claim American citizenship for his people. A yearning to belong might be combined with the right to fight in a struggle that blacks could view as their very own. Of course, not all the thousands of blacks who would later serve in the Union forces necessarily viewed the question of loyalty in Douglass' grand terms. Many would not require the war rhetoric of a black orator in order to enlist; their motives would be as complex or practical as those of any other group of soldiers. But many would need to be inspired by the call to arms of black recruiters. In 1861–62, however, the task was not only to convince the black soldier to come forth; it was also to persuade white northerners to fight a war against slavery with the aid of their black brothers.

To this end Douglass used the issue of loyalty, defining *true* loyalty narrowly by equating it with abolitionist sentiment. There were two conflicting kinds of loyalists to the Union cause, Douglass maintained. One group was "for putting down the rebellion if that can be done by . . . force alone, and without abolishing slavery," while the other was "for putting down the rebellion by putting down slavery upon every rod of earth which shall be made sacred by the footprints of a single loyal soldier." To be truly "loyal," Douglass held, was to acknowledge slavery as the cause and abolition the remedy of the conflict. "Our enemies are those of our own household," Douglass announced in February, 1862, striking a note he would repeat many times. His own loyalty to the Union was genuine, though tempered by his radical abolitionism. He knew all too well that a person could be loyal to the Union without being against slavery, but the war made this a distinction he no longer had to accept, and one he rarely recognized.[13]

As the war progressed and took on an antislavery character, Douglass stepped up his rhetoric about loyalty. With the prospect of emancipation and black enlistment imminent, he could more starkly separate his two conceptions of Union loyalty. At times, his language took on a conservative nationalistic tone, not unlike many other northern

---

12. Fredrickson, *Inner Civil War*, 130–50.
13. "The Future of the Negro People of the Slave States," 214. In "The Slave Power Still Omnipotent at Washington," Douglass calls the group who would preserve slavery and the Union "simply traitors in the disguise of loyalty."

opinion leaders. "If this Government of ours fails to subdue the rebel States, and to cause its authority to be respected over the whole country," Douglass asserted in November, 1862, "it will not be because the South is united and strong, but because the North is divided and weak." In words no black leader could have uttered before emancipation and black enlistment were likely, Douglass called for "liberty and country first, everything else afterward."[14] For the first time, black freedom and equality were hitched to the nation's survival. Douglass' loyalty was to a promised America, a nation he now believed the war could produce.

During the first several months of 1863, great joy swept through abolitionist ranks because of the Emancipation Proclamation, but because of military setbacks and war weariness, it was also a dark time for the Union cause. Dissatisfaction with the war spread in the North, especially in the Midwest. Peace Democrats gained an increasing audience, and Copperheads were being arrested in alarming numbers. Douglass joined this debate over internal dissent. In February, after a month-long, two-thousand-mile speaking tour of jubilee meetings, he confessed that the country generally was demoralized. He denounced the "frightful growth of disloyalty in the northern states" and urged that it be rooted out. Calling for the repression of dissent and untroubled by Lincoln's suppression of civil liberties, Douglass demanded "sufficient nerve and intelligence" in the government "to weed out the army, and cleanse it of all disloyalty." He declared that he might be hopeless about northern morale were it not for the decisive turn toward emancipation—a war against slavery would weaken the morale of the South as no other measure could. But to Douglass, "the most hopeful sign of the times" was the "growing disposition to employ the black men of the country in the effort to save it from division and ruin." Black soldiers were Douglass' answer to war weariness. They were the freshest and, to him, the most effective resource the North could employ against the South.[15]

The timing of these two phenomena—northern demoralization and black enlistment—Douglass found significant. Official recruit-

14. "The Slave Democracy Again in the Field," *DM*, November, 1862, in Foner (ed.), *Life and Writings*, III, 295–96. For the conservative opinion leaders and the doctrine of loyalty, see Fredrickson, *Inner Civil War*, 135–46.

15. Wood Gray, *The Hidden Civil War: The Story of the Copperheads* (New York, 1942), chap. 6; Voegeli, *Free But Not Equal*, 26, 56, 127–28; Frank L. Klement, *The Copperheads in the Middle West* (Chicago, 1960); "Condition of the Country," *DM*, February, 1863, in Foner (ed.), *Life and Writings*, III, 314–16.

ing of black troops began in the spring of 1863. Meanwhile, increasing dissatisfaction with the war made northerners more favorable toward letting black men fight. The more desperate the military situation, the more pliant common northerners became to the revolutionary strokes of emancipation and arming blacks. The Conscription Act of March, 1863, by subjecting the mass of white northerners to the draft, also created a greater willingness to use black soldiers—that blacks could "stop a bullet as well as any white man" became a common attitude in the North. Moreover, the rise of the Copperheads gave a black spokesman like Douglass an effective contrast for his assertion of black loyalty. Black people who "did not cease to love their country, though rudely dealt by" and who were "waiting to be honorably invited forward" compared well with Copperheads, whom Douglass defined simply as "men who hate the Negro more than they love their country."[16] Thus could Douglass make his authoritarian appeals to loyalty and nationalism.

Although he never espoused the "divine right" doctrine of government authority held by many conservative northern intellectuals, Douglass did believe the government had earned black allegiance. The "government" was now something precious and "rebellion" against it a heinous act; abolition and black citizenship depended upon its preservation. In his famous broadside "Men of Color to Arms!" written in March, 1863, Douglass tried to make this message clear to his fellow blacks. "I urge you to fly to arms," he pleaded, "and smite with death the power that would bury the government and your liberty in the same hopeless grave." A reverence for authority and hostility to dissent are natural results of war, but demands for loyalty rarely coexist with appeals to the right of revolution. From Douglass' perspective, however, blacks could demonstrate allegiance to country as well as make revolution against the old order. The black soldier was the embodiment of both themes.[17]

In 1863, along with several other black leaders and abolitionists, Douglass threw himself into the recruiting of black troops. He thrilled at the opportunity to make his people warriors. Language had always been the primary means by which he could vent his rage against slavery and racism, but now he could convert rhetoric into

16. *Ibid.*, 316.
17. "Men of Color to Arms!" March 21, 1863, in *ibid.*, 318. On the "divine right" doctrine of loyalty, see Fredrickson, *Inner Civil War*, 136–46.

action and apply his literary and oratorical skills to the specific purpose of recruiting black men to make war on slaveholders. Recruiting would become Douglass' own means of active service.

Massachusetts led the way in the cause of black enlistment. Its governor, John Andrew, was a staunch antislavery Republican and worked vigorously to convince the Lincoln administration to allow him to mobilize black troops. In January, 1863, he received authorization from Secretary of War Stanton to recruit a regiment. Stanton promised equal pay and treatment for black soldiers but denied Andrew's request for black commissioned officers. Although Stanton's promise would not be kept and the denial of officer's rank caused deep resentments, the recruiting process began for the famous 54th Massachusetts Infantry Regiment. The Massachusetts legislature appropriated funds to pay recruiters and transport troops, and Andrew called on the wealthy Boston abolitionist, George Luther Stearns, to direct the recruiting. For the remainder of the war Stearns devoted himself and a fair portion of his own money to the cause of black enlistment across the North and in the border states. Shortly after joining Stearns's corps of recruiters, Douglass remarked that Massachusetts was "not only the most direct way to the heart of our slaveholding rebellion, but she is the colored man's way to . . . political and civil liberty." An antislavery state had opened the door to freedom and dignity; Douglass' task was to convince black men to march through it.[18]

Stearns quickly established recruiting posts all across the North and enlisted as agents other black leaders such as Charles Lenox Remond, John Mercer Langston, William Wells Brown, Henry Highland Garnet, and Martin R. Delany. Douglass first met with Stearns in late February; within days he issued "Men of Color to Arms!" and began barnstorming the towns of western and upstate New York. In April he traveled to New York City and Philadelphia to speak at large recruiting meetings. Douglass pledged to raise one company for the new regiment, and two of his sons, Charles and Lewis, were his first recruits. He had traveled this lecture circuit many times before, but never with such a purpose. In town after town, the black orator appealed to young blacks to join up. By mid-April Douglass had sent more than one hundred men off to Readville, Massachusetts, the training site of the 54th.[19]

18. "Massachusetts," *DM*, April, 1863. On the role of Massachusetts and Stearns's organization of recruiters, see McPherson, *Struggle for Equality*, 202–206.

19. The frantic activity of the recruiting process is illustrated in George Stearns to Douglass, March 24, 1863, in FD Papers (LC); "Movers," *DM*, April, 1863. Stearns paid

It is a telling scene, indeed, to imagine Frederick Douglass standing before gatherings of blacks, exhorting his people to grasp the opportunity to fight. His listeners were wary and sometimes openly distrustful—would a black soldier really be treated fairly in the Union army? At times, though, Douglass' appeals to patriotism and self-interest must have been irresistible. At the end of some of his speeches he broke into song and led the assembled in a rendition of "John Brown's Body." He recruited twenty-five men in Syracuse, and twenty-three more followed him away from his lectures in Glen Falls, Little Falls, and Canajoharie. But in other places he was less successful—the war had caused full employment, even among blacks, in many northern communities. Privately, Douglass admitted to some initial "hesitation" about black enlistment due to the denial of officer's status, but for the moment, he told Gerrit Smith, blacks "should hail the opportunity of getting on the United States uniform as a very great advance." Publicly, Douglass counseled "Action! Action! not criticism." "Words are now useful only as they stimulate to blows," he stated in "Men of Color to Arms!"[20]

Douglass had clearly found the most meaningful use for war rhetoric, and at every stop he offered his potential volunteers an elaborate list of reasons why they should enlist. Some were pragmatic; some stirred the soul and gave meaning to the war as nothing else could. Douglass urged enlistment for the following practical ends: self-defense through learning the "use of arms"; self-respect by proving the manhood and courage of black people; self-involvement by controlling their own destiny and making their own history; and finally—perhaps the ultimate act of self-interest—retribution against slaveholders. In Douglass' view, these ends were tied to larger and nobler purposes. He encouraged blacks to join "for your own sake," but always with an eye on the "more inviting, ennobling, and soul enlarging work . . . of making one of the glorious band who shall carry liberty to your enslaved people."[21]

Letters he received from the front in 1863 must have encouraged Douglass as a recruiter. A George Evans wrote to him in June asking for a recommendation to Governor Andrew for a commission as lieu-

---

Douglass' expenses at ten dollars per week. This was less than Douglass believed his services were worth, and, although he raised no public objection, he did complain privately. See Douglass to Smith, March 6, 1863, in Gerrit Smith Papers; Smith to Douglass, March 10, 1863, in FD Papers (LC).

20. *DM*, April, 1863; "Men of Color to Arms!" 318.
21. "Why Should a Colored Man Enlist?" *DM*, April, 1863, in *ibid.*, 340–44.

tenant in the newly organized black 55th Massachusetts Infantry Regiment. Describing the situation in Virginia in that pivotal summer of the war, Evans wondered about "the future of the immense multitudes of the flying fugitive slaves . . . thronging the roads with their bundles upon their heads not knowing which way to go." Evans observed many slaves being sent south, thousands "throwing up rifle pits—and building fortifications for the rebels," and still more "swallowed up in death" by the contending armies. Evans described this scene as "an amazing subject for our thoughts." Douglass, no doubt, must have agreed.[22]

As a war propagandist, Douglass had done more than his part to create the hated enemy. The war provided him ample opportunity to vent his own lifelong rage against slaveholders, and now he was inviting younger black men to do the work of slaying them. In a recruiting speech at New York City in late April, Douglass supplied a combination of nationalistic, noble, and pragmatic motives, but he ended with a direct appeal for vengeance against slaveholders. "Retribution," cried Douglass, was what blacks "owe to the slaveholders." The long-awaited chance had arrived: "Now the government has given authority to . . . black men," he concluded, "to shoulder a musket and go down and kill white rebels." Douglass understood that the path to glory was served by vengeful as well as noble aims. Like any clever propagandist, he kept his image of the enemy simple, never bothering to acknowledge that most southern soldiers were non-slaveholders.[23] Through the biting language of war rhetoric, he could exploit a legitimate means to settle a personal score.

To Douglass, a compelling reason for enlistment was the black soldier's capacity to secure the rights of citizenship. Through military participation blacks could finally have their nationality recognized, command respect, and guarantee their liberty; they could belong as never before. "To fight for the Government in this tremendous war," Douglass claimed, "is . . . to fight for nationality and for a place with all other classes of our fellow citizens." He tried to sow the deepest seeds of nationalism in his recruits by linking black patriots of the Civil War with their white counterparts in the American Revolution: "The white man's soul was tried in 1776," wrote the zealous re-

22. George Evans to Douglass, First Mass. Light Artillery, Army of the Potomac, on the Rappahannock, Virginia, June 6, 1863, in FD Papers (LC).

23. "Great Meeting at Shiloh Church," *DM*, July, 1863. This meeting took place on April 27 and was presided over by Henry Highland Garnet. On Douglass' hatred of southern whites and his need for retribution, see my discussion in chapter 4, and Davis, *Leadership, Love, and Aggression,* 26–58, 74, 79, 90–91.

cruiter, "the black man's is tried in 1863. The first stood the test, and is received as genuine—so may the last." Douglass promised his charges that their sacrifice would pay the greatest dividends. Pleading with them to have faith, he contended that once a black man could "get upon his person the brass letters U.S. . . . , an eagle on his button, and a musket on his shoulder, and bullets in his pocket, there is no power on earth . . . which can deny that he has earned the right of citizenship in the United States." Douglass was eager to rush as many black men into uniform as possible. To him they were the symbol of an apocalyptic war, liberating warriors who alone made suffering meaningful, a physical force that gave reality to millennial hopes.[24]

But Douglass and other recruiters faced many obstacles in convincing young black men to enlist in a war already prolonged and bloody. In June, 1863, the War Department added insult to injury in its discriminatory treatment of black soldiers. To the denial of commissions for blacks, it added the policy of unequal pay. White privates were paid thirteen dollars per month, while blacks were to receive ten dollars from which three dollars would be deducted to cover the expense of clothing. This policy was shabbily justified on the grounds that the Militia Act of 1862 had empowered the president to enlist black troops at a standard pay of ten dollars, and previous pledges of equal pay by Stanton, generals Butler, Saxton, and Hunter, Governor Andrew, and numerous recruiting agents were simply disregarded. In March, Douglass himself had boldly declared that he was authorized to assure his recruits "the same wages, the same rations, the same equipments, the same protection, the same treatment, and the same bounty secured to the white soldiers." These assurances, which Douglass had personally sought from George Stearns, would collapse in bitter protest before the end of 1863.[25]

As enlistment moved into the border states and the Deep South, protest against unequal pay swelled. Black troops began to refuse their pay altogether while it remained unequal, some regiments accepting no wages at all well into 1864. Discriminatory pay was a desperate problem for impoverished blacks, and the hardships, even starvation, of their families back home and in freedmen's camps only fueled their outrage at the government's policy. Noncommissioned

---

24. "Another Word to Colored Men," *DM*, April, 1863, in Foner (ed.), *Life and Writings*, III, 344–45; "Address for the Promotion of Colored Enlistments," speech in Philadelphia, July 6, 1863, in *ibid.*, 365.

25. "Men of Color to Arms!" 319. For early doubts and warnings about unequal pay, see *Christian Recorder*, July 26, 1862, February 14, 1863.

officers were especially angered when they realized that the highest ranking black sergeant earned less than a white private. Letters and petitions from outraged black soldiers streamed into the offices of Stanton, Lincoln, and state governors. Typical of the more eloquent of these letters was one penned to Lincoln in September, 1863, by James Henry Gooding, a black corporal from Massachusetts. Gooding told the president that he and his comrades had been "obedient . . . , patient, and solid as a wall." "Now your Excellency," he asserted, "we have done a Soldier's Duty, Why can't we have a Soldier's pay?" Letters of protest also poured into Washington from the white commanders of black regiments, as well as from soldiers' wives. Rachel Ann Wicker, wife of an Ohio soldier, wrote to "President Andrew" in 1864 that she, her mother, and other women were "suffering for want of money to live on." She demanded to know "why it is that you still insist upon them [black soldiers] takeing 7 dollars a month when you give the Poorest White Regiment that has went out 16 dollars." These direct appeals spoke the anguish of betrayal and deprivation. Black protest reached heroic and tragic proportions in the fall of 1863, when whole units threatened mutiny. In November, led by Sergeant William Walker, the men of one company of the 3rd South Carolina Volunteers stacked their rifles in front of the tent of their regimental commander, Colonel Augustus G. Bennett, refusing to do further duty until the pay controversy was settled. Bennett was sympathetic, but he pressed charges of mutiny nonetheless. In February, in one of the ugliest episodes of the war, a firing squad executed Walker in front of his entire brigade.[26]

Not until June, 1864, did Congress respond to the flood of protest by passing a bill that authorized equal pay for black troops retroactive to January 1 of the same year. The equal-pay struggle galvanized the black community in the North and served as a symbol of a new-found sense of dignity among southern freedmen. Douglass' lofty appeals for black enlistment in the spring and summer of 1863 must be seen in the context of this wave of indignation over the government's discrimination. He had a deep sense of irony about his people's place in America, but rarely had Douglass confronted such a predicament between principle and expediency.

26. On the equal-pay struggle, see Berlin (ed.), *Freedom*, Ser. 2, pp. 17–21, 362–68; Cornish, *Sable Arm*, 181–96; Higginson, *Army Life*, 267–76; McPherson (ed.), *Negro's Civil War*, 193–203; Herman Belz, "Law, Politics, and Race in the Struggle for Equal Pay During the Civil War," *Civil War History*, XXII (September, 1976), 197–222. Gooding and Wicker are quoted in Berlin (ed.), *Freedom*, Ser. 2, pp. 386, 402. On the execution of Walker and the documents pertaining to his trial, see *ibid.*, 365–66, 391–94.

Prior to the government's enactment of the unequal-pay policy (before July, 1863), Douglass steadfastly maintained that blacks should enlist in spite of the restrictions against commissions. Although a little uneasy about this position, he was ready to reconcile it with an argument black leaders used throughout the nineteenth century: that blacks faced two enemies of comparable significance— southern slavery and northern racism. "We shall be fighting a double battle," he said, "against slavery at the South and against prejudice and prescription at the North." By refusing military service because of discrimination, blacks would allow one enemy to prevent them from exploiting an opportunity to destroy the other, but by enlisting with their heads high and eyes open they might through example and valor discredit, if not defeat, both adversaries. "Colored men going into the army and navy of the United States," Douglass warned in February, "must expect annoyance. They will be severely criticized and even insulted—but let no man hold back on this account." A month later Douglass attacked the "cowardly meanness" at the root of the provision against officer status. Although angered by such discrimination, he wrote a rousing appeal for enlistment as a means of blotting it out: "To say we won't be soldiers because we cannot be colonels is like saying we won't go into the water until we have learned to swim. A half a loaf is better than no bread—and going into the army is the speediest way to overcome the prejudice that has dictated unjust laws against us. . . . Let us take this little the better to get more. . . . Once in the United States uniform and the colored man has a springing board under him by which he can jump to loftier heights." Pull together now as citizen soldiers, Douglass was telling his people, and after the war freedom and equality would be possible.[27]

Douglass' concept of a "double battle" against slavery and racism is strikingly similar to the messages of W. E. B. Du Bois in World War I and many black newspaper editors during World War II. In 1918, as editor of the NAACP's *Crisis*, Du Bois called on blacks to "Close Ranks" with white Americans, enlist in the army, and fight to save democracy abroad before returning to demand it at home. In 1942, the Pittsburgh *Courier* first launched the "Double V" campaign, a call for victory over fascism abroad and racism at home. Although much was different in circumstances and degree, a unifying theme runs through all three concepts: Douglass' "double battle," Du Bois' "Close

27. "Condition of the Country," *DM*, February, 1863; "Another Law Against Common Sense," *DM*, March, 1863.

Ranks," and the black press's "Double V." Each contains the premise that blacks would fight to save the nation, while militantly asserting their rightful place in it. Loyalty and sacrifice in war offered a unique chance to demand equality and justice in peace.[28]

This awareness of the dual enemies thwarting black advancement is a constant theme in Douglass' Civil War thought. His fellow recruiters expressed the same sentiment of "double battle." "This is the time God has given your race to conquer its freedom from northern prejudice and southern pride and avarice," declared Stearns to potential recruits, "you must fight . . . to obtain the right to fight on terms of equality." Military service rapidly became the readiest argument for those demanding black equality after emancipation. Hence the dual nature of the black soldier's fight, as proposed to him by recruiters, was both a burden and an opportunity.[29]

Attitudes toward enlistment varied widely among blacks. For southern slaves, the most powerful inducement to join was, of course, freedom itself, and for many, persuasion was unnecessary; they joined at the first chance. In some Union-occupied regions, though, conscription practices became brutal as northern state agents roamed widely to fill their quotas. But ex-slaves filled the Union ranks, providing 141,000 of the 179,000 blacks who served. The motives of northern free blacks were more complex. Some had education and respectable jobs; they were free but not equal, and the appeal to a "double" struggle against slavery and racism fell on attentive ears. The northern states supplied 33,000 (approximately 18 percent) of the total black soldiers, and in many districts blacks served in higher proportion than whites. Yet when Douglass spoke at a series of recruiting meetings in New York in April, 1863, he confronted hesitation and resistance to enlistment. The inequality within the army was a tough pill for some to swallow while risking their lives for the hope of more complete justice down the road.[30]

28. For Du Bois's "Close Ranks" argument, see *Crisis*, XVI, July, September, 1918. The Pittsburgh *Courier* launched the "Double V" slogan in the spring of 1942, carrying it on the masthead of the paper. None of Douglass' biographers have stressed this connection with future wars. The problem of divided loyalties and dual enemies has been prevalent in every war for blacks.

29. Stearns is quoted in McPherson, *Struggle for Equality*, 203. Douglass' comments on the notion of dual enemies are too numerous to cite. For a further discussion of the theme, see Berlin (ed.), *Freedom*, Ser. 2, pp. 21–22.

30. Berlin (ed.), *Freedom*, Ser. 2, pp. 14–15. For the government's estimates about the proportions of black and white enlistments, see Doc. 27, Joseph C. G. Kennedy, Superintendent of the Census Office, to J. P. Usher, Secretary of the Interior, Washington, D.C., February 11, 1863, in *ibid.*, 87–88.

These New York meetings, presided over by Henry Highland Garnet, offer interesting images of the conflict that many blacks felt toward the enlistment issue, even before equal pay became the focus of controversy. At the first gathering (April 20), Garnet counseled against enlistment because of the denial of promotion and honor. At the second and much larger meeting (April 27), Douglass issued his call for "retribution" against slaveholders and for soldiering as the means to manhood. This time Garnet shifted and joined Douglass with his own eloquent endorsement of enlistment. The Reverend James W. C. Pennington did the same. But when they finished, only one young man walked forward from the audience to sign up. Embarrassed but undaunted, Douglass addressed a third session three days later (April 30). He acknowledged the government's policy as grounds for "hesitation and . . . indifference." Black enlistment had come about by a "tardy, back-door manner," he admitted, and his own "blood boiled at the discriminations." He invited a frank discussion of the objections to enlistment, but nevertheless argued strongly that blacks should take a larger view, bear up, and join the 54th Massachusetts.[31]

Quite likely, many of the young men Douglass faced in these recruiting meetings simply did not share his need for retribution, and the call to kill slaveholders may not have had the same urgency to those born free in the North. As individuals, black soldiers had few certainties and much to fear from military service. Capture could have dire consequences in the slaveholding South, and inequality, familiar enough in civilian life, was no more tolerable in the military. The remarkable fact is that so many thousands of free blacks volunteered to serve the Union even after the unequal-pay policy was in force.

In early July, shortly after the unequal-pay policy began, Douglass spoke at a recruiting rally in Philadelphia—his last attempt for some time to reconcile enlistment with discrimination. His speech was a powerful effort to chart the pragmatic course. He told the skeptics that he agreed with their principled stand against unequal pay, but he proposed that more justice could be gained by fighting in the war than by sitting it out. The speediest way to earn the justice they sought, he contended, was by helping to save the nation. Douglass counseled enlistment, even if the government "offered nothing more as an inducement . . . than bare subsistence and arms." Unconvincingly, he

31. All three New York meetings are reported in *DM*, June, 1863. On the hesitation of blacks to enlist, also see Berry, *Military Necessity and Civil Rights Policy*, 72–73.

urged his listeners to rely on the faith that all existing discriminations in the military would be overturned by war's end.[32]

But Douglass soon found it impossible to continue recruiting young men for a discriminatory army. On July 13, one week after his Philadelphia speech, draft riots broke out in New York City in which at least a dozen blacks were lynched by mobs. The inequality issue became harder and harder to explain away.

Even more important, Douglass became deeply discouraged over the treatment of black prisoners of war by the Confederacy. As early as November, 1862, Confederate Secretary of War James A. Seddon had ordered the death penalty for blacks taken as prisoners, and five months later the Confederate Congress authorized each state to treat captured blacks and their white officers as insurrectionists, thus subject to death. The Union government's apparent lack of response to this harsh treatment angered Douglass even further. In two editorials written sometime in late July, he viciously attacked Lincoln's silence on Confederate killings of black prisoners, as well as threats of their enslavement. "The slaughter of blacks taken as captives," wrote an outraged Douglass, "seems to affect him [Lincoln] as little as the slaughter of beeves for the use of his army." Douglass wanted an eye for an eye—one southerner put to death for every black soldier killed as a prisoner of war. Lincoln, like most northern leaders, had little stomach for the kind of retaliation Douglass suggested, but these threats did not go unanswered. Two weeks after the assault on Fort Wagner in South Carolina (which occurred on July 18, 1863), where many black soldiers of the 54th Massachusetts were slain or captured, Lincoln issued his retaliatory order. It contained a one-for-one policy, including one rebel soldier put at hard labor for every Union soldier sold into slavery. Following Lincoln's retaliatory proclamation, few black soldiers were actually enslaved after capture, though some were killed. For the moment, however, Douglass had run out of arguments as a black recruiter, so in frustration he lashed out at Lincoln.[33]

Similarly, Douglass attacked Secretary of State William H. Seward's claim that blacks should do their duty as soldiers without "hesitating about pay or place." This had essentially been Douglass' position as well, but after four months of counseling expediency, he could

32. "Address for the Promotion of Colored Enlistment," 362.
33. "The Commander-in-Chief and His Black Soldiers," *DM*, August, 1863, in Foner (ed.), *Life and Writings*, III, 370–72. For a discussion of the retaliation issue, see Quarles, *Lincoln and the Negro*, 173–76. Lincoln ordered his cabinet to investigate ways to protect black troops in February, 1863.

no longer defend it. As principles, "pay" and "place" were important, and Douglass felt he could no longer talk about duty without equal stress on rights.[34]

As yet unaware of Lincoln's retaliatory proclamation, Douglass officially withdrew from recruiting in a letter to Stearns on August 1, 1863. Deeply distressed, he said he felt he owed it to his people, especially those he had enlisted, "to expose their wrongs and plead their cause." Douglass had abruptly switched hats, temporarily ceasing his role as war propagandist and government recruiting agent while returning to the role of black leader. "When I plead for recruits," he told Stearns, "I want to do it with all my heart, without qualification. I cannot do that now." Douglass seemed to be atoning for his promises of equal treatment in the army and admitted to helping foster a "false estimate" of the Union government's generosity.[35]

In the letter Douglass seemed not only discouraged but somewhat confused. His zigzag on this issue no doubt reflects the strain of travel and recruiting before increasingly reluctant audiences. Moreover, his son Lewis had participated in the assault on Fort Wagner and another, Charles, had taken ill at the front, which may have curbed his enthusiasm for recruiting. In a letter to an abolitionist friend, Martha Greene, Douglass described his sons as fighting "with halters about their necks." Greene, whose own son had been wounded in the war, wrote back expressing her sympathy for Douglass as a black parent: "The white mothers and fathers think it hard to send our sons to fight, with every assurance of their protection—how little we know the depth of earnestness it must require in you to send yours." Douglass still believed in his "double battle" strategy, but temporarily he had lost the will to argue it before black audiences.[36]

Douglass' inner conflict on this issue was probably typical of most black leaders during the Civil War. He possessed many conflicting ideals—national loyalty versus black self-interest, temporary gains versus extended justice, country versus race—and he wanted to wed all these opposites. Emancipation and military service seemed to provide the connecting links, if only blacks were patient enough. But by 1863, unprotected from barbarous treatment, paid inferior wages, and standing no chance of promotion, blacks had waited long enough, Douglass angrily told Stearns. For the time being, he could no longer

34. "Duty of Colored Men," *DM*, August, 1863, in Foner (ed.), *Life and Writings*, III, 372–73. Seward's claim was in a letter to John Mercer Langston, which was the basis of Douglass' reaction in his paper.
35. Douglass to Stearns, August 1, 1863, in *ibid.*, 367.
36. Martha Greene to Douglass, July 7, 1863, in FD Papers (LC).

in clear conscience urge young black men to enlist. So Douglass quit recruiting and resumed agitation.

But Stearns did not allow his most famous recruiter to step aside easily. He sent Douglass the news of Lincoln's retaliatory proclamation and urged him to go to Washington and present the black soldiers' grievances to Lincoln himself. On August 10, 1863, Douglass visited Washington for the first time, meeting with the president and the secretary of war. In a businesslike, thirty-minute interview with Stanton, Douglass raised the issues of equal pay and promotion, and Stanton assured him that he believed wholeheartedly in the black soldier's right to both, and that he had been working to bring them about. Stanton ended the interview by proposing that Douglass take his recruiting skills to Vicksburg and organize black troops among the freedmen of the Mississippi Valley.

At the White House, Douglass met Lincoln for the first time. The president received the ex-slave cordially, and Douglass quickly felt at ease with what he later called Lincoln's "honest . . . countenance." Lincoln listened attentively as the black spokesman raised the issues of pay, promotion, and treatment of prisoners, responding that he understood the complaint on unequal pay but considered it a "necessary concession" in order to achieve the larger aim of getting blacks into the army. Defending his policies and his pace, Lincoln declared that "popular prejudice" had prevented an earlier retaliatory proclamation, since he had feared that too many northern whites simply would not accept the killing of southern whites to avenge the deaths of blacks. Black heroism on the battlefield, as Douglass recalled the interview, was Lincoln's idea of the "necessary preparation of the public mind for his proclamation" about retaliation. Douglass was most impressed, though, when Lincoln assured him that once he took a position (emancipation or black enlistment), he would not retreat from it.[37]

Douglass got a political education from his meeting with Lincoln, and he came away better informed about the complexity of the president's responsibilities. Lincoln responded frankly and respectfully to the black leader's questions. "Though I was not entirely satisfied with his views," Douglass wrote of the Lincoln meeting, "I was so

37. Douglass to Stearns, August 12, 1863, in Abraham Barker Papers, Historical Society of Pennsylvania, Philadelphia. For a longer recollection of the meetings, see Douglass, Life and Times, 346–50. Douglass' two major biographers, Foner and Quarles, describe the interviews in the order of Lincoln first and Stanton second. I have reversed the order because that is the way Douglass himself describes them in his August 12 letter to Stearns.

well satisfied with the man and with the educating tendency of the conflict that I determined to go on with the recruiting." Trust in the man fostered increased patience with his policies. "My whole interview with the President was gratifying," Douglass wrote to Stearns, "and did much to assure me that slavery would not survive the war and that the country would survive both slavery and the war."[38]

Most important, Douglass' meeting with Lincoln had personal meaning. He had received a hearing at the highest level of power, and whatever pangs of conscience he possessed about recruiting soldiers for a discriminatory army were largely put to rest. He gained reassurance that the "double battle" strategy was still tenable. Moreover, the meeting was a personal triumph for Douglass—the former slave who grew up across Chesapeake Bay on the Eastern Shore of Maryland—as he sat in the president's office, spokesman of his people. His determination to resume recruiting, which he probably made before the meeting in Washington, could only be firmer in the afterglow of the interview with Lincoln. Douglass reveled in opportunities to tell the story of his first meeting with the president. Describing the scene in a speech at Philadelphia several months later, he left no doubt of his pride in the occasion: "I tell you I felt big there!" he assured his audience.[39] The black leader and the government recruiting agent could be the same person again, because the citizen and the activist had been treated as one man, causing a sense of recognition that Douglass—like all black leaders—sorely needed.

Douglass also left Washington with what he thought was the promise of a commission in the United States Army. According to Douglass, Stanton promised to appoint him assistant adjutant on the staff of General Lorenzo Thomas, who was in Mississippi organizing black troops. His faith renewed, Douglass returned to Rochester in high spirits. He quickly decided to cease publication of his newspaper, the *Douglass Monthly*, rushing a final "Valedictory" issue into print. After sixteen years as editor of his own newspaper—along with being an orator, the only vocation he had ever known—this was a momentous decision. Douglass was ready for active service and insisted on an officer's rank. He received orders to report to Thomas at Vicksburg, as well as a character reference signed by, among others, Lincoln himself, and his transportation was arranged at government

38. Douglass, *Life and Times*, 349; Douglass to Stearns, August 12, 1863, in Abraham Barker Papers.
39. "Our Work Is Not Done," 383.

expense. But to Douglass' great disappointment, the commission never arrived. Apparently, Stanton (perhaps Lincoln as well) had second thoughts about commissioning a black man, an act that might be too far in advance of public opinion. On August 14 Douglass wrote to the War Department, inquiring as to the "conditions" of his service. The reply one week later discussed only his remuneration and instructed him to report to General Thomas, where he would be expected to exercise his "influence" with the freedmen.[40]

Without the commission, Douglass would not go to Mississippi. An interesting question arises from this sequence of events: why would Douglass not budge from Rochester without the commission? Moreover, why had he not already enlisted in active service? Other black recruiters had done just that. Why not take the recruiting crusade into the heart of the South among the thousands of freedmen, whether honored with rank or not? In *Life and Times*, Douglass' explanation of why he would not go without a commission is somewhat lame: "I knew too much of camp life and the value of shoulder straps in the army to go into the service without some visible mark of my rank." Yet this is exactly what he had urged thousands of younger blacks to do. There is no question that Douglass was sincere in his willingness to go South, join the war, and radically alter his own career, but there is also some evidence that he was again confused about his own priorities. As late as August 19 (before receiving his final communication from the War Department), Douglass told a correspondent of his disappointment that no commission had arrived. "I shall obey, however," he said, "hoping that all will be well in the end." But before the end of the month, he decided not to obey and stayed in Rochester. The conflicting ideals were at war in him again.[41]

There are several possible explanations of Douglass' refusal to go South. His personal circumstances offer some reasons. His sons, Charles and Lewis, were in the army. His third son, Frederick, was already in Mississippi serving as a recruiter of black troops; he would soon be back home, ill and convalescing. Douglass' daughter Rosetta,

40. Douglass received several communications from the War Department regarding his appointment to go to Mississippi. See FD Papers (LC) for the following: C. W. Foster to Douglass, August 13, August 21, 1863; C. W. Foster to Brig. Gen. Daniel H. Rucker, August 13, 1863, authorizing Douglass' transportation; Department of the Interior, To Whom It May Concern, August 10, 1863, Douglass' character reference, signed by Senator Samuel Pomeroy and President Lincoln; Stearns to Douglass, August 29, 1863; Asst. Adj. Gen. C. W. Foster to Douglass, August 21, 1863.

41. Douglass, *Life and Times*, 350; Douglass to Thomas Webster, August 19, 1863, in Foner (ed.), *Life and Writings*, III, 377.

who had been a troubled child, was soon to marry; she and her husband, Nathan Sprague, would move into the Douglass family home in Rochester. The forty-six-year-old Douglass and his beleaguered wife Anna had a growing flock for which to provide. Douglass had considered abandoning the newspaper and starting a farm at least as early as 1862. Although it was the primary occupation of his life, the paper had always been a burden, and quite likely much relief accompanied the final issue of the *Douglass Monthly*. In late summer, 1863, Douglass was a man without a secure occupation, his sons were under the daily peril of war, and his own sense of identity, no doubt, was under some question.[42]

Douglass often referred to his sons as if they were his surrogates at war. Frequently, he expressed a father's pride that Charles and Lewis had been his first recruits. He corresponded with them often, sending them money and buoying their spirits. In July, 1863, a correspondent to the *Anglo-African* called Douglass to task for sending his sons to a war he would not fight himself. More than once Douglass was questioned about his failure to enlist, but in reply he characterized this challenge as "malicious." He disclaimed any ability as a soldier. "When have I been heard as a military man?" Douglass asked in response to the claim that his failure to enlist had caused many blacks to hesitate. He felt no compulsion to join the army, he said, until his fellow blacks found someone "to fill my place at the North." Irked at the suggestion that he allowed his sons to do his fighting for him, Douglass simply replied: "I am proud to refer to my two sons." There is no concrete evidence that Douglass actually saw his sons playing out a role he might crave for himself—liberating slaves and killing slaveholders—but their enlistment may have diminished his own desire to join. As soldiers, the sons were symbols of the father's conception of the meaning and purpose of the war. Besides, the father had other roles to play.[43]

Douglass' "Valedictory" statement also provides some clues about the choices he made. Written while waiting to receive his commis-

42. Julia Griffiths Crofts to Douglass, December 5, 1862, Leeds, England, in FD Papers (LC). On Anna and difficulties in the Douglass home, see Rosetta Douglass Sprague, "My Mother as I Knew Her," published speech delivered before the WCTU, Washington, D.C., May 10, 1900, reprinted 1923, in FD Papers (LC), reel 1.

43. Charles R. Douglass to Douglass, September 8, 18, 1863, in FD Papers (LC); Douglass to *Anglo-African*, July 27, 1863, in Foner (ed.), *Life and Writings*, III, 360–61. For further illustrations of the importance of Douglass' sons in the war, see Douglass, *Life and Times*, 350. After lengthy description of the commission matter, he ends the chapter: "Meanwhile, my three sons were in the service." Douglass had also been urged

sion, his last editorial was both somber and exhilarated. Clearly, the newspaper had been the center of Douglass' life; for sixteen years he had found hope, identity, and prestige as its editor. He owed many debts to his friends in England and in the American abolitionist community whose moral and financial support had kept the paper afloat. The editorial pages had always afforded Douglass a mouthpiece to the world, but he could now give it up because there were several other papers that welcomed his writing—in New York, the *Tribune,* the *Independent,* and the *Anglo-African.* At the end of the piece, Douglass told his readers that he was going South to recruit black troops. Although he ended with another direct appeal for retribution against slaveholders and asserted that it was time for him to play a "physical" as well as "moral" part in the war, the self-portrait Douglass conveyed in this statement was consistent with the past: he was still writer, orator, leader.[44]

Douglass was a reformer, not a soldier. As an adjutant, recruiting among refugee freedmen, he may have envisioned himself a fish out of water. Also, he may have imagined himself stultified under a general's orders—since leaving the Garrisonians, he had never operated under anyone's direction. How could he continue to reach the widest possible audience with his message of "abolition war" if stationed in the Deep South? How could he continue to touch the highest levels of power in Washington—something Douglass relished—if he became a recruiter in Dixie? Questions of this sort must have crossed his mind as he pondered whether to enlist with commission or without. Simply put, perhaps Douglass was too proud to go South without a commission; moreover, the whole proposition conflicted with his sense of self as black symbol and spokesman. So he decided to stay where he could best fulfill that role.

Douglass received a great deal of reinforcement for his self-image from friends and supporters, especially those in England. His most devoted friend, Julia Griffiths Crofts (companion and business man-

to enlist by H. Ford Douglas in January, 1863. After describing how he had enlisted himself six months earlier, H. Ford Douglas urged Douglass to join as well: "They say we will not fight. I want to see it tried on. You are the one to me of all others, to demonstrate this fact." See H. Ford Douglas to Douglass, January 8, 1863, Collinsville, Tenn., in *DM*, 1863.

44. "Valedictory," August 16, 1863, *DM*, August, 1863, in Foner (ed.), *Life and Writings,* III, 374–77. On the availability of other papers to Douglass' writings, see Theodore Tilton to Douglass, April 30, 1862, in FD Papers (LC). Tilton was the editor of the *Independent.*

ager of his paper from 1849 to 1855, married and now living in Leeds, England), raised a great deal of money for Douglass in Britain throughout the war, and as his most faithful correspondent she counseled him on every aspect of his life. She vehemently discouraged his plans about farming and urged him not to give up the paper. She also pleaded with him not to join the army. Griffiths Crofts had her own agenda; the *Douglass Monthly* was a primary means for her and her British antislavery friends to communicate with Douglass, as well as the object of their continued fund-raising. Although very few of Douglass' letters to her survive, Griffiths Crofts's letters to him tell us a good deal about the self-sustaining nature of their relationship. Douglass no doubt made up his own mind, but when he pondered how best to direct his energies, he had plenty of guidance from his old friend to rely upon if he wished. As early as September, 1862, she was adamant about what she perceived as her friend's purpose: "Do not I beseech you be hurried away into taking up arms . . . your work is with your pen, not with a sword or gun." In February, 1863, Douglass wrote to her expressing his personal interest in enlisting if the New York legislature would grant "equal rights" to black soldiers. "By everything dear to you my friend," Griffiths Crofts responded, "do not *take any commission* that leads you personally into the fighting ranks . . . never go South—or killed you most assuredly will be . . . you are . . . a *marked man.*" This argument about his personal vulnerability must have weighed heavily on Douglass' mind when he made his decision not to go South. By December, 1863, the Englishwoman could write of her relief that "the dangerous task of recruiting in the South is given up," but she was distressed over Douglass' abandonment of the newspaper, wondering how he would carry on his work without it. By then Douglass was back on the lecture circuit, spreading his views on the meaning of the war more widely than ever.[45]

Late 1863 brought a personal turning point for Douglass. He was no longer a journalist, and black recruiting in the North pretty well ran its course in 1863—for the rest of the war, most black soldiers came from the South. Down to Appomattox, Douglass served the Union war effort and his people primarily as an orator and by raising funds for freedmen's aid societies. He remained in the roles he knew best: teacher, preacher, and writer. Douglass did not need the adventure of war to assert his manhood, nor did he feel any noble obligation to be a

45. Julia Griffiths Crofts to Douglass, September 1, 1862, April 3, 1863, December 10, 1863, all in FD Papers (LC).

soldier. He possessed numerous sources of self-esteem, and through language he had his own mode of retribution against slaveholders. He could take greater satisfaction from organizing black soldiers than from being one. As thousands of black men entered the army, Douglass cheered them on. They took the abstraction out of the slogan "abolition war" and gave it reality.

8/ABOLITION WAR—ABOLITION PEACE

> I end where I began—no war but an Abolition war; no peace but an Abolition peace.
> —Frederick Douglass, "The Mission of the War," 1864

FOR FREDERICK DOUGLASS, the Civil War was a transforming event, a stage in his life that forever changed him. On the eve of the conflict, he was a frustrated leader of an enslaved people, flirting with support for emigration schemes. Four years later at war's end, the slaves were emancipated, and black soldiers were stationed all over a defeated South. A new era in race relations was about to begin, though few could envision the nature of its struggles. During the final bloody year of the war, Douglass pondered at great length the meaning of the conflict, both for himself and his people, and well before the war ended, the issues of Reconstruction captured his attention, especially as they concerned the welfare of the freedmen in the postwar order.

In the winter of 1863–64, Douglass joined the lecture circuit with a speech entitled "The Mission of the War," which was perhaps his fullest expression of what the Civil War meant to him. If northerners would resist weariness, endure further sorrow, and comprehend the war's true mission, he argued, then genuine "national regeneration" was possible. Douglass was at his apocalyptic best: "If sharp and signal retribution, long protracted . . . and overwhelming can teach a great nation respect for the . . . claims of justice, surely we shall be taught now and for all time to come." Douglass wanted a "new order," a new definition of American nationality. Indeed, he envisioned a new country built on the ashes of the old one, freed from slavery and sectionalism. The Declaration of Independence would no longer be "a lie"; free thought and literacy would reign in all sections. Anticipating the Radical Republican vision of Reconstruction, Douglass favored "transplanting the whole South with the higher civilization of the North," and he reasoned that "the New England schoolhouse is bound to take the place of the Southern whipping post." He called for a new definition of citizenship that would include blacks, and "mean as much as it did to be called a Roman citizen in the palmiest days of the Roman Empire."[1] In this appeal for nationalism and liberty, Doug-

1. "The Mission of the War," 395–97.

lass captured the twin desires of most blacks: to be free, and to belong. By 1864 the Civil War had made both aims possible.

As part of his "Mission" speech, Douglass presented what he called his "platform of principles," which was a black abolitionist's plan for racial justice in war and peace. He demanded four points: (1) an "Abolition War"; (2) an "Abolition Peace"; (3) full rights of citizenship for blacks; and (4) black suffrage and an end to all racial discrimination. Grandiose and perhaps oversimplified, these principles nevertheless represented the abolitionists' conception of the war's objectives. They were revolutionary in scope and anticipated the Radical Republican aims for Reconstruction. Douglass knew that the transition from slavery to freedom for blacks would be long and arduous; he was also well aware that the military contest was far from over. In the election year of 1864, he questioned the resolve of Republicans and feared the power of Peace Democrats. Douglass was not insensitive to the death and suffering the country had endured, and he spoke with compassion about the "agony at a million hearthstones," the "stumps of men" wandering the land, and "200,000 rudely formed graves."[2] But in 1864 he scorned all peacemakers, continued to create a hated enemy, and demanded a war that would finish the work begun.

In practical terms, what Douglass meant by "abolition war" was a military conquest of the South, complete emancipation, continued enlistment of black soldiers without discrimination, and legal guarantees of black freedom and equal rights at war's end. In the aftermath, an "abolition peace" would mean the subjugation of the South's slaveholding leadership, black citizenship and enfranchisement, and a strong role for the federal government in protecting the freedmen and in restructuring southern society. One could conclude that this represents Douglass the dreamer, calling for a racial justice that might not occur for several generations, but Douglass' vision was shared by many Republicans and was the substance of much of Radical Reconstruction. As an abolitionist, he saw the war as a moral crusade; as a black leader, he saw it as the "Negro's hour," a whole people rising from bondage to dignity; and as an American nationalist, he saw the conflict in millennial terms: a nation redeemed from an evil past to a second beginning. The meaning of the Civil War for blacks was never better expressed than when Douglass called for "no war but an Abolition War; no peace but an Abolition Peace; liberty for all, chains for none; the black man a soldier in war, a

2. *Ibid.*, 393–94, 388.

laborer in peace; a voter at the South as well as at the North; America his permanent home, and all Americans his fellow countrymen. Such fellow citizens, is my idea of the mission of the war. If accomplished, our glory as a nation will be complete, our peace will flow like a river, and our foundations will be the everlasting rocks."[3] To Douglass, the Civil War was for liberty *and* Union, reborn and redefined.

As early as the fall of 1862 Douglass turned his attention to the postwar reconstruction. He predicted a turbulent period and held no illusions about the difficulties blacks would face after emancipation. Indeed, the problems of peace appeared much greater than the problems of war. After the fighting, Douglass suggested, "will come the time for the exercise of the highest of all human faculties. A profounder wisdom, a holier zeal, than belongs to the prosecution of war will be required." He wondered about the use of federal authority in the reconstruction of state governments, calmly predicting that Charles Sumner's plan to revert the seceded states to territories would be adopted. Douglass' early views on Reconstruction indicate that he also agreed with those Radicals like Thaddeus Stevens and Albion Tourgée who advocated that the southern states endure an extended probationary period before being readmitted to the Union. Douglass also envisioned Reconstruction as a long ideological struggle. "The work before us is nothing but a radical revolution," he declared, "in all the modes of thought which have flourished under the . . . slave system." A new order in race relations could not happen overnight—"there is no such thing as immediate Emancipation either for the master or for the slave," Douglass asserted. The "invisible chains of slavery" in black-white relations might take generations to break. Douglass seemed fully aware that the Civil War held the potential for untold racial struggle as well as hope.[4]

Naturally, Douglass' wartime concern with Reconstruction centered upon the welfare of the freedmen. His answer to the question of what was to be done with the emancipated slaves was, "do nothing with them." "Your *doing* with them is their greatest misfortune," Douglass told his white countrymen; "just let them alone." In May, 1862, he expressed further doubts about the wisdom of freedmen

3. *Ibid.*, 403.
4. "The Work of the Future," *DM*, November, 1862, in Foner (ed.), *Life and Writings,* III, 290–92. These same sentiments about the time required for a new order in race relations were expressed in "A Day for Poetry and Song," speech at Zion Church, Rochester, December 28, 1862, in *ibid.*, 311. "Slavery has existed in this country too long and has stamped its character too deeply and indelibly, to be blotted out in a day or a year, or even a generation," Douglass maintained.

relief efforts. Denouncing the "old clothes system of benevolence," he said he did not want the freedmen to "depend for their bread and raiment upon the benevolence of the North," and he argued that the freedmen could make it on their own if left alone. "The great need of the Negro in this country," Douglass asserted, "is the consciousness that he is somebody." Although he was quite right about his people's need for self-esteem, these insensitive remarks about northern benevolence were shortsighted. Later, in the 1870s, Douglass did preach a black self-reliance and a laissez-faire individualism that echoed the reigning Social Darwinism of the day, but during the war he soon found that the fate of the freedmen was a much more complex and demanding problem than his "do nothing" rhetoric would imply.[5]

The tension between the doctrine of self-reliance and the necessity of government philanthropy for the freedmen remained a paradox in Douglass' thought throughout the war and the postbellum era. He never stopped arguing that the legacy of slavery would require federal aid to the freedpeople, but he also never relinquished his commitment to laissez-faire individualism. He simply advanced both doctrines at once, a position of stark contradiction in an age decreasingly receptive to humanitarian reform. Douglass seemed no more willing than most of his Radical Republican contemporaries to convert the federal government into a long-term, aggressive engine of social welfare, and he was prepared to lead no revolutions in economic thinking, though he would later conclude that the failures of Reconstruction were primarily economic. But while expecting a rugged self-reliance from his own people, he demanded justice and fairness from the nation—prescriptions that would be difficult enough to achieve in the racial atmosphere of Reconstruction.[6]

Embedded in each of his discussions of the welfare of the freedmen was Douglass' demand that the nation "deal justly" with blacks. What he meant, in large part, by the "do nothing" dictum was "do justice." Coupled with his calls to let the freedmen simply help themselves were demands for education, wages, protection in the work

5. "What Shall Be Done with the Slaves If Emancipated?" *DM*, January, 1862, in *ibid.*, 188. For another full expression of this "do nothing" idea, see "The Future of the Negro People of the Slave States." "Arms Not Alms for the Contrabands," *DM*, May, 1862. On the conditions of and federal policies toward the freedmen, see Gerteis, *From Contraband to Freedman.*

6. On Douglass' mingling of government responsibility and laissez-faire individualism during Reconstruction, see Martin, *Mind*, 67–70. My analysis confirms Martin's contention that "this paradox between self-reform and outside philanthropy at times confounded his [Douglass'] conception of Reconstruction, thereby undermining its viability" (67). For good examples of the contrast between Douglass' advocacy of

place, civil rights, and suffrage. All of these aims would require extraordinary use of federal power, new laws, and fundamental changes in social attitudes. "We would not for a moment check . . . any benevolent concern for the future welfare of the colored race in America," wrote Douglass in 1862, "but . . . we earnestly plead for justice above all else." From northerners, Douglass wanted less pity and more ballots, less benevolence and more black landownership. Like most black leaders in both North and South, Douglass would not support radical plans for widespread confiscation and redistribution of Confederate land; instead, he wanted his people to obtain land by means consistent with the sanctity of private property and the doctrine of self-improvement, and in his view the government should have a primary role in securing and arranging the sale of such lands. With time, Douglass would applaud virtually every function of the Freedmen's Bureau, including its relief efforts, but during the war years he prepared his white audiences for emancipation with a blunt message:

What shall be done with the four million slaves if emancipated. I answer, deal justly with them; pay them honest wages for honest work; dispense with the biting lash, and pay the ready cash; awaken a new class of motives in them; remove those old motives of shriveling fear of punishment which benumb and degrade the soul, and supplant them by the higher and better motives of . . . self-respect . . . and personal responsibility. Reverse the whole current of feeling in regard to them. They have been compelled hitherto to regard the white man as a cruel, selfish, and remorseless tyrant. . . . Now, let him see that the white man has a nobler and better side to his character.

The substance of Douglass' message to white Americans, therefore, was *change yourselves*. The new order was as much for whites to give as it was for blacks to take.[7]

---

black self-improvement and the demand for government protection and assistance during Reconstruction, see the following three speeches delivered in the period 1873–75: "Address at the Third Annual Fair of the Tennessee Colored Agricultural and Mechanical Association," Nashville, September 18, 1873; "The Color Question: Past and Present Status of the Negro—The Great Change in His Condition—How Shall He Work Out His Destiny," Hillsdale, New York, July 5, 1875; and "Address at the Centennial Celebration of the Abolition Society of Pennsylvania," Philadelphia, 1875, all in FD Papers (LC), reel 15. On the decline of humanitarian reform in the postwar period, see Fredrickson, *Inner Civil War*, 183–98.

7. "What Shall Be Done With the Slaves If Emancipated?" 190–91; "The Future of the Negro People in the Slave States," 222. Douglass expressed this in almost identical terms in "What the Black Man Wants," speech at the annual meeting of the Massachusetts Antislavery Society, Boston, April, 1865, in Foner (ed.), *Life and Writings*, IV, 164. On Douglass' call for justice rather than generosity, see Huggins, *Slave and Citizen*, 105–106; Martin, *Mind*, 70–71. Douglass placed great emphasis on freedmen's

The expectations that lay beneath the "do nothing" idea demonstrate that it was not merely a negative approach to government policy or individual action. When he urged white Americans to leave the freedmen alone, Douglass was also asking them to be vigilant in securing the war's higher abolitionist goals. Moreover, implicit in the "do nothing" dictum was Douglass' desire to allay white fears of emancipation, so he portrayed blacks as self-reliant, hard-working people who only needed a chance, arguing that freedom and land-ownership would only make each of them "a better producer and a better consumer." Northerners need not fear massive migrations, vagrancy, or criminality from the freedmen, Douglass contended; if given equality before the law, blacks would be both peaceful and productive. Those who failed deserved their fate; it was nature's law. Douglass knew that the prospect of emancipation needed sweetening for northern ears, but his belief in the necessity of black self-reliance was a sincere and consistent view he had held since the early 1850s. It is also possible that Douglass was somewhat out of touch with the plight of the growing thousands of freedmen, for although he received a great deal of information about the welfare of the freedmen through his newspaper and correspondence, only late in the war did he visit refugee camps near Washington, D.C. But Douglass was no crass Social Darwinist; rather, he was concerned that blacks had been an "exception" too long and wanted to prevent their becoming permanent social pariahs. What "do nothing" meant was free the slave, without colonizing or subjugating him as a racial caste; give him equality before the law and allow him to learn, work, and vote. This was a prescription for widespread social action, not merely a call to let the freedmen live or die by their own pluck.[8]

Douglass knew that the southern freedmen would live in a deeply hostile postwar society, and he feared a "vindictive spirit sure to be roused against the whole colored race." Calling on northern reform-

---

education but did not squarely confront that issue until after the war. On Douglass and the question of land redistribution, see Martin, *Mind*, 71–72. For the anticonfiscation views of black leaders generally, especially in the South, see Leon F. Litwack, *Been in the Storm Too Long: The Aftermath of Slavery* (New York, 1979), 521–22.

8. "The Future of the Negro People of the Slave States," 218, 222–24; *DM*, November, 1862; H. Oscar to Douglass, September 25, 1862, a letter describing the growing numbers of freedmen at Cairo, Illinois, in 1862, in "Facts Concerning the Contrabands," *DM*, March, 1863; George Evans to Douglass, First Mass. Light Artillery, Army of the Potomac, on the Rappannock, Virginia, June 6, 1863, in FD Papers (LC); "What Shall Be Done With the Slaves If Emancipated?" 190. Douglass also converted this defense of black values into a vehement argument against colonization.

ers to "ameliorate the condition" of the former slaves, he repeatedly cautioned his audiences that abolitionists' work would not cease when the war ended. "The whole South," Douglass declared, "as it never was before the abolition of slavery will become missionary ground." Capturing the spirit of the numerous freedmen's aid societies as well as the humane vision of Radical Reconstruction, Douglass urged northerners to "walk among these slavery-smitten columns of humanity and lift their forms towards Heaven." No "do nothing" doctrine motivated these sentiments—the freedmen's needs, Douglass believed, would require the work of "all the elevating and civilizing institutions of the country."[9]

In Douglass' early Reconstruction thought, he gave great importance to black suffrage. He revived the demand for the franchise in 1863 and, defending blacks against all claims that they were not ready to vote, called for immediate and unconditional suffrage. "I will hear nothing of degradation and ignorance against the black man," Douglass said. "If he knows enough to be hanged, he knows enough to vote . . . if he knows enough to take up arms in defense of this Government . . . , he knows enough to vote." Black military service made the most effective argument for abolitionists who advocated black suffrage. Douglass was fond of Irish jokes, and he made special use of them on the suffrage issue. He often entertained his lecture audiences with tales of drunken Pat, "fresh from the Emerald Isle . . . leaning upon the arms of two of his friends," staggering into the polls to vote. If a black man knew "as much when sober as an Irishman knows when drunk," Douglass claimed, "he knows enough to vote." Moreover, the black orator urged Republicans to see the pragmatic politics of black suffrage in the postwar South. "I tell you the Negro is your friend . . . your best defender . . . ," Douglass told an antislavery convention, "against the traitors and the descendants of those traitors, who will inherit the hate . . . all over the South." He predicted that blacks would soon be in Congress and garnered applause and laughter by declaring himself "a candidate already."[10]

9. Douglass to An English Correspondent, June, 1864, *Liberator*, September 16, 1864, in Foner (ed.), *Life and Writings*, III, 404; "A Day for Poetry and Song," 312. Douglass warned that the freedman's "enemies will endeavor to make him the slave of society." On the hardships and suffering, see "What Shall Be Done With the Freed Slaves," *DM*, November, 1862, in Foner (ed.), *Life and Writings*, III, 297–98; "The Work of the Future."

10. "Our Work is Not Done," 382–83. On Douglass and the suffrage issue, also see "The Cause of the Negro People," address of the Colored National Convention to the People of the United States, Syracuse, October 4–7, 1864, in Foner (ed.), *Life and Writings*, III, 418–20.

As the war was ending in April, 1865, Douglass gave a lecture in Boston entitled "What the Black Man Wants" in which he outlined at length the reasons his people needed the vote. Douglass envisioned the freedmen as strangers in their own land in the postwar South, and the ballot would serve them as protection from white racism, a means of education, and a source of self-esteem. Douglass discussed black suffrage with a special sense of urgency at the end of the war; the same opportunity might never come again. "This is the hour," Douglass declared, "our streets are in mourning . . . and under the chastisement of this Rebellion we have almost come up to the point of conceding this great, this all-important right of suffrage." Hence, with prophetic insight, Douglass urged abolitionists to harness the extraordinary forces the war had unleashed. "I fear that if we fail to do it now . . . ," he said, "we may not see, for centuries to come, the same disposition that exists at this moment."[11] Reconstruction would, indeed, become a struggle characterized by changing dispositions toward the freedmen and the conquered South.

In the election year of 1864 Douglass continued to be troubled by the policies of the Lincoln administration. The equal-pay controversy burned until midsummer, and the Union government showed no disposition to grant black suffrage in such occupied southern states as Louisiana. Increasing war weariness and the rising popularity of the Peace Democrats placed President Lincoln's reelection in jeopardy; whether an "abolition war" could ever be waged to its conclusion seemed in doubt. Douglass reacted angrily to Lincoln's refusal to sign the Wade-Davis Bill and called the president's 10 percent plan "an entire contradiction of the constitutional idea of the Republican Government." In a letter to his British friends, he declared his patience thin. Lincoln, he said, had adopted an unworthy rule of statesmanship: "Do evil by choice, right from necessity." Lincoln's promises of leniency and speedy readmission to the Union for the southern states, Douglass contended, did not bode well for the freedpeople. It seemed to Douglass that after the government had asked "the Negro to espouse its cause" and "turn against his master," it now planned to "hand the Negro back to the political power of his former master, without a single element of strength to shield himself." Douglass bristled at northern hostility to black suffrage, found even among Radical Republicans; the Wade-Davis Bill itself, Congress's radical

11. "What the Black Man Wants," 158–60.

proposal for Reconstruction, failed to include black voting rights. Douglass did take heart, however, in that most abolitionists were beginning to speak loudly for black suffrage.[12]

In May, 1864, some four hundred Radical Republicans gathered in Cleveland to nominate John C. Frémont and John Cochrane (nephew of Gerrit Smith) for president and vice president, respectively. Initially, Douglass joined in this move to force an alternative to Lincoln and endorsed the call for the convention. Responding to a request to explain his position on the dump-Lincoln movement, he revealed that his support directly reflected his demand for an "abolition war":

I mean the complete abolition of every vestige, form and modification of Slavery in every part of the United States, perfect equality for the black man in every state before the law, in the jury box, at the ballot box and on the battlefield: ample and salutary retaliation for every instance of enslavement or slaughter of prisoners of color. I mean that in the distribution of offices and honors under this Government no discrimination shall be made in favor of or against any class of citizens, whether black or white, of native or foreign birth. And supposing that the Convention which is to meet in Cleveland means the same thing, I cheerfully give my name as one of the signers of the call.[13]

However, Douglass did not attend the convention. During the summer of 1864, with the war in a bloody stalemate in Virginia, he maintained his criticism of the Lincoln administration, giving every sign that he would work against the president's reelection in the fall. But in August, Lincoln invited Douglass to the White House for an urgent meeting. The president was under heavy criticism from all sides: Copperheads condemned him for pursuing an abolitionist war; some abolitionists sought to replace him because of his leniency toward the South and his disinterest in black rights. Lincoln seemed genuinely concerned that the war might end without complete victory and abolition, so he sought Douglass' advice on how best to answer his critics. Lincoln had drafted a letter, denying that he was standing in the way of peace and declaring that he could not sustain a war to abolish slavery if Congress and the people did not support it, but Douglass strongly urged the president not to respond with anything that would be construed as an abandonment of the antislavery policy.

12. Douglass to An English Correspondent, 404. On abolitionists' advocacy of black suffrage during the last year of the war, see McPherson, *Struggle for Equality*, 239–43, 294–99, 301–29.
13. Douglass to E. Gilbert, May 23, 1864, in Foner (ed.), *Life and Writings*, III, 403. This letter was also published in the New York *Times*, May 27, 1864.

Whether Douglass had influence or not, events quickly changed the balance of power, and Lincoln never published the letter.[14]

The second and more important reason Lincoln summoned Douglass was to enlist his aid in a scheme suggestive of John Brown and Harpers Ferry. As Douglass later reported the meeting, "the President said he wanted some plan devised by which he could get more of the Slaves within our lines. He thought now was their time—and that such only of them as succeeded in getting within our line would be free after the war was over. This shows that the President only has faith in this proclamation of freedom during the war, and that he believes the operation will cease with the war." In Douglass' judgment, the president also feared that the Emancipation Proclamation would lack legality once the war ended. Lincoln asked the black leader to become general agent of a campaign to mobilize the slaves behind Confederate lines and spirit them to freedom.[15]

Because military fortunes shifted dramatically in late 1864 and this plan for a government-sponsored underground railroad never commenced, Douglass' biographers have paid little attention to it. But it is remarkable that Lincoln suggested such a scheme to Douglass; it would have forged an unprecedented alliance between black leadership and federal power for the purpose of emancipation. On August 29, 1864, Douglass wrote to Lincoln, outlining a plan where twenty-five agents would work at the front, channeling slaves into Union lines. After his meeting with Lincoln, he had discussed the plan with several other black leaders; all believed in the "wisdom" of the idea, Douglass reported, but only "some" thought it "practicable." Although he seemed willing to lead such an operation and committed himself to Lincoln, it is unlikely that Douglass had much enthusiasm for it. Organizing his "band of scouts," as he referred to the plan in his autobiography, must have been a daunting prospect. Events, however, quickly rendered the whole scheme unnecessary.[16]

The Democrats' nomination of George B. McClellan at the end of August and the fall of Atlanta on September 2 suddenly made Lincoln's reelection look better to abolitionists like Douglass. McClellan and the Democrats' peace-at-any-price platform put Lincoln's moderation in a different light. By late September, Frémont withdrew from

14. On Douglass' meeting with Lincoln, see Huggins, *Slave and Citizen*, 99–100; Quarles, *Douglass*, 216–17; Quarles, *Lincoln and the Negro*, 214–16.

15. Douglass, *Life and Times*, 358.

16. Douglass to Lincoln, August 29, 1864, in Foner (ed.), *Life and Writings*, III, 405–406. The best record of the meeting is Douglass to Theodore Tilton, October 15, 1864, in *ibid.*, 422–24.

the race and the choice was simplified. "When there was any shadow of a hope that a man of a more decided antislavery conviction . . . could be elected, I was not for Mr. Lincoln," Douglass wrote to Theodore Tilton. "But as soon as the Chicago [Democratic] convention, my mind was made up, and it is made still. All dates changed with the nomination of Mr. McClellan." Douglass did not actively campaign for Lincoln, though many other abolitionists did. Sensing the Republican desire not to be identified as the "N-r party," he stayed away from the stump. "The Negro is the deformed child . . . ," he complained to Tilton, "put out of the room when company comes." But like virtually all abolitionists, Douglass rejoiced in Lincoln's reelection. Copperheads were silenced and the back of the Confederacy had been broken.[17]

Douglass spent the last months of the war performing in his customary dual roles: black leader and national patriot. In October, 1864, he wrote the "Address" of the Colored National Convention held in Syracuse. "We shall speak . . . for our race . . . ," Douglass declared, "but we speak not the less for our country." For so long Douglass had wanted to make the black cause the same as the nation's, and that goal now seemed within grasp. The nation's "welfare and permanent peace," he lectured the American people, "can only result from . . . wise and just measures towards our whole race." Douglass was still a Jeremiah warning against backsliding on emancipation, still cautioning against a backlash of postwar racism, still conditional with his trust in the Republican party. But by the fall of 1864 and increasingly into the next year, he saw a new day dawning for black people: "The change is great, and increasing," he announced, "and is viewed with astonishment and dread by all those who had hoped to stand forever with their heels upon our necks." The last months of the Civil War were a time when Douglass could combine race advocacy with nationalism as never before.[18]

In 1865 Douglass shared with his people a great sense of jubilation. An unparalleled turning-point in their history had been reached— black troops were among the first to enter the fallen cities of Charleston and Richmond, and in February Congress removed any

17. Douglass to Tilton, October 15, 1864, in Foner (ed.), *Life and Writings*, III, 424. On the abolitionists' stumping for Lincoln, see McPherson, *Struggle for Equality*, 383–84.

18. "The Cause of the Negro People," 410. A good example of one of Douglass' jeremiads about the extent of postwar racism is in "What the Black Man Wants," 160.

legal doubt about the future of emancipation. Douglass must have been moved by the letter his son Charles wrote from Washington, describing the celebration of the passage of the Thirteenth Amendment: "I wish you could have been here the day that the constitutional amendment was passed forever abolishing slavery in the United States," Charles wrote from his job at a freedmen's hospital, "such rejoicing I never before witnessed, cannons firing, people hugging and shaking hands, white people I mean, flags flying. . . . I tell you things are progressing finely . . . if only they will give us the elective franchise."[19]

Although its extent could not be predicted, a revolution in American race relations was underway. Douglass had said as much in a triumphant return to his native Maryland in November, 1864. Just sixteen days after slavery was abolished by law in Maryland, he journeyed to Baltimore for the first time in twenty-six years. In a dramatic and emotional address to an emancipation celebration at the AME church where he first experienced organized religion as a slave boy, Douglass set aside his bitterness toward slaveholders. He came "not to condemn the past," he told the racially mixed gathering, "but to commend and rejoice over the present." He felt almost "awed into silence" at the changes the war had wrought. This was not Douglass the propagandist or the moral reformer; it was a homecoming, as Douglass said, "hailed with the joy of an exiled son." He spoke with deep affection for Maryland, his only true "native soil," and rejoiced that his return was possible. That Maryland was now a free state seemed to verify that "the revolution is genuine, full and complete."[20]

Douglass held no illusions that those on the bottom rung would suddenly rise to the top of the American social ladder, and he seemed aware that the abolition peace he desired would come harder than the abolition war. The freedmen's integration into American society would require power, commitment, and patience that would be difficult to sustain in the postwar period. Emancipation in America had occurred more as an imperative of total war than as a result of national policy forged through the political process. Nevertheless, chattel slavery had been destroyed. In Douglass' vision, racial democracy

19. Charles R. Douglass to Douglass, Washington, D.C., February 9, 1865, in FD Papers (LC).
20. The Bethel AME Church speech was printed in full in a pamphlet, "A Friendly Word to Maryland: A Lecture Delivered by Frederick Douglass, Esq., in Bethel Church on the 17th of November, 1864" (Baltimore, 1864), quoted in Preston, *Young Frederick Douglass*, 162–63.

was the next step in the nation's rebirth, though he knew it would not come easily. His old despair of the late-1850s seemed far in the past. Expended in the fury of war, the old hatred of slaveholders had also subsided. Conditioned to view history in a millennial framework and living through what appeared to be a rapid succession of revolutionary changes, Douglass believed the country had received an apocalyptic education in the war. Only small numbers of Americans would have willed emancipation in 1861; none could stop it in 1864–65. Few might will the racial democracy Douglass advocated in 1865; but with time, might that not also become a national imperative? The last months of the Civil War and the early stage of Reconstruction were a season of hope for blacks.

Douglass often pointed to Lincoln's example in speaking of the educative nature of the war. Although frequently one of the president's fiercest critics, he acknowledged Lincoln's ability to change on racial issues. "If he did not control events," Douglass said of Lincoln, "he had the wisdom to be instructed by them. When he no longer could withstand the current, he swam with it."[21] The black orator expressed these sentiments both before and after Lincoln's death. The idealist in Douglass saw this educative feature of the war as the bridge from wartime emancipation and black enlistment to peacetime racial democracy, but the realist in him knew that this final goal could only be reached through power politics, against a resurgent racism, and on behalf of a needy and largely illiterate population of ex-slaves.

But what a beginning had been made! There were 170,000 blacks in uniform, marching as conquerors across the South, while slavery— the institution from which all blacks were forced to derive social identity—was abolished. Many slave quarters had been converted to freedmen's schools, and the federal government seemed ready to pay for at least some of the transition to freedom through a Freedmen's Bureau. Substantial land redistribution seemed a real possibility along the coast of the Carolinas, and streetcar segregation and other "black laws" were being repealed in some northern states and cities. John Rock, a black lawyer from Boston, was admitted to practice before the U.S. Supreme Court, and Douglass found himself an invited guest at Lincoln's second inauguration. Black people everywhere, for the first time, could have a sense of belonging in the land of their birth. Whether he was a former fugitive slave who had become

21. "Abraham Lincoln—A Speech," December, 1865 (handwritten), in FD Papers (LC).

an internationally famous orator and writer or a fieldhand in the Sea Islands of South Carolina, half-broken by age, work, and despair, every black American in the last months of the Civil War could realize that something profound had changed his relationship to white people, to the land, to the government, and to the country.

When news of Lincoln's assassination reached Rochester on April 13, 1865, Douglass had just returned from speaking engagements in the East, where he had seen in many towns great joy at the war's ending. He shared the shock of fellow northerners at how a springtime of relief turned overnight into horror and mourning. A throng of Rochester citizens gathered at City Hall, as Douglass remembered, "not knowing what else to do in the agony of the hour." Douglass was called upon to speak and, although he described his own emotions as "stunned and overwhelmed," he held forth nonetheless. "I had resided long in Rochester, and had made many speeches there which had more or less touched the hearts of my hearers," he recalled, "but never to this day was I brought into such close accord with them. We shared in common a terrible calamity, and this touch of nature made us more than countrymen, it made us Kin."[22]

Douglass' use of the words *countrymen* and *kin* is revealing. Perhaps this tells us as much as anything what the war had meant to Douglass. In common grief with his fellow citizens (mostly white), the black orator felt his fullest sense of belonging. The war had provided a common sense of nationhood; Lincoln's death, a common sense of family. Douglass saw himself as America's representative "exiled son." Out of a common search for meaning in Lincoln's violent death at the dawning of peace, Douglass felt a unity with other Americans theretofore unrealized. Most blacks would have a long way to go to achieve Douglass' status and good fortune, but were not all black leaders (and to a certain extent the slaves as well) exiles in their own land, a people denied a birthright and a social identity? To Douglass, the Civil War offered a rare moment in history when that older circumstance could be overturned. The "exiled son" who triumphantly returned to the free state of Maryland in late 1864 was the same exiled son who returned to Rochester in April, 1865, to share the grief of his fellow citizens. Both were homecomings: one to his native Maryland, and the other to his adopted western New York. His two lives and two homes were no longer divided. Douglass' quest for kinship with his countrymen found reality in the Civil War.

22. Douglass, *Life and Times*, 371–72.

9/Fragile Jubilee: Douglass and the Meaning of Reconstruction

The man who does not hate with an implacable hate the whole system of bondage which for two hundred and fifty years ground down his race in this country cannot truly love his newly acquired liberty, or be depended upon to properly guard that liberty. We insist upon it, and fire will not burn it out of us, that no colored voter shall either forget or forgive the men who have enslaved him until they have repented, and given evidence of that repentance by doing justice to the colored race.
—Frederick Douglass, *New National Era*, December 22, 1870

> Emancipation: 1865
> Sighted through the
> Telescope of dreams
> Looms larger,
> So much larger,
> So it seems,
> Than truth can be.
>
> But turn the telescope around,
> Look through the larger end—
> And wonder why
> What was so large
> Becomes so small
> Again.
> —Langston Hughes, "Long View: Negro," 1965

FREDERICK DOUGLASS EMERGED from the Civil War years with renewed faith in his people's future in America. That faith would be sorely tested again and again down to the end of his life in 1895, but now it was rooted in experience as well as in ideology and spirit. The apparent revolutionary changes brought by the war strengthened Douglass' nationalism, made him ultimately a loyal Republican, provided an opportunity to vent some—though not all—of his rage against slaveholders, and gave him an increasingly prestigious social identity. To Douglass, the war's results were a precious legacy, a heritage in which he could claim ownership. His greatest tasks in postwar America were to find new roles for himself in a society that no longer needed abolitionists and, most important, to find ways to protect the results and preserve the meaning of the war as it receded into memory. At the first task he was a great success. Preserving the legacy of the war as the aging orator interpreted it, however, proved to be an almost desperate endeavor.

Douglass remembered the immediate aftermath of the Civil War as a time of "vast changes" and personal ambivalence. "A strange and perhaps perverse feeling came over me," he wrote in 1881, admitting that his great joy over the abolition of slavery had been "tinged with a feeling of sadness." Douglass had always been enlivened by struggle and necessity, and his autobiographical descriptions indicate that he may have experienced a depression once a major portion of the struggle for abolition seemed over. "I felt that I had reached the end of the noblest and best part of my life," he lamented. "The antislavery platform had performed its work, and my voice was no longer needed. Othello's occupation was gone."[1] Douglass' career as an orator, reformer, and black leader was hardly over—he would play new roles in the postwar society, some with great distinction and some without, and he would eventually make a comfortable living, largely from his exhaustive lecture tours. But to a certain extent, the "noblest and best" work of Douglass' life was indeed behind him in 1865. It is revealing that sixteen years after Appomattox, he would remember the aftermath of the war in such terms.

Douglass saw Reconstruction as a continuation of the purpose of the Civil War and envisioned it as a grand opportunity rooted in the Emancipation Proclamation and the Thirteenth Amendment, and as a sacred responsibility to the Union dead. President Andrew Johnson's leniency toward the South, his commitment to states'-rights doctrine, and his hostility to black civil and political rights outraged Douglass. Along with George T. Downing of Washington, D.C., he led a delegation of five blacks who obtained an interview with Johnson on February 7, 1866. The president was cordial but delivered what appeared to be a prepared address in which he self-righteously declared himself ready to be the "Moses" of the freedpeople. Johnson brandished his fear of race war, stressed the virtues of majority rule, coldly rebuked Douglass' advocacy of black suffrage, and suggested that colonization was the best option for the freedpeople. During the interview, Douglass attempted several times to interject the issue of black suffrage or to simply engage the president in discussion, but Johnson sought no discussion with black leaders. In a formal reply published immediately after the interview, Douglass was restrained but clear in his denunciation of Johnson's policies, which "would arm

1. Douglass, *Life and Times,* 373.

the strong and cast down the defenseless." The president's Recon-struction plans reflected motives that were anything but "just, fair, or wise." One can only imagine Douglass' thoughts as he sat across the room from Andrew Johnson in the White House, less than a year after Appomattox, and heard the president declare "the feelings of my own heart . . . have been for the colored man. I have owned slaves and bought slaves, but I never sold one."[2]

Douglass made no distinction between Johnson's white supremacy and slavery itself. In one of his earliest postwar speeches, Douglass asserted that even when every southern state had ratified the Thir-teenth Amendment, "while the black man is confronted in the legis-lation of the South by the word 'white', our work as abolition-ists . . . is not done." Douglass anticipated the passage of the "black codes"—laws proscribing the basic human rights of the freedpeople in most southern states—that flowed from new state governments reconstructed under Johnson's authority. Only such a "system of un-friendly legislation," Douglass contended, could result from govern-ments ruled by ex-Confederates. Moreover, with other Radicals, Douglass made black suffrage the great crusade of Reconstruction. "Slavery is not abolished until the black man has the ballot," he lectured his fellow abolitionists in May, 1865. In Douglass' reasoning, as long as Johnson controlled Reconstruction policy, the war was not really over. Douglass' early postwar thought provides one stark exam-ple of the political and moral distance between Johnson and the Radi-cals, as well as a portent of the great conflicts on the immediate horizon.[3]

When the Fourteenth Amendment was passed in May, 1866, Doug-lass followed the lead of Wendell Phillips and Gerrit Smith in oppos-ing it on the grounds that it did not provide for black suffrage. Re-publicans were deeply divided by the issue of black suffrage while preparing for the crucial congressional elections of 1866. If they pressed the measure, they feared the loss of northern votes and, there-

2. "Interview with President Andrew Johnson," and "Reply of the Colored Delega-tion to the President," both in Foner (ed.), Life and Writings, IV, 185–91, 191–93. On the meeting between the black delegation and Johnson, see McPherson, Struggle for Equal-ity, 343, 346–47. On President Johnson's views toward blacks, especially the questions of suffrage and civil rights, see Eric L. McKitrick, Andrew Johnson and Reconstruction (Chicago, 1960), 55–61, 313–15; and especially LaWanda Cox and John H. Cox, "John-son and the Negro," in Kenneth M. Stampp and Leon F. Litwack (ed.), Reconstruction: An Anthology of Revisionist Writings (Baton Rouge, 1969), 59–82.

3. "The Need for Continuing Antislavery Work," speech at the Thirty-Second An-nual Meeting of the American Antislavery Society, May 9, 1865, in Foner (ed.), Life and Writings, IV, 166–69.

fore, the failure to wrest Reconstruction policy away from Johnson. But in the South the newly created Republican party depended largely upon potential black voters. There was also the vexing question of whether American citizenship could be guaranteed without the right to vote. To Douglass, such a proposition rendered his "equal" citizenship "but an empty name": "To say that I am a citizen to pay taxes . . . obey laws . . . and fight the battles of the country, but in all that respects voting and representation, I am but as so much inert matter, is to insult my manhood." With time, the Fourteenth Amendment and its guarantee of "equal protection of the laws" would become a cherished and controversial part of the Civil War legacy. Without the influence of Radical Republicans, ironically even those who opposed it, the Fourteenth Amendment, perhaps the most momentous constitutional change wrought by the Civil War, could never have been adopted in the nineteenth century. It was the product of a unique historical moment, one that Douglass would soon be struggling to preserve and revive. But until linked with suffrage, citizenship and equal protection seemed hollow measures in the political climate of 1866.[4]

In September, 1866, circumstances gave Douglass the center stage in pushing the cause of black suffrage. In August, the National Union Convention, a coalition of conservative elements from all sections of the country, met in Philadelphia to rally around the policies of Andrew Johnson. Appalled by this display of obeisance to the former Confederate states, and against the backdrop of the bloody antiblack riots in New Orleans and Memphis that spring and summer, Republicans decided to convene their own convention of "Southern Loyalists" in Philadelphia. Hundreds of northern Republicans attended as honorary delegates, including Douglass, who was unexpectedly elected by his fellow party members in Rochester.

Douglass' presence at the convention was the subject of controversy even before he arrived in Philadelphia. Aboard a train somewhere in eastern Pennsylvania, a group of fellow delegates visited him and, after expressing their high regard, urged him not to participate in the convention. The "undesirableness" of his presence, they

4. *National Antislavery Standard* (New York), July 7, 1866; Kenneth M. Stampp, *The Era of Reconstruction, 1865–1877* (New York, 1965), 12–13. For background analysis of the complex origins of the Fourteenth Amendment, I have relied upon Harold M. Hyman, *A More Perfect Union: The Impact of the Civil War and Reconstruction on the Constitution* (Boston, 1975), 446–71; and McKitrick, *Andrew Johnson*, 326–63. The political climate of 1866 was charged by race riots in Memphis and New Orleans, and by Johnson's vetoes of the Freedmen's Bureau and Civil Rights bills.

declared, was dictated by northern racial prejudice. In the contest for votes in the fall elections, these Republicans believed they must dodge the "cry of social and political equality" sure to be raised against them, and even such an earnest Radical as Thaddeus Stevens would later worry privately about the untimeliness of Douglass' role in the convention. Although he must have found such reactions disconcerting, Douglass remembered warning his detractors that should they persist in excluding him, they would be "branded . . . as dastardly hypocrites." Not to have participated, he wrote, "would contradict the principle and purpose of my life."[5] Since the 1840s, Douglass' life and work had been a symbolic presence in America, but rarely had his physical presence caused such a stir in the house of his friends.

On September 3, nearly three hundred delegates gathered at Independence Hall for a grand procession, two abreast, through the streets of Philadelphia. Having failed to exclude Douglass, most Republicans resolved to openly ignore him. Awkward and conspicuous, Douglass stood alone as the lines formed; the delegates, he recalled, "seemed to be ashamed or afraid of me." To Douglass' rescue came Theodore Tilton, a friend and an editor of the New York *Independent.* During the lengthy procession, Douglass' and Tilton's arm-in-arm march garnered tumultuous cheers from the large crowds and the scowls of some tense Republicans. The event would also become the subject of great ridicule in the Democratic party and pro-Johnson newspapers.[6]

For three days southern and northern delegates met separately and attacked Johnson and the Democrats. Trouble began on the fourth day when Douglass, Tilton, and Anna Dickinson, the young Quaker orator, entered the hall of the southern loyalists. Border state delegates opposed black suffrage and tried to force adjournment, whereas delegates from the former Confederate states, directly dependent on black votes, held out for a suffrage resolution by the convention. The decisive moments came when Dickinson and Douglass were called upon to speak. Dickinson, a mere twenty-four years old and already heralded as the Joan of Arc of the abolitionist platform, urged black suffrage as an inevitable step in human progress, an act of considerable courage and irony, since the right of women to vote was nowhere recognized. The content of Douglass' speech is not known, but we do know that he invoked thunderous cheers with his appeal for the franchise. "I . . . responded with all the energy of my soul," he later

5. Douglass, *Life and Times,* 387–89; McPherson, *Struggle for Equality,* 361.
6. Quarles, *Douglass,* 230–31; McPherson, *Struggle for Equality,* 361.

wrote, "for I looked upon suffrage to the Negro as the only measure which would prevent him from being thrust back into slavery." Some border state delegates bolted the convention, declaring its business finished. Meanwhile, the mass of southern delegates reconvened the next morning, expressed public thanks to Douglass and Dickinson, and then forthrightly endorsed black suffrage. Douglass experienced few such opportunities to truly influence public policy, either before or after the Southern Loyalists Convention. Although the Fifteenth Amendment was still two years away, its momentum swung into motion at Philadelphia in 1866, and Douglass must have reveled in the irony, as he put it, of how "the ugly and deformed child of the family" had won a "victory" over fear and expediency.[7]

Douglass' ideas about Reconstruction fell squarely into the Radical Republican camp. He also confronted the revolutionary changes brought by the war from his customary apocalyptic outlook. The great challenge before the new Republican-controlled Congress in 1866–67, Douglass believed, was to determine "whether the tremendous war so heroically fought . . . shall pass into history a miserable failure, barren of permanent results," or whether the victors would gain the "rightful reward of victory over treason . . . a solid nation, entirely delivered from all contradictions . . . based upon loyalty, liberty and equality." The war, he contended, was "an impressive teacher, though a stern and terrible one." The American people were in the midst of overturning an old and evil age, and if properly "instructed" by their suffering, they might experience a lasting and glorious rebirth. Radical Reconstruction, Douglass asserted in words that echoed his wartime rhetoric, was the "great work of national regeneration and entire purification."[8]

The war had refurbished Douglass' faith in the doctrine of progress and had sustained his apocalyptic view of history, but as for policy, Douglass saw Reconstruction as a largely political problem. He approached the restoration of the Union as a matter of political and moral will. The Confederacy, its political and military leadership, and all that sustained slavery and its ideology were to Douglass like "deadly upas" that must be "root and branch, leaf and fibre, body and sap . . . utterly destroyed." Concurrently, his principle goal for the freedpeople was political liberty, created and sustained by federal law.

7. Douglass, *Life and Times*, 390–91; Quarles, *Douglass*, 232–34; McPherson, *Struggle for Equality*, 128–32.

8. "Reconstruction," *Atlantic Monthly*, December, 1866, in Foner (ed.), *Life and Writings*, IV, 198–99, 201.

Douglass infused the suffrage with all-pervasive significance. The best way to reconstruct the Union, Douglass maintained, was not to give the federal government "despotic power" or to "station a federal officer at every crossroad." "The true way," he urged, was to "give to every loyal citizen the elective franchise—a right and power which will be ever present, and will form a wall of fire for his protection." This proposition, however, was one of the paradoxes in Douglass' Reconstruction thought; it was just such a "despotic power" that he desired from the federal government in order to protect the freedpeople, to build a larger and more effective Freedmen's Bureau, and eventually to eradicate the Ku Klux Klan. He wholeheartedly supported the military measures legislated by Congress in 1867 and cheered on the Radicals in the impeachment crisis of 1868. The Radicals' brief but ill-fated desire to remake the South fit comfortably into Douglass' conception of the war and its meaning—in late 1866 he urged Congress to approach the former Confederate states "with a clean slate, and make clean work of it."[9]

Rooted in liberal political ideology, Douglass' vision of Reconstruction lacked thoroughgoing economic analysis. This hardly made him an exception, even among Radical Republicans, but his most basic assumptions created several unresolved contradictions in his postwar thought: a fierce belief in the sanctity of private property while demanding land for the powerless freedpeople; laissez-faire individualism and black self-reliance coupled with demands for federal aid to the freedpeople; and political liberty viewed as the a priori path to economic independence and social equality. These conflicts reflect a continuity between Douglass' prewar and postwar thought. Political and moral phenomena had always dominated his mind; liberty for a fugitive slave rising to fame as a reformer had always been an intensely individualistic affair. Much of Douglass' autobiographical writing stressed his personal triumph of will and his political education. Indeed, American individualism had few better proponents than the postwar Douglass who celebrated "self-made men" in a famous lecture delivered countless times.[10] Thus, though deeply committed to the welfare of the freedpeople, Douglass was limited in his assessment of the economic complexity of their lot and, as the years of

9. *Ibid.,* 201, 200, 203.
10. "Self-Made Men," speech by Douglass delivered during numerous postwar lecture tours, in FD Papers (LC), reel 18. On Douglass' Reconstruction ideas as well as his conception of self-made men, see Martin, *Mind,* 66–71, 253–78.

Reconstruction passed, he fell somewhat out of touch with their plight. He did not lack commitment or understanding; rather, he lacked creative prescriptions for the welfare of America's recently enslaved peasantry in an age rapidly growing intolerant to humanitarian reform and hostile to government philanthropy.

Throughout Reconstruction, Douglass mixed his customary optimism with emphasis on the legacy of slavery and the immensity of what his people had to overcome. Slavery, Douglass contended in 1866, had left the Negro "physically, a maimed and mutilated man," had "twisted his limbs, shattered his feet, deformed his body and distorted his features." Repeatedly, Douglass stressed that the black man's "speed in the new race of life" should not be measured from "the heights which the white race has attained, but from the depths from which he has come." Although Douglass never tired of celebrating the glory of emancipation, he never ceased to observe—often lament—the lack of progress among his people. Ten years after the war, Douglass observed the economic and physical well-being of the freedpeople with both anger and awe: "The world has never seen any people turned loose to such destitution," he argued, "as were the four million slaves of the South. . . . We gave them freedom and famine at the same time."[11]

The ravages of slavery were thrown into stark contrast for Douglass as the war made possible a series of emotional reunions with his own siblings who had remained in bondage. During the black orator's triumphant first return to Baltimore in late 1864, he encountered his fifty-two-year-old sister Eliza Mitchell, who had traveled sixty miles to hear Douglass lecture. They had not communicated with each other since 1836, the year Douglass left the Eastern Shore for good, and one year before his escape from slavery. Eliza was a sturdy woman who had purchased her own freedom and had mothered nine children, one of whom she named Mary Douglass Mitchell in honor of her famous brother. Douglass, the urbane citizen of the world in a moment of public triumph, learned privately from his illiterate sister that many of his Bailey kin had "been sold and scattered through the rebellious slave states." An even more compelling reunion occurred in 1867, when Douglass' older brother Perry and his family of six came to Rochester. Perry had been nearly fifty-six years a slave, much

11. "The Future of the Colored Race," *North American Review,* May, 1866, in Foner (ed.), *Life and Writings,* IV, 194; "Speech on the Occasion of the Centennial Celebration of the Abolition Society of Pennsylvania," Philadelphia, 1875, in FD Papers (LC), reel 15. For similar sentiments, also see Douglass, *Life and Times,* 377.

of that time in Texas, where he had followed his wife after she was sold. Through kindly intermediaries in New Orleans and New York, Perry contacted Douglass by letter and made his way to the North. In July, Douglass returned from a lecture tour to find Perry's family at his home in Rochester. "The meeting of my brother after nearly forty years of separation is an event altogether too affecting for words to describe," he wrote. "How unutterably accursed is slavery, and how unspeakably joyful are the results of the overthrow!" Such reunions in the wake of the war, Douglass concluded, were a "subject of the deepest pathos." He spent much of the summer of 1867, the period of heady ascendency for the Radical Republicans, building a small house for Perry's family. But Douglass' sons and daughter, all grown to adulthood, did not take well to their strange relatives, and the contrasts between the family of freedpeople and the family of northern, middle-class blacks were striking and disruptive. Douglass' son Charles, distressed by what he had "heard of their conduct," wrote to his father, wondering "in what way those people you have at home are related to you." Perry's family stayed in Rochester until 1869, whereupon they moved back to the Eastern Shore of Maryland.[12]

Douglass found these reunions a source of both joy and unresolved anguish. The social distance between himself and his close relatives could only have reminded him of his own strange and exceptional life while at the same time forcing him to face the brutal legacy of slavery. His brother Perry had come to him, Douglass wrote to Theodore Tilton, "as if he had lived on another planet." He might have written a "narrative" of Perry's bondage "if slavery were not dead, and I did not in some sort wish to forget its terrible hardships . . . and shocking horrors." His brother's story he would leave unwritten, perhaps because he was busy with his lecturing career, perhaps because there was much in the story he could never reconstruct, or perhaps because there was much that he did not wish to confront at this juncture in his life. "Let the old system go!" Douglass declared in rejoicing over his brother's freedom. "I would not call its guilty ghost from the depths into which its crimes have cast it. I turn gladly from the darkness of the past to the new better dispensation now dawning."[13] His own life

12. Letter from Douglass, in New York *Independent*, March 2, 1865; Douglass to J. J. Spelman, July 11, 1867, in *ibid.*, July 25, 1867; Charles R. Douglass to Douglass, August 16, 1867, in FD Papers (LC), reel 2. The intermediary in New Orleans was the Rev. T. W. Conway. On both reunions, see Preston, *Young Frederick Douglass*, 163–64, 175–77.

13. Douglass to Theodore Tilton, New York *Independent*, September 12, 1867, in Foner (ed.), *Life and Writings*, IV, 205–206.

was, of course, one of profound and heroic change, and the nation, he could only reason, had just experienced something similar. But these terrible contrasts between the public and private elements of his life often left him grasping for explanation. Douglass' life and thought would always be characterized by this timeless, troublesome problem of understanding just how powerful the spell of the past over the present was.

In spite of his occasional hostility to private benevolent societies, Douglass fully supported the efforts of the Freedmen's Bureau. Indeed, he almost became its director in 1867 when Andrew Johnson, as a political ploy against his Radical foes, indirectly offered Douglass a chance to head the agency that the president detested. Douglass declined the appointment, knowing full well that Johnson's offer was only part of the bitter machinations between the president and the Radicals. When the incident became public, Douglass' friends made the most if it; "the greatest black man in the nation," declared Theodore Tilton, "did not become the tool of the meanest white."[14] Douglass, however, remained committed to the work of the Freedmen's Bureau, even as he watched it die an early death with so much work left undone and so much promise unfulfilled.

Douglass was especially concerned with the issues of education and land for the freedpeople. He applauded all the educational efforts of the Freedmen's Bureau, including the hundreds of small schools established in the hinterland of the South, as well as colleges such as Howard University in Washington, D.C. Charles Douglass, who worked as a clerk at the agency's headquarters in Washington, sent his father volumes of information, including "a file of all the reports issued from this office since the commencement of the bureau" on the topic of freedmen's education.[15] Douglass had always been driven by the quest for knowledge; nothing had given more meaning to his life than the freedom, self-understanding, and power he had attained through language and learning. Education, therefore, was indispensable to his social reform philosophy, as well as to his vision of Reconstruction.

14. William Slade to Douglass, July 29, August 18, 1867; Charles R. Douglass to Douglass, July 18, September 2, 1867; Douglass to Slade, August 12, 1867, all in FD Papers (LC), reel 2. Charles worked as a clerk at the Freedmen's Bureau and was approached by a Carter Stewart about whether Douglass would accept the job as head of the agency. Charles hoped his father would take it because "the work is easier than lecturing and traveling." The Tilton letter is from the New York *Independent*, September 12, 1867.

15. Charles R. Douglass to Douglass, August 12, 1868, in FD Papers, (LC), reel 2. On freedmen's education, see Litwack, *Been in the Storm*, 472–501.

By the end of the war Douglass had long been a proponent of free public schools and a fierce opponent of educational segregation, but he had begrudgingly—and he hoped temporarily—accepted separate black schools founded in the spirit of self-reliance. The depth of American racism and the need for industrial education for blacks, he reasoned, dictated such a position, although "present circumstances are the only apology." Since the 1850s, Douglass had advocated manual labor schools and had preached the virtues of farming for blacks. He is, therefore, often cited as a precursor of the educational and social philosophy of Booker T. Washington.[16]

Although there is ample evidence for this enduring strain in Douglass' thought advanced during Reconstruction and beyond, it is equally true that emancipation invoked a deeper, more classical educational vision from Douglass. In a lecture in October, 1865, at the dedication of the Douglass Institute—a black school in Baltimore founded in his honor—Douglass spoke emotionally of "the rise of a people long oppressed . . . and bound in chains of ignorance to a freer and higher plane of life . . . and civilization." He rejoiced that Baltimore blacks would "dare here and now to establish an institute devoted to all the higher wants and aspirations of the human soul." The school would be their very own "from foundation to roof," and it would contradict the claim among white supremacists that blacks lacked the "consciousness" essential to human moral and intellectual aspiration. The challenge of black education, Douglass declared, was no less than the cultivation of just such an historical consciousness. "Man learns from the past," Douglass asserted, "improves upon the past, looks back upon the past, and hands down his knowledge of the past to after-coming generations. . . . To lack this element of progress is to resemble the lower animals, and to possess it is to be men." These were hardly the sentiments of one devoted merely to industrial education. In words that anticipated the educa-

16. "The Douglass Institute," lecture at inauguration of the Douglass Institute, Baltimore, October, 1865, in Foner (ed.), *Life and Writings*, IV, 178–79; Douglass to W. J. Wilson, August 8, 1865, in *ibid.*, 172; Martin, *Mind*, 192–93. Martin points to Douglass' strong advocacy of black manual-labor schools in the 1850s to demonstrate this link to Washington; moreover, he finds it inherently inconsistent with Douglass' advocacy of free public schools for all children regardless of color during the postwar period. But such ambiguity or contradiction in nineteenth-century black educational thought was common, perhaps unavoidable, given the racist social and legal context. Douglass advocated both strains of black educational thought until the end of his life: Du Boisian classical education and Washingtonian industrial education. For Douglass' views on farming, see "Away to the Country," *New National Era*, September 22, 1870; "Address at the Third Annual Fair of the Tennessee Colored Agricultural and Mechanical Association," September 18, 1873, Nashville, in FD Papers (LC), reel 14.

tional philosophy of W. E. B. Du Bois far more than that of Booker T. Washington, Douglass announced the mission of the Douglass Institute:

We who have been long debarred the privileges of culture may assemble and have our souls . . . lifted to the skies on the wings of poetry and song. Here . . . we can have our minds enlightened upon the whole circle of social, moral, political and educational duties. Here we can come and learn true politeness and refinements. Here the loftiest and best eloquence which the country has produced, whether of Anglo-Saxon or African descent, shall flow as a river, enriching . . . and purifying all who will lay in its waters. Here may come all who have a new and unpopular truth to unfold and enforce. . . . Here, from this broad hall, shall go forth an influence which shall at last change the current of public contempt for the oppressed, and lift the race into the popular consideration which justly belongs to their manly character and achievements.[17]

Such lofty optimism fit the occasion and reflected the new hope among blacks in the immediate aftermath of the war. The Douglass Institute, however, did not achieve distinction among black institutions. Such noble language withered in the face of the bitter struggle of Maryland blacks to achieve true dignity and economic freedom out of the legacy of slavery—a story ably analyzed in the recent work of historian Barbara J. Fields—but Douglass was determined to set the highest standard of aspiration in an educational institution that he described as "a free arena for the strife of mind." Even if frustrated in implementing his ideas, he never lacked eloquence in identifying the largest goals of his people. In the postwar period, he often led best by providing the vocabulary of the new era, rather than by accomplishing specific strategies.[18]

On a more pragmatic level, Douglass perceived land ownership among the freedpeople as a need equal to the ballot and the schoolhouse. Across the South in 1865 the expectation of land ownership, whether imaginary or real, swelled the hopes of ex-slaves, and the promise of land redistribution, explicit in some federal action and implicit in the meaning of emancipation, caused the greatest conflict of the early Reconstruction period. No action so illustrated this fact as did General William T. Sherman's famous Field Order 15, issued in

17. "The Douglass Institute," 176–82. In the spring of 1865, an association of thirty-four Baltimore blacks purchased a building, formerly called the Newton University, for sixteen thousand dollars. Called the Douglass Institute, the school's purpose was to be "the intellectual advancement of the colored portion of the community." See Foner (ed.), *Life and Writings,* IV, note 5, p. 544.

18. Barbara J. Fields, *Slavery and Freedom on the Middle Ground: Maryland During the Nineteenth Century* (New Haven, 1985), 90–166.

January, 1865, which set aside the South Carolina Sea Islands and a long stretch of coastline for the exclusive settlement of the freedpeople. During the spring and summer of 1865, thousands of black families were relocated on these abandoned lands with the direct assistance of the Union army and the Freedmen's Bureau. But after planting a crop and experiencing freedom and independence as they had never known it, promise turned to betrayal as President Johnson rescinded Sherman's order, requiring the land to be returned to its original owners. All observers knew that land ownership meant economic liberty for the freedpeople, but the newly pardoned planters struggled mightily to maintain the economic dependence of their former slaves, and a wide range of wage labor, contract, and tenant schemes began to replace the old order in the South. As one of the Civil War's greatest promises slipped away over the years of Reconstruction, the freedpeople left a compelling story of just how vehemently they asserted their right to the land. In varying ways, blacks claimed the land they worked by the labor theory of value, a position never more eloquently stated than by a freedman named Bayley Wyatt, at a contraband camp in Virginia in 1866:

We has a right to the land where we are located. For why? I tell you. Our wives, our children, our husbands has been sold over and over again to purchase the lands we now locates upon; for that reason we have a divine right to the land. . . . And den didn't we clear the land, and raise de crops ob corn, ob cotton, ob tobacco, ob rice, ob sugar, ob everything. And den didn't dem large cities in de North grow up on de cotton and de sugars and de rice dat we made . . . ? I say dey has grown rich and my people is poor.[19]

Such an appeal represented the central truth of Reconstruction as blacks understood it; no leader of any persuasion could fail to grasp its import.

Douglass never advocated widespread confiscation and redistribution of southern land—that would have necessitated an economic

19. On the freedpeople's quest for land, see Litwack, *Been in the Storm*, 398–408; Edward Magdol, *A Right in the Land: Essays on the Freedmen's Community* (Westport, Conn., 1977), 131–32, 139–73; Eric Foner, *Nothing But Freedom: Emancipation and Its Legacy* (Baton Rouge, 1983), 44–45, 55–58, 82–84; Eric Foner, *Reconstruction: America's Unfinished Revolution, 1863–1877* (New York, 1988), 104–106, 302, 374–77; Armstead L. Robinson, "The Difference Freedom Made: The Emancipation of Afro-Americans," in Darlene Clark Hine (ed.), *The State of Afro-American History: Past, Present, and Future* (Baton Rouge, 1986), 60–64; Rose, *Rehearsal for Reconstruction*, 200–204, 213–14, 282–96. On the abolitionists' efforts to achieve land for the freedpeople, see McPherson, *Struggle for Equality*, 407–16. On the economics of emancipation for blacks, see Roger L. Ransom and Richard Sutch, *One Kind of Freedom: The Economic Consequences of Emancipation* (London, 1977), 1–105. Bayley Wyatt, *A Freedman's Speech* (Philadelphia, 1867), quoted in E. Foner, *Nothing But Freedom*, 56.

revolution he was not prepared to lead, and would have demanded a level of coercion that few in capitalist America could accept. But he did call for direct federal assistance to the freedpeople to enable them to purchase land. In 1869 he sketched a plan for a National Land and Loan Company, which would be created and funded by Congress. The company would sell stock and purchase large tracts of land in the South, small portions of which would be sold to freedmen on easy terms. Douglass demanded "capital" and "small farms . . . sold to the colored people, who with proper instructions can then go to work and make themselves homes." "They will do it," Douglass argued, "and do it successfully if they have a fair chance. . . . Unless something of this kind is done thousands, I fear, will continue to live a miserable life and die a wretched death." No such land policy ever emerged from Radical Reconstruction, a fact Douglass would later deeply lament. The freedpeople, he said in 1880, "were sent away empty handed, without money, without friends, and without a foot of land to stand upon."[20]

By 1870 Douglass seemed to be trapped in a paradox on the land question. A lecture tour of northern Virginia took him to the town of Vienna, where he visited a community of freedpeople living in poverty. "They neither have land nor money," he sadly observed. "They live in narrow and imperfectly built shanties and their children are poorly clad and mostly running wild." How such people lived and yet remained "cheerful" was "a mystery" to Douglass. He counted sixty black children in Vienna and not a single school. But one week after recording these sobering observations of landless poverty, Douglass wrote an editorial, "Away to the Open Country," where he vehemently appealed to blacks to leave cities and go back to the land. For the freedman, he argued, "the great thing is to have him settle upon the land, and obtain a permanent interest in it."

However, Douglass had only fuzzy suggestions for implementing such a scheme. He called for an Emigration Committee in Washington to place black youths on farms and looked to "philanthropic associations" for funding. Just how that precious land was to be provided, Douglass never really specified; he only knew that it should be, and called for a "true missionary" who would "rescue these people from their wretchedness, and open to them the way to knowledge, plenty, and independence." He must have experienced acute frustration from his own contradictory appeals to urban blacks, as well as

20. "A Plan to Buy Land to Be Sold to Freedmen," in FD Papers (LC); P. Foner, *Frederick Douglass,* 253–54; "Speech at Elmira, New York," delivered at a celebration of West Indian Emancipation, August 1, 1880, in FD Papers (LC), reel 15.

those in southern shanty towns, to go "back to the land" that they had no means to purchase. Like virtually everyone else, Douglass lacked viable solutions on the land question.[21]

Throughout the postwar era, Douglass coupled his discussion of all issues regarding the freedpeople with resounding appeals for black self-reliance. In his opening piece as editor of the *New National Era* in 1870, Douglass declared that "the time has come for the colored men of the country to assume the duties and responsibilities of their own existence." Whites had done much through "benevolence and sympathy," he argued, "but respect and confidence are called into life by the vigorous assertion of manly power, self-reliance, and independence."[22] Douglass saw the *New National Era*, which he purchased and operated with two of his sons, as just such a model of black enterprise and self-improvement, but despite exhaustive efforts to make the paper a truly national weekly, it lasted only three years—a deep disappointment Douglass carried with him into the waning days of Reconstruction.

To Douglass, black self-reliance meant adherence to the traditional values of thrift, sobriety, and a work ethic, and as the years passed he became a self-styled proponent of the Gospel of Wealth. At a black agricultural and mechanical fair in Tennessee in 1873, he declared that the great question left unanswered by the war was "whether the black man will prove a better master to himself than his white master was to him." Blacks must stake their own claim to civilization and must build their own culture, Douglass asserted; otherwise they would continue "wearing the old clothes left by a bygone generation." They would have "no science nor philosophy of their own . . . neither history nor poetry." The first step for blacks, argued the orator, was to "accumulate property." Poverty rendered blacks helpless and despondent, whereas "money" could purchase "the only condition upon which any people can rise to the dignity of genuine manhood." Property also made leisure possible, and "without leisure," Douglass concluded, "there can be no thought . . . no progress." He ended his speech with a ringing call for the work ethic. All knowledge and culture, he claimed, were "founded on work, and the wealth which work brings."[23]

21. "Across the Potomac," *New National Era*, September 15, 1870; "Away to the Country," *ibid.*, September 22, 1870.

22. "Salutatory of the Corresponding Editor," *ibid.*, January 27, 1870.

23. "Address at the Third Annual Fair of the Tennessee Colored Agricultural and Mechanical Association." On Douglass and self-reliance, see Martin, *Mind*, 67–72, 254–55.

A decade after the Emancipation Proclamation, Douglass found himself speaking to more and more such gatherings of freedpeople, trying to strike the difficult balance between unrequited black claims on American society and the everlasting necessity of self-reliance. In an 1875 speech, he mixed his oft-repeated demand upon the American people for "justice and fair play" with an equally stern appeal to blacks for self-help and self-respect. "We must not beg men to do for us what we ought to do for ourselves," he argued. "The prostrate form, the uncovered head, the cringing attitude, the bated breath, the suppliant outstretched hand of beggary does not become an American freedman."[24] Douglass never tired of coaxing his people to stand up and assert their own dignity, no matter what level of racism confronted them. He seemed to have concluded from his own experience that, whether in a moral or an economic context, justice and black self-reliance were sometimes separate categories. Indeed, what America has owed to blacks and what blacks have built for themselves have caused one of the deepest tensions faced by black leaders throughout American history.

Douglass was constantly reminded of this tension by the agonizing struggle for self-reliant success within his own family. The postwar letters between Douglass and his three sons, Lewis, Frederick, and Charles, and his daughter Rosetta, reverberate with financial distress, bitter family rivalry, and dependence upon the father's money. Rosetta, the eldest, though well educated, married a fugitive slave named Nathan Sprague, who turned out to be a shiftless ne'er-do-well. Rosetta's growing family became directly dependent upon Douglass' homestead in Rochester as her marriage deteriorated and Nathan failed in one menial job and business scheme after another. By the mid 1870s, Nathan was openly despised by Douglass' sons, while his many creditors sued Rosetta and her father. Lewis had served with merit in the famous 54th Massachusetts Infantry during the war, but both he and Frederick, Jr., were unsuccessful in establishing themselves in business. They went west to Colorado in 1866 and tried to make a living with a laundry business and a "lunch room," but eventually returned to the East, discouraged and dependent upon their father. Lewis' and Frederick's experience with journalism under their father had prepared them to be the printers and publishers of the *New National Era* from 1870 to 1873, but in the end, the paper turned out to be a major loss of ten thousand dollars to the elder Douglass.[25]

The youngest son, Charles, was perhaps the most acute example of

24. "The Color Question," speech delivered July 5, 1875, in FD Papers (LC), reel 15.
25. Nathan Sprague to Douglass, March 26, 1867, Rosetta Sprague to Douglass,

this anguish in the Douglass family. Charles, only eighteen when he enlisted in the 54th Massachusetts in 1863, worked the small farm in Rochester in the aftermath of the war. Eager to make it on his own, he took a job as a clerk at the Freedmen's Bureau in Washington, D.C.—a door his father helped to open. Along with a young wife and baby, he managed to purchase a lot and build a small house of which he was exceedingly proud, but he did so with loan after loan from his father, a level of indebtedness that exceeded one thousand dollars by 1870. Charles' letters are full of an almost desperate need, not only for his father's cash but also for his approval. Charles was very defensive about his debts but sometimes rationalized them through his scorn for Nathan, declaring to his father that "none of us lie buried as deep in your pockets as he [Nathan] does." Although Charles always acknowledged Douglass' constant pleas for thrift and hard work and declared how "unspeakably grateful" he was, he fell deeper and deeper in debt. His circumstances seem to have been caused by a combination of relatively low wages, bad investments, foolish extravagance, and an apparent hypochondria.[26]

By the mid 1870s, Charles' debts damaged the trust in the father-son relationship and caused some of his creditors to threaten legal action and adverse publicity against Douglass. Charles sought a new job with the State Department, hoping for a foreign appointment and perhaps a chance to dodge the creditors. "I know how you feel toward me," Charles wrote to his father in 1875, "and would do anything to change that feeling." Undoubtedly, Douglass experienced great distress and embarrassment over his son's difficulties. From his new position at a forsaken outpost in Santo Domingo in 1876, Charles wrote to his father in despair: "Under the circumstances of my many failures in life," he declared, "I have felt my letters were not desired. I wrote again, however, risking the result. It seems that under any circumstances I am to fail in my undertakings, and my life is to be one series of blunders. I have been here nearly a year and I don't know how I have lived."[27]

Douglass must have deeply pondered the financial distress and singular lack of economic independence in his own family when he made his public appeals for hard work and self-reliance. The greatest

April 11, 1867, February 18, 1869, March 10, 1869, September 17, 1876, Lewis Douglass to Douglass, Denver, Colorado, October 29, 1866, all in FD Papers (LC), reels 2, 3.

26. Charles R. Douglass to Douglass, September 2, 7, 11, 22, 1868, October 27, 1868, May 6, 10, 1870, June 9, 16, 1870, all in *ibid.*, reels 2, 3.

27. Charles R. Douglass to Douglass, July 28, 1875, W. B. Shaw to Douglass, February 7, 1876, Charles R. Douglass to Douglass, Puerto Plata, Santo Domingo, August 5, 1876, all in *ibid.*, reel 3.

need of blacks, Douglass announced in 1873, was "regular and lucrative employments"; their quickest means to independence, he maintained, was to get money, "to work for it, and save it when you get it." In his writings and speeches, Douglass maintained a strict separation between the public and private aspects of his life, but to this champion of the self-improvement formula, the failures of his own children were a haunting irony.[28]

In the long run, Douglass subsumed his economic understanding of Reconstruction in a political world-view. More often than not, he analyzed the plight of the freedpeople, as well as America's growing labor strife, in political terms. He chastised the leaders of labor unions for denouncing capitalism itself as the cause of working-class poverty: "We think that real pauperism, wherever it is found," Douglass wrote in 1871, "can always be traced back to faulty political institutions." He urged workingmen to put their faith in the protectionist policies of the Republican party and in the "great law of trade, which controls the price of labor and everything else." Political liberty and the right political associations would do far more, he contended, "than all the trade unions, eight-hour leagues, and other combinations . . . till the end of time can ever accomplish."[29]

The extent to which political considerations dominated Douglass' economic thought was demonstrated even further by his insensitive and faulty understanding of the southern black exodus to Kansas in 1879–81. Virtually alone among black leaders, he opposed the exodus, which had grown out of intolerable economic conditions and white repression in the lower Mississippi Valley. Refusing to accept that the plight of the freedpeople was "so desperate" as exodus advocates maintained, Douglass based his opposition on a misplaced optimism that with time and patience the "rights" of blacks would be "fully protected in the South." He denounced the movement as an "apostleship of despair" and "a premature, disheartening surrender" of all that had been achieved for freedom and equality since the war. But this legacy of freedom that Douglass now felt so compelled to defend against the idea of black migration was, for him, a largely political affair. As a source of forbearance, Douglass reminded each

28. "Address at the Third Annual Fair of the Tennessee Colored Agricultural and Mechanical Association." On Douglass and the dependence of his children, see Huggins, *Slave and Citizen*, 153–54. On the conflict between the public and private in Douglass' autobiography, see Donald B. Gibson, "Reconciling Public and Private in Frederick Douglass' Narrative," *American Literature*, LVII (December, 1985), 549–69.

29. *New National Era*, April 20, 1871, November 16, 1871.

freedman of his "standing in the supreme law of the land" through the Fourteenth and Fifteenth amendments. Hope should be sustained because "the permanent powers of the government are all on his side." To the displaced, half-starved victims of white violence on the wharves of a Mississippi River port town, these appeals would have seemed like so much hollow delusion—a realization Douglass himself reached later in life—but, blinded by liberal political ideology and, for a time at least, out of touch with the fate of ordinary southern blacks, Douglass clung to the power of the ballot and to the promise of the Constitution. His position on the exodus demonstrated his growing estrangement, not only from other black leaders but from economic reality as well.[30]

Although never at his best in economic analysis, the postwar Douglass was quite at home in political affairs. Throughout the early years of Reconstruction, he traveled and labored exhaustively for black suffrage; his two- and three-month lecture tours, which took him from New England to the Great Plains, had no more dominant theme than national politics. When the Fifteenth Amendment passed Congress in 1869 and was ratified by March, 1870, giving blacks the right to vote, Douglass was one of the leading voices in the chorus of celebration among former abolitionists. Although he would have preferred a broader amendment that would have prohibited qualification tests for suffrage, he nevertheless rejoiced in its passage. In the spring of 1870, he spoke at ratification celebrations all over the North. At the final meeting of the American Antislavery Society in New York in April, Douglass spoke of his amazement at the historic changes of the previous decade: "I seem to myself to be living in a new world," he remarked. "The sun does not shine as it used to."[31]

The largest celebration of the Fifteenth Amendment was held in

30. "The Exodus as Policy," handwritten manuscript, 1879, in FD Papers (LC), reel 15. For Douglass' views on the Exodus, also see "Frederick Douglass on the Exodus," a series of resolutions submitted by Douglass at a meeting in Hillsdale District of Columbia, 1879, in FD Papers (LC), reel 15; "Oration at the Second Annual Exposition of the Colored People of North Carolina," Raleigh, October 1, 1880, in ibid., reel 15; "The Negro Exodus from the Gulf States," address before convention of the American Social Science Association, Saratoga Springs, September 12, 1879, in Foner (ed.), *Life and Writings*, IV, 324–42. For Douglass' realization of the folly of his position on the Exodus, see "Southern Barbarism," speech on the occasion of the twenty-fourth anniversary of Emancipation, Washington, D.C., 1886, in ibid., IV, 437–38. For further analysis of Douglass' ideas about the Exodus, see Nell Irvin Painter, *Exodusters: Black Migration to Kansas After Reconstruction* (New York, 1977), 247–50; Martin, *Mind*, 73–77.

31. Quoted in P. Foner, *Frederick Douglass*, 267. On abolitionists and the Fifteenth Amendment, see McPherson, *Struggle for Equality*, 424–30.

Baltimore in mid-May. Twenty thousand blacks marched in a parade with brass bands, and an audience of six thousand listened to a long series of speeches. In his remarks Douglass pointed to three great symbols of black progress: the "cartridge box," the "ballot box," and the "jury box." It was a compelling moment as Douglass stood in the central square of his old home town of Baltimore—the former slave city from which he had escaped to freedom—and addressed a cheering throng of his people claiming their birthright as soldiers, voters, and citizens. "We have a future," Douglass shouted as he concluded, "everything is possible to us!" Despite the uncertainties over whether the Fifteenth Amendment could truly protect black suffrage against white subterfuge, the celebration allowed Douglass some moments of triumph and a sense of closure. The gathering did not adjourn until it passed several resolutions, one of which recognized him as the "foremost man of color in the times" and appealed to him to lead blacks "to a higher, broader, and nobler manhood."[32] So much of Douglass' life had been devoted to the struggle to establish and to feel just such freedom, dignity, and a sense of future.

Douglass soon took a more sober approach to the meaning of the Fifteenth Amendment. A growing indifference toward the freedpeople among northern whites, the rise of the Ku Klux Klan in the South, the resurgence of the Democratic party, and the readmission to the Union of the former Confederate states put all questions of black rights in a cloud of uncertainty even before the celebrations had finished. Douglass entered the 1870s urging blacks to distinguish between what was "seeming" and what was "real" in their prospects, and he cautioned his people not to be absorbed by a "delirium of enthusiasm." The struggle to secure black equality and rights had only begun: "Slavery has left its poison behind it," he warned in October, 1870, "both in the veins of the slave and in those of the enslaver." Citing the Declaration of Independence and the Bill of Rights, he urged his readers to remember America's historic conflict between law and practice. "The settled habits of a nation," Douglass asserted, are "mightier than a statute." With both a strong sense of history and prophetic vision, Douglass warned against the growing penchant to forgive and forget the war and to ignore the freedpeople. The national responsibility to his people, in his view, had only deepened with the passage of the Civil War amendments. He summed up the challenge: "Press, platform, pulpit should continue to direct their energies to the removal of the hardships and wrongs which continue

32. *New National Era*, May 26, 1870. On Douglass and the Fifteenth Amendment celebrations, see Quarles, *Douglass*, 249–51.

to be the lot of the colored people . . . because they wear a complexion which two hundred and fifty years of slavery taught the great mass of the American people to hate, and which the fifteenth amendment has not yet taught the American people to love."[33] Thus did Douglass anticipate the 1870s and 1880s as a time when America would either begin to conquer its historic racism or be overwhelmed by it.

After 1870 Douglass' career underwent major changes, but the central fact of his life and work was that he became a stalwart Republican. He moved permanently to Washington, D.C., in 1872 after his home in Rochester burned in a tragic case of probable arson. In addition to editing the *New National Era* (a weekly), serving as president of and ushering to its demise the ill-fated Freedmen's Savings Bank, and continuing a dizzying lecture schedule, Douglass set himself up in Washington as America's leading black spokesman. He cultivated relationships with congressmen, senators, and virtually every postwar president until his death in 1895. Moreover, he sought prestige and appointive office, something he did not really achieve until 1877, when President Rutherford B. Hayes appointed him marshall for the District of Columbia. Subsequent appointments as recorder of deeds for the District of Columbia (1881–86) and minister to Haiti (1889–91) continued a pattern that gave the aging orator a place—albeit largely emblematic—in Washington officialdom through most of the last third of his life. Ironically, despite his steadfast support of Ulysses S. Grant during both terms of his presidency (1869–77), Douglass received only an appointment as a secretary to the Santo Domingo Commission in 1871. He accompanied the commission to the island but was greatly disappointed when he served only an observer's role, one he later described to Secretary of State Hamilton Fish as "inconsiderable and unimportant."[34]

33. "Seeming and Real," *New National Era*, October 6, 1870, in Foner (ed.), *Life and Writings*, IV, 226–28.

34. On the fire, see *New National Era*, June 6, 13, 1872. On Douglass and the bank, see Quarles, *Douglass*, 268–71; Douglass to S. L. Harris, March 30, 1874, Douglass to Henry Highland Garnet, March 19, 1874, Douglass to John Jay Knox, Controller of Currency, February 12, 1874, Douglass to unknown, May or June, 1874, all in FD Papers (LC), reel 2. "The truth is," Douglass wrote in the final letter, "I have neither taste nor talent for the place, and when I add as I must that the condition of the bank is not prosperous and possibly not sound, you will appreciate my ill fortune. I am only persuaded to remain in it for the present with a view to restore confidence and save the depositors from themselves." On Douglass and the Santo Domingo Commission, see Quarles, *Douglass*, 254–58. Douglass to Hamilton Fish, April 3, 1871, in Foner (ed.), *Life and Writings*, IV, 240.

Neither the fact that he was the victim of Jim Crow restrictions in the dining room of a steamer on the return voyage nor President Grant's failure to invite him to a White House dinner for the commissioners deflected Douglass from wholehearted support of the annexation of Santo Domingo. Douglass claimed that the Civil War had completely changed his views on United States expansionism. Before the war, the nation was cursed by slavery and therefore "could not be confined within limits too narrow," but the new nation, as Douglass conceived it, reborn "under the rule of liberty and justice," must advance "the ideas and institutions with which it is her mission to bless the world."[35] Douglass had always believed in American mission, but after the war his nationalism flowered as never before, and he found it much more comfortable to speak the language of imperialism.

Just as he saw Reconstruction policy as a direct extension of the issues over which the Civil War was fought, Douglass viewed political party conflict in the same way. To him, the Republican party had been a reluctant, though conclusive, author of emancipation, the embodiment of Union victory, and the custodian of black citizenship. By the time of Grant's first term, Douglass considered the Republican party the only conceivable political home for blacks, and he looked upon elections as referendums on the meaning of the war and the durability of the Reconstruction laws. "If the war for the preservation of the Union was important," Douglass wrote on the eve of the congressional elections of 1870, "and the great measures of reconstruction . . . are of the transcendent value they have hitherto been taken to be, the elections to take place . . . are of surpassing importance." In 1871, defending Grant against growing opposition, and in the context of Ku Klux Klan violence, Douglass simplified American politics to a contest between good and evil. "There are but two real parties in the country," he wrote. "One is the party loyal to liberty, justice, and good order, and the other is the party in sympathy with the defeated rebellion. . . . Between these two parties we have no option." The Republican party had been the defender against the rebellion of 1861; it would now have to be the protector against "Ku Kluxism . . . the pestilence that walketh in darkness."[36] Thus, Douglass forced upon himself the impossible tension of maintaining the Radical-

35. "Annexation of Santo Domingo," *New National Era*, January 12, 1871. For Douglass' views on Santo Domingo annexation, also see *New National Era*, March 30, 1871, April 6, 13, 20, 27, 1871, and May 18, 1871.

36. "November Elections," *ibid.*, November 3, 1870; "Demands of the Hour," *ibid.*, April 6, 1871.

humanitarian vision of the Republican party at the very time it was vanishing.

There can be no doubt that Douglass' loyalty to the Republican party was at times motivated by personal ambition and sustained by faulty analysis. He was a paid stump speaker for Grant in 1872, and he sought office and influence as a return for his efforts. But his political rhetoric in the 1870s reveals a good deal about Douglass' deepest conception of the meaning of the Civil War and Reconstruction. His analysis of the resurgent Democrats of the 1870s differed little from his wartime condemnation of slaveholders—both represented the same hated enemy. For Douglass, "waving the bloody shirt" possessed more than mere political motives. Fond of reviving the passions of the war years, he never missed an opportunity to brand the Democrats as the party of "treason." What Douglass resisted most was the growing desire in the country to forget the agony of the war issues and to get on with sectional reconciliation. In 1870 he provided a list of "great truths" that the nation should never forget: that the "Copperhead Democracy" had started the war "for the purpose of extending and rendering perpetual the foul curse of slavery"; that in the war "these rebel Democrats slaughtered a quarter of a million brave loyal men"; that "they wounded and disabled a quarter of a million more"; that "they made full a million of widows and orphans"; and that "these same rebel Democrats" now demanded that they be restored to power. By invoking these images, Douglass demonstrated that the "bloody shirt," at least for him, appealed for more than votes; it searched for the depths of collective memory where all great historical change must be preserved. Democrats, Douglass warned with characteristic harshness, "are the apostles of forgetfulness . . . and no wonder, for their pathway has been strewn with the whitened bones of their countrymen."[37]

Douglass' party loyalty was often as much a measure of his fear and loathing of southerners as it was of his admiration for the Republicans. His old rage against slaveholders, tempered by a victorious war, had not altogether dissipated, and during the Ku Klux Klan crises

37. *New National Era*, November 7, 1872; "The South Still Bent on Treason," *ibid.*, November 2, 1871; "Never to be Forgotten," *ibid.*, September 8, 1870; "New Names But Old Faces," *ibid.*, December 15, 1870. The New York *Tribune* had attacked Douglass for receiving large amounts of money for his speeches. Douglass responded that he had received only $500 from the Republican party and $3,700 from other literary societies during the lecture season of 1872. Also see Douglass to "son" (Lewis or Frederick, Jr.), *New National Era*, August 29, 1872. In this letter, Douglass informed his readers that he had made seven speeches in one week in Maine on behalf of Grant.

of the early 1870s, he devoted many columns of his newspaper to the story of murder, destruction, and intimidation from the South. He equated Democrats with the "old ex-slaveholding oligarchy of the South." The Klan was merely a tool; its real source was the "besotted madness . . . blind rage . . . the degrading stupidity growing out of the barbarism of slavery." To criticism of his "intolerant, bitter hostility" to Democrats, Douglass contended that no "fanaticism" was too strong in opposing the revival of that party. "We are . . . entitled," he argued, "to call the Democratic party a party of murder, robbery, treason, dishonesty, and fraud." Douglass was further outraged at the extension of universal amnesty to ex-Confederates, whom he believed had "forfeited their right to life, liberty, and property" and were still alive only because of the grace of the Republican party. He even registered his regret that "no rebel has either been hung or deprived of his liberty." These were the strong words of a practiced political propagandist, but they were also the sentiments of a black leader who believed that the power to forgive belonged to those most wronged. The old moral reformer in Douglass cried out for a repentance from the heart, something that the South not only would not give, but from which the Democratic party would now safely protect them.[38]

Douglass' loyalty to the Republican party stemmed from several motives. The party was the primary vehicle through which he could pursue his own political ambitions and develop his growing political consciousness, but he also imbued it with deeper, historical meanings, seeing it as the vessel of progress and the custodian of the Civil War's legacy. In the 1870s he promoted and defended the party with an almost desperate zeal, as if only through that organization could the meaning of the war, emancipation, and Radical Reconstruction be preserved. In 1870, on behalf of his newspaper, Douglass gave a "pledge of fidelity" to the Republicans "without reserve," and he idealized the party as the power that "saved the nation, conquered the rebellion, put down the slaveholders' war, and liberated four million of bondmen." Although this was political rhetoric directed at black as well as white voters, it represented Douglass' personal crusade to thwart the backsliding of Republicans and the resurgence of Democrats. To him, the political struggles of the 1870s were between those who won and those who lost the war. He made this point emphat-

38. *New National Era*, January 26, 1871, February 2, 9, 16, 23, 1871, March 2, 9, 16, 23, 30, 1871; "Barbarism Against Civilization," *ibid.*, April 6, 1871; "Toleration and Indifference," *ibid.*, May 11, 1871; "What Universal Amnesty Will Accomplish," *ibid.*, February 2, 1871.

ically in a speech in Rochester in November, 1870, on the eve of the congressional elections. "Talk of dead issues!" he angrily declared. "The Republican party will have living issues with the Democratic party until the last rebel is dead and buried—until the last nail of the last coffin of the last rebel is driven."[39]

For Douglass, the Republican party represented the best hopes of his people, hopes that he tried to sustain in the 1870s by urging blacks to consider the alternatives. He reminded his black readers in 1871 that though they were often "slighted" by Republicans, they were "murdered" by Democrats, and he insisted that the interests of blacks could be "more easily accomplished inside than anywhere outside the Republican party."[40] Although often disappointed, since the 1850s Douglass had viewed the Republicans as the party of hope. Their "antislavery tendency" had been enough to gain his allegiance. Now, in the early 1870s, as the Radical leadership began to fade away, Douglass clung to the Republicans as the party of memory.

In the presidential election of 1872, Douglass steadfastly supported Grant and vehemently denounced Horace Greeley and the Liberal Republican movement. What he most objected to in the Liberals' program was their hostility to Grant's southern policy and their desire for sectional reconciliation. The Liberal Republicans were a motley coalition driven by a complexity of motives, but especially after their candidate—Greeley—joined hands with the Democratic party in the summer of 1872, Douglass viewed them as apostates and enemies. The Liberal Republicans' "chief topic," he argued in September, 1872, " . . . is the clasping of hands across the bloody chasm, the great love feast of reconciliation cooked by Mr. Greeley, on which occasion our southern brethren are indirectly promised the first seats at the common table." The welfare of the freedpeople, the cause of black equality, the very meaning of the Civil War and Reconstruction were at risk in Douglass' conception of the Liberal Republican movement and the resurgence of the Democrats. "The fruits of ten years of labor, suffering, and loss are at stake," he declared as the campaign of 1872 commenced. Loyal Republicans, he believed, should not be thrown off guard by "the deceitful cry that all the questions raised by the war for the Union and liberty are now settled," and he warned his readers again and again about the fragility of past victories and about

39. Martin, *Mind*, 86; "Has the Republican Party Accomplished Its Mission?" *New National Era*, September 8, 1870; speech at Rochester City Hall, *ibid.*, November 10, 1870.
40. "A Word on Mr. Downing's Letter," *ibid.*, June 8, 1871.

the revival of the South. "The slave demon still rides the southern gale," he wrote in May, 1872, "and breathes out fire and wrath . . . the smouldering embers of the Lost Cause show themselves in shouts for . . . Horace Greeley."[41] Ever fighting the struggles of the present, Douglass cast his gaze to the past in order to find resolve and understanding.

The Liberal Republicans' concern over corruption in the Grant administration and in southern carpetbag governments, as well as their advocacy of civil service reform, also met with Douglass' scorn. He found these issues increasingly difficult to explain, however, especially in the wake of the election when the Crédit Mobilier scandal rocked the administration and the Republican party. By 1874 he wrote to Gerrit Smith describing the "moral atmosphere" in Washington as "rotten," full of "avarice, duplicity . . . , corruption . . . , fawning and trickery of all kinds." He divided Washington politicians into two groups, "the class used" and the "class that uses them," and cynically declared himself one of the "used." But in the heat of the 1872 campaign, Douglass defended Grant against all claims of corruption. In language he must have later regretted, he claimed that there had "never been an administration since the government existed . . . which could better endure the most searching scrutiny" on questions of corruption. "Whatever defects or delinquencies there have been," Douglass argued, "the President himself has been the most earnest in ferreting out, and the first to condemn."[42]

41. "Swinging Around the Circle," *ibid.*, September 26, 1872; "What the National Convention of Philadelphia Ought to Do," *ibid.*, May 30, 1872. On the Liberal Republican movement, see William Gillette, *Retreat from Reconstruction, 1869–1879* (Baton Rouge, 1979), 56–72; Richard A. Gerber, "The Liberal Republicans of 1872 in Historiographical Perspective," *Journal of American History,* LXII (June, 1975), 40–73; Matthew T. Downey, "Horace Greeley and the Politicians: The Liberal Republican Convention in 1872," *Journal of American History,* LIII (March, 1967), 727–50; James M. McPherson, "Grant or Greeley? The Abolitionist Dilemma in the Election of 1872," *American Historical Review,* LXX (October, 1965), 43–61; Patrick W. Riddleberger, "The Break in the Radical Ranks: Liberals vs. Stalwarts in the Election of 1872," *Journal of Negro History,* XLIV (April, 1959), 142–58.

42. Douglass to Gerrit Smith, Washington, D.C., September 24, 1874, in Gerrit Smith Papers; "The Account Fairly Stated," *New National Era,* March 14, 1872. On civil service reform, see Ari A. Hoogenboom, *Outlawing the Spoils: A History of the Civil Service Reform Movement, 1865–1883* (Urbana, 1961). Douglass received many visitors and letters asking for political favors and for the use of his influence. See, for example, Julia Foster Sagendorf to Douglass, July 13, 1873, in FD Papers (LC), reel 2. Sagendorf was a young woman with a small child, begging Douglass to help her get a job in the Treasury Department. "Oh! Mr. Douglass, if you could!" she wrote, "if you only could . . . I will teach my child to worship you."

Such blind defenses of the Grant administration seem lame and incredulous in retrospect, but for a black leader like Douglass, as for many other stalwart Republicans, Grant represented the only hope of continuity with Union victory and the work of Reconstruction. "The Republican Party cannot be broken up at this juncture," he wrote to Cassius M. Clay, "without . . . putting in peril not only the freedmen of the South, but the honor and safety of the country." Whether politically inept or not, Grant was popular and could hold the votes of several crucial constituencies—veterans, midwestern farmers, the rising business elite, and the freedpeople—and he was a symbolic leader, the custodian president and standardbearer of the only political organization that could preserve the legacy of the Civil War against those who would return the country to a status quo antebellum. Douglass' efforts on behalf of Grant in 1872 were more often arguments about the meaning of the war than they were about the president himself—a political persuasion and a rewritten Constitution had to be preserved; slavery, injustice, and treason were suppressed but not conquered; and Grant was merely the vessel by which to preserve the cause. So certain was Douglass that Republican disunity could lead to the doom of black freedom that he declared it "better to put a pistol to my head and blow my brains out, than to lend myself in any wise to the destruction or defeat of the Republican party."[43]

Douglass had found a political home, the sense of belonging he so desired, and perhaps even the appointive office he pursued. Personally, he never knew Grant very well; whether of experience or ideology, the soldier and the black reformer shared little in common. Douglass knew Grant from a distance as the heroic general and symbolic statesman, and he defended Grant's patronage record and contributed a good deal to the popular image of the warrior-president who stood apart from all the spoilsmen of Washington. Because Grant had worked for passage of the Fifteenth Amendment and had wielded federal power to stop the Ku Klux Klan, he seemed to Douglass committed to the "progress and completion of the great work devolved upon the nation by the late war," as Douglass put it in late 1871. Douglass could hardly claim a place for Grant in the abolitionist tradition, but he could still attempt to do so for the Republican party. In the end, he wholeheartedly supported Grant in 1872 for a reason

43. Douglass to Cassius M. Clay, Rochester, July 26, 1871, in Foner (ed.), *Life and Writings*, IV, 252. On the election of 1872 and Grant's skills as a politician, see William S. McFeely, *Grant: A Biography* (New York, 1981), 380–99.

similar to his more restrained support of Lincoln in 1860—Grant was the candidate the South and the resurgent Democrats feared most, and Douglass had learned long ago that, politically, what southerners most feared and opposed, blacks ought to embrace. Hence he concluded his official endorsement of Grant in 1872 by stating that "long ago we adopted the maxim 'never to occupy ground which our enemies desired us to occupy' if we could help it."[44] Such a maxim does not indicate that Douglass practiced negative politics in the 1870s, but it does illuminate why his loyalty to Grant and the Republicans was so enduring.

Throughout the 1870s and beyond, Douglass lamented the waning zeal for what he considered the original mission of the Republican party, and he returned to the jeremiadic tradition in his political rhetoric, calling upon Republicans to cease their indifference toward the freedpeople and curb their sentimentality for sectional reconciliation. In the early 1870s, he saw that the Republican party was also losing its influence. "The earth appears to be gradually crumbling away beneath its foundations," he lamented in describing the party's electoral reverses in his own state of New York. What Republicans most needed, he argued, were "fresh vows of fidelity to principle." Grieving at the party's loss of "the influence of its radical element" and offended by what he called "this cry of peace! peace! where there is no peace," Douglass urged Republicans to abandon any further thought of concessions to the South. "We have already placed in their hands by our weak lenience," he declared in 1871, "nearly all the power they need to render the success of our armies a barren victory. Shall we still . . . aid them in their new war against our rights and the existence of the Union?" But as the decade passed, Douglass' chastisements of his fellow Republicans, as well as his appeals for steadfastness in the cause of black equality and for vigilance against the South, increasingly fell upon deaf ears.[45]

The collapse of his newspaper in 1873, the failure of the Freedmen's Savings Bank in 1874, and the political process of "southern redemption" all cast a pall over the normally sanguine Douglass. In a speech in 1875, he anticipated America's impending centennial celebration as a time when the nation would "lift to the sky its million voices in

44. "U. S. Grant, 1872," *New National Era*, December 7, 1871.
45. "The November Elections," *ibid.*, November 17, 1870; "Maintain the Republican Party in the District of Columbia," *ibid.*, October 26, 1871; "The South Still Bent on Treason," *ibid.*, November 2, 1871.

one grand Centennial hosanna of peace and good will to all the white race . . . from gulf to lakes and from sea to sea." As a black citizen, he dreaded the day when "this great white race has renewed its vows of patriotism and flowed back into its accustomed channels." Proud but worried, Douglass looked back upon fifteen years of unparalleled change for his people. "If war among the whites brought peace and liberty to the blacks," he wondered, "what will peace among the whites bring?" Douglass feared that "justice" and "reconstruction" did not have a deep enough hold upon the nation. In an understatement, he warned his fellow blacks that "the signs of the times are not all in our favor." From rich experience and with great solicitude, Douglass envisioned the road to reunion paved only for whites.[46]

By the late 1870s, Douglass was still campaigning for Republican candidates, but with less confidence and with a sense of lost opportunity. In 1876 he worked hard for the election of Rutherford B. Hayes, serving as a stump speaker wherever the Republican party needed him. Appointed marshall of the District of Columbia in the wake of Hayes's disputed election, Douglass found himself truly an official insider for the first time, and he rejoiced in continued Republican control of the presidency. But in a short time Douglass found it difficult to countenance the "end" of Reconstruction and the Hayes administration's "hands off" policy toward the South. Politically adroit, he always separated Hayes as a man from the president's policy—a technique he had practiced a great deal during the Grant years—and he argued that the government's policy of peace and reconciliation was based on faulty assumptions and driven by false hopes. Northern Republicans, he claimed, had been for too long "meanly, sneakingly, and grossly deceived" by an ungrateful and unrepentant South, and had failed—or had refused—to understand the depth of southern white supremacy. Campaigning for Alonzo B. Cornell, Republican candidate for governor of New York in 1879, Douglass asserted that the issues of the current election were "precisely those old questions which gave rise to our late civil war, and no other." Too many Republicans had caved in, he charged, to the charms of reunion and forgiveness, and he chastised "this tender forbearance, this amazing mercy, and generous oblivion to the past." Douglass wanted the nation to confront its recent history and not to run from it. The greatest mistake Republicans ever made, he declared, was to

46. "The Color Question," speech at Hillsdale, Washington, D.C., July 5, 1875, in FD Papers (LC), reel 15.

allow the "loyal North" to turn "away from the ghastly scene of war and the past," to "let bygones be bygones," to "forgive and forget and to make the rebel South feel at home and comfortable under the flag against which they fought." Douglass did not want national reunion; he wanted racial justice, promised in law, demonstrated in practice, and preserved in memory.[47]

47. See Zachary Chandler to Douglass, August 11, 1876, in *ibid.*, reel 3; "Campaign speech on behalf of Alonzo B. Cornell," 1879, in *ibid.*, reel 15.

10/Douglass and the Struggle for the Memory of the Civil War

Fellow citizens: I am not indifferent to the claims of a generous forgetfulness, but whatever else I may forget, I shall never forget the difference between those who fought for liberty and those who fought for slavery; between those who fought to save the republic and those who fought to destroy it.
> —Frederick Douglass, "Decoration Day," Rochester, 1883

We fell under the leadership of those who would compromise with truth in the past in order to make peace in the present and guide policy in the future.
> —W. E. B. Du Bois, *Black Reconstruction*, 1935

What you have as heritage,
Take now as task;
For thus you will make it your own.
> —Goethe, *Faust*

IN THE FIRST WEEK OF JANUARY, 1883—the twentieth anniversary of the Emancipation Proclamation—Frederick Douglass was honored at a banquet in Washington, D.C., by a distinguished group of black leaders. The banquet was an act of veneration for Douglass, an acknowledgment of the aging orator's indispensable role in the Civil War era, a ritual of collective celebration, and an opportunity to forge historical memory and transmit it across generations. The nearly fifty guests included black leaders from many backgrounds—college professors, congressmen, state politicians, bishops, journalists, and businessmen; virtually every southern state and six northern states were represented. Rivalries and ideological disputes were suppressed for the moment. Senator Blanche K. Bruce chaired the event. Robert Smalls, Edward Blyden, the Reverend Benjamin T. Tanner, Professor Richard T. Greener, the young historian George Washington Williams, and the journalist T. Thomas Fortune were just a few of the notables at this remarkable gathering.

After a sumptuous dinner, numerous toasts were offered to Douglass and to nearly every major aspect of black life: to "the colored man as a legislator"; to "the Negro press"; to "the Negro author"; to "the Republican Party"; to "the Exodus from the South"; to "the A. M. E. church"; to "orators"; and so forth. Douglass himself finally ended the joyous round of toasts by offering one of his own: to "the spirit of the young men" by whom he was surrounded. Many of the guests were men who had come of age since the Civil War; for them, slavery, abolitionism, and even the war itself were the history beyond memory. Douglass in his toast captured an essential meaning of the occasion—the young gathering in tribute to the old. But as they met to celebrate and to understand the pivotal event in their history—emancipation—the meaning of that event was being passed to a new generation of black leaders.[1]

In his formal remarks at the banquet, Douglass demonstrated that during the last third of his life one of the most distinguishing features of his leadership was his quest to preserve the memory of the Civil War, as he believed blacks and the nation should remember it. He viewed emancipation as the central reference point of black history, but the nation also, in his judgment, had no greater turning point and no better demonstration of national purpose. On this twentieth anniversary, Douglass sought to infuse emancipation and the war with the sacred and mythic qualities by which he had always interpreted them. "This high festival . . . ," Douglass declared, "is coupled with a day which we do well to hold in sacred and everlasting honor, a day memorable alike in the history of the nation and in the life of an emancipated people." In these broad images, Douglass drew deeply from his apocalyptic view of history and from his enduring American nationalism. Emancipation day, he believed, ought to be a national celebration in which all blacks—the low and the mighty—could claim a new and secure social identity, but it also represented an "epoch" full of lessons and responsibilities about the meaning of historical memory. "Reflection upon it [emancipation] opens to us a vast wilderness of thought and feeling," Douglass suggested. "Man is said to be an animal looking before and after. To him alone is given the prophetic vision, enabling him to discern the outline of his future through the mists of the past." Warming to the occasion, he challenged his fellow black leaders to remember the Civil War with awe. "The day we celebrate," he said, "affords us an eminence from which we may in a measure survey both the past and the future. It is one of those days which may well count for a thousand years." This was

1. *People's Advocate*, Washington, D.C., January 6, 1883, copy in the Leon Gardiner Collection, Pennsylvania Historical Society, Philadelphia. The banquet was organized by Professor J. M. Gregory of Howard University. Conspicuous by his absence at the banquet was John Mercer Langston of Ohio, a black political leader with whom Douglass had had a long-standing feud.

more than mere banquet rhetoric. It was Douglass' attempt to inspire his colleagues with the idea Robert Penn Warren would later express when he wrote that "the Civil War is our only *felt* history—history lived in the national imagination." Douglass was trying to forge memory into action that could somehow save the legacy of the Civil War for blacks—freedom, citizenship, suffrage, and dignity—at a time when the nation appeared indifferent or hostile to that legacy.[2]

The richly symbolic Emancipation Day banquet of 1883 occurred at the beginning of the year when the United States Supreme Court struck down the Civil Rights Act of 1875, rendering the Civil War amendments "sacrificed," as the dissenting justice John Marshall Harlan put it, and opening the door for the eventual triumph of Jim Crow laws across the South. The ruling in *United States* v. *Stanley*— or the civil-rights cases, as the decision is better known—declared that the equal protection clause of the Fourteenth Amendment applied only to states; a person wronged by racial discrimination, therefore, could look for redress only from state laws and courts. In effect, the decision would also mean that the discriminatory acts of private persons were beyond the safeguards of the Fourteenth Amendment.[3]

At a mass meeting in Washington, D.C., in the immediate aftermath of the decision, Douglass tried to capture the sense of outrage felt by his people. "We have been, as a class, grievously wounded, wounded in the house of our friends," Douglass proclaimed. In the Supreme Court's decision, Douglass saw the oldest foe blacks had faced in America. "The whole essence of the thing," he declared, "is a studied purpose to degrade and stamp out the liberties of a race. It is the old spirit of slavery, and nothing else." Moreover, Douglass interpreted the civil-rights cases as a failure of historical memory and national commitment. Reflecting upon the Supreme Court decision in his final autobiography, he contended that "the future historian will turn to the year 1883 to find the most flagrant example of this national deterioration." White racism among individuals and in national policy, he remarked, seemed to increase in proportion to the "increasing distance from the time of the war." Douglass blamed not only the "fading and defacing effects of time," but, more important, the spirit of reconciliation between North and South. Justice and

2. *Ibid.*; Warren, *Legacy of the Civil War*, 4. On Douglass' apocalyptic conception of the Civil War, see David W. Blight, "Frederick Douglass and the American Apocalypse," *Civil War History*, XXXI (December, 1985), 309–28.

3. Rayford W. Logan, *The Betrayal of the Negro: From Rutherford B. Hayes to Woodrow Wilson* (New York, 1965), 114–18.

liberty for blacks, he maintained, had lost ground from "the hour that the loyal North . . . began to shake hands over the bloody chasm."[4] Thus, Douglass saw the Supreme Court decision as part of a disturbing pattern of historical change. Historical memory, he had come to realize, was not merely a problem of the passage of time, it was a struggle between rival versions of the past, a question of will, of power, of persuasion. The historical memory of any transforming or controversial event emerges from cultural and political competition, from the choice to confront the past and debate and manipulate its meaning.

Ever since the war, Douglass had increasingly exhibited a keen sense of history. "I am this summer endeavoring to make myself a little more familiar with history," he wrote to Gerrit Smith in 1868. "My ignorance of the past has long been a trouble to me." From the early days of Reconstruction, but especially by the 1870s, Douglass seemed acutely aware that the postwar era might ultimately be controlled by those who could best shape interpretations of the war itself. Winning the peace would be a matter of power, but it would also be a struggle over moral will and historical consciousness. In the successful rise of the Democratic party, Douglass saw that the South was beginning to win this struggle. The American people were "destitute of political memory," he complained in 1870, and he demanded that his readers not allow the country to "bury dead issues," as the Democrats wished. "The people cannot and will not forget the issues of the rebellion," Douglass angrily admonished. "The Democratic party must continue to face the music of the past as well as of the present."[5]

Some of Douglass' critics accused him of living in the past. American politics would "leave Mr. Douglass behind . . . ," declared a Liberal Republican newspaper in 1872, "vociferating the old platitudes as though the world had stopped eight years ago." But to these criticisms Douglass always had a ready answer: he would *not forgive* the South and he would *never forget* the meaning of the war. At the Tomb of the Unknown Soldier in Arlington Cemetery, on one of the first observances of Memorial Day (1871), Douglass declared where he stood:

We are sometimes asked in the name of patriotism to forget the merits of this fearful struggle, and to remember with equal admiration those who struck at

4. "Speech at the Civil Rights Mass Meeting," Lincoln Hall, Washington, D.C., October 22, 1883, in Foner (ed.), *Life and Writings*, IV, 393, 402; Douglass, *Life and Times*, 539.

5. Douglass to Gerrit Smith, August 24, 1868, in Gerrit Smith Papers; *New National Era*, November 24, 1870.

the nation's life, and those who struck to save it—those who fought for slavery and those who fought for liberty and justice. I am no minister of malice . . . , I would not repel the repentant, but . . . may my tongue cleave to the roof of my mouth if I forget the difference between the parties to that . . . bloody conflict. . . . I may say if this war is to be forgotten, I ask in the name of all things sacred what shall men remember?[6]

The Union had been saved, and Douglass often appealed to that fact in glowing, nationalistic tones. But in the last third of his life, Douglass repeatedly demonstrated that the Civil War had also left many bitter elements of memory. Around this pledge to "never forget," Douglass organized his entire postwar effort to shape and preserve the legacy of the Civil War.

By intellectual predilection and by experience, Douglass was deeply conscious that history mattered. He had cultivated deep furrows into his own memory as the author of three autobiographies by the 1880s, and to a large degree the Frederick Douglass who endures as an unending subject of literary and historical inquiry—because of the autobiographies—is and was the creature of memory. Moreover, Douglass deeply understood that peoples and nations are shaped and defined by history, which he knew was a primary source of identity, meaning, and motivation. He seemed acutely aware that history was both burden and inspiration, something to be both cherished and overcome. Douglass also understood that winning battles over policy or justice in the present often required an effective use of the past. He came to a realization that in late nineteenth-century America blacks especially needed a usable past. "It is not well to forget the past," Douglass warned in an 1884 speech. "Memory was given to man for some wise purpose. The past is . . . the mirror in which we may discern the dim outlines of the future and by which we may make them more symmetrical."[7]

6. *The Golden Age*, quoted in *New National Era*, August 8, 1872; "Address at the Grave of the Unknown Dead," Arlington, Virginia, May 30, 1871, in FD Papers (LC), reel 14.

7. "Speech at the Thirty-Third Anniversary of the Jerry Rescue," Syracuse, 1884, in FD Papers (LC), reel 15. On the nature and importance of historical memory, see Hayden White, *Tropics of Discourse: Essays in Cultural Criticism* (Baltimore, 1978), 26–50; Eric Hobsbaum and Terence Ranger (eds.), *The Invention of Tradition* (New York, 1983); Jaroslav Pelikan, *The Vindication of Tradition* (New Haven, 1984), 43–82; Michael Kammen, *A Season of Youth: The American Revolution and the Historical Imagination* (New York, 1978); Ulric Neisser (ed.), *Memory Observed: Remembering in Natural Contexts* (San Francisco, 1982); David Lowenthal, *The Past Is a Foreign Country* (London, 1985). On the Civil War in the northern memory, see Paul H. Buck, *The Road to Reunion, 1865–1900* (New York, 1937), 228–309; Aaron, *Unwritten War;* Oscar Handlin, "The Civil War as Symbol and as Actuality," *Massachusetts Review,* III (Autumn, 1961), 133–43; James M. McPherson, *The Abolitionist Legacy: From Reconstruction to the NAACP* (Princeton, 1975), 95–139, 333–38.

To all who look to history for meaning, these premises may seem obvious, but in the 1880s—and perhaps in all eras of American history—such simple dicta had immediate relevance. According to Douglass, blacks occupied a special place in America's historical memory as participants and as custodians. He understood the psychological need of his people not to dwell upon the horrors of slavery, but the slave experience was so immediate and unforgettable, Douglass believed, because it was a history that could "be traced like that of a wounded man through a crowd by the blood." Douglass urged his fellow blacks to keep *their* history before the consciousness of American society; if necessary, they should serve as a national conscience. "Well the nation may forget," Douglass said in 1888, "it may shut its eyes to the past, and frown upon any who may do otherwise, but the colored people of this country are bound to keep the past in lively memory till justice shall be done them."[8] But as he learned, such historical consciousness was as out-of-date in Gilded Age America as the racial justice he demanded.

In his retrospective thought about the Civil War, Douglass' real intention was to forge enduring historical myths that could help win battles in the present. The deepest cultural myths—ideas and stories drawn from history that, through symbolic power, transcend generations—are the essence of historical memory. Douglass hoped that Union victory, black emancipation, and the Civil War amendments would be so deeply rooted in recent American experience, so central to any conception of national regeneration, so necessary to the postwar society, that they would become sacred values, ritualized in memory. Douglass dearly wanted black freedom and equality—the gift from the Union dead, memorialized every Decoration Day—to become (as Richard Slotkin puts it) one of those "usable values from history . . . beyond the reach of critical demystification."[9] Douglass' hope that emancipation could attain such indelible mythic quality

8. "Speech at the Thirty-Third Anniversary of the Jerry Rescue"; "Address Delivered on the Twenty-Sixth Anniversary of Abolition in the District of Columbia," April 16, 1888, in FD Papers (LC), reel 16.

9. Richard Slotkin, *The Fatal Environment: The Myth of the Frontier in the Age of Industrialization, 1800–1890* (New York, 1985), 19. For my understanding of the structure of cultural myth, as well as its uses and misuses by historians, I have relied upon Slotkin, *Fatal Environment,* 3–32; Bruce Kuklik, "Myth and Symbol in American Studies," *American Quarterly,* XXIV (October, 1972), 435–50; Bercovitch, *American Jeremiad,* xi–xii, 132–220; Clifford Geertz, *The Interpretation of Cultures: Selected Essays* (New York, 1973), 28–30, 33–141, 213–20; Kammen, *Season of Youth,* 3–32, 221–58; Warren I. Susman, *Culture as History: The Transformation of American Society in the Twentieth Century* (New York, 1984), 3–26.

was rooted in his enduring faith in the doctrine of progress and in his moral determinism. Repeatedly, he criticized the claim that emancipation came only by "military necessity" during the war. "The war for the Union came only to execute the moral and humane judgment of the nation," he asserted in 1883. "It was an instrument of a higher power than itself." What drew northerners to Memorial Day observances, Douglass maintained in 1878, was the "moral character of the war . . . , the far-reaching . . . , eternal principles in dispute, and for which our sons and brothers encountered . . . danger and death."[10] By continuing to stress the sacred and ideological qualities in the legacy of the Civil War, he exposed both his deepest sense of the meaning of the conflict and his fear that such meaning would be lost over time.

Douglass' pledge to "never forget" the meaning of the Civil War stemmed from at least five sources in his thought and experience. First, he never softened his insistence that the Civil War had been an ideological conflict with deeply moral consequences. Douglass abhorred the nonideological interpretation of the war that was gaining such popularity by the 1880s, when the spirit of sectional reunion fostered a celebration of martial heroism, of the strenuousness and courage best expressed perhaps by Oliver Wendell Holmes, Jr., and later popularized by Theodore Roosevelt. Holmes experienced and therefore loathed the horror of combat, yet to him the legacy of the Civil War rested not in any moral cause on either side but in the passion, devotion, and sacrifice of the generation whose "hearts were touched with fire." To Holmes, the true hero—the deepest memory— of the war was the soldier on both sides, thoughtless of ideology, who faced the "experience of battle . . . in those indecisive contests." Indeed, the very face of battle, suffering, and death can blunt or deny ideology altogether. Teleological conceptions of war are rarely the luxury of individual soldiers; the veteran's memory rarely focuses on the grand design. Ideology, though always at the root of war, is left to the interpreters, those who will compete to define the meaning and legacy of the wartime experience. "In the midst of doubt, in the collapse of creeds," said Holmes, "there is one thing I do not doubt, and that is that the faith is true and adorable which sends a soldier to throw away his life in obedience to a blindly accepted duty, in a cause

10. "Speech on Emancipation Day," Rochester, September, 1883, in FD Papers (LC), reel 15. For Douglass' attacks on the idea of "military necessity," also see "The Black Man's Progress on This Continent," New National Era, July 27, 1871; "Speech in Madison Square," Decoration Day, New York, 1878, in FD Papers (LC), reel 15.

which he little understands, in a plan of campaign of which he has no notion, under tactics of which he does not see the use."[11] By the 1880s Holmes's memory of the war became deeply rooted in American culture. What mattered most was not the content of the cause on either side but the acts of commitment to those causes, not ideas but the experience born of conflict over those ideas. Whoever was honest in his devotion was *right*.

Although Douglass' Memorial Day addresses were full of tributes to martial heroism—albeit only on the Union side—they were primarily testaments to the abolitionist conception of the war. He demanded a teleological memory of the war. The conflict, Douglass insisted in 1878, "was a war of ideas, a battle of principles . . . a war between the old and new, slavery and freedom, barbarism and civilization."[12]

After Reconstruction, Douglass was one of a small band of old abolitionists and reformers (led by Wendell Phillips and Albion Tourgée) who struggled to sustain an ideological interpretation of the Civil War. Northern thinkers like Douglass were not merely trying to "keep alive conflict over issues time was ruthlessly discarding," as Paul Buck wrote in 1937.[13] Belligerency was not the primary motive of those who argued for an ideological memory of the Civil War. Theirs was a persuasion under much duress by the 1880s, a collective voice nearly drowned out by the chorus of reconciliation. They understood the need for healing in the recently divided nation; they could acknowledge the validity of veterans' mutual respect. But they distrusted the sentimentalism of both North and South, and they especially feared Holmes's notion of the "collapse of creeds." Most of all, those northerners who stressed ideas in the debate over the memory of the war saw America avoiding—benignly and aggressively— the deep significance of race in the verdict of Appomattox.

Douglass' voice was crucial to the late nineteenth-century debate

11. Mark De Wolfe Howe (ed.), *The Occasional Speeches of Justice Oliver Wendell Holmes, Jr.* (Cambridge, Mass., 1962), 4–5, 76. Excellent discussions of Holmes are found in George M. Fredrickson, *The Inner Civil War: Northern Intellectuals and the Crisis of the Union* (New York, 1965), 218–21; Cruce Stark, "Brothers At/In War: One Phase of Post-Civil War Reconciliation," *Canadian Review of American Studies*, VI (Fall, 1975), 174–81; and Aaron, *Unwritten War*, 161–62.

12. "Speech in Madison Square."

13. Buck, *Road to Reunion*, 242. On Tourgée, see Otto H. Olsen, *Carpetbagger's Crusade: The Life of Albion Winegar Tourgée* (Baltimore, 1965); Richard Nelson Current, *Those Terrible Carpetbaggers: A Reinterpretation* (New York, 1988), 367–82, 401–406; and Aaron, *Unwritten War*, 193–205. On Phillips, see Fredrickson, *Inner Civil War*, 196–98.

over the legacy of the Civil War. As Edmund Wilson wrote in analyzing the significance of "detached" American writers of the Civil War era, "they also serve who only stand and watch. The men of action make history, but the spectators make most of the histories, and these histories may influence the action." Douglass had acted in history, but his principal aim now was to help shape the histories. Unlike Holmes, he had not served on the battlefield. But he had served in slavery, on the abolitionist platform, and with his pen and voice as few other black leaders had during the war. Douglass' war was a deeply intellectual and spiritual experience; his action had been more an inner struggle than a physical test. Unlike some other northern intellectuals, perhaps his remoteness from the carnage enabled him to sustain an ideological conception of the war throughout his life. The war "was not a fight between rapacious birds and ferocious beasts," Douglass maintained, "a mere display of brute courage and endurance, but it was a war between men of thought, as well as of action, and in dead earnest for something beyond the battlefield."[14]

The second source of Douglass' quest to preserve the memory of the Civil War was his refurbished nationalism. At stake in this debate was his sense of nationhood, the secure social identity that he hoped emancipation and equality would one day offer every black in America. Douglass expressed this connection between nationalism and memory in his famous speech at the unveiling of the Freedmen's Memorial Monument to Abraham Lincoln in Washington, D.C., in April, 1876. The Freedmen's Memorial speech is too easily interpreted as merely eulogistic, part of Douglass' contribution to the myth of Lincoln as Great Emancipator. Attended by President Grant, his cabinet, Supreme Court justices, and numerous senators, the ceremony was as impressive as the bright spring day, which had been declared a holiday by joint resolution of Congress.[15]

After a reading of the Emancipation Proclamation and the unveiling of the statue (which Douglass later admitted he did not like because "it showed the Negro on his knees"), Douglass took the

14. Wilson, *Patriotic Gore*, 669; "Speech in Madison Square."

15. See Quarles, *Douglass*, 276–78. Quarles maintains that the Freedmen's Memorial speech was "distinctly not one of his best." Also see Huggins, *Slave and Citizen*, 102–103. Huggins contends that in delivering eulogies to Lincoln, Douglass merely "played his part in the creation of the Lincoln myth. As is so often the case with myths, this one came to have more vitality than the real man. In time Douglass came to forget that there was a difference." This analysis underestimates Douglass' understanding of the meaning and use of cultural myths. The Lincoln myth served an important and a genuine purpose in Douglass' rhetoric, in the Freedmen's Memorial Address and elsewhere.

podium as the orator of the day. His address included strong doses of the rail-splitter Lincoln image, the "plebeian" who rose through honesty, common sense, and the mysterious hand of God to become the "great liberator." But he also understood that the occasion was a moment to forge national memory and practice civil religion. Through most of the speech, he spoke to and for blacks; the monument had been commissioned and paid for almost entirely by blacks. But the monument was not only to Lincoln; rather, it was to the *fact* of emancipation. The occasion honored Lincoln, but Douglass equally stressed the *events* that transpired "under his rule, and in due time." Most important, in contributing to the Lincoln myth and in commemorating emancipation in such a symbolic way, Douglass was staking a claim to nationhood for blacks. "We stand today at the national center," he said, "to perform something like a national act." Douglass struck clear notes of civil religion as he described the "stately pillars and majestic dome of the Capitol" as "our church," and rejoiced that "for the first time in the history of our people, and in the history of the whole American people, we join in this high worship." Douglass was trying to make Lincoln mythic and therefore useful to the cause of black equality, but the primary significance of his Freedmen's Memorial address lies in its concerted attempt to forge a place for blacks in the national memory, to assert their citizenship and nationhood. "When now it shall be said that the colored man is soulless . . . ," Douglass concluded, "when the foul reproach of ingratitude is hurled at us, and it is attempted to scourge us beyond the range of human brotherhood, we may calmly point to the monument we have this day erected to the memory of Abraham Lincoln." What Lincoln himself had once called the "mystic chords of memory" as a source of devotion to the Union, Douglass now claimed as the rightful inheritance of blacks as well. He did so through language, the essence of cultural myth, and the only secure means he possessed.[16]

The third cause of Douglass' concern over the memory of the Civil War was the resurgent racism in the country and the rise of the "Lost Cause" mentality. Since its origins as a literary and political device immediately after the war, the Lost Cause has been an enigmatic phrase in American history. Historians have defined the Lost Cause

16. "Oration in Memory of Abraham Lincoln," delivered at the unveiling of the Freedmen's Memorial, Lincoln Park, Washington, D.C., April 14, 1876, in Foner (ed.), *Life and Writings*, IV, 317–19, 314, 310–11, 319. For the "mystic chords" quotation, see Lincoln's "First Inaugural Address," March 4, 1861, in Basler (ed.), *Collected Works of Lincoln*, IV, 271.

in at least three different ways: one, as a public memory, shaped by a web of organizations, institutions, and rituals; two, as a dimension of southern and American civil religion, rooted in churches and sacred rhetoric as well as secular institutions and thought; and three, as a literary phenomenon, shaped by journalists and fiction writers from the die-hard Confederate apologists of the immediate postwar years, through the gentle romanticism of the "local color" writers of the 1880s, to the legion of more mature novelists of the 1890s and early twentieth century who appealed to a national audience eager for reconciliation.[17]

In the midst of Reconstruction, Douglass began to realize the potential power of the Lost Cause sentiment. Indignant at the universal amnesty afforded ex-Confederates and appalled by the national veneration of Robert E. Lee, he attacked the emerging Lost Cause. "The spirit of secession is stronger today than ever," Douglass warned in 1871. "It is now a deeply rooted, devoutly cherished sentiment, inseparably identified with the 'lost cause,' which the half measures of the Government towards the traitors has helped to cultivate and strengthen." He was disgusted by the outpouring of admiration for Lee in the wake of the general's death in 1870. "Is it not about time that this bombastic laudation of the rebel chief should cease?" Douglass wrote. "We can scarcely take up a newspaper . . . that is not filled with *nauseating* flatteries of the late Robert E. Lee." Douglass had no interest in honoring the enemy. "It would seem from this," he asserted, "that the soldier who kills the most men in battle, even in a bad cause, is the greatest Christian, and entitled to the highest place in heaven."[18]

Douglass' harsh reactions to the veneration of Lee are a revealing measure of his enduring attitudes toward the South, as well as his conception of the meaning of the war. He seemed to relish the opportunity to lecture his readers about their former enemies. "The South has a past not to be contemplated with pleasure," Douglass cautioned in 1870, "but with a shudder. She has been selling agony, trading in blood and in the souls of men. If her past has any lesson, it is one of

17. Gaines M. Foster, *Ghosts of the Confederacy: Defeat, the Lost Cause, and the Emergence of the New South, 1865–1913* (New York, 1986), 4–5, 36–46, 104–14; Charles Reagan Wilson, *Baptized in Blood: The Religion of the Lost Cause, 1865–1920* (Athens, Ga., 1980), 12–14, 37–78; Thomas L. Connelly and Barbara L. Bellows, *God and General Longstreet: The Lost Cause and the Southern Mind* (Baton Rouge, 1982), 39–72. On the Lost Cause, also see C. Vann Woodward, *The Origins of the New South, 1877–1913* (Baton Rouge, 1951), 154–58.

18. "Wasted Magnanimity," *New National Era*, August 10, 1871; "Bombast," *ibid.*, November 10, 1871.

repentance and thorough reformation." As for proposed monuments to Lee, he considered them an insult to his people and to the Union, and he feared that such monument building would only "reawaken the confederacy." Moreover, in a remark that would prove more ironic with time, Douglass declared in 1870 that "monuments to the Lost Cause will prove monuments of folly." But as the Lost Cause myth sank deeper into southern and national consciousness, Douglass found that he was losing ground in the battle for the memory of the Civil War.[19]

Douglass never precisely clarified just how much "repentance" or "reformation" he deemed necessary on the part of the South before he could personally extend forgiveness. He merely demanded "justice," based on adherence to the Civil War amendments and to the civil rights acts. Given the strength of his nationalism and his own southern roots, Douglass' vindictiveness toward the South probably would have softened more with time had not events worked the reverse effect. What Douglass most despised was the resurgent racism of the 1880s, fueled by the spirit of sectional reunion. "A spirit of evil has been revived . . . ," Douglass declared in a eulogy to William Lloyd Garrison in 1879, "doctrines are proclaimed . . . which were, as we thought, all extinguished by the iron logic of cannon balls." In the political victories of the southern Democrats and in the increasing oppression of the freedmen, Douglass saw a "conflict between the semi-barbarous past, and the higher civilization which has logically and legally taken its place." He lamented the passing of so many of the old abolitionists like Garrison, whose services would be needed in what Douglass called "this second battle for liberty and nation."[20]

From his position as a stalwart Republican, Douglass' condemnations of resurgent racism often seemed in stark contradiction to his allegiance to the party that increasingly abandoned blacks. He was not as aggressive as some black leaders in their efforts to preserve black rights outside or inside the political system, and his allegiance to and criticism of the Republican party could emerge in bewildering

19. "Bombast"; "The Survivor's Meeting–A Soldier's Tribute to a Soldier," and "Monuments of Folly," both in *ibid.*, December 1, 1870. Douglass was also outraged by southerners' attempts to write the Lost Cause outlook into American history textbooks. "They have taken to making rebel schoolbooks and teaching secession and disloyalty in their primary schools," Douglass reported. See "Still Firing the Southern Heart," *ibid.*, February 23, 1871.
20. "Speech on the Death of William Lloyd Garrison," at Garrison Memorial Meeting, 15th Street Presbyterian Church, Philadelphia, June 2, 1879, in FD Papers (LC), reel 15.

extremes. In an 1880 speech, he declared: "Of the Republican party . . . it is the same as during and before the war; the same enlightened, loyal, liberal and progressive party that it was. It is the party of Lincoln, Grant, Wade, Seward, and Sumner; the party to which today we are indebted for the salvation of the country, and today it is well represented in its character and composition by James A. Garfield and Chester A. Arthur." Such superficial political rhetoric sometimes shifted to harsher and more realistic assessments when Douglass faced the bitter truth. In an 1888 speech, he accused the federal government (and therefore the Republicans) of treating the freedman as "a deserted, a defrauded, a swindled outcast; in law, free; in fact, a slave; in law, a citizen; in fact, an alien; in law, a voter; in fact, a disfranchised man." Douglass finally acknowledged that his party had lost its ideals. "I am a Republican, I believe in the Republican party . . . ," he asserted. "But while I am a Republican and believe in the party, I dare to tell that party the truth. In my judgment, it can no longer repose on the history of its grand and magnificent achievements. It must not only stand abreast with the times, but must create the times."[21]

Whatever he thought of the Republican party, the aging Douglass never wavered in his hatred or his understanding of racism. "The tide of popular prejudice" against blacks, Douglass said in 1884, had "swollen by a thousand streams" since the war. Everywhere, he lamented, blacks were "stamped" with racist expectations. Douglass expressed the pain of being black in America: wherever a black man aspired to a profession, "the presumption of incompetency confronts him, and he must either run, fight, or fall before it." Lynching and the alleged rapes by black men of white women were, to Douglass, manifestations of the South's invention of a new "crime" to replace its old fear of "insurrection." In a speech in 1884, commemorating the rescue of fugitive slaves in the 1850s, Douglass chastised his Syracuse audience for preferring sectional peace over racial justice. "It is weak and foolish to cry PEACE when there is no peace," he stated. "In America, as elsewhere, injustice must cease before peace can prevail."[22]

The fourth argument Douglass employed in the debate over the memory of the Civil War was his claim that the country had been seduced into "national forgetfulness," a peculiar American condi-

21. "Emancipation," speech in Rochester, August 4, 1880, in *ibid.*, reel 15; "Address Delivered on the Twenty-Sixth Anniversary of the Abolition of Slavery in the District of Columbia."
22. "Speech at the Thirty-Third Anniversary of the Jerry Rescue."

tion of historical amnesia. In his numerous retrospective speeches in the 1880s, Douglass discussed the limitations of memory. He knew that memory was fickle and admitted that people must live "in the hurry, bustle, and tumult of the ever-changing . . . present." He even admitted that his own "slave life . . . has lost much of its horror, and sleeps in my memory like the dim outlines of a half-forgotten dream." But Douglass' greater concern was with collective historical memory, not merely with personal recollection. He was striving against one of the strongest currents in American thought and experience, for Americans had always been a people who rejected the past and relished their newness. Douglass was learning to appreciate one of Alexis de Tocqueville's great observations about American society: in America each generation is a new people, and "no one cares for what occurred before his time." American individualism, wrote Tocqueville in 1831, makes "every man forget his ancestors . . . hides his descendants and separates his contemporaries from him; it throws him back forever upon himself alone and threatens in the end to confine him entirely within the solitude of his own heart." To Douglass, this larger individualism that bred indifference, coupled with the more specific racism that bred oppression, provided the twin enemies of those who wished to preserve an abolitionist memory of the Civil War.[23]

Douglass' laments about historical amnesia often echoed Tocqueville's prescience, but he laid the blame upon the spirit of sectional reunion, as well as upon national character. One of the ambiguities in Douglass' postwar thought is that he was an outspoken proponent of laissez-faire individualism and a celebrator of "self-made men," yet with equal vehemence he attacked the surging indifference of northerners who wished to forget the war, forgive ex-Confederates, and abandon the freedmen. Perhaps it was his abiding nationalism and his faith in political solutions that pushed Douglass into this contradiction. Perhaps there was no other solution for a black leader like Douglass, who had to preach self-reliance to his people while at the same time demanding national commitments from the government and from society at large. Or perhaps Douglass was one of Tocqueville's

23. "Thoughts and Recollections of the Antislavery Conflict," speech, undated, in FD Papers (LC), reel 19; Alexis de Tocqueville, *Democracy in America*, ed. Thomas Bender (New York, 1981), 115, 397. On the significance of Tocqueville in understanding American individualism and the rejection of the past, see Robert Bellah *et al.*, *Habits of the Heart: Individualism and Commitment in American Life* (New York, 1985), 27–31, 255–307.

Americans, trapped between the country's historic racism, on the one hand, and his own embrace of individualism on the other.[24]

Most assuredly, though, Douglass was not one of those Americans who rejected the past. He believed that individualism could coexist with social justice, that getting on in the world released no one from the weight of history. "Well it may be said that Americans have no memories," Douglass said in 1888. "We look over the House of Representatives and see the Solid South enthroned there; we listen with calmness to eulogies of the South and of traitors and forget Andersonville. . . . We see colored citizens shot down and driven from the ballot box, and forget the services rendered by the colored troops in the late war for the Union." More revealing still was Douglass' contempt for northern sympathy with the Lost Cause. He believed northern forgiveness toward the South shamed the memory of the war. "Rebel graves were decked with loyal flowers," Douglass declared, "though no loyal grave is ever adorned by rebel hands. Loyal men are building homes for rebel soldiers; but where is the home for Union veterans, builded by rebel hands . . . ?" Douglass had never really wanted a Carthaginian peace, but it seemed that he was left out of the nation's happy reunion, that the deep grievances of his people—both historic and current—were no longer heard. At the very least, Douglass seemed to be demanding that the power to forgive should be reserved for those most wronged.[25]

Thus Douglass worried about historical amnesia not because the debate over the meaning of the war was merely a question of remembering or forgetting. He worried because his version of that memory faltered next to the rival memories that resonated more deeply with the white majority in both North and South. Douglass may never have fully appreciated the complexity of the experience of the Civil War and Reconstruction for whites. The overwhelming number of white northerners who voted against black suffrage shared a bond of white supremacy with southerners who rejected the racial egalitarianism of Radical Reconstruction. The thousands of white Union veterans who remembered the war as a transforming personal experience, but not as the crucible of emancipation for four million slaves, had much in common with white Georgians who had found

24. Martin, *Mind*, 253–78.
25. "Address Delivered on the Twenty-Sixth Anniversary of Abolition in the District of Columbia"; "Thoughts and Recollections of the Antislavery Conflict," speech, undated, in FD Papers (LC), reel 19.

themselves in the path of Sherman's march to the sea. There were many rival memories of the war and its aftermath, and there was much need for forgetting and healing. As Friedrich Nietzsche suggested, personal happiness often requires a degree of forgetting the past. "Forgetting is essential to action of any kind," wrote Nietzsche. "Thus: it is possible to live almost without memory . . . but it is altogether impossible to live at all without forgetting . . . there is a degree of the historical sense which is harmful and ultimately fatal to the living thing, whether this living thing be a man or a people or a culture." Nietzsche captured elements of both truth and danger in this vision of human nature. Douglass focused his efforts on the dangers of collective forgetting, not on its personal or cultural necessity. Confined to minority status and living at the margins of society, Douglass knew that his people could rarely afford the luxury of forgetting. Although he may not have thoroughly discriminated between the rival memories he confronted, he became fully aware of their power and their threat. Thus, with ever fewer sympathetic listeners by the late 1880s, Douglass was left with his lament that "slavery has always had a better memory than freedom, and was always a better hater."[26]

These were not merely words of nostalgia by a man out of touch with changing times. In a sense, Douglass *was* living in the past during the last part of his life; the Civil War and Reconstruction were the reference points for the black experience in the nineteenth century, and all questions of meaning, of a sense of place and of a future for blacks in America, drew upon the era of emancipation. Hence, the fifth source of Douglass' pledge to "never forget": a tremendous emotional and psychological investment in his own conception of the legacy of the conflict. As an intellectual, he had grown up with the abolition movement, the war, and its historical transformations; his career and his very personality had been shaped by these events. Douglass' effort to preserve the memory of the Civil War was a quest to save both the freedom of his people and the meaning of his own life.

The preservation of memory, therefore, was a duty no less important than what I have earlier referred to as the duty of hope that

26. Friedrich Nietzsche, "On the Uses and Disadvantages of History for Life" (1874), in *Untimely Meditations*, trans. by R. J. Hollingdale, with an introduction by J. P. Stern (New York, 1983), 62; "Thoughts and Recollections of the Antislavery Conflict," speech, undated, FD Papers (LC). On the concept of historical forgetting, see Lowenthal, *The Past*, 204–206. On northerners and black suffrage, see C. Vann Woodward, *American Counterpoint: Slavery and Racism in the North-South Dialogue* (Boston, 1964), 173–83.

Douglass embraced before the Civil War. In an 1883 speech in his old home town of Rochester, Douglass was emphatic on this point: "You will already have perceived that I am not of that school of thinkers which teaches us to let bygones be bygones; to let the dead past bury its dead," he declared. "In my view there are no bygones in the world, and the past is not dead and cannot die. The evil as well as the good that men do lives after them. . . . The duty of keeping in memory the great deeds of the past and of transmitting the same from generation to generation is implied in the mental and moral constitution of man."[27] But what of a society that did not widely share this sense of history, and much preferred a different version of the past, if any at all? Douglass' answer was to resist the Lost Cause by arguing for an opposite and, he hoped, deeper cultural myth—the abolitionist conception of the Civil War and black emancipation as the source of national regeneration.

In trying to forge an alternative to the Lost Cause, Douglass drew upon America's reform tradition and constantly appealed to the Constitution and to the rule of law. Moreover, reversing a central tenet of the Lost Cause—the memory of defeat—Douglass emphasized the memory of northern victory, the sacrifices of the Union dead, and the historical "progress" he believed inherent in emancipation. This is what Douglass meant in a Memorial Day speech in Madison Square in New York in 1878, when he declared that "there was a right side and a wrong side in the late war which no sentiment ought to cause us to forget."[28]

In some of his postwar rhetoric, Douglass undoubtedly contributed to what Robert Penn Warren has called the myth of the "Treasury of Virtue." He sometimes imbued Union victory with an air of righteousness that skewed the facts, and his insistence on the "moral" character of the war often neglected the complex, reluctant manner in which emancipation became the goal of the Union war effort. Douglass could be as selective as his Lost Cause adversaries in structuring historical memory, and his persistent defense of the Republican party after Reconstruction caused him to walk a thin line of hypocrisy. His millennialist interpretation of the war had caused him to see the conflict as a cleansing tragedy, wherein the nation had been redeemed of its evil by lasting grace. Douglass knew that black freedom had emerged *from* history perhaps as much as human agents had created that history, but winning the battle over the legacy of the

27. "Speech on Emancipation Day."
28. *Ibid.;* "Speech in Madison Square."

Civil War demanded deep cultural myths that were at least half true. He knew that the struggle over memory was always, at least in part, a debate over the present. In his view, emancipation and black equality under law were, in fact, the great result of the war; hence, while urging old abolitionists not to give up their labors in 1875, Douglass contended that "every effort should now be made to save the result of this stupendous moral and physical contest." Nine years later, Douglass warned that unless an abolitionist conception of the war were steadfastly preserved, America would "thus lose to after-coming generations a vast motive power and inspiration to high and virtuous endeavor." Douglass labored to shape the memory of the Civil War, then, as a skillful propagandist, as a black leader confident of the virtue of his cause, and as an individual determined to protect his own identity.[29]

In his book, *The Unwritten War: American Writers and the Civil War*, Daniel Aaron observes that very few writers in the late nineteenth century "appreciated the Negro's literal or symbolic role in the war." Black invisibility in the massive Civil War fictional literature—the absence of fully realized black characters, even in Mark Twain or William Faulkner—was yet another striking illustration that emancipation and the challenge of racial equality overwhelmed the American imagination in the postwar decades. Slavery, the war's deepest cause, and black freedom, the war's most fundamental result, remain the most conspicuous missing elements in the American literature inspired by the Civil War. This black invisibility in America's cultural memory is precisely what Douglass struggled against during the last two decades of his life. Obviously, he was no novelist himself and was not about to write the great Civil War book, but memories and understandings of great events, especially apocalyptic wars, live in our consciousness like monuments in the mind. The aging Douglass' rhetoric—his speeches and his writings—was an eloquent attempt to forge a place on that monument for those he deemed the principal characters in the drama of emancipation: the abolitionist, the black soldier, and the freedpeople. Perhaps the best reason the Civil War remained, in Aaron's words, "vivid but ungraspable" to literary imagination was that most American writers avoided or were

29. Warren, *Legacy*, 59–76; "The National Lincoln Monument Association," *New National Era*, October 27, 1870; "Address at the Centennial Celebration of the Abolition Society of Pennsylvania," Philadelphia, 1875, in FD Papers (LC), reel 15; "Speech at the Thirty-Third Anniversary of the Jerry Rescue."

confounded by slavery and race, the deepest moral issues in the conflict.[30]

The late nineteenth century was an age when white supremacy flourished amidst vast industrial and social changes. The nation increasingly embraced sectional reunion, sanctioned Jim Crow, dreamed about technology, and defined itself by the assumptions of commerce. Near the end of his monumental work *Black Reconstruction* (1935), W. E. B. Du Bois declared himself "aghast" at the way historians had suppressed the significance of slavery and the black quest for freedom from the literature on the Civil War and the Reconstruction era. "One is astonished in the study of history," wrote Du Bois, "at the recurrence of the idea that evil must be forgotten, distorted, skimmed over . . . The difficulty, of course, with this philosophy is that history loses its value as an incentive and example; it paints perfect men and noble nations, but it does not tell the truth."[31]

As Du Bois acknowledged, it was just such a use of history as "incentive and example" for which Douglass had labored. Although his jeremiads against the Lost Cause myth and his efforts to preserve an abolitionist memory of the conflict took on a strained quality, Douglass never lost hope in the regenerative meaning of the Civil War, which he believed was such a great divide, such a compelling reference point, that the nation would in time have to face its meaning and its consequences. In an 1884 speech, Douglass drew hope from a biblical metaphor of death and rebirth—the story of Jesus raising Lazarus from the dead. "The assumption that the cause of the Negro is a dead issue," Douglass declared, "is an utter delusion. For the moment he may be buried under the dust and rubbish of endless discussion concerning civil service, tariff and free trade, labor and capital . . . but our Lazarus is not dead. He only sleeps."[32]

Douglass' use of such a metaphor was perhaps his recognition of temporary defeat in the struggle for the memory of the Civil War, but

---

30. Aaron, *Unwritten War,* 332–33, 340; Robert A. Lively, *Fiction Fights the Civil War: An Unfinished Chapter in the Literary History of the American People* (Chapel Hill, 1957). On black literature and memory in the nineteenth and early twentieth centuries, see Arlene A. Elder, *The "Hindered Hand": Cultural Implications of Early African-American Fiction* (Westport, Conn., 1978). For the power of war over the imagination, especially in literary forms, see Paul Fussell, *The Great War in Modern Memory* (New York, 1975), 310–35.

31. W. E. B. Du Bois, *Black Reconstruction in America, 1860–1880* (1935; repr. New York, 1972), 725, 722.

32. "Speech at the Thirty-Third Anniversary of the Jerry Rescue."

it also represented his belief that, though the struggle would outlast his own life, it could still be won. Douglass gave a Memorial Day address in 1883 at Mount Hope Cemetery in Rochester, where he would himself be buried some eleven years later. The sixty-five-year-old orator delivered an angry disavowal of the "doctrine of forgiveness and forgetfulness" that seemed to be sweeping the country. He feared that Decoration Day would become an event merely of "anachronisms, empty forms and superstitions." One wonders if the audience in Rochester on that pleasant spring afternoon thought of Douglass himself as somewhat of an anachronism. In a country reeling from labor unrest, worried about Gilded Age corruption, the farmers' revolt, and the disorder of growing cities, one wonders if Douglass' listeners (even in his old home town) could see beyond the symbolic trappings of the occasion, cultivate their twenty-year-old memory of the war and all its sacrifice, and face the deeper meanings Douglass demanded.

The aging Douglass could still soar to oratorical heights on such occasions. He asked his audience to reflect with him about their "common memory." "I seem even now to hear and feel the effects of the sights and the sounds of that dreadful period," Douglass said. "I see the flags from the windows and housetops fluttering in the breeze. I see and hear the steady tramp of armed men in blue uniforms. . . . I see the recruiting sergeant with drum and fife . . . calling for men, young men and strong, to go to the front and fill up the gaps made by rebel powder and pestilence. I hear the piercing sound of trumpets." These were more than Whitmanesque pictures of bygone peril and glory. In a nation soon to acquiesce in the lynching of his people and shattering of their hopes with disfranchisement and segregation, Douglass appealed to history, to what, for him, was authentic experience, to the recognition scenes that formed personal and national identity. On an ideological level, where Douglass did his best work, he was still fighting the war; he was as harsh as ever in his refusal to concede the Confederate dead any equal place in Memorial Day celebrations. "Death has no power to change moral qualities," he argued. "What was bad before the war, and during the war, has not been made good since the war." A tone of desperation entered Douglass' language toward the end of his speech. Again and again he pleaded with his audience not to believe the arguments of the Lost Cause advocates, however alluring their "disguises" may seem. He insisted that slavery had caused the war, that Americans should never forget that the South fought "to bind with chains millions of the human race."[33]

No amount of nationalism, individualism, or compassion could ever change Douglass' conception of the memory and meaning of the Civil War. His pledge to "never forget" was both a personal and a partisan act, an assertion of the power of memory to inform, inspire, and compel action. Douglass was one of those nineteenth-century thinkers who, by education, temperament, and especially by experience, believed that history was something living and useful. Even in the twilight of his life, when his leadership and his ideas seemed, at times, selfishly out of touch, there was no greater voice than Douglass' for the old shibboleth that the Civil War had been a struggle for union *and* liberty. "Whatever else I may forget," Douglass told the assembled at Mount Hope Cemetery, "I shall never forget the difference between those who fought for liberty and those who fought for slavery; between those who fought to save the Republic and those who fought to destroy it." The jubilee of black freedom in America had been achieved by agitation, through forces in history, through a tragic war, and by faith. Through the power of language and historical imagination, Douglass fought to preserve that jubilee in memory and in reality. In such public acts as the speech in a Rochester cemetery he stood with the Union dead, waved the last bloody shirts of a former slave, a black leader, and a Yankee partisan, and anticipated the dulling effects of time and the poet Robert Lowell's vision of "the stone statues of the abstract Union soldier" adorning New England town greens, where "they doze over muskets and muse through their sideburns."[34]

33. "Decoration Day," May, 1883, in FD Papers [LC], reel 17, pp. 3, 6–8 (typescript misdated 1894).
34. *Ibid.*, 9; Robert Lowell, "For the Union Dead," in *Norton Anthology of American Literature* (New York, 1980), I, 842.

EPILOGUE

And so the Civil War draws us as an oracle, darkly unriddled and portentous, of personal, as well as national fate.
—Robert Penn Warren, *The Legacy of the Civil War*, 1961

AT THE END OF HIS THIRD AUTOBIOGRAPHY, Douglass declared that he had "lived several lives in one: first, the life of slavery; secondly, the life of a fugitive from slavery; thirdly, the life of comparative freedom; fourthly, the life of conflict and battle; and fifthly, the life of victory, if not complete, at least assured."[1] The fourth stage ("conflict and battle") encompassed the Civil War era, a time that was as pivotal in Douglass' life as it was for the nation. With an autobiographer's sense of self-importance, Douglass wanted to demonstrate the struggle and achievement in his life. He had suffered and overcome, we are told. He had persevered through hopelessness, led his people through a trial, and in the end triumphed. These are the images of an aging man trying to sum up his life and control his historical reputation. To some extent they are apocalyptic images, cast in the same way as Douglass' spiritual interpretation of the war. As the nation had suffered, experienced God's retribution, and then triumphed over itself, so too had the fugitive slave risen to racial leader been regenerated. Autobiography must be interpreted with caution, but the stages Douglass gave his life are instructive. They represent the turning points that define his career. They also suggest the significance of the Civil War in his long and divided life.

Douglass saw in the Civil War an apocalyptic power that forever changed the relationship of blacks to America. Through that conflict, he believed, the national millennium had come; the old Union had been destroyed and a new one created. Blacks were "opening a new account with the American people and with the whole human family," Douglass said in 1863. Douglass always believed that he voiced the deepest yearnings of his people when he demanded their freedom and their birthright as American citizens, and the war allowed him to glimpse a future transformed, a society where blacks would belong and prosper, a time when race might dissolve into nationality. These were ambitious and improbable dreams, but Douglass could not resist his refurbished hope. After all, as Edmund Wilson has written, the apocalyptic vision, in the midst of the Civil War, "had imposed

---

1. Douglass, *Life and Times*, 479.

itself." The last lines of a wartime speech by Douglass on the future of blacks in America burned with apocalyptic imagery and the desire to overcome racial prejudice: "Tonight we stand at the portals of a new world, a new life and a new country," he declared. "We have passed through the furnace and have not been consumed. During . . . two centuries and a half, we have survived contact with the white race. . . . We have illustrated . . . that the two most opposite races of men . . . can live in the same latitudes . . . and that . . . there is reason to believe that we may permanently live under the same skies, brave the same climate, and enjoy liberty, equality and fraternity in a common country."[2]

Douglass' apocalypticism may have conditioned him to see the war as more conclusive than it really was, and his belief in the transforming nature of the conflict may also have caused him to expect too much from the postwar period.[3] The idea of national regeneration forged in the war may have blinded him to some of the economic dilemmas and subsequent failures of Reconstruction and the Republican party. The nation did indeed regenerate, but after 1870 it hardly followed the humanitarian and egalitarian paths that Douglass had imagined. Although he should not be faulted for his great expectations, perhaps the postwar Douglass, trapped in the paradox of trying to be both a black activist and a stalwart Republican, was thwarted by his own perception of what he called the "undreamed of changes" the war had wrought.[4]

Out of the Union victory and the experience of war, many northern intellectuals demanded a more organized and disciplined society. Wars typically cause the consolidation of thought and action, allowing authoritarianism to reign over individual liberty, and Douglass was no exception to this trend in wartime thinking. As early as September, 1861, he declared that "the grand object . . . and aim of government is the preservation of society, and from nothing worse than anarchy." Douglass did not appeal for social order in the same ways as some conservative nationalists who saw in the war an opportunity to discipline the passions of the masses, circumscribe reform, and reassert the power of authority over individualism. His principle goal in the war and in its aftermath was to see the preservation of the Union

2. Wilson, *Patriotic Gore*, 106; "The Present and Future of the Colored Race in America."
3. Moorhead, in *American Apocalypse*, 242–44, makes this point about the war's conclusiveness for northern Protestants in general.
4. "Reminiscences of the Antislavery Conflict," speech delivered during the lecture season, 1872–73, in FD Papers (LC), reel 14.

linked with the cause of abolition and black equality. Once that seemed likely, Douglass defended social order and condemned southerners for destroying "the existence among the whole people of a fraternal good will, an earnest spirit of cooperation for the common good." Douglass had never before been a voice for such conservative notions as social cohesion and government authority, but he had long yearned for a secure place among the governed and had long desired to see his people recognized as part of the social fabric. Herein lies the irony of his defense of social order during the Civil War era. As he contemplated the winning of the war and the tasks of Reconstruction, Douglass saw "great duties and responsibilities" before the American people. "Liberty, order, and civilization," he asserted in November, 1862, "are staked against a slaveholding despotism and social anarchy." Douglass had always compared the evils of slavery to the liberating influences of free institutions, but now, through the crucible of the war, he wanted to "unify and reorganize" those free institutions forever.[5]

By late 1865, Douglass' nationalism had flowered as never before. In a speech eulogizing Lincoln, he rejoiced that the "ship of state" was now safe, that the "country was never stronger," and that the "national will" had prevailed over the South's rebellion. Douglass' nationalistic sentiments had always stemmed from a deep personal longing to be recognized as a citizen in his own land, and he also shared his generation's sentimental attachments to the Union. He wanted a country built on egalitarian humanism, and most of all he wanted the country to be his own. He said this clearly in his "Mission of the War" speech in 1864: "What we now want is a country—a free country—a country not saddened by the footprints of a single slave—and nowhere cursed by the presence of a single slaveholder. We want a country which shall not brand the Declaration of Independence a lie. We want a country whose fundamental institutions we can proudly defend before the highest intelligence and civilization of the age . . . a country in which . . . patriotism shall not conflict with fidelity to justice and liberty."[6] This seminal speech represents Douglass the visionary, but it also demonstrates the black orator's grasp of how the Civil War was truly a struggle for liberty and union.

5. Fredrickson, *Inner Civil War*, 104–106, 183–94; "Cast Off the Millstone," *DM*, September, 1861, in Foner (ed.), *Life and Writings*, III, 155–56; "The Work of the Future"; "The Mission of the War."

6. "Abraham Lincoln—A Speech," December, 1865, in FD Papers (LC), reel 14. For another excellent example of the flowering of Douglass' nationalism during the postwar period, see the speech "Composite Nation," a lecture first delivered in the Parker Fraternity Course, Boston, 1867, in *ibid.* "The Mission of the War."

Among Douglass' deepest psychological conflicts were his divided racial and social identities, which combined to cause a divided self that he may never have fully resolved. He was half-white and half-black; he was an American, but also a former slave denied a place in the national family. The historian Peter Walker's analysis of the first of these conflicts—the alleged, unresolved racial identity—is both fascinating and debatable. In Walker's view, Douglass yearned to escape his blackness and suffered from a "hopeless secret desire to be white." Through successive autobiographies, Douglass engaged in an unending quest to discover his "lost past," argues Walker, especially his white patrimony. Clearly, Douglass sought a usable past, both as a heroic spokesman for his people and in order to build a secure sense of self-definition. As an orphan struggling through the many transformations in his life, he needed to know who he was, which may have required confirmation of his blackness and his whiteness in the white world that he embraced in the 1840s. In Douglass there lived two people and two cultures; he was perhaps the nineteenth century's most conspicuous example of the black "double self" about which W. E. B. Du Bois wrote so insightfully.[7] Whether Walker's conclusions about Douglass' racial identity are correct will, like all major assertions in psychohistory, remain open to speculation and debate. The argument undoubtedly requires a certain leap of faith with the evidence; namely, that Douglass' embrace of the white world of American abolitionists and English-Scottish reformers was a craving for "whiteness" (literally a new racial identity), rather than merely a fervent desire to overcome the debilitating effects of slavery and racism.

In any case, Douglass' unrelenting quest to preserve a black-abolitionist memory of the Civil War during the final third of his life does underscore his crucial desire for a usable history. For Douglass—and, he reasoned, for all blacks—the deep personal meaning derived from the war, emancipation, and the promises of Reconstruction became the past with which the present and the future could be securely faced and judged. However his inner conflict over racial identity may have been manifested, Douglass never relinquished his self-perception nor his pride as a black man and leader. Interpreting the public and private dimensions of Douglass' life, over which he tried to exercise so much control, will always be the most intriguing challenge to his biographers.

Through the experience of the Civil War, Douglass found a reconciliation of the second of these psychological conflicts—his need for

7. Walker, *Moral Choices*, 224–28, 244–61; Du Bois, *Souls*, 45.

a secure social identity. This process was clearly revealed in his wartime nationalism and in his postwar struggle to preserve the meaning and memory of the war. In the war for emancipation, Douglass found a personal union with the legacy of the Founding Fathers, as the struggle to free the slaves and preserve the Union turned into a black person's war as well. The war in all its apocalyptic force also offered Douglass a perfect outlet for his millennial nationalism and an opportunity to unleash a deeply felt revenge against slaveholders. In the black soldier, he helped create the symbol of black manhood and a ready justification for future citizenship. In the realization of an "abolition war" and the hope of an "abolition peace," Douglass staked his own claim to citizenship in a nation reborn and reunified. And by preserving his version of the legacy of the war, he hoped to forge an eternal, mythic place in America's historical memory for abolitionism, black regiments, emancipation, the Civil War amendments, and the millions of nameless freedpeople striving for land and the free exercise of their rights. Douglass dearly hoped that his own sense of self, so inextricably tied to the crusade against slavery and to the tradition of reform, would rest securely in new national traditions that he helped create.

Peter Walker has argued that Douglass' first abolitionist speech at Nantucket in 1841 was "the great reference point" of his postslavery life. If by launching his public life as a reformer Nantucket provided the reference point for Douglass' struggle over his personal and racial identity, then the Civil War was surely the reference point for his social identity. By 1865, Douglass' longing to "have a country" was full of promise. For the rest of his life, he was a black leader whom all, friend and foe alike, associated with the war and the nation's struggle to end slavery. If Douglass harbored an inner conflict over race, he only revealed it in subtle and largely unintentional ways, but from the beginning of his political awakening in the early 1850s through the struggles of Reconstruction and beyond, he openly exposed the second half of his divided soul. Douglass embraced his native soil and preached American mission; his nationalism was never without a fierce demand for racial justice and human rights, nor did it lack the rhetoric of manifest destiny. He entered the Civil War in 1861 with a tattered but unbroken faith in his version of a promised America, and he emerged from the fury in 1865 with a sense of nationhood. The successes and failures of Reconstruction severely tested but ultimately enriched this new sense of belonging. As an individual, Douglass achieved a lasting social identity. It must have been the resolution of this part of his inner conflict that Douglass had in mind when he wrote in 1881 that "whatever of good or ill the future may have in store for me, the past at least is secure."[8]

Douglass' self-assurance about his own social identity notwithstanding, his increasingly desperate struggle to preserve an abolitionist memory of the Civil War late in life betrays an acute realization that the collective social identity of black people was much less secure. As an autobiographer, he could continue to explore and shape his own past into a usable fabric, even though it may never have attained the "sense of completeness" he suggested. But for his people collectively, that task was much more formidable; their social identity—indeed their survival—depended upon a vigilant struggle, as Douglass said in an Emancipation Day address in 1883, of "making the nation's life consistent with the nation's creed."[9] In such phrases, Douglass captured as well as any of his contemporaries the legacy of emancipation and the meaning of the Civil War for himself, for black people, and for the nation.

8. Walker, *Moral Choices*, 236–37, 225; Douglass, *Life and Times*, 407.
9. Douglass, *Life and Times*, 407; "Speech on Emancipation Day."

BIBLIOGRAPHY

PRIMARY SOURCES

MANUSCRIPT COLLECTIONS

Boston Public Library, Boston, Massachusetts.
  Garrison, William Lloyd. Collection.
  Weston Family. Papers.
Library of Congress, Washington, D.C.
  Douglass, Frederick. Papers. Microform.
  Fleetwood, Christian A. Papers.
Moorland-Spingarn Research Center, Howard University, Washington, D.C.
  Douglass, Frederick. Collection.
Pennsylvania Historical Society, Philadelphia, Pennsylvania.
  Barker, Abraham. Papers.
  Chase, Salmon P. Papers.
  Dreer, Ferdinand J. Collection.
  Gardiner, Leon. Collection.
  Gravely, William B. "Report on the Christian Recorder in the Archive of Mother Bethel A.M.E. Church." Microform.
Public Record Office, London, England.
  Correspondence Respecting the Emigration of Free Negroes from the United States to the West Indies, CO 884/2, June 19, 1863. Confidential Print.
State Historical Society of Wisconsin, Madison, Wisconsin.
  Doolittle, James R. Papers.
Syracuse University Library, Syracuse, New York.
  Smith, Gerrit. Papers. Microform.
Yale University, New Haven, Connecticut.
  Douglass, Frederick. Papers.

PUBLISHED WORKS

Aptheker, Herbert, ed. *A Documentary History of the Negro People in the United States.* Vol. I of 3 vols. New York, 1968.
Basler, Roy P., ed. *The Collected Works of Abraham Lincoln.* 8 vols. New Brunswick, N.J., 1953.
Beale, Howard K., ed. *Diary of Gideon Welles, Secretary of the Navy Under Lincoln and Johnson.* Vol. II of 3 vols. New York, 1960.
Bell, Howard Holman, ed. *Minutes of the Proceedings of the National Negro Conventions, 1830–1864.* New York, 1969.

Berlin, Ira, *et al.*, eds. *Freedom: A Documentary History of Emancipation, 1861–1867.* Series 2. *The Black Military Experience.* New York, 1983.

Blassingame, John W., ed. *The Frederick Douglass Papers.* Series 1. *Speeches, Debates, and Interviews.* Vols. I and II of 3 vols. to date. New Haven, 1979, 1982.

Blassingame, John W., Mae G. Henderson, and Jessica M. Dunn, eds. *Antislavery Newspapers and Periodicals: Annotated Index of Letters, 1817–1871.* Vol. III, *1836–1854,* of 5 vols. New York, 1981.

Brotz, Howard, ed. *Negro Social and Political Thought, 1850–1920: Representative Texts.* New York, 1966.

Brown, William Wells. *The Negro in the American Rebellion.* 1867; rpr. New York, 1971.

Chambers, William. *American Slavery and Colour.* New York, 1857.

Delany, Martin R. *The Condition, Elevation, Emigration, and Destiny of the Colored People of the United States.* 1852; rpr. New York, 1968.

Donald, David, ed. *Inside Lincoln's Cabinet: The Civil War Diaries of Salmon P. Chase.* New York, 1954.

Douglass, Frederick. *The Life and Times of Frederick Douglass: Written By Himself.* 1881; rpr. New York, 1962.

———. *My Bondage and My Freedom.* 1855; rpr. New York, 1969.

———. *Narrative of the Life of Frederick Douglass, An American Slave, Written By Himself.* 1845; rpr. New York, 1963.

Du Bois, W. E. B. *The Souls of Black Folk.* 1903; rpr. New York, 1969.

Foner, Philip S., ed. *The Life and Writings of Frederick Douglass.* 5 vols. New York, 1950.

Garnet, Henry Highland. *An Address to the Slaves of the United States of America.* 1848; rpr. New York, 1969.

Goodell, William. *Slavery and Antislavery.* 1852; rpr. New York, 1968.

———. *Views of American Constitutional Law in Its Bearing upon American Slavery.* N.p., 1844.

Griffiths, Julia, ed. *Autographs for Freedom.* 2 vols. Rochester, N.Y., 1854.

Higginson, Thomas Wentworth. *Army Life in a Black Regiment.* New York, 1969.

McLoughlin, William G., ed. *The American Evangelicals, 1800–1900: An Anthology.* New York, 1968.

McPherson, James M., ed. *The Negro's Civil War: How American Negroes Felt and Acted During the War for the Union.* New York, 1965.

Marsh, Luther R., ed. *Writings and Speeches of Alvan Stewart on Slavery.* New York, 1860.

Proceedings of the Radical Abolition Convention, June 26–28, 1855. New York, 1855.

Redpath, James. *Echoes of Harpers Ferry.* 1860; rpr. New York, 1969.
————, ed. *A Guide to Hayti.* Boston, 1860.

Richardson, James D. *A Compilation of the Messages and Papers of the Presidents, 1789–1897.* Vol. VI of 10 vols. Washington, D.C., 1897.

Ruchames, Louis, ed. *The Letters of William Lloyd Garrison.* Vol. IV of 4 vols. Cambridge, Mass., 1976.

Spooner, Lysander. *The Unconstitutionality of Slavery.* 2nd ed. 1845; rpr. New York, 1965.

Sprague, Rosetta Douglass. *My Mother As I Recall Her.* Washington, D.C.: Library of Congress, 1900. Microform.

Statutes At Large of the United States of America, 1789–1873. 17 vols. Boston, 1850–1873.

Storing, Herbert, ed. *What Country Have I? Political Writings of Black Americans.* New York, 1970.

Stuckey, Sterling, ed. *The Ideological Origins of Black Nationalism.* Boston, 1972.

Tocqueville, Alexis de. *Democracy in America.* Edited by Thomas Bender. New York, 1981.

Walker, David. *Walker's Appeal in Four Articles.* 1830; rpr. New York, 1969.

Ward, Samuel Ringgold. *Autobiography of a Fugitive Negro.* 1855; rpr. New York, 1968.

Washington, Booker T. *Up From Slavery.* 1903; rpr. New York, 1965.

NEWSPAPERS AND PERIODICALS

Anglo-African Magazine. New York, 1859–60.
Christian Recorder. Philadelphia, 1854–65.
Douglass Monthly. Rochester, 1859–63.
Frederick Douglass's Paper. Rochester, 1851–59.
Liberator. Boston, 1845–65.
National Antislavery Standard. New York.
New National Era. Washington, D.C., 1870–73.
New York Independent.
North Star. Rochester, N.Y., 1847–51.

SECONDARY SOURCES

PUBLISHED WORKS

Aaron, Daniel. *The Unwritten War: American Writers and the Civil War.* New York, 1973.

Ahlstrom, Sydney. *A Religious History of the American People.* New Haven, 1972.

Albrecht, Robert M. "The Theological Response of the Transcendentalists to the Civil War." *New England Quarterly,* XXXVIII (March, 1965), 21–34.

Anderson, James William. "The Methodology of Psychological Biography." *Journal of Interdisciplinary History,* XI (Winter, 1981), 455–75.

Andrews, William L. "Frederick Douglass, Preacher." *American Literature,* LIV (December, 1982), 592–96.

Baker, Houston A., Jr. *The Journey Back: Issues in Black Literature and Criticism.* Chicago, 1980.

Beck, Warren A. "Lincoln and Negro Colonization in Central America." *Abraham Lincoln Quarterly* (September, 1950), 162–83.

Bellah, Robert N. "Civil Religion in America." *Daedalus,* 98 (Winter, 1969), 1–21.

Bellah, Robert N., et al. *Habits of the Heart: Individualism and Commitment in American Life.* New York, 1985.

Belz, Herman. "Law, Politics, and Race in the Struggle for Equal Pay During the Civil War." *Civil War History,* XXII (September, 1976), 197–222.

Bennett, Lerone, Jr. "Was Abe Lincoln a White Supremacist?" *Ebony,* XXIII (February, 1968), 35–38, 40, 42.

Bercovitch, Sacvan. *The American Jeremiad.* Madison, 1978.

Berry, Mary Frances. *Military Necessity and Civil Rights Policy: Black Citizenship and the Constitution, 1861–1868.* Port Washington, N.Y., 1977.

Blackett, R. J. M. *Beating Against the Barriers: Biographical Essays in Nineteenth-Century Afro-American History.* Baton Rouge, 1986.

———. *Building an Antislavery Wall: Black Americans in the Atlantic Abolitionist Movement, 1830–1860.* Baton Rouge, 1983.

Blassingame, John W. "Black Autobiographies as History and Literature." *Black Scholar,* V (1973–74), 2–9.

Blassingame, John W., and Mary Frances Berry. *Long Memory: The Black Experience in America.* New York, 1982.

Blight, David W. "Frederick Douglass and the American Apocalypse." *Civil War History,* XXXI (December, 1985), 309–28.

————. "In Search of Learning, Liberty, and Self-Definition: James McCune Smith and the Ordeal of the Antebellum Black Intellectual." *Afro-Americans in New York Life and History*, IX (July, 1985), 7–25.

Boritt, G. S. "The Voyage to the Colony of Linconia: The Sixteenth President, Black Colonization, and the Defense Mechanism of Avoidance." *Historian*, XXXVII (August, 1975), 619–33.

Boyd, Willis D. "James Redpath and American Negro Colonization in Haiti, 1860–1862." *Americas*, XII (October, 1955), 169–82.

Bradley, David Henry, Jr. *A History of the A.M.E. Zion Church, 1796–1872*. Vol. I of 2 vols. Nashville, 1956.

Breiseth, Christopher. "Lincoln and Frederick Douglass: Another Debate." *Illinois State Historical Society Journal*, LXVIII (1975), 9–26.

Brown, Ira. "Watchers for the Second Coming: The Millennial Tradition in America." *Mississippi Valley Historical Review*, XXXIX (December, 1952), 441–58.

Bruss, Elizabeth. *Autobiographical Acts*. Baltimore, 1976.

Buck, Paul H. *The Road to Reunion, 1865–1900*. New York, 1937.

Butterfield, Stephen. *Black Autobiography in America*. Amherst, 1974.

Buttrick, George A., ed. *The Interpreter's Dictionary of the Bible*. Vols. I, IV of 4 vols. Nashville, 1957, 1962.

Channing, Stephen. *Crisis of Fear: Secession in South Carolina*. New York, 1970.

Cherry, Conrad, comp. *God's New Israel: Religious Interpretations of American Destiny*. Englewood Cliffs, N.J., 1971.

Clebsch, William. "Christian Interpretations of the Civil War." *Church History*, XXX (June, 1961), 212–22.

Connelly, Thomas L., and Barbara L. Bellows. *God and General Longstreet: The Lost Cause and the Southern Mind*. Baton Rouge, 1982.

Cooke, Jacob E. *Frederic Bancroft: Historian*. Introduction by Allan Nevins. Norman, Okla., 1957.

Cooper, Frederick. "Elevating the Race: The Social Thought of Black Leaders, 1827–1850." *American Quarterly*, XXIV (December, 1972), 604–25.

Cornish, Dudley T. *The Sable Arm: Negro Troops in the Union Army, 1861–1865*. New York, 1956.

Cox, LaWanda. *Lincoln and Black Freedom: A Study in Presidential Leadership*. Columbia, S.C., 1981.

Current, Richard Nelson. *Those Terrible Carpetbaggers: A Reinterpretation*. New York, 1988.

Davidson, James West. *The Logic of Millennial Thought: Eighteenth-Century New England.* New Haven, 1977.

Davis, Allison. *Leadership, Love, and Aggression.* New York, 1983.

Davis, David Brion. *The Slave Power Conspiracy and the Paranoid Style.* Baton Rouge, 1969.

Demos, John. "The Antislavery Movement and the Problem of Violent Means." *New England Quarterly,* XXXVII (December, 1964), 501–26.

Donald, David. *The Politics of Reconstruction, 1863–1867.* Baton Rouge, 1965.

Downey, Matthew T. "Horace Greeley and the Politicians: The Liberal Republican Convention in 1872." *Journal of American History,* LIII (March, 1967), 727–50.

Du Bois, W. E. B. *Black Reconstruction in America, 1860–1880.* 1935; rpr. New York, 1972.

Dyer, Brainerd. "The Treatment of Colored Union Troops by the Confederates, 1861–1865." *Journal of Negro History,* XX (1935), 272–86.

Elder, Arlene A. *The "Hindered Hand": Cultural Implications of Early African-American Fiction.* Westport, 1978.

Erikson, Erik H. *Childhood and Society.* New York, 1963.

———. "On the Nature of Psycho-historical Evidence: In Search of Gandhi." *Daedalus,* 97 (Summer, 1968), 695–730.

Farrison, William E. *William Wells Brown: Author and Reformer.* Chicago, 1969.

Fehrenbacher, Don E. *The Dred Scott Case: Its Significance in American Law and Politics.* New York, 1978.

———. "Only His Stepchildren: Lincoln and the Negro." *Civil War History,* XX (December, 1974), 293–310.

Field, Phyllis F. *The Politics of Race in New York: The Struggle for Black Suffrage in the Civil War Era.* Ithaca, 1982.

———. "Republicans and Black Suffrage in New York State: The Grass Roots Response." *Civil War History,* XXI (June, 1975), 136–47.

Fields, Barbara J. *Slavery and Freedom on the Middle Ground: Maryland During the Nineteenth Century.* New Haven, 1985.

Foner, Eric. *Free Soil, Free Labor, Free Men: The Ideology of the Republican Party Before the Civil War.* New York, 1970.

———. *Nothing But Freedom: Emancipation and Its Legacy.* Baton Rouge, 1983.

———. *Reconstruction: America's Unfinished Revolution, 1863–1877.* New York, 1988.

Foner, Philip S. *Frederick Douglass.* New York, 1964.

Fordham, Monroe. *Major Themes in Northern Black Religious Thought, 1800–1860.* Hicksville, N.Y., 1975.

Forgie, George B. *Patricide in a House Divided: A Psychological Interpretation of Lincoln and His Age.* New York, 1979.

Foster, Gaines M. *Ghosts of the Confederacy: Defeat, the Lost Cause, and the Emergence of the New South, 1865–1913.* New York, 1986.

Franklin, H. Bruce. "Animal Farm Unbound." *New Letters,* XLIII (1977), 25–48.

Franklin, John Hope. *The Emancipation Proclamation.* Garden City, N.Y., 1963.

Fredrickson, George M. *The Black Image in the White Mind: The Debate on Afro-American Character and Destiny, 1817–1914.* New York, 1971.

———. *The Inner Civil War: Northern Intellectuals and the Crisis of the Union.* New York, 1965.

———. "A Man But Not a Brother: Abraham Lincoln and Racial Equality." *Journal of Southern History,* XLI (February, 1975), 39–58.

———. "Self-Made Hero." *New York Review of Books,* XXXII (June 27, 1985), 3–4.

Friedman, Lawrence J. "Antebellum American Abolitionism and the Problem of Violent Means." *Psychohistory Review,* IX (1980), 26–32.

———. "The Gerrit Smith Circle: Abolitionism in the Burned-Over District." *Civil War History,* XXVI (March, 1980), 18–38.

———. *Gregarious Saints: Self and Community in American Abolitionism, 1830–1870.* New York, 1982.

Fulkerson, Gerald. "Exile as Emergence: Frederick Douglass in Great Britain, 1845–1847." *Quarterly Journal of Speech,* LX (February, 1974), 69–82.

Fussell, Paul. *The Great War in Modern Memory.* New York, 1975.

Gara, Larry. "Slavery and the Slave Power: A Crucial Distinction." *Civil War History,* XV (March, 1969), 5–18.

Gates, Henry-Louis, Jr. "Binary Oppositions in Chapter One of Narrative of the Life of Frederick Douglass an American Slave Written by Himself." In *Afro-American Literature: The Reconstruction of Instruction,* edited by Dexter Fisher and Robert B. Stepto. New York, 1979. Pp. 212–32.

———. "Frederick Douglass and the Language of the Self." *Yale Review,* LXX (Summer, 1981), 592–611.

Geertz, Clifford. *The Interpretation of Cultures: Selected Essays.* New York, 1973.

Gerber, Richard A. "The Liberal Republicans of 1872 in Historiographical Perspective." *Journal of American History*, LXII (June, 1975), 40–73.

Gerteis, Louis S. *From Contraband to Freedman: Federal Policy Toward Southern Blacks, 1861–1865*. Westport, Conn., 1973.

Gibson, Donald B. "Reconciling Public and Private in Frederick Douglass's Narrative." *American Literature*, LVII (December, 1985), 549–69.

Gienapp, William E. *The Origins of the Republican Party, 1852–1856*. New York, 1987.

Gillette, William. *Retreat from Reconstruction, 1869–1879*. Baton Rouge, 1979.

Goldstein, Leslie Friedman. "Violence as an Instrument for Social Change: The Views of Frederick Douglass." *Journal of Negro History*, LXI (1976), 61–72.

Gray, Wood. *The Hidden Civil War: The Story of the Copperheads*. New York, 1942.

Griffith, Cyril E. *The African Dream: Martin R. Delany and the Emergence of Pan-African Thought*. University Park, Pa., 1975.

Grimké, Francis J. "The Second Marriage of Frederick Douglass." *Journal of Negro History*, XIX (July, 1934), 324–29.

Handlin, Oscar. "The Civil War as Symbol and as Actuality." *Massachusetts Review*, III (Autumn, 1961), 133–43.

Harding, Vincent. *There Is a River: The Black Struggle for Freedom in America*. New York, 1981.

Harlow, Ralph Volney. *Gerrit Smith: Philanthropist and Reformer*. New York, 1939.

Hatch, Nathan O. "The Origins of Civil Millennialism in America: New England Clergymen, the War with France, and the Revolution." *William and Mary Quarterly*, XXXI (July, 1974), 407–30.

———. *The Sacred Cause of Liberty: Republican Thought and the Millennium in Revolutionary New England*. New Haven, 1977.

Hedin, Raymond. "The Structuring of Emotion in Black American Fiction." *Novel*, XVI (Fall, 1982), 35–54.

Hobsbaum, Eric, and Terence Ranger, eds. *The Invention of Tradition*. New York, 1983.

Holland, Frederic May. *Frederick Douglass: The Colored Orator*. 1891; rpr. New York, 1969.

Holt, Thomas C. *Black Over White: Negro Political Leadership in South Carolina During Reconstruction*. Urbana, 1978.

Hoogenboom, Ari A. *Outlawing the Spoils: A History of the Civil Service Reform Movement, 1865–1883*. Urbana, 1961.

Howard-Pitney, David. "The Enduring Black Jeremiad: The American Jeremiad in Black Protest Rhetoric, from Frederick Douglass to W. E. B. Du Bois, 1841–1919." *American Quarterly,* XXXVIII (Fall, 1986), 481–92.

Howe, Mark De Wolfe, ed. *The Occasional Speeches of Justice Oliver Wendell Holmes, Jr.* Cambridge, Mass., 1962.

Hudson, Winthrop S. *Nationalism and Religion in America: Concepts of American Identity and Mission.* New York, 1970.

Huggins, Nathan I. "Afro-Americans." In *Ethnic Leadership in America,* edited by John Higham. Baltimore, 1978. Pp. 91–118.

———. *Slave and Citizen: The Life of Frederick Douglass.* Boston, 1980.

Hughes, Langston. *The Panther and the Lash: Poems for Our Times.* New York, 1974.

Hyman, Harold M. *A More Perfect Union: The Impact of the Civil War and Reconstruction on the Constitution.* Boston, 1975.

Jordan, Winthrop D. *White Over Black: American Attitudes Toward the Negro, 1550–1812.* Baltimore, 1969.

Kammen, Michael. *A Season of Youth: The American Revolution and the Historical Imagination.* New York, 1978.

Klement, Frank L. *The Copperheads in the Middle West.* Chicago, 1960.

Kohut, Heinz. "Thoughts on Narcissism and Narcissistic Rage." In *The Search for the Self: Selected Writings of Heinz Kohut,* edited by Paul H. Orenstein. New York, 1978. Vol. II of 2 vols. Pp. 615–58.

Kousser, J. Morgan, and James M. McPherson, eds. *Region, Race, and Reconstruction: Essays in Honor of C. Vann Woodward.* New York, 1982.

Kraditor, Aileen S. *Means and Ends in American Abolitionism: Garrison and His Critics on Strategy and Tactics, 1834–1850.* New York, 1967.

Kraut, Alan M., ed. *Crusaders and Compromisers: Essays on the Relationship of the Antislavery Struggle to the Antebellum Party System.* Westport, 1983.

Kren, George M., and Leon H. Rappoport, eds. *Varieties of Psychohistory.* New York, 1976.

Kuklik, Bruce. "Myth and Symbol in American Studies." *American Quarterly,* XXIV (October, 1972), 435–50.

Langer, William L. "Presidential Address to the American Historical Association." [1958]. In *Psychoanalysis and History,* edited by Bruce Mazlish. Englewood Cliffs, 1963. Pp. 87–107.

Levesque, George A. "Boston's Black Brahmin: Dr. John S. Rock." *Civil War History,* XXVI (December, 1980), 326–46.

Lewis, R. W. B. *The American Adam: Innocence, Tragedy, and Tradition in the Nineteenth Century.* Chicago, 1955.

Litwack, Leon F. *Been in the Storm Too Long: The Aftermath of Slavery.* New York, 1979.

———. "The Emancipation of the Negro Abolitionist." In *The Antislavery Vanguard: New Essays on the Abolitionists,* edited by Martin Duberman. Princeton, 1965. Pp. 137–55.

———. *North of Slavery: The Negro in the Free States, 1790–1860.* Chicago, 1961.

Lively, Robert A. *Fiction Fights the Civil War: An Unfinished Chapter in the Literary History of the American People.* Chapel Hill, 1957.

Lofton, Williston. "Northern Labor and the Negro During the Civil War." *Journal of Negro History,* XXXIV (July, 1949), 251–73.

Logan, Rayford W. *The Betrayal of the Negro: From Rutherford B. Hayes to Woodrow Wilson.* New York, 1965.

Lowell, Robert. "For the Union Dead." 1964. In *The Norton Anthology of American Literature.* New York, 1980.

Lowenthal, David. *The Past Is a Foreign Country.* London, 1985.

Lowi, Theodore J. *The Politics of Disorder.* New York, 1971.

Mabee, Carleton. *Black Freedom: The Non-Violent Abolitionists from 1830 Through the Civil War.* London, 1970.

McFeely, William S. *Grant: A Biography.* New York, 1981.

McKitrick, Eric L. *Andrew Johnson and Reconstruction.* Chicago, 1960.

Maclear, J. F. "The Republic and the Millennium." In *The Religion of the Republic,* edited by Elwyn A. Smith. Philadelphia, 1971. Pp. 183–216.

McPherson, James M. "Abolitionists and Negro Opposition to Colonization During the Civil War." *Phylon,* XXVI (1965), 391–99.

———. *The Abolitionist Legacy: From Reconstruction to the NAACP.* Princeton, 1975.

———. "Grant or Greeley? The Abolitionist Dilemma in the Election of 1872." *American Historical Review,* LXX (October, 1965), 43–61.

———. *The Struggle for Equality: Abolitionists and the Negro in the Civil War and Reconstruction.* Princeton, 1964.

Magdol, Edward. *A Right to the Land: Essays on the Freedmen's Community.* Westport, Conn., 1977.

Man, Albon P. "Labor Competition and the New York Draft Riots of 1863." *Journal of Negro History*, XXXVI (1951), 375–405.

Marsden, George M. *The Evangelical Mind and the New School Presbyterian Experience: A Case Study of Thought and Theology in Nineteenth-Century America*. New Haven, 1970.

Martin, Waldo E. *The Mind of Frederick Douglass*. Chapel Hill, 1984.

Mathews, Donald G. *Slavery and Methodism: A Chapter in American Morality, 1780–1845*. Princeton, 1965.

Mays, Benjamin E. *The Negro's God: As Reflected in His Literature*. New York, 1973.

Meier, August. "Frederick Douglass's Vision for America: A Case Study in Nineteenth-Century Protest." In *Freedom and Reform*, edited by Harold M. Hyman and Leonard W. Levy. New York, 1967. Pp. 127–48.

Miller, Floyd J. "The Father of Black Nationalism: Another Contender." *Civil War History*, XVII (December, 1971), 310–19.

———. *The Search for a Black Nationality: Black Emigration and Colonization, 1787–1863*. Urbana, 1975.

Miller, Perry. *Errand into the Wilderness*. Cambridge, Mass., 1958.

———. *The New England Mind: From Colony to Province*. Boston, 1961.

Mitgang, Herbert. "Was Lincoln Just a Honkie?" *New York Times Magazine*, February 11, 1968, pp. 34–35, 100–107.

Mohr, Clarence L. "Southern Blacks in the Civil War: A Century of Historiography." *Journal of Negro History*, LXIX (1974), 177–95.

Moorhead, James H. *American Apocalypse: Yankee Protestants and the Civil War, 1860–1869*. New Haven, 1978.

———. "Between Progress and Apocalypse: A Reassessment of Millennialism in American Religious Thought, 1800–1880." *Journal of American History*, LXXI (December, 1984), 524–42.

Moses, Wilson Jeremiah. *Black Messiahs and Uncle Toms: Social and Literary Manipulations of a Religious Myth*. University Park, Pa., 1982.

———. *The Golden Age of Black Nationalism*. Hamden, Conn., 1978.

Nagel, Paul C. *One Nation Indivisible: The Union in American Thought, 1776–1861*. New York, 1964.

Neely, Mark E., Jr. "Abraham Lincoln and Black Colonization, Benjamin Butler's Spurious Testimony." *Civil War History*, XXV (January, 1979), 77–83.

Neisser, Ulric, ed. *Memory Observed: Remembering in Natural Contexts.* San Francisco, 1982.

Nietzsche, Friedrich. "On the Uses and Disadvantages of History for Life." In *Untimely Meditations,* translated by R. J. Hollingdale, with an introduction by J. P. Stern. New York, 1983.

Nye, Russell B. *This Almost Chosen People: Essays in the History of American Ideas.* East Lansing, 1966.

Oates, Stephen B. *To Purge This Land with Blood.* New York, 1970.

Olsen, Otto H. *Carpetbagger's Crusade: The Life of Albion Winegar Tourgée.* Baltimore, 1965.

O'Meally, Robert G. "Frederick Douglass's 1845 Narrative: The Text Was Meant to be Preached." In *Afro-American Literature,* edited by Dexter Fisher and Robert B. Stepto. New York, 1979. Pp. 192–211.

Osterweis, Rollin G. *The Myth of the Lost Cause, 1865–1900.* Hamden, 1973.

Painter, Nell Irvin. *Exodusters: Black Migration to Kansas After Reconstruction.* New York, 1977.

Paludan, Phillip S. *A Covenant with Death: The Constitution, Law, and Equality in the Civil War Era.* Urbana, 1975.

Pascal, Roy. *Design and Truth in Autobiography.* Cambridge, Mass., 1960.

Payne, Walter A. "Lincoln's Caribbean Colonization Plan." *Pacific Historian,* VII (May, 1963), 65–72.

Pease, Jane H., and William H. Pease. "Boston Garrisonians and the Problem of Frederick Douglass." *Canadian Journal of History,* II (September, 1967), 29–48.

———. "Confrontation and Abolition in the 1850s." *Journal of American History,* XLVIII (March, 1972), 923–37.

———. *They Who Would Be Free: Blacks' Search for Freedom, 1830–1861.* New York, 1974.

Pelikan, Jaroslav. *The Vindication of Tradition.* New Haven, 1984.

Perry, Lewis. "Psychohistory and the Abolitionists: Reflections on Martin Duberman and the Neoabolitionism of the 1960s." *Reviews in American History,* II (September, 1974), 309–22.

———. *Radical Abolitionism: Anarchy and the Government of God in Antislavery Thought.* Ithaca, 1973.

Potter, David M. *The Impending Crisis, 1848–1861.* New York, 1976.

———. *Lincoln and His Party in the Secession Crisis.* New Haven, 1942.

Preston, Dickson J. *Young Frederick Douglass: The Maryland Years.* Baltimore, 1980.

Quarles, Benjamin. "Abolition's Different Drummer: Frederick Douglass." In *The Antislavery Vanguard: New Essays on the Abolitionists*, edited by Martin Duberman. Princeton, 1965. Pp. 123–34.

———. *Allies for Freedom: Blacks and John Brown*. New York, 1974.

———. *The Black Abolitionists*. New York, 1969.

———. *Frederick Douglass*. 1948; rpr. New York, 1968.

———. "Letters from Negro Leaders to Gerrit Smith." *Journal of Negro History*, XXVII (October, 1942), 450–56.

———. *Lincoln and the Negro*. New York, 1962.

———. *The Negro in the Civil War*. New York, 1953.

Raboteau, Albert J. *Slave Religion: The Invisible Institution in the Antebellum South*. New York, 1978.

Ransom, Roger L., and Richard Sutch. *One Kind of Freedom: The Economic Consequences of Emancipation*. London, 1977.

Rice, C. Duncan. *The Scots Abolitionists, 1833–1861*. Baton Rouge, 1981.

Richey, Russell E., and Donald G. Jones, eds. *American Civil Religion*. New York, 1974.

Riddleberger, Patrick W. "The Break in the Radical Ranks: Liberals vs. Stalwarts in the Election of 1872." *Journal of Negro History*, XLIV (April, 1959), 142–58.

Robinson, Armstead L. "The Difference Freedom Made: The Emancipation of Afro-Americans." In *The State of Afro-American History: Past, Present, and Future*, edited by Darlene Clark Hine. Baton Rouge, 1986. Pp. 51–74.

Rose, Willie Lee. "Killing for Freedom." *New York Review of Books*, December 3, 1970, pp. 12–19; February 11, 1971, pp. 43–44.

———. *Rehearsal for Reconstruction: The Port Royal Experiment*. New York, 1964.

Schor, Joel. "The Rivalry Between Frederick Douglass and Henry Highland Garnet." *Journal of Negro History*, LXIV (Winter, 1969), 30–38.

Schwartz, Hillel. "The End of the Beginning: Millennarian Studies, 1969–1975." *Religious Studies Review*, II (July, 1976), 1–15.

Sewell, Richard H. *Ballots for Freedom: Antislavery Politics in the United States, 1837–1860*. New York, 1976.

Sheips, Paul J. "Lincoln and the Chiriqui Colonization Project." *Journal of Negro History*, XXXVII (October, 1952), 418–53.

Shepperson, George. "Frederick Douglass and Scotland." *Journal of Negro History*, XXXVIII (July, 1953), 307–21.

Shick, Tom W. *Behold the Promised Land: A History of Afro-American Settler Society in Nineteenth-Century Liberia.* Baltimore, 1977.

———. "A Quantitative Analysis of Liberian Colonization from 1820 to 1843 with Special Reference to Mortality." *Journal of African History,* XII (1971), 45–59.

Shore, Miles F. "Biography in the 1980s: A Psychoanalytic Perspective." *Journal of Interdisciplinary History,* XII (Summer, 1981), 89–113.

Slotkin, Richard. *The Fatal Environment: The Myth of the Frontier in the Age of Industrialization, 1800–1890.* New York, 1985.

Smith, David E. "Millennarian Scholarship in America." *American Quarterly,* XVII (Fall, 1965), 535–49.

Smith, Elwyn A., ed. *The Religion of the Republic.* Philadelphia, 1971.

Smith, George W. "Broadsides for Freedom: Civil War Propaganda in New England." *New England Quarterly,* XXI (September, 1948), 291–312.

Smith, Henry Nash. *Virgin Land: The American West as Symbol and Myth.* Cambridge, Mass., 1950.

Sorin, Gerald. *The New York Abolitionists: A Case Study of Political Radicalism.* Westport, 1971.

Stampp, Kenneth. *And the War Came: The North and the Secession Crisis, 1860–1861.* Baton Rouge, 1950.

———. *The Era of Reconstruction, 1865–1877.* New York, 1965.

Stampp, Kenneth M., and Leon F. Litwack, eds. *Reconstruction: An Anthology of Revisionist Writings.* Baton Rouge, 1969.

Stannard, David E. *Shrinking History: On Freud and the Failure of Psychohistory.* New York, 1980.

Stanton, William. *Leopard's Spots: Scientific Attitudes Toward Race in America, 1815–1859.* Chicago, 1960.

Stark, Cruce. "Brothers At/In War: One Phase of Post–Civil War Reconciliation." *Canadian Review of American Studies,* VI (Fall, 1975), 174–81.

Staudenraus, P. J. *The African Colonization Movement, 1816–1865.* New York, 1961.

Stepto, Robert B. *From Behind the Veil: A Study of Afro-American Narrative.* Urbana, 1979.

———. "Narration, Authentication, and Authorial Control in Frederick Douglass' Narrative of 1845." In *Afro-American Literature: The Reconstruction of Instruction,* edited by Dexter Fisher and Robert B. Stepto. New York, 1978. Pp. 178–91.

Sterling, Dorothy. *The Making of an Afro-American: Martin Robison Delany, 1812–1885.* Garden City, N.Y., 1971.

Stewart, James Brewer. *Holy Warriors: The Abolitionists and American Slavery.* New York, 1976.

Stone, Albert. "Identity and Art in Frederick Douglass' Narrative." *CLA Journal*, XVII (1973), 192–213.

Storing, Herbert J. "Frederick Douglass." In *American Political Thought: The Philosophic Dimension of American Statesmanship*, edited by Morton J. Frisch and Richard G. Stevens. New York, 1971. Pp. 145–66.

Strickland, Arvarh E. "The Illinois Background of Lincoln's Attitude Toward Slavery and the Negro." *Illinois State Historical Society Journal*, LVI (Autumn, 1963), 474–94.

Strout, Cushing. *The New Heaven and New Earth: Political Religion in America.* New York, 1974.

Strozier, Charles B. *Lincoln's Quest for Union: Public and Private Meanings.* New York, 1982.

Susman, Warren I. *Culture as History: The Transformation of American Society in the Twentieth Century.* New York, 1984.

Sweet, Leonard I. *Black Images of America, 1784–1870.* New York, 1976.

Takaki, Ronald T. *Violence in the Black Imagination: Essays and Documents.* New York, 1972.

ten Broek, Jacobus. *The Antislavery Origins of the Fourteenth Amendment.* Berkeley, 1951.

Toll, William. *The Resurgence of Race: Black Social Theory from Reconstruction to the Pan-African Conferences.* Philadelphia, 1979.

Trefousse, Hans. *The Radical Republicans: Lincoln's Vanguard for Racial Justice.* Baton Rouge, 1975.

———. *Reconstruction: America's First Effort at Racial Democracy.* New York, 1971.

———, ed. *Lincoln's Decision for Emancipation.* Philadelphia, 1975.

Tuveson, Ernest Lee. *Redeemer Nation: The Idea of America's Millennial Role.* Chicago, 1968.

Van Deburg, William L. "Frederick Douglass: Maryland Slave to Religious Liberal." *Maryland Historical Magazine*, LXIX (Spring, 1974), 27–43.

Voegeli, V. Jacque. *Free But Not Equal: The Midwest and the Negro During the Civil War.* Chicago, 1967.

Wagandt, Charles L. *The Mighty Revolution: Negro Emancipation in Maryland, 1862–1864.* Baltimore, 1964.

Wahle, Kathleen O'Mara. "Alexander Crummell: Black Evangelist and Pan-Negro Nationalist." *Phylon*, XXIX (Winter, 1968), 388–95.

Walker, Clarence E. *A Rock in a Weary Land: The African Methodist Episcopal Church During the Civil War and Reconstruction.* Baton Rouge, 1982.

Walker, Peter F. *Moral Choices: Memory, Desire, and Imagination in Nineteenth-Century American Abolition.* Baton Rouge, 1978.

Warren, Robert Penn. *The Legacy of the Civil War.* Cambridge, Mass., 1983.

Weisman, Stephen M. "Frederick Douglass, Portrait of a Black Militant: A Study in the Family Romance." *Psychoanalytic Study of the Child*, XXV (1975), 725–51.

Welter, Rush. *The Mind of America, 1810–1860.* New York, 1975.

Wesley, Charles H. "Lincoln's Plan for Colonizing the Emancipated Negroes." *Journal of Negro History*, IV (January, 1919), 7–21.

White, Hayden. *Tropics of Discourse: Essays in Cultural Criticism.* Baltimore, 1978.

Wiecek, William M. *The Guarantee Clause of the U.S. Constitution.* Ithaca, 1972.

_____. *The Sources of Antislavery Constitutionalism in America, 1760–1848.* Ithaca, 1977.

Wiggins, William H., Jr. *O Freedom! Afro-American Emancipation Celebrations.* Knoxville, 1987.

Wiley, Bell I. *Southern Negroes, 1861–1865.* New Haven, 1938.

Williams, T. Harry. *Lincoln and the Radicals.* Madison, 1941.

Wilson, Charles Reagan. *Baptized in Blood: The Religion of the Lost Cause, 1865–1920.* Athens, Ga., 1980.

Wilson, Edmund. *Patriotic Gore: Studies in the Literature of the American Civil War.* 1962; rpr. Boston, 1984.

Wilson, Major L. *Space, Time, and Freedom: The Quest for Nationality and the Irrepressible Conflict, 1815–1861.* Westport, 1974.

Wood, Forest G. *Black Scare: The Racist Response to Emancipation and Reconstruction.* Berkeley, 1968.

Wood, Gordon. *The Creation of the American Republic, 1776–1787.* New York, 1969.

Woodward, C. Vann. *American Counterpoint: Slavery and Racism in the North-South Dialogue.* Boston, 1964.

_____. *The Origins of the New South, 1877–1913.* Baton Rouge, 1951.

Zoellner, Robert H. "Negro Colonization: The Climate of Opinion Surrounding Lincoln, 1860–1865." *Mid-America*, XLII (July, 1960), 141–45.

UNPUBLISHED MATERIALS

Boyd, Willis D. "Colonization in the National Crisis, 1860–1870." Ph.D. dissertation, University of California in Los Angeles, 1953.

Goldstein, Leslie Friedman. "The Political Thought of Frederick Douglass." Ph.D. dissertation, Cornell University, 1974.

Raboteau, Albert J. "Ethiopia Shall Soon Stretch Forth Her Hands: Black Destiny in Nineteenth-Century America." University Lecture in Religion, Arizona State University, January 27, 1983.

Riach, Douglas C. "Ireland and the Campaign Against American Slavery, 1830–1860." Ph.D. dissertation, University of Edinburgh, 1975.

Siegler, Phil S. "The Attitudes of Free Blacks Towards Emigration to Liberia." Ph.D. dissertation, Boston University, 1969.

Van Deburg, William L. "Rejected of Men: The Changing Religious Views of William Lloyd Garrison and Frederick Douglass." Ph.D. dissertation, Michigan State University, 1973.

INDEX